THE SEQUEL TO HIS BEST SELLING BOOK

BAGMAN 2
COLIN BYRNE

"I parted company with Retief Goosen late last year. A couple of weeks after our separation my ex-boss went on to win a tournament in Malaysia, with a local caddie on the bag...

Sod's bloody law, eh?"

Further tales and observations on the weird and wonderful world of professional golf, from one of the world's most respected caddies, featuring work from his weekly, acclaimed columns in

THE IRISH TIMES

D0280553

PUBLISHED BY RED ROCK PRESS

For Joan

Colin Byrne and Retief Goosen strolling up the 18th at Doha Golf Club during the Qatar Masters in 2007 which Goosen won. "Retief's three-wood to the par-five 18th ended up on the fringe of the green about 40 feet from the pin. O'Hern's shoulders collapsed as Retief's ball charged into the hole at high speed for an eagle three. It is, of course, how champions finish off a tournament."

BAGMAN 2
BY COLIN BYRNE
First published 2009

Red Rock Press

Claremont Road

Howth

Dublin 13

Ireland

redrockpress@eircom.net

www.redrockpress.ie

A catalogue record for this book is available from the British Library.

ISBN: 978-0-9548653-8-2

Printing

J.F. Print Limited, Sparkford, Somerset.

Printing liaison

Hugh Stancliffe.

Photographs

Featuring the work of Getty Images photographers and that of Matthew Harris (pages 24 and 25).

WITH THANKS

With thanks to my current bag,
Alex Noren, my previous bag
Retief Goosen, and to all the players for
whom I have toiled over the last
three decades. In particular to
David Feherty for his generous and
much appreciated foreword.

To my fellow caddies and
partners in crime.
Our reward will come – tomorrow.

To my family, father **Cyril**,
mother **Joan**, sister **Carolyn**,
partner **Christine**, and to all my friends
at home and abroad.

To all of those involved in the tour at
every level for providing the nuggets for
my weekly jottings – and to The Irish
Times and its sports editor
Malachy Logan.

To all of you who play and love the
game of golf – go in hope rather than in
expectation. I trust you find something
in this book that shaves a shot or two
off your round.

Now – go hit the damn thing.

October 2009

Caddie, author and seven handicap amateur, striding across the Alps at Crans-sur Sierre, en route to taking his player, Alex Noren, across the winning line at the European Masters, September 2009.

Catching the early bird: Steve Williams of New Zealand, Tiger Woods's porter and probably the best known caddie of the world, marches down the fifth fairway during the final day of practice for the World Golf Championships at the Doral Golf Resort and Spa, in 2009.

THE CHAPTERS

2005

Colin's second year on Retief Goosen's bag, during which Retief went into the last round of the US Open with a three shot lead, only to see it disappear over the hugely demanding Pinehurst No 2.
See page 66

2006

The British Open returns to Hoylake after an absence of 29 years, and Tiger Woods destroys the field with a brilliant strategy that sees him take irons from virtually every tee.
See page 114

2007

At the Open Championship played at Carnoustie, Padraig Harrington pulls off an amazing up and down on the 72nd to get into a playoff against Sergio Garcia, from where he would go on to win.
See page 164

2008

Having successfully defended his Open Championship title despite a damaged hand, Padraig Harrington goes on to win his third Major, the US PGA title at Oakland Hills, in truly majestic style.
See page 218

2009

A new season, a new player in Alex Noren, and back to where it all began – the European Tour – during a year marred by injury, but one which ends with a richly earned victory.
See page 295

David Feherty on the 18th tee at St Andrews during the 1990 Dunhill Cup. Feherty and team mates Philip Walton and Ronan Rafferty would go on to win the tournament for Ireland. Feherty is widely known and respected for his golf commentary on CBS television in the USA, where he lives with his wife Anita and their five children. Mystery continues to surround the disappearance of the Scottish Open trophy which he won in 1986. Neither the player, nor his then caddie, are implicated in any way whatsoever, in any of the events surrounding its disappearance despite words published herein that may give rise to...

FOREWORD
by
DAVID FEHERTY

I

vaguely remember the first time Colin carried my bag, although details of the Eighties are sketchy to me at best, recalled through swirling vapors of Bushmills and a narcotic filter, which at one time made the Old Course at

CONTINUED ON NEXT PAGE

St. Andrews look a bilious shade of mauve through my bloodshot eyes.

Mine wasn't the easiest sack to pack either, and the author of this book took more than his fair share of abuse, which he bore with the grace and dignity of a scrawny intellectual who may well have been bullied in his formative years by various schoolyard versions of me, or worse still, an ecumenically exempt example Jesuit teacher.

Colin Byrne is the rarest kind of caddie, for while many of them look like a homeless version of Guevara or Trotsky, few if any have actually read anything by

David Feherty on the job for CBS.

either, never mind Gabriel García Márquez.

In fact, "Trotsky," was the first nickname I gave him, with others to follow, like, "Tosspot, Dickbox" and "Gobshite."

But in the words of another of my favourite Irish golf writers, the great Dermot Gilleece, this man was, "no ordinary gobshite".

The fact that Colin chose caddying for a living should have been no surprise to anyone who knew him. The boy had the wanderlust, and it was a great way to escape the limits of Ireland to see the world, and some countries that were actually finished. But most of us thought that it was something he had to get out of his system, like the year-long adolescent lust that afflicts so many of our young'uns after they've survived college.

But young Collywobbles stayed with it, even though from the start it seemed obvious he was destined to do far more intelligent things, like write a book, become a bhuddist, and orchestrate a bloodless coup in the Isle of Man, or maybe Dollymount.

Then oddly enough he wrote a book and – odder yet – I read it. *Bagman*, is undoubtedly by far the best account of the glory days of the European Tour ever written, and I don't refer to the standard of the golf that was played either, although by coincidence it was also the time we began to win both major championships and the Ryder Cup on a regular basis.

No, that was glorious all right, but more relevant was a time of difficult yet hilarious travel, of talented yet tragic characters, of shitty golf courses in dreadful condition on absurd islands and third-world countries, and of players dropping pantloads in Asia and Africa. Or maybe that was just bad ice cubes and my pants. Like I said, details are sketchy.

Of course, few of us even knew that Colin was moonlighting as a writer for that disreputable and disgusting rag, *The Irish Times*. By disreputable and disgusting, I mean *The Irish Times* occasionally actually tells the truth, a quality that most players and all caddies righteously feared at the time, as the truth, rather than setting us free, could in most of the countries in which we played, get us thrown in the nearest pokey.

When *Bagman* hit the shelves, the first few hundred copies were anxiously stolen by those who could possibly have faced indictment, but the initial shock was that he had managed to get Retief Goosen to write a foreword that contained more words than any of us had ever heard him speak – cumulatively.

Other than that, Colin had seemingly managed the impossible. He had written an accurate and entertaining account of daily life on tour for both caddies and players, without dropping anyone in the sheepshit. As far as I was concerned, this was a literary and moral achievement to rival W.B.Yeats, and surpass Oscar Wilde (well morally, anyway).

And all this from the man who had carried my bag to a Scottish Open victory in a three-way playoff with Sir Ian Ball-Acher Flinch, and Christy O'Connor Jr. The Scottish Open is the oldest trophy in professional sports, and within hours of the prize giving, during a drunken bender that somehow included at least one member of Led Zepplin, I had lost it.

And yes, it's still lost, as are the two days after the event (from my memory).

Colin could have written about this ghastly moment in the history of the great game, but he didn't, for one of two fairly obvious reasons.

1. He cared enough about his boss, and he kept mum for humanitarian reasons.

2. The worthless f***** has the Scottish Open Trophy locked up somewhere.

3. (Okay, so mathematics is not a strong point either.) I gave it to him – he lost it.

So anyway, here it is. To be honest, my career on the golf course was a mixed bag of luck, laziness, lack of talent, an even greater lack of the courage needed to be great, and enough sense to know I never would be, occasional brilliance followed by comas, induced by heavy drinking, and hilarity of a quality few people ever have the privilege to experience, which often lasted for days.

There are few things of which I can be proud and for which I can actually claim responsibility, but I am happy to say that I was the one who got Colin Byrne into caddying at the professional level, and perhaps as a result, he became a writer.

Whatever... I'm saying it's true. Colin was a great man to have on the bag, and he remains one of my favourite writers and friends.

I hope this book sells a million, and the rotten, black-hearted bastard gives me my Scottish Open Trophy back.

David Feherty, Dallas 2009.

David Feherty's rich and varied career has been punctuated by virtuoso acts of creativity including the writing of three books, *A Nasty Bit of Rough*, *Somewhere in Ireland a Village Is Missing an Idiot*, and *David Feherty's Totally Subjective History of the Ryder Cup*.

INTRODUCTION

by

COLIN BYRNE

WE

won in September. High up in the Swiss Alps my man, the Swede Alex Noren who became my employer in January 2009, put on a virtuoso performance in the final round to win by two shots.

He pulled off some outrageous shots in that final round: big accurate tee shots, holed bunker shots, really eye-popping stuff that had "winner's enclosure" written all over them. As ever I was there in the centre of things – but ultimately at the periphery. Draw as I did on over 25 years' worth of caddying experience, I knew that ultimately all I could do was watch as my player went

CONTINUED ON NEXT PAGE

Sweden's Alex Noren for whom Colin began working at the start of 2009. A big shift in emphasis towards his short game bore fruit in September 2009 when he won the Omega Masters at Crans-sur-Sierre, Switzerland.

about his business.

I am not sure that – on both a personal and professional level – if I can recall ever being as hopeful of victory as I was for Alex.

Since we played our first tournament back in January, I have enjoyed every moment of his company both on and off the course. Anecdotally I knew that he was very much liked on tour – what a pleasure it was to find out why.

He's a delightful guy. Warm, funny, crazy about golf and a generous human being – courteous not just to me, but to everyone with whom he comes in contact.

He also has a profound and innate understanding not just of the rules of golf, but the *spirit* in which the game ought to be played.

Let me tell you what I mean by that: earlier in the year Alex found himself on the 72nd hole with a 10 foot putt which, if holed, might have got him into a play-off in the Jakarta Indonesian Open.

The greens were strong, grainy and wiry – typical of the region and very difficult – not the sort of greens with which most people who play golf in Europe would be familiar. It was hard to distinguish between scuff marks and pitch marks.

Directly on his line was a big bump that looked like a poorly repaired pitch mark – but he wasn't sure if that's what it was.

So he called for a rules' official who studied the blemish, shrugged his shoulders and said that it was what he, Alex, thought it was.

In other words, you have to decide. If you think it's a pitch mark you are fully entitled to repair it – if not – don't.

Over the years I have seen many players who would have assessed the situation in their favour, rather than take the more considered and thoughtful approach that Alex did.

They would have said, right that's a pitch mark and got on with the business of repairing it. Not cheating – by the way – just assessing the

"He's a delightful guy. Warm, funny, mad about golf and a generous human being – courteous not just to me, but to everyone with whom he comes in contact."

Alex in full swing during the Omega European Masters at Crans-sur-Sierre. As good a striker of the ball as Colin has seen.

balance of possibilities and reaching a conclusion that would go in their favour.

Alex demurred – he couldn't convince himself that the mark, which looked like a pitch mark in my eyes, was in fact that.

So he left it unrepaired, stood over the ball and tried to hit it around the lump. Sure enough – given that he was putting "off line" it failed to drop, leaving him out of the running for a play-off: as it turned out missing that putt made no difference to the outcome of the tournament – Thongchai Jaidee won the title by two shots.

I was hugely impressed with the choice he made: it was the wrong one to make in his immediate self interest, but *absolutely* the right one to make in his broader self interest and that of the integrity of the game.

Reflecting on that moment after the close of play, I hoped that such honourable behaviour would be rewarded. I know that others might have been tempted to call it differently – such was the fine margin of choice on offer – and that they would have had no qualms in doing so. When the possibility of victory is within one's grasp – then human nature might tend towards the most expedient outcome. Not cheating – just an expedient outcome.

> "They began to come to the conclusion that the least best developed part of his game, was around and on the greens."

And in the world of professional golf where the chance of victory is a rare and beautiful thing, where the stakes are so high, choosing the expedient option might sometimes be the easy one to take.

The tour is littered with players who play the game really well, have terrific technique, hit the ball a mile and putt well. But they rarely if ever make it to the winner's rostrum.

That gap, between outstanding tour-pro and winning tour-pro, is as big as the gap between a scratch amateur golfer and a 12 handicapper.

Sometimes a good tour pro will make the breakthrough and can go on to greater things. Many do win, but then slip down the rankings into relative obscurity, happy to take home good cheques for relatively uninspired and mundane performances.

But it's the hungry, ambitious, "want-to-get-on-at-all-costs" players that are the ones who for whom you want to be looping. And, by and large, they tend to be challenging people; difficult, tough, hard-working and totally driven in a way that can be slightly scary to those who haven't come across such people in their daily lives.

Strangely, as circumstances were to prove later in the year, this theory was totally turned on its head. Alex not only has the technical ability to win tournaments, he also has great mental depth and strength. And he does prove the old saying that the good guys *do* and *can* win.

As the season progressed with Alex, I found myself in an unusual position which is, unfortunately, something I'm going to have to live with as the years progress. He's 26 – and I'm not. And, to be frank, I felt something like a gnarled veteran when we first teamed up. I had to face the fact that I'm nearly old enough to be his father.

In the first few months of our relationship I found my "world weariness" slip away under constant exposure to his enthusiasm and the sheer pleasure that he derived from the game. I was also enjoying being back in Europe again with its more intimate, varied lifestyle on tour.

Alex had a really outstanding career before he teamed up with me. He spent eight years competing for the Swedish amateur team before he turned pro in 2005, at the age of 21 and after he had achieved a Business Marketing degree from Oklahoma State University where he also ruled the golfing roost.

I was hugely impressed with his ball striking, honed to perfection with hours and hours on the practice range. And it was this that began to nag at me: if he's such a fine athlete (more of which anon) and if he's hitting the ball so damn well, how come he wasn't getting the results that so many predicted would come his way?

The answer was short – short game. Not bad, but not nearly good enough to make the jump from middle of the table pro with potential – to winning pro not just once, but twice, three times and on.

We talked about this a lot and with his team, coach Pete Cowen and his assistant Mike Walker, and they began to come to the conclusion that the least best developed part of his game, was around and on the greens. His technique was quite good but he needed to work on choosing the right shot to play.

And the only way to fix that was to alter the balance of time assigned to his work off course, and that meant dramatically reducing the amount of time spent on the range – and significantly increasing the workload on his short game.

Getting him away from the driving range was like weaning an addict off his fix and I am sure he doubted the wisdom of what we were saying.

I told him that his striking game was magnificent, but that he hadn't developed sufficient technique or imagination around the greens, and that it was this, more than anything, this was holding him back.

Coming from a caddie – albeit a caddie with 25 years' experience – this might have caused some upset: but he took the observations on board and made the big switch in terms of priorities.

We devised a routine during tournament weeks that saw us eschew the range in favour of going out onto the course in the late afternoon when no-one was about, and spending our time working our way around the 18 greens on the course.

We would head to the 1st and figure out where the pin positions were going to be over the four days and then play a variety of chips shots – many from deliberately poor lies – and then hole them out.

We would pace around the green looking at breaks and borrows and the shape of things, trying to visualise all the time how the ball would react under different circumstances and different angles.

And thus it would go for the 18 greens – chipping, putting, playing out of greenside bunkers, all the time building our store of knowledge and our feel for what would happen in tournament play.

Off the course we devised putting routines on the practice green. He worked hard holing from two to three feet over and over and over and over again.

The premise was this: you're more likely to hole longer putts if they are going at the hole at pace. If you're babying them to the hole they are much more likely to take borrow as they lose speed. So getting the ball to the hole at pace became an imperative.

The downside of being aggressive with pace is that you can leave yourself beyond the hole by maybe three feet. But if you're happy and confident from three feet then that really doesn't present a problem – one simply has to build confidence from that distance.

And build it he did. We would spend an age on these putts building up his expectation and subconscious sense of certainty that he would hole them. And hole them he did. Over and over and over again.

This wasn't a technical issue – his technique was fine – but one of repetition and habit. We wanted to be in the habit of hearing the ball drop from this distance so that when faced with this type of putt in a pressure situation – the habit of knocking them in would simply flood both mind and body with the resulting positive outcome.

And he worked diligently at improving his visualisation of chip shots and his feel for the best option and how to get the best result.

Mid-way through the season Alex was struck down with a wrist injury that may have been a blessing in disguise, although it didn't seem like it at the time.

But with his wrist damaged he couldn't practice his long game and was forced to concentrate on his work around the greens.

Meanwhile, I found myself at something of a loose end which saw me playing plenty of golf at my home club of Royal Dublin, buttressing my reduced income with easy pickings from my publisher who's a total sucker for complicated bets that he doesn't understand and which he invariably loses.

But you get itchy feet when you're a caddie.

Thus I found myself spending a remarkable couple of weeks with the Colombian golfer, Camilo Villegas, during which we played the Scottish Open and then the British Open at Turnberry where I was hugely impressed with the level of preparation and attention to detail that the super-fit Villegas brought to the championship.

That experience left me hankering to get back to Alex who was emerging from his injury both physically fit – he is a fantastic looking athlete – and mentally very strong.

Our evolving approach to focusing on his short game really began to pay dividends when we got to the serene Crans-sur-Sierre in Switzerland, one of my favourite, and one of the tour's favourite destinations.

I had repeatedly said to him during the course of the year that he was going to win, that his game was good enough and, with an improved short game, we just had to be patient and wait until the opportunity presented itself – and we'd be away.

Our opening round at Crans was a joy with Alex shooting a six-under-par 65 –

and that was with a relatively poor putting round where he notched up a total of 31 – simply too many for a pro in the modern game.

But it was in the second day that the work we had been doing paid dividends – strangely enough in his worst round of the week which turned into a one-under-par 70.

Most great players have at least one round in a four round tournament when the going gets tough, when ball striking is, relatively speaking poor, and when you have to grind out a result in the face of mediocre golf.

It really separates the good players from the great players.

And Alex showed that resolve on the second day during which he played his worst golf of the week hitting only 11 greens in regulation – average by his standards. But his short game saved him, with four out of seven up and downs and a total of 28 putts in the round.

A round that could have been 74/76 was turned into a round of 70. Not great but not bad and certainly proof that the work we were doing was bearing fruit.

And on the third round it came together magnificently with a really exhilarating 63 which included seven birdies and one eagle. Great ball striking, brilliant course management, and positive assured putting – only 26 for the round.

> "And he worked diligently at improving his visualisation of chip shots and his feel for the best option and how to get the best result."

He slept poorly on his two shot lead but when I hooked up with him the following morning and as we began our pre-round preparation, I had that lovely instinctive feeling that today was going to be his – and our day. Not that Bradley Dredge was going to let us have a free run at the title, one that he had won just two years previously.

Alex got off to a cracking start with a couple of birdies to give him a four shot advantage before Dredge came back at him with some sparkling golf that saw him draw level.

But then Alex pulled out one of those tournament-changing shots when he holed out a really tricky bunker shot at the 15th for an eagle. That simply stopped Dredge in his tracks and from then on there was ever only going to be one name on the trophy – Alexander Noren.

Showered with champagne he very graciously acknowledged my small part in his victory attributing the short game work as the single most decisive factor in his maiden victory.

Later on that evening – as Alex was dutifully attending a sponsor's event from which he might have been forgiven for wanting to duck out – I was standing at the Taxi Bar in Crans Montana enjoying one of those classic European post-tournament get togethers that I enjoy so much and which rarely – if ever – you get on the US tour.

Caddies, players, tour officials, a whole mix of people, were enjoying a few

"I've no doubt that Danny Willet and Tano Goya have the same utterly focused approach to their fitness and to their game. That combined with a highly ordered lifestyle in every facet of their lives is now the norm on tour rather than the exception... of course there are exceptions to the rule...."

Main photograph: Danny Willet, former World Number One amateur – physically and mentally honed for the game.
Left: Argentina's Tano Goya. Opted to join the professional ranks early rather than go through the college system in the USA.
Above: the incomparable exception to the rule, Spain's Miguel-Angel Jiménez who plays the game with imagination, creativity and panache.

drinks in a glorious setting and savouring the atmosphere that this lovely event creates.

Time and time again people came over to have a chat with me and to congratulate – in his absence – Alex on winning the title. As ever I basked in the reflected glory and mumbled the usual "nothing to do with me really" line with as much sincerity as I could muster.

But what really struck me that evening was the sincerity of the good wishes: it was clear to me this was more than just plámás. People genuinely like Alex, find him hugely agreeable, approachable and an all round nice fellow – rare enough in life, very rare in the world of professional golf.

The next day was a classic of its kind in the old fashioned sense of caddying and how I remember it from when I first began on tour in the eighties.

Caddies up and on the bus – some slower than others – at 8.00am and down to the train station of Sion, where some bought coffee and others tucked a few sharpeners away, before boarding the train to Cologne en route to the Mercedes Championship.

A glorious train journey through some of the most spectacular scenery in Europe with a bunch of colleagues all intent on having a laugh and celebrating the best and worst that this bizarre circus we call the pro tour flings at us week in, week out.

After all these years I still got a great kick out of the sense of camaraderie that we still share: how lucky to be involved in a sport that allows you to keep on playing and caddying well beyond the years where other sportspeople are forced to retire.

I was really disappointed to reach Cologne and for the party to break up as we decanted ourselves from the train and made our way to our respective hotels to gather our wits and prepare for another week of hope, expectancy, pleasure, work – or a possible firing – at Gut Lärchenhof.

By the time Alex made it to Cologne I could see that he was mentally exhausted. Winning, the mental effort more than the physical, takes its toll on a golfer and in that regard Alex was no different.

He just couldn't muster the energy to mount any serious sort of challenge during the course of the week and I wondered whether the old maxim – win one week take the next one off – might have applied in these circumstances.

During the course of that week we were paired with another couple of young-bloods in the form of England's Danny Willett and Argentina's Tano Goya.

Willet joined the pro ranks in 2008 after a glittering career as an amateur achieving world number one status off a handicap of +5. Goya turned pro in 2007 at the tender age of 19, opting to learn his craft on tour rather than at college in the US. In early 2009 he took the big leap forward winning the Madeira Islands Open.

Looking at Willet, Goya and Alex I was struck by their physical conditioning and athleticism. The three of them could put on singlets and wouldn't look out of place in Olympic competition.

They were simply superb physical specimens honed, conditioned and built to play golf at the highest level.

My mind wandered back to my early days on tour when the idea of going to a gym simply didn't exist. The first time I noticed anyone on the European tour taking the slightest interest in their fitness was an old player of mine, Anders Forsbrand.

I remember the looks of disbelief when word got out that he was attaching weights to his ankles in an attempt to build stamina.

Twenty years on from that I was looking at a trio of golfers who couldn't conceive of life on tour without daily access to a gym – and their personal trainers.

If you go to Alex's website, *www.alexandernoren.com*, and read his blog you'll quickly pick up on the effort and intensity of the work-outs he does and the pain he puts himself through to get to where he feels he ought to be.

"Really tired again after yesterday's work out. Hope the soreness will be gone by tomorrow morning...we'll see," is a pretty standard entry.

"Totally dead when I woke up this morning! Pierre (his trainer) absolutely killed me yesterday during our work out. We have a plan we follow for each tournament. We go really hard on Monday and Tuesday, easy on Wednesday and Thursday. Hard on Friday and easy on Saturday. Relax Sunday. This make me feel really sore on Wednesday and a little sore on Thursday morning but it doesn't affect my game negatively. Then I feel great Friday and pumped up for the weekend

after the harder work out Friday night," reads another.

You'll also find really interesting material as to how he feels his body is working, how "well" he feels based on his food and drink intake and what remedial steps he takes if he's not feeling right.

In short – it's a highly regimented and focused programme designed to extract the maximum from his body in order to deliver peak performance as a golfer.

I've no doubt that Danny Willet and Tano Goya have the same utterly focused approach to their fitness and to their game. That combined with a highly ordered lifestyle in every facet of their lives is now the norm on tour rather than the exception.

And it's down to Tiger. Where he went others naturally followed. In a world where fractions matter, Tiger surged ahead of the rest of the tour with his relentless quest for physical and mental preparedness.

And when the results flowed from his complete devotion to winning and what was required to win, it was inevitable that others would follow. You can't argue with success.

Of course there are exceptions to the rule – the wonderful Miguel Angel Jiménez chomping on his cigar, his ample tummy suggesting an affinity with the good things in life, springs to mind. But even he is not immune from the pressure of gym work and though he may fight against it, you can rest assured that the Spaniard can be found on the treadmill from time to time.

It has been in this area that I have seen the biggest transformation in professional golfers over the last two decades. When I started out there were great players of the game as there are now great players. Now there are great players who are supremely fit, ripped with muscles and capable of maintaining their stamina right through a tournament without feeling in any way tired or run-down.

Mental tiredness is a different thing altogether and it was that which Alex was suffering from when he hit Cologne – the body was willing but the mind was not.

But an athlete like Alex is not long in the recovery room and the enthusiasm and commitment to the game and his desire to squeeze every last drop out of his ability is quite life affirming. Unlike the journeymen pros – the winning pros are desperate to succeed. Not in a panicky sort of way, but in a mind-set of complete self-belief.

It is as though they feel that winning is their destiny and anything that falls short of that mark is really quite an affront to their commitment at all levels to the game and their chosen profession.

And while amateurs – even top amateurs – can't absorb themselves so completely in either the game or themselves – it is possible to harness much of what the pros do and apply it your own game. That's what I am hoping to do over the next number of pages, and while I am no coach you cannot but come to some view as to what works for golfers and what doesn't, after 25 years as a tour caddie. Hopefully what I touch on is of some benefit. Most of all I would suggest that you should *lower* your expectations and stop being so hard on yourself.

Now read on...

BLOOD, SWEAT AND FEARS

Alex Noren grimacing during a vigorous workout under the watchful eye of his personal trainer, Pierre Johansson, during the Dunhill Links Championship in Scotland. Noren, like the vast majority of today's professional golfers, spends a considerable amount of time in the gym developing core strength.

by

COLIN BYRNE

THE

high winds that had been
predicted for Scotland earlier in the
week of the Dunhill Links Championship, duly arrived on the
Saturday in such force as to
warrant the cancellation of play for
the day. By the time I sauntered
down to the practice ground at St
Andrews, my man, Alex Noren,
CONTINUED ON NEXT PAGE

was punching balls into the southwest wind that howled across the range from the left side. It was of course a hopeless and detrimental wind to practice in.

It was mainly the Swedes who tried to defy the elements and actually learn something from hitting balls in a forty-mile-an-hour wind. The Scandinavians are dogged by relentless and – frequently – an inefficient work ethic. It was simply not a day for constructive practice.

Alex had his personal trainer with him that week, Pierre Johansson. He travels with Alex and some other Swedish players and is usually present at events every other week. Pierre, like most trainers, is a walking advertisement for keeping yourself in shape. He spent much of the 1990s in America working as a physical therapist. He then returned to Sweden and joined the Swedish Olympic Committee working with athletes of Olympic standard.

Alex has been conditioning himself throughout his career for the optimum physical performance on the golf course. Until earlier this year, he was advised by an Australian based trainer. Naturally enough, and being in Europe, hands on direction for Alex was not readily available. So he decided to join Johansson and get more immediate attention on a regular basis.

I took myself down the Fife coast to the town of Leven and headed for Dowie's Gym nestled among a sleepy looking residential area. Amongst the packed red weight machines, with power music pumping across the gym, I found Alex popping a 40 kilo weight bar above his head in quick six-rep succession and looking invigorated after each exercise. Although I was chatting to Pierre during the routines, he never once took his eyes off his pupil while he was in action.

"Alex is not particularly big – he weighs about 75 kilos and stands at 1.8 metres. But when it comes to striking and launching his golf ball, he punches well above his modest weight. "

Pierre advised me that you need good balance and control. It is not the exercise itself that is dangerous, rather how you do it. My first thought was, how on earth are these guys going to lift a cup of tea tomorrow, let alone play a round of golf, after such a demanding workout.

Alex is not particularly big – he weighs about 75 kilos and stands at 1.8 metres. But when it comes to striking and launching his golf ball, he punches well above his modest weight. He is one of the longer hitters on tour averaging just over 290 yards off the tee. This is because he has a good technique and is very well conditioned.

Sceptics may question the alliance between swing coaches and physical trainers. However you have to look no further than the standard bearer of physical and technical prowess, the greatest golfer in the world Tiger Woods, who has developed himself into such a superior physical condition, enabling him to swing the club as hard as he possibly can, while exercising a huge degree of control, without injuring himself.

There is of course a valid argument that his knee did not stand up to the

The spoils of victory: Alex with the Omega European Masters trophy.

demands his aggressive swing required from the lower half of his body. Serious surgery, lengthy convalescence, and six wins later would suggest that the ultimate golfing machine in the history of the game is very much back in control. It is simply a sign of the times that the standard of the modern game is such that it is worth risking possible injury in order to reach ever-increasing standards.

What Johansson and his colleagues on the modern tour are trying to accomplish with their players is the ability for them to be able to practice enough to improve as golfers. They want minimum limitation and maximum possibility. If a coach has a player who cannot get into a vital swing position, Pierre can do exercises with the player to gradually and carefully get him to that position. He can get them to tolerate more time on the range with more quality.

As with every aspect of the game of golf, the trick is to do everything in moderation. Golfers, and particularly ambitious golfers, can be frequently obsessive. So it is important that someone monitors their work rate. Alex is very flexible, this is something I have observed in many exceptional golfers; when they are warming up, they look like rubber-men. Pierre's physical goal for Alex is to get his mid-section stronger, to use his legs more and thus generate greater power.

Johansson clearly understands the important divide between the golfer and the physical specimen. He clearly sticks to non-golf specific physical training, leaving the golfer to get on with what he does best, namely swing the club.

He gets his pupils to work with heavy weights so that they can fire their appropriate muscles. There are two ways to increase speed or power; either use really light weights and accelerate fast or, use heavy weights which will trigger signals in the body to respond well to heavy loads. The biomechanics of the golf swing combine *stability* with *mobility*. In other words what joints in the system should be *stable* and what should be *mobile?*

Working core strength with tight players can work against them. So the training entails constant monitoring because the individual's core strength and mobility will change on a monthly basis depending on their work rate.

Naturally there are all body types in golf. The physical therapist's goal is to assess non-athletic golfers and see if he/she can make them better. Johannson is specifically trying to eliminate compensatory movements in a golfer's swing. With the correct physical guidance, he can get rid of the compensations made for a restricted swing.

Alex will spend at least 15 minutes stretching, or being stretched, before he plays. If Pierre is with him he will be set up in the locker room a couple of hours before Alex is due to tee off.

The routine is not as simple as a rub down with an oily rag – it's more intense. Some of the positions that Pierre forces Alex into, confirms my view that the modern pro is made of rubber.

If Pierre is not around then Alex can avail of the extensive facilities of the Tour Physio unit which is present and on site each week.

Inside the unit, the physiotherapists are available to help players loosen up before their practice sessions. If Alex finds himself without access to any of the above assistance, he will go through his own stretching routine. Whatever the circumstances, he will *always* go through an extensive stretching routine before playing. These young players are finely tuned athletes and will do everything to ensure that they can push their swings to the limit without risking injury.

Of course this is all highly structured and focused and technical and whether the average golfer can extrapolate any benefit from the professional's approach is a moot point.

My own personal experience – and I am off a handicap of seven – is that it can – to a certain level.

Go on, stretch yourself

The simplest, most inexpensive way to improving your round of golf – is to begin stretching. Not the jump out of the car, run to the first tee with bits and pieces falling out of your golf bag, followed by a bit of grunting and putting your hands over your head, and reaching for the sky three times type of stretching.

No, what I mean is the sort of stretching that Tom Watson referred to when he said that, given the option of hitting a basket of balls on the range as part of his pre-round preparation, and doing some stretching exercises – he'd opt for the stretch.

I'd hazard a guess that if I asked you, the reader, right now, whether you did any stretches before a round of golf – the vast majority of you would say no. And if I asked those who said yes how much time they dedicated to those stretches, I'd suggest that the vast majority of you would be in the one minute mark.

So what if you were to do the following: take ten minutes before your next round to do a series of five different exercises of two minutes each. This is hardly going to tax you from a time perspective, nor is it going to leave you puffing and panting before you go to the course.

On the contrary, stretching and increasing your potential for flexibility on the course is actually going to relax you before your round *if* you do it in a calm, ordered and methodical way.

It really isn't too much to ask of yourself. After all you're going to spend up to four-and-a-half hours (yes I know it's too long for a round of golf but that's what they're averaging these days) out on the course. So all I am suggesting is that ten minutes – a mere four per-cent of the time you are going to spend on the course – is going to be far more beneficial physically *and* mentally to you than whacking 30 golf balls in a rush on the practice ground.

But of course you're an amateur – and I know what will happen. You'll start with good intentions, do a few hamstring stretches, a few shoulder rotations and then get edgy and impatient to do something more *meaningful* – or at least what you think is more meaningful – like having a chat with the next person who turns the corner in the locker room about the weather. Or how difficult the rough is. Or how wretched the economy is.

Fine and noble sentiments about the nature of golf – but not withstanding Jean Van de Velde's Gallic sense of irony – one cannot but think that the prospect of this infamous shot out of the burn at Carnoustie, on his 72nd hole of the 1999 Open Championship, hardly presented itself as a "fun" option.

And there's another mental difference between the amateur and the pro. The pro is utterly and totally focused on himself and what he has to do on the course. Nothing will interfere with their pre-round preparation, whether it is on the range, around the green or in their heads. They will be utterly committed to themselves in the most extraordinarily selfish way, oblivious to any external force that might impede their preparation.

Again, Tiger is the most brilliant exponent of this state of mind. No autographs, no interviews, no interruptions. As far as he is concerned he is there for himself and for himself alone. Anything that has the potential to get in his way is not even noticed, doesn't enter into his field of vision.

It's like a giant force field of will, containment and focus that encircles him prior to his round. It's quite a phenomenon to experience and witness it close up – almost scary spiritual – and hugely impressive. He's there not only to do his job as he sees it, but to deliver on his remarkable talent. And whatever it takes to deliver that result is what will be done.

Of course the amateur, you and me alike, has neither the wherewithal nor the mental strength to replicate Tiger: if you tried it – you'd probably become either the laughing stock of the club or the player to be most avoided such would be the parody. But why not take a leaf out of his approach – firstly with the exercises and secondly by just finding a few minutes of calm on your own prior to going to the first tee.

No last minute phone calls to see are the kids all right, no final check-ups to see whether the package has arrived or that lodgement has been made, just a quiet three minutes breathing gently through your nose and exhaling through your mouth and blanking your mind from the outside world and all its noise. I guarantee you that if you devote three minutes – properly – to this, you'll arrive at the first tee in a far more ready state of mind.

> "Because that's what playing the game of golf is – an ongoing series of challenges and interesting shots that you have to get on with. It's the next one that's fun – not the one you've just hit."

Nor does learning from the professional's selfishness mean that you have to become the club's most anti-social player. On the contrary, it's the professional who can switch off between shots that is likely to come out ahead over time.

Chat away with your playing partners when you're between shots. But when you get towards the ball that's when you need to start mentally focusing beginning with a series of questions.

Is that my ball? How is it lying? Where is it lying? How far to the pin? Where is the wind from? What is my expectation from this shot? What is the risk factor? Can I execute this shot nine times out of ten? Am I ready to choose a club and commit?

If yes the answer – stand over the ball, think of nothing but the target and hit the ball with conviction. And move on instantly. It's over – and now you're faced with another exciting challenge.

Because that's what playing the game of golf is – an ongoing series of challenges and interesting shots that you have to get on with. It's the next one that's fun – not the one you've just hit.

Time and time again in the company of amateurs I see their heads go down after a few poor shots over the opening holes. What baffles me is what they thought they were going to achieve and what expectations they had when they arrived to the course, poorly prepared, in poor physical condition, dragging the stress of the outside world along with them, and in the absence of any ongoing, *intelligent* practice.

In those circumstances, it is utterly delusional to expect anything other than your fair share of poor shots. Even more so when you consider the professional golfer is mentally prepared for poor shots – they are, after all, an integral part of the game.

Indeed the professional golfer is expecting at least one poor round during the course of 72 holes. It's how they manage themselves during that poor round – that separates the winners from the pack.

So if the professional brings this attitude to his game – how then can the amateur bring even higher expectations to the weekly round of golf?

And if you do insist on raising the bar to such an unreasonable height, it will not only affect the management of your round, it will severely undermine the pleasure you take from your weekly outing.

All of these things are a question of balance – and it's been my experience that the professional and amateur golfers who fare best, tend to have achieved a really good sense of balance between the myriad of competing issues that create the entire golfing experience.

Get the most from practice – or don't practice at all

There's nothing wrong with practice – it's just what you practice, and where you practice, and with what kind of balls you practice, and off what surface you practice, that makes a difference. Personally I hate driving ranges while fully understanding that it's the only facility of which many golfers can avail.

Why, for instance, have so many driving ranges got no – or very mediocre – putting and chipping facilities? It would be the cynic who might posit the view that's because there's no money in chipping and putting, while at €8 the basket of 70 the driving range proprietor is making a living.

I hate the sound, look and feel of driving ranges – so alien are they from the actual theatre where the game is played, out in the open, in natural and beautiful surroundings. And off grass. Don't underestimate that difference – hitting off mats gives you an entirely unrelated experience to hitting off the genuine article.

But they're a necessary evil, I guess, so if it is the only way you can hone your game, then it's important that you approach your practice with some focus, some sense of realism and some discipline. You do run the risk of doing damage to your game, and your confidence, by simply whacking ball after ball into a field.

First and foremost, you must force yourself to take a break between shots. I have watched men and women hit four shots in 60 seconds and do so over a period of 15 minutes, totally exhausting themselves, working themselves into a frenzy and a state of bewilderment in the process. And then they'll rush off to get another basket to try and put things to rights! A recipe for disaster.

So you have to take a break between each shot you hit. I was out helping a reasonably useful club golfer on a driving range recently and I made him hit a shot, walk away, have a chat and put a minimum of 60 seconds between each shot – our session lasted an hour.

During that period we talked about visualisation, changes to technique and – most importantly – target assessment.

I forced the player to pick out flags on the range at different distances and to combine the technical changes we were making to target attack. I would make him hit an eight iron, then a five iron, then a three iron, and a driver *at* targets rather than into the void of the range field.

That forced him to adopt an attitude and approach similar to that on the course. We were using the range to its maximum potential. The change in approach resulted in a far more productive use of time for both me, and the player.

Professionals can fall into the same trap as amateurs, confusing quantity over quality and getting themselves into a comfort zone bashing out 100 perfect five irons, which is totally and utterly meaningless in the context of playing the game on the course.

Numerous professionals spend hours and hours on the range when their time would be far better spent working on their short game drills and working on meaningful competition. By that I mean saying, if I fail to get up and down three times out five, it's going to cost me €10 payable to my caddie.

That immediately puts a player under some pressure and builds a link between what happens on the practice green and what will happen in tournament play – failed up and downs cost money, both in practice and in play.

What is absolutely essential in all of this is that amateurs practice their short game. While I appreciate that most amateurs – actually most golfers – would prefer to work on their long game, it's from 60 yards in that is going to transform your scores.

You simply have to make the commitment to working on this area of your game to the extent that if you are lucky enough to have an hour's practice a week, then I would suggest that you devote 20 minutes to hitting your long irons/driver, 10 minutes to pitching and the remaining 30 minutes to chipping and putting.

And don't just throw down 20 balls beside the green and play shot after shot. Put one ball in a decent lie, the next in a poor lie, the next downhill, the next from a different position and so on.

And change your clubs. Hit little five iron bump and runs as well as eight iron chips and use your pitching wedge as well. All of this will help you form a vision and understanding of how the ball reacts in different circumstances and with different clubs – the results of which will then form part of your store of knowledge and experience when you get to the course.

This is practice for playing – not practice for practice sake.

And maybe stop using that 60-degree lob wedge around the green all the time. They require really good technique and if you're playing off a handicap of 18 you are simply putting yourself under too much pressure with that club.

I remember asking Andy Prodger, who caddied for Nick Faldo in his first Masters victory at Augusta, what Faldo did that was so special in order to conquer the National. Amongst many things, he mentioned his chipping as being a major contributor.

What Faldo did – and still does – when chipping, is to keep the ball as low to the ground as possible with as little spin as possible. Many of us are lured into chipping with the most lofted wedge we have in the bag. This is rarely necessary unless you are constantly getting stuck behind bunkers or other hazards. So put the lob wedge away and work with an easier instrument and chart your progress.

Spend that 30 minutes working on getting up and down and note the results, the percentage of times that you made the save. And over a period of four weeks, if you stay focused on your practice, you should see a gradual improvement that will travel to the golf course and onto your score card.

So use your time carefully and manage your practice sessions to squeeze as much out of yourself as you possibly can.

Putting practice

Probably the best bit of general advice I can give in relation to putting practice is to concentrate from six feet in – that's where the average amateur struggles. Start from two feet out and get used to the sound of hearing your ball drop, get accustomed to holing out time and time again. Get confident about standing over the ball and expect – almost demand of yourself that the ball is going to drop. Will it in.

It won't always, of course, and the fact that it might occasionally slide by doesn't make you a bad putter – far from it. But if you get into the habit of knocking them in from short distances, in particular from three feet in, you'll be a lot more confident and aggressive over your longer putts.

And when you're practising those longer putts, try and get them running at the hole at speed. Don't try to cosy them up to the cup, give it a go and putt with purpose and confidence and intent.

More often than not it's better to work on *attitude* rather than technique when you're practicing your putting.

Retief Goosen, who has one of the most beautiful strokes I've ever seen, has a very methodical routine to his putting. He hits medium length putts of about 15 to 20 feet, both right to left and left to right. He then hits shorter putts, up to six feet, from various positions around the hole.

This way he gets to practice straight, right to left, left to right, uphill and downhill putts. He will then hit some longer putts of 30 feet and up. He might finish with some two-footers. The average session before he plays in competition would be about 15 minutes. After his round he might spend half an hour on the practice green. Tell your playing partners that you're heading to the practice putting green rather than the bar after your Saturday competition and watch the reaction.

If Retief is putting badly he spends as long as it takes to work into a position that he is more comfortable with. It's methodical and logical. He will run through a checklist of hand and eye positions in relation to the ball. He will check his posture and then assess whether the putter is working along the correct line. He tends to take the putter a little bit inside the line on the way back and brings it through straight to the target. If he is off, the putter tends to be deviating off this line at some point.

It is usually something in his set-up that causes him to move from his regular stroke. Like the average golfer, the reason for a pro putting badly is likely to be down to set-up. What the pros work on is trying to almost mindlessly repeat the same stroke time after time, until their muscles remember the desired feeling.

And don't be afraid to go to a coach for putting lessons. Strangely there appears to be this weird suspension of logic – particularly amongst men – when it comes to getting help with putting. They just don't seem to get the idea that putting and the short game is the secret to scoring.

Ask any teaching pro how what percentage of club golfers walk through their door and ask for a putting lesson, and they'll tell you about five percent. It's a shocking statistic – truly amazing when you consider that the putter is the most *used* club in the bag. Actually the most *overused* club in the bag.

But, hey, we're blokes and we like to hit things long and hard. That short game stuff is for wimps.

In coach we trust

Virtually every aspirant golfer starts off with a coach whether at their home club or at the range. And just as there are good players and poor players, there are good coaches and poor coaches. Having said that the quality of club coaches has improved considerably over the last number of years – mainly due to significant improvements in the PGA exam system which is considerably more demanding both in its practical and theory elements, than in years gone by. By and large, unless you're very unlucky, you're not going to fall into the hands of someone who will ruin your game.

Students of the game and the tour will know that there's a hierarchy of coaches and they'll be able to name the star coaches and who their players are: Hank Haney and Tiger Woods. Butch Harmon and Phil Mickelson. Bob Torrance and Padraig Harrington. David Leadbetter and Trevor Immelman.

Coaches have been around for years and they'll be around for years although there is no question but that their involvement with players is far more intense and hands on than it was two decades ago.

To what extent that is a result of genuine technical need on the part of players or simply the players needing psychological support, is a moot point. Hitting golf balls on your own can be a lonely old station; maybe it just suits players to have a bit of company with the odd bit of technical advice thrown in, to offer some sort of confirmation that they are heading in the right direction.

And fashions come and fashions go: one year the buzz words on the range might be "wide arc", the next it could be "counter rotation".

All of this theoretical stuff has its place and it can be quite entertaining – particularly if you know how to separate the wheat from the chaff, which

> "By and large I find that amateurs in this category are not looking for any major changes in what they do, they are simply looking for a "banker" shot, one that they can execute with reasonable degree of confidence."

most skilled practitioners of the game can do. If you're playing the game to a reasonable standard you're more likely to have a better understanding of what is total nonsense and what is not. Although I have seen a fair share of thinking professionals totally lose the plot by adopting some theory and approach advanced by what could only be generously described as a crackpot.

So the good golfer is not immune to having both his head and his swing wrecked by over-analysis. But it's the golfer at the other end of the scale that I really pity. The ones playing off 22 who resort to trying every conceivable trick thrown at them whether in books (ah, like this one), magazines and now the web where grainy image meets dubious advice and where you can tie yourself up in knots in no time at all.

To them the advice is simple: STOP. Simplify your life and go find yourself a coach who is not going to talk at you about swing planes, decisive impact, hands at the top, long thumb versus short thumb, pivot points and the like. One who will quietly have a look at you, suggest one, possibly two things for you to do, and will then urge you to get on with it.

By and large I find that amateurs in this category are not looking for any major changes in what they do, they are simply looking for a "banker" shot, one that they can execute with reasonable degree of confidence.

That's precisely the time you do need to get to a coach who will show you the correct technique – most importantly one that you can use over and over again –

David Leadbetter – with impeccably creased trousers (left) and Trevor Immelman – equally smart turn-out (right) doing there thing on the practice range.

for, say, bunker play, so that you're not feeling like a total fool having taken three swipes to get out from the sand.

It's that sort of simple, "here's-how-you-do-it" approach, that can relieve the fear that higher handicap golfers have of certain types of shots, particularly for the likes of bunker play which feature high on that list of scary shots for the average player.

Chipping is another area of torture, indeed most high handicap golfers find they get the hee-be-geebees in or around the green and that's where they get most demoralised. Strangely they don't seem to care if they knock six drives out of town – bizarrely that's kind of acceptable and doesn't tend to affect the ego of the high handicapper.

But see the head slump when Mr 20 duffs a chip shot or double hits a lob-wedge, and you can begin to understand the fragility of the mind when it comes to expectations – and the male ego in particular.

Later in the book you'll come across Neil Manchip, the national coach to the Golfing Union of Ireland, who has had the likes of Rory McIlroy and Shane Lowry through his hands, but who also puts his hands onto very ordinary amateur golfers.

Neil has always had a very simple, restrained approach to coaching. I should know as I have taken some lessons from him in the past. His current philosophy (no bad thing that – good coaches are constantly re-evaluating their message) is minimalist almost to the point of non-existence.

Find the ball, hit it, find it again and hit it again.

This mantra's underlying philosophy is that he is trying to un-clutter a player's mind and divest him of all thoughts, bar hitting the ball to a target. His view is that good players can let their conscious mind get in the way of executing the shot by virtue of thinking too much and not letting the body, drilled as it has been, get on with doing the work.

Playing with freedom and without the burden of thought and expectation is a pretty elevated plain to be working on – but it's one that the professional golfer aspires to.

I do appreciate how difficult this is for the amateur. How often have you been engaged in an actual, conscious discussion with yourself just prior to hitting a shot? And what tends to be the result? Yes, awful.

So try and divest yourself of swing thoughts and try and just imprint the target into your mind and let it and yourself go.

If you go to a regular tour event early in the week you would do worse than spend an hour closely watching the preparation that professionals go through in order to perform at the highest level.

It is quite staggering the amount of balls these already hugely talented golfers hit, and the workload they get through in order to get themselves into a position to win.

That is what they are doing; preparing to be able to hit the shot they need on the 72nd hole to win a golf tournament. You'll probably also be surprised by the amount of 'others' that surround the players. The swing coach has become a regular feature of the modern golfer's entourage. Many of the coaches will leave by Wednesday but some see the whole week through. There are varying opinions about the presence of a swing coach at an event.

The old school would argue that you 'have to dance with the one you brought', or rely on the swing you have, and trust your golfing brain, or savvy, to deal with temporary deficiencies.

If you look at what Tiger does at an event it is clearly minimal practice. It seems that he does his serious practice away from tournaments. When he is at an event he is concentrating on understanding the course and, above all, scoring.

It is the constant challenge for good golfers; balancing the search for the perfect swing with the necessity to bring in a score. So if the professional does bring a swing coach on tour, it's important that they are experienced enough to understand the subtleties of the fine balance between scoring and swinging.

And I think the same goes for amateurs. Once you get to the course for a competition you really must focus on getting the ball into the hole. That's what you're there to do – not to execute the perfect swing.

My man Alex has worked with the much respected swing coach Pete Cowen, and his assistant Mike Walker, for about three years now. One of them is usually on tour each week keeping an eye on one of their many pupils.

Pete Cowen, according to many top European professionals is as knowledgeable a coach as you will find on any range in the world. Depending on his player's requirements, he can go deep into the mechanics of the golf swing all of course with the aim of improving the golfer's swing and in turn his scores.

His assistant Mike Walker feels privileged to have learnt his top end swing teaching from the best. Both Cowen and Walker played golf at a high level and, in Mike's case, he realised from an early age that he was not made as a golf performer but recognised his ability to convey to others how to improve their swings. He admits that he was always more interested in how the swing worked rather than performing.

If you saw these coaches at work, often lurking on the back of a cold, windy and frequently wet range waiting for the next casualty to arrive looking for some emergency surgery, you could be forgiven for seeing them as golf perverts. Mike admits to sleeping, eating and breathing golf. He has done so for six years now.

Despite both Pete and Mike's technical expertise they can speak from experience. Cowen competed on tour for years but more importantly he was a range rat, hitting thousands of balls a day.

His own experience has taught him that it is not the way of the future for his young alumni. He would now recommend physical exercise ahead of hitting that extra 500 range balls. The combination of the physical, modern, athletic golfer and the technical and talented one is very much in the advanced coaches' plan when honing today's top golfers.

There are only a handful of events that you can compete in today if you do not have length in your game. This is now the inescapable fact of tour life. I remember

Hal Sutton discussing the modern era of the golfer back in the late nineties. He took the view that someone coaching a young golfer should show them a strong grip and then get them to hit the ball hard – as hard as they could. After that basic lesson and only after they were *hitting* the ball, would he introduce them to the finer details of the game.

Swings are notoriously difficult to change. The key now is to get the talent early, and mould it from there.

You can segregate practice into three categories; technical, shots and course shots. The technical aspect is, in mechanical terms, the car being stripped down into individual parts and being worked on individually. The coach may take the right wrist movement and identify what the player wants that wrist to do within the swing. The technical aspect is obviously the area that should not be tampered with during an event. Given the examination of minutiae it is understandable why.

Working on such detail is fed into the golfers swing by introducing it through the short game and thus it should flow into the longer swing. The emphasis is on having the same principals at work in both the short and long games.

It is difficult to achieve improvements at high speed. Naturally with the use of technology in the form of video analysis, the coach can slow down the swing and practice moves in isolation so that the player can feel the change and get better feedback throughout the process. The key with tour players is that they must be kept in a playable condition. Given the amount of events there are each year there is never time for major reconstruction.

A top player has nine different shots. This array consists of low, medium and high shots. With a fade, straight or with a draw. There are nine possibilities with the above array. The golfer wants control of all nine shots. Perhaps he may only play three or four of them but, with experience, at least he will know his strengths and weaknesses.

Again Mike emphasises that the understanding of these nine shots comes from the short game. Crucially there should be no conflict between the short and long game.

A recognition of the critical relationship and mutual dependence between swing coaches and the bio-mechanists has emerged in recent years. Mike admits that his knowledge of golf technique has been enhanced by the physiotherapists and their physiological expertise. It is not *technical perfection* that you should seek but *technical efficiency*. You can achieve success with a diversity in technique.

A player like Alex can get orthodox tuition because he has an orthodox technique. If you get a less orthodox player you need to look at why his swing works and not why it should be perfect. A really good coach will understand what to interfere with and what to accept.

The coach on tour also knows that players need to be handled with care when they are at tournaments. I have overheard many 'lessons' by coaches to their star players during events and you would be staggered at how facile the advice is.

They are one liners – uncomplicated words of encouragement – not detailed monologues about the intricacies of the golf swing.

Less IS *more* for these guys.

It's something that amateurs need to be aware of when they feel their heads are about to explode with an overload of technical jargon from the coach who is simply showing off his technical understanding while prattling on in the driving range.

Be wary of the coach who goes into too much detail, particularly if you're just starting out in the game.

The good coach is tapping into the psyche of the golfer, trying to align his perception with reality. Players need to play to their strengths even though they may not be aware of what their strengths are. When it comes to shot making, the player wants complete control of the flight – both trajectory and deviation.

So when the coach is dealing with a player at an event, he deals more with the shots he will hit and – in particular – the course shots he will hit. When the coach and player are working away from the tournament scene, they will concentrate more on the purely technical aspects of the game.

At a tournament with a player like Alex Noren, you are dealing with maintenance and supervision. The hard work has been already done.

When discussing technique and theory, Ben Hogan and Sam Snead are the templates that modern coaches use as their reference.

Nicklaus came along and people tried to interpret his technique: more often than not, it was misinterpreted and misunderstood. His was the 'rock and block' era.

We have recently gone through a brief spell of 'stack and tilt' theory which appears to have lost some momentum this year despite previously attracting a lot of attention.

Swing coaching has probably turned full circle and we are now back to using the classic Hogan swing as a model to emulate when it comes to moulding young golfers.

It seems with the swing, no matter what fads and creative ideas that coaches dream up, the more we change the more we stay the same.

The most important question any golfer must ask themselves is 'what do I want to get out of it'.

It is a question I frequently ask myself given that I never practice. Expectation must always match preparation. And if you can't devote the time to develop and improve your game at all levels, then really you have no business going onto the course with expectations of even playing to your handicap. So stop beating yourself up. Go out, sniff the air, and *enjoy* yourself.

In Neil Manchip's simple words, perhaps it's best just to 'turn, hit and celebrate'.

Colin Byrne, Dublin 2009.

BAGMAN 2
2005
ON TOUR

"Tiger approached Marc in the locker room on Wednesday and asked him how his hand was. He didn't have a bandage on it, so it wasn't that obvious; Tiger had somehow found out about his injury. Marc was touched. On Thursday morning as they headed down the 10th fairway together, Marc was already starting to feel at ease with Woods, whom he describes as humble, very human, friendly and intensely focused when it came to his shot."

Page 74

Tiger Woods beaming during the second round of the 2005 PGA Championship at Baltusrol Golf Club, New Jersey, and at full extension off the tee during the same round. Woods finished tied 4th behind eventual winner Phil Mickelson.

COLIN BYRNE

Everyone wants Wie piece of a rare talent

JANUARY 18: 'Go Michelle" badges adorned the sea of sponsors' hats outside the ropes at the Sony Open in the Waialae Country Club, Honolulu, Hawaii, last week. Michelle mode had taken on a life of its own.

The buzz fizzed around south-east Oahu as audible as the swoosh of the wind through the lanky palms that surround the seaside golf course.

The 15-year-old prodigy Michelle Wie was making her second appearance at the event having missed last year's cut by one shot. The local expectation was bigger than a child's on Christmas Eve. Unfortunately the six-foot tall youth missed the halfway cut more convincingly, by eight shots, this year.

I got the chance to observe the Hawaiian wunderkind first hand last Tuesday in a local charity six-hole foursome shoot-out involving some of the participating pros (including Retief Goosen) accompanied by qualifying young amateurs from the area. What a tough position the talented adolescent Wie is in.

Everyone wants a piece of her and her handlers are willing to give them as much as they want. She is articulate and seemingly mature beyond her years, so when she is asked yet another question she replies almost better versed than the last answer. All this for a young girl who has effectively bunked off high school to play in a men's professional golf tournament.

Kids screamed when she was introduced on the first tee. Adults looked in amazement at the height of her. In a country that is keen to elevate as many young talented people as they can to heroic status and subsequently destroy them with unnecessary adulation, I could not help but feel concerned for the hugely-talented youngster.

'Team Michelle' was ever present. David Leadbetter, the famed coach, was by her side at every practice session early in the week. Jimmy Johnson, Nick Price's regular caddie, had been flown in from Texas to carry her bag and offer his advice for the big occasion. Her parents were there, friends, sponsors and the obvious predators waiting to pounce on any potential good deal.

That is if she ever gets to the starting blocks of professional golf without being run off the track along the way.

I remember the hooha surrounding teenager Justin Rose after his fourth-place finish as an amateur in the British Open at Birkdale in 1998. His immediate future was doomed by hyper attention and arguably not enough protection from the predators. The best thing that Wie could have learned last week would have come from a brief conversation with Justin Rose.

Rose took a fall from the relative heights of his Open performance for the next few years and battled his way back to serious contention out of the wilderness of mismanagement. Some would contend that he was just learning his trade in those dark years, others argue he should have been protected a little more.

I was asked in a questionnaire for visitors if Wie's presence at the event had influenced my decision to come to Honolulu. To which I naturally replied that the Irish winter and Retief Goosen had more to do with that decision. It was a indication of how the sponsors viewed the local starlet.

Fair play to them or shame on them? If they were really interested in the welfare of the young Wie they would invite her to play at their event and let her do it on her terms to give herself the best chance of performing to the best of her ability. With the circus surrounding the local girl, quite frankly she had very little chance of making the cut. But the sponsors got more than their money's worth out of her in the process.

The badge for next year should be "Let Wie be". The teenager is a prodigious talent, give her a chance to develop and don't use her specifically as a promotional tool.

From a personal point of view we substituted whale watching in Maui to tree spotting on the golf course last week. Things were not quite going to plan on the short grass which gave me a chance to deviate to the impressive foliage that border the fairways of Waialae.

They are proud of their trees at the country club to the extent that they have put name plaques on many of the thick-leaved exotic trees dotted around the course.

As you enter the clubhouse grounds a huge sprawling Benjamin tree from India acts as a canopy for a large part of the car park. Moving from the locker-room towards the practice ground a Paper Bark tree with a trunk that looks like crumpled dried sheets of paper catches your eye. Then you pass an Autograph Tree from Florida, a Tropical Almond from Malaysia and a Money Tree from Madagascar.

Out on the course the only advantage of an errant drive is that you are likely to improve your knowledge of tropical trees. With Silver Trumpets and Monkey Pod Raintrees you could be forgiven for thinking you are were in a botanical garden. The marshals' dream tree would have to be the Be Still tree from central America with its beautiful yellow flower. The Vertical Wili Wili from the Polynesian Islands leads to some giggling from the less mature among us.

Michelle Wie may look like a well developed woman who needs no sheltering from the perils of a commercial world, but much like the exotic saplings that were planted in Waialae years ago and which stand so elegantly and strong today, they would not be there without a formative stage of protective nurturing.

Alarm bells ring as pro-am cooks the Goose

FEBRUARY 22: Short on daylight and big on amateurs who want to partake in the Nissan Open, as soon as you can see the first fairway the pro-am starts. That was at 6.40am west coast local time. My player, Retief Goosen, was supposed to be the leader of the first group of enthusiastic amateurs last week at Riviera Country Club. Unfortunately, he was still sleeping as Woody Austin, the first alternate for the pro-am, took his place.

Given that the pro-am is a necessary evil for the higher ranked players on the PGA Tour, it would be misleading to say that the pro leaps out of bed on a Wednesday morning with unbridled enthusiasm about playing with "four new friends". But of course they like playing for the prize money that the new friends add to the generous purses on the US Tour.

It was to be our first week back after a month's break, and effectively it was to be the unofficial start of Retief's year. I waited, as we caddies do at most events on the US Tour, outside the clubhouse. The trouble with Riviera is that there are three doors from which the players can exit the locker-room.

Given that it was my first time to Riviera, I was not too sure which door my man would appear through.

I stood outside the exit I assumed he would walk through at about 6am. Stephen Ames's coach was showing me the morning paper, with the news that Paul Casey is receiving therapy for the psychological trauma of playing in America after his anti-American comments of late last year.

> "Steve Williams was explaining what he remembered of his accident in a car race back in New Zealand three weeks ago. I was cringing at the look of his left hand, with over 50 stitches..."

Steve Williams was explaining what he remembered of his accident in a car race back in New Zealand three weeks ago. I was cringing at the look of his left hand, with over 50 stitches, heavily bandaged and very swollen, when I realised that maybe I should have made an effort to get hold of my player.

There was no answer on his mobile. As luck wouldn't have it, the range was quite a way from the clubhouse. On the way, I bumped into Andy Prodger, KJ Choi's caddie, who was also on the look out for his man. The range was empty. I had assumed that Retief was going to go straight to the tee, given that the range was a distance away and that it was still quite dark. As I expressed concern to those around me that I had not seen my player yet, with only 20 minutes to tee off, nobody hinted at the implications of missing your pro-am time.

I got hold of a tour official who had also tried to contact Retief, with no success. It was only then that I was made aware of our disqualification from the event as a result of tardiness. Obviously, I feel somewhat responsible for not being able to rouse my man from his slumber. I suppose it could be argued that I should have known the rule which was introduced last year as a result of a host of players not showing up for their pro-am time. I didn't, nor did the people I had been chatting to outside the locker-room. Otherwise I would have had more of a sense of urgency about shaking my man from his jet-lagged rest.

Retief awoke at 6.40. He immediately phoned me and I passed him over to

Mark Russell, a tour official, who explained to him that he was disqualified from the tournament. He had no idea that this was the punishment either until that chilling moment early Wednesday morning last.

He arrived in his soon-to-be-handed over Nissan car, driving up Capri Avenue and into the players' car-park. He was still assuming that the already mooted punishment of disqualification from the Nissan Open could be turned around.

A call was made to Tim Finchem, the Tour Commissioner, straight to the top. Tim was unavailable. His right-hand man, Henry Hughes, was available, but only to confirm to Retief that there was no compromise: he was out of there.

An hour later we were on our way south on Interstate 5, destination Carlsbad, in plenty of time for the Accenture Matchplay Championship, due to start exactly seven days later. Golf pros do not hang around when their skill is no longer of value at a venue. There is always next week, so just an hour after his abrupt dismissal from the Nissan he was already mentally preparing for the matchplay event.

The LA radio show hosts gave Retief a defamatory pasting. On Tuesday evening, there had been a launch in the clubhouse for Retief's endorsement of Grey Goose vodka. Talk about bad timing. Never let the truth get in the way of a good story, they say, and the word on Thursday morning talk radio was that the Goose got Grey Goosed on vodka on Tuesday night and couldn't make it out of bed. Retief is not a drinker and traditionally punctual, so naturally there was no truth to the rumour. Just a simple alarm clock technical difficulty. It didn't ring at 5am on Wednesday last.

We interrupted our trip to San Diego with a visit to an electrical store to buy a new alarm clock.

As we continued our trip south we came to the conclusion that perhaps the rule of disqualification for innocently missing your pro-am time is a bit harsh. In an equitable justice system the punishment should fit the crime. A call from Finchem last Friday would suggest that an exception clause will be written into the rule book to avoid such an occurrence in the future.

Anyway, judging by the weather complications at Riviera last week, the faulty alarm clock may well have done us a favour.

I'd recommend a tree-iron, boss

MARCH 1: I was squatting low to the right of the eighth fairway during the World Matchplay at La Costa last Friday looking for my player's ball.

It was the shortest distance I ever remember having to scour the ground for – the shot only travelled about 40 yards. The rough was brutally tough. A mixture of seemingly endless rain and a truck load of fertiliser meant that you needed a shovel to extract your ball from it.

Retief is about as strong a player as you can get and even he could only manage to shift his ball this short distance when he missed the fairway well right in our second round match against Fred Couples. The ground was obviously starting to decay in the swamp that Retief's shot disappeared into. I resorted to fumbling around the stinking, soupy mess with my fingertips in order to locate his ball. We found it, but lost the hole to Freddie, so it was a waste of finger fumbling.

You tend to get one hole on a course that somehow causes regular problems. It was the eighth for us last week. In the semi-final against Chris DiMarco, Retief sprayed his tee shot a bit right of the fairway and it came to rest in a stubbly pine tree. We arrived at the tree to find a gaggle of marshals wondering where to put their little flag.

You see, the marshals have flags to stick by errant balls that come to rest in the calf-high rough. Most of them stick it by the ball and stand bolt upright and expressionless waiting for the player to come and claim it, as opposed to years back when most of them had enlightening insight into the lie and how bad it actually was. They were always dying to tell the already irate golfer just how hopeless the situation was.

The way around this is the little flag and the stance of silent attention. The trouble was Retief's ball had entered the tree and didn't reappear.

So the flag remained tentatively in the marshal's hand. The ball, meanwhile, was still unidentified, up the tree. Being the loyal porter I am, I took it upon myself to leg it up the tree and see if I could either identify our ball or somehow dislodge it.

A golf tournament is obviously a fairly dull event if the sight of a caddie climbing up a tree in search of his master's golf ball is a noteworthy occurrence. Apart from the hoots and hollers from the crowd, half of them already the worse for drink, I was feeling a little unsteady given it has been quite a few decades since I used to scale apple trees in summertime in the traditional Irish youthful pastime of robbing orchards.

I took the two-iron with me in order to give the old branches a stir. It's amazing how resilient a relatively small tree is. All I was doing was making myself dizzy and increasing the volume of the cheering crowd.

The mind wanders in these situations. A number of tunes entered my head.

Peter Gabriel's *Shaking The Tree* as I rattled furiously. *Autumn Leaves*, as the foliage started to dislodge due to my disturbing it. *Living On The Ceiling* by Blancmange seemed particularly appropriate as I looked down on the amused heads below me.

The line: "Up and down, I'm up the wall, I'm up the bloody tree" seemed apt as the official said I had less than a minute to shake the ball free.

The directors below could see one ball wedged between some debris near where I was waving my two-iron and they were trying to guide me towards it. I managed to dislodge it only to be told as it fell at Retief's feet that it was indeed a Titleist but not the one he had hit off the tee.

By the time I scurried down the trunk, the gaggle of observers had dispersed and we were marching up the fairway having conceded the hole. It seemed to mark the end of our contention of the semi-final as Retief never performed anywhere near his capability after that.

I had my suspicions about the semi-final when the honorary observers (people who walk inside the ropes with the match because they pay a lot of money or are invited by sponsors) were announced on the first tee.

The starter spoke like a raconteur with not much of a story to tell, but whose voice and deliberate delivery were the most important part of the spiel.

The players were laboriously announced, then the official, and finally the observers who turned out to be Mr and Mrs Angst from California.

They got a bigger welcome from the crowd than Retief or DiMarco. The Angsts turned out to be perfectly charming people and nowhere near as anxious as their name might have suggested.

I squatted low and leaped high in an effort to save my man a shot last week in the Accenture World Matchplay championship at La Costa, Carlsbad, California.

Just some of the many duties we are called upon to perform in the mystery tour that is professional caddying.

Best hole and we all get chance to play it

MARCH 29: It was 6.20 Wednesday morning last, and the night was slowly yielding to day as I set the angle for the car parking position in the alternative caddie parking lot at Sawgrass, Ponte Vedra beach near Jacksonville, Florida. I had been instructed to be ready for action for 6.30am by my boss the previous night. It's top security at the Players Championship, the fifth major as they like it to be known; the security guards are not waiting for dawn to check passes, they are vigilant 24 hours a day.

I interrupted the volunteers at the caddie shack below the clubhouse as they were setting up breakfast for us. The New York Times had already been delivered and the weather channel was painting a grim picture of the early morning.

As some other early morning cads started to roll into the lounge, a tour official wandered in bearing the all too familiar information of "weather delay". The sun rises at 6.30, that's usually Tiger's tee-off time. We were informed that the range would not be open till seven o'clock and the first and 10th tees at 7.30.

So Retief interrupted me from my Danish pastry, coffee and newspaper to drag me out to the first tee at 7.15 to try to beat the 7.30 rush. There wasn't even a marshal on the tee when we got there. One arrived soon after as Goosen did a make-shift warm-up by swinging a couple of clubs. The marshal arrived with the obligatory, "I want to say something to the pro comment".

At 7.23 some spectators started to assemble around the tee. At 7.24 Tiger arrived through the grandstand tunnel. He is traditionally the first to tee off in a practice round and he was surprised to see Retief ahead of him. Are you going to go, his caddie Steve asked, to which Retief, who has had a bad run with tour rules lately, replied that we could not go till 7.30.

Tiger flushed a three-wood down the first fairway and Goosen followed with a flushed drive, and so we wandered off the tee for our first practice round with Tiger. As we approached the fairway I had a sudden realisation of what this meant.

Today was "caddie shot at the 17th" day. It was the traditional annual caddie shot day at Sawgrass, when the caddies get a chance at hitting it closest to the pin for a wad of dollars that the players put in a jar beside the tee.

This meant that I was going to have to not only hit a shot in front of all the people that follow Tiger, but also the great man. Is there any chance that Retief might only want to play nine?

Maybe Tiger will want to go on and play by himself? The electronic board by the second green flashed a weather warning sign. My prayers had been answered, and so soon. We were going to have to go in and I was not going to have to hit a scank off the 17th tee in front of the most famous golfer in the world.

But the sign was not correct, the clouds lifted, there was not a rumble of thunder and we were getting closer to the 17th. The world's number two and five were getting along nicely in their impromptu practice round. Tiger was seeing a side of Retief that he does not show when he is playing a competitive round.

> "The fact that Tiger is actually so personable and casual to play a practice round with managed to calm my twitching right hand as I started to tee the ball up on the 17th tee."

There is a rule on the US Tour that players can not tee-off the 10th tee (as their first hole) after 8.30. Of course when we got to the 10th tee after an uninterrupted front nine two players were on the fairway, obviously not paying much attention to the 10th-tee rule. So we got to wait for every shot on the back nine.

I got to prolong my agony just a little longer. There must have been well over a thousand people around as we approached the 16th green.

I was nervous, but the fact that Tiger is actually so personable and casual to play a practice round with managed to calm my twitching right hand as I started to tee the ball up on the 17th tee. It all happened very quickly, I had decided not to go through too many pre-shot preambles.

Retief suggested using his eight-iron. At 132 yards to the pin and the wind straight off the right, it may have sounded like too much club. Given that you could build your house on the shafts that my boss plays with, distance is irrelevant. I took a swipe at the well teed-up ball, made contact somewhere off the bottom groove, close to the hosel, and watched the ball float limply in the direction of the flag but just short of the green and into the water. The shot wasn't good enough to get an applause and not bad enough to get a giggle. In short it was nondescript, which suited me just fine.

Chris Jones, who caddies for Kevin Na, hit his shot to one and a half feet and took the loot. The prize was limited to $1,000 and a watch. The remainder of the pot was matched by the tour and donated to the ALS charity (some $10,000 in all), "Driving for Life".

We spent the rest of the week in the environs of the clubhouse waiting patiently to play the Players Championship. In fact, by the time you have read this, the chances are we will still be trying to finish the longest event at which I have ever caddied.

Ryan puts us right on subtle changes

APRIL 8: There are courses that we return to every year on tour that you get to feel familiar with, so going back is a bit like going home. Augusta National is one of those pretty predictable places.

You know what to expect when you pull up to Magnolia Lane, or gate seven down the side street as us toters do: there are few surprises. But the difference at Augusta, is that there are usually some very subtle changes that only the astute, or pre-warned, will be aware of.

A few weeks ago we were fortunate enough to play with Nick Faldo in the Tavistock Cup at Isleworth in Orlando. Nick had his present caddie Ryan with him – Ryan is a local caddie at Augusta.

So we got chatting at Isleworth. As Faldo – a former Masters champion continued to grind out scores in the manner that he always has – Ryan told me about some of the changes at the National.

Now we all know that there were some major alterations to the course a few years back to make it more of a challenge for today's pro. The mystique that surrounded the proposed changes was intriguing and well discussed; there were stories of helicopters flying overhead with cameramen trying to get photos of the developments.

Well this time there have been a couple of changes that a forensic scientist would be hard pressed to notice. But if you hit your ball in the wrong place around where the subtle alterations have occurred you, will notice them.

So, as myself and Retief Goosen stood on the fourth tee last Tuesday evening, looking down towards the green, we both agreed that the right side of the green looked different; the bamboo that used to encroach the right edge of the green had been moved back.

When we got to the green we noticed that a run-off area had been introduced so that a ball that missed the green right would run back about 20 yards instead of into the bush. If you were not pre-warned or paying attention you would be hard pressed to notice such changes.

The next change became apparent when we got to the 15th green. The front right of the green had been raised so that a ball landing on the front of the green is guaranteed to run back into the water. The back left of the green has been extended and a more severe run off area developed to bring the water behind the green into play.

The one thing that remains constant at the National is the age of the patrons. An elderly couple sat where they have probably positioned themselves for the past four decades in early April, behind the seventh green.

As Joakim Haeggman approached the green in a garish pair of orange shiny nylon-looking trousers, as only a Swede would dare leave the house in, the elderly gentleman remarked to his partner that Haeggman looked like 'one of those queers'.

His wife apparently corrected him and said that he was wrong, he wasn't queer, just European. To which he replied that he still looked like a 'faggot' to him.

After days of disruption due to bad weather, the second round was finally completed by lunchtime on Saturday. The forecast was good for the rest of the weekend and the future looked bright. The third round was scheduled to start at three o'clock. It was to be a two-tee start in twoballs.

So those players who thought they would be one of the first pairings to go off both tees prepared themselves for play at the advised time. At 3pm last Saturday about 20 players were assembled on the practice putting green waiting for the word from the organisers to commence the third round.

Bearing in mind that the latest that light would permit us to play was 7.45pm, there was some anxiety amongst the players who had hung around all week waiting for the weather to clear; if they started play at 3pm there was a good chance that about 20 players might complete their third rounds by sundown. We were all very aware of that.

We eventually got going by 3.30pm, which meant that only a few groups completed their rounds before darkness meaning the rest would have to return early on Sunday to finish off the third round.

A long day on Sunday saw us finish in joint third alongside Luke Donald, while Tiger overwhelmed Chris DiMarco in a playoff. Close – but no cigar.

The attention to detail at Augusta runs all the way through the tournament and not just on the course. For many of us there is a tradition and a permanence at Augusta, with just the very minute changes most years that draw us back to partaking in a very rich part of golfing culture.

Yes it's golf in China, but not as we know it

MAY 3: To those of us without an eye for detail China can look pretty similar to Japan when it comes to buildings, people and urban infrastructure. You look at the symbols of Chinese characters displayed on neon signs and billboards and wonder if it all really means something apart from the aesthetic and exotic pleasure the colours and shapes give those unfamiliar with Asian languages.

The people somehow find their little pockets of space amongst the 13 million who inhabit Beijing in seemingly impossible circumstances. Watching the nation move through a busy city centre intersection would make you believe in a greater controlling force – if you did not already.

A loaded old electric-powered bus vying with the latest chauffeur-driven S-Class Mercedes, a Wacky Races motorised tri-bike and a gang of cyclists, all heading at once for the one lane on the opposite side of the road, is something you soon get used to, or perish, in modern China. The system mysteriously works.

Of course, China is not Japan. Particularly now the two countries are rediscovering old hatreds; there were numerous riots in Beijing outside the Japanese embassy when we were there for the Johnnie Walker tournament a couple of weeks ago. However, when you go to a golf course in China, you cannot help but see the similarities in how golf is run in Asia, if I may be permitted to make such a sweeping generalisation.

The clubhouses tend to be lavish, the courses impeccably maintained, the on-course set-up similar, with workers in uniform, and a sense of regimented order pervading. There is one marked difference, however, as against the order of Japan, chaos reigns in China. Especially when there is a big international event on. The crowd that attended the event in Beijing were out of control. It was the first time in a year and a half caddying for Retief, that I have heard my player asking me to keep the crowd somewhat under control. Normally he is oblivious to distractions on the course.

It was impossible to ignore the antics of the young-to-golf Chinese spectators. Talking, mobile phone use, extremely active cameras, video-recorders and generally poor spectator etiquette prevailed over the four days.

One spectator – standing just three yards away from Thomas Bjorn – decided to zip up his noisy rain jacket and adjust it as Bjorn was mid-chip. Perhaps it is time to look at the rigid demands for absolute silence amongst golf spectators, China would be the place to start – in fact, it already has begun. By the end of the week there were certain on-course noises that seemed normal that would not be tolerated in a more sophisticated golfing land.

There has been frenetic development of courses over the past couple of years and the construction of hundreds of courses was halted early last year because of a lack of control. Land owners with small holdings were volunteering or being persuaded to sell off their livelihoods to enable developers to plough new golf holes instead of crops. The result for the farmers was a quick influx of cash and a long time to do nothing after the cash and land had gone.

It was no wonder then that when some of the star golfers at the Beijing event were invited for dinner with the owner of the opulent Pine Valley Resort they were in the company of, amongst other army general friends of the owner, the daughter of Deng Xiao Ping, the deceased former Communist Party chairman. When you asked anyone how the owner had made his fortune, the polite reply was by starting the Red Bull company. Given the polite smiles and raised eyebrows of the respondents, I got the rich aroma of another kind of bull.

When we stayed around Beijing last week to partake in a special day's golf for Deutsche Bank and their clients, the guest list included the movers and shakers of the local business world. All were decked out with the latest equipment and, judging by the shots they were hitting, very new to the game. Despite China having two permanent members on the Asian Professional Tour and three others in the wings, the amateur game is very raw.

They say 300,000 Chinese play the game with a further 14.5 million interested in taking it up, and just under 60 per cent of those are under 34. In 2005 there will be in excess of 10 Asian Tour events of which four are co-sanctioned with the European Tour held in China, offering over $7 million in prize money. China has gone into the game head first at the top end; at grass roots, in the Hutongs (neighbourhoods) it does not exist. It seems to be gearing itself towards a tourist market and elite Chinese clientele and little else.

With the Chinese economy growing rapidly and the unbridled embracing of the game of golf, there is no doubt that, without Asia, the European Tour would have a big hole in its schedule. It may look like golf here, but it is golf Chinese style.

If they are putting up the prize funds I suppose they are entitled to do so with a distinctive local touches. Be warned, it's golf for the intrepid only.

Swing in to action with tips from the top

MAY 10: The evenings are stretching to the point where you might fit in 18 holes after work. What an invigorating thought having been cooped up in the office all day.

If time does not permit a round there is plenty of time to at least whack a few balls on the range or in some remote field somewhere. How often have you played your best golf when you just stole out by yourself with no expectation and no self-consciousness? It might be a state to try to emulate when next in competition.

Anyway if you do find yourself with an hour to figure out the finer points of the swing you might benefit from what I gleaned from some pretty good players a few weeks ago in Asia.

When I was in Thailand for the Tiger Skins game, part of the four competitors' obligations was to give a clinic to some of the chosen guests. Usually myself and the other attending caddies tend to switch off when we are not directly involved.

This time, for some unknown reason I happened to listen to what my man Retief Goosen, Colin Montgomerie, Thomas Bjorn and Grace Park had to say. I actually found it quite insightful. Not only from a playing point of view but also from a professional angle. Their thoughts on hitting the golf ball could give the observant toter clues as to what to look for in their player's swing when they complain of not hitting the ball the way they would like to.

Retief's lesson was pretty much what I have understood him to emphasise in the swing, namely the basic set-up and address position. Whenever he feels he is off his game he always looks at his set-up. It is an instinctive thing with talented golfers to feel good or bad when they stand over the ball.

If Retief feels uncomfortable he spends as long as he needs to on the range trying to regain his equilibrium. This, of course, is what he told the guests during his lesson. You can never put enough emphasis on basic set-up and alignment. This is why choosing a target is so important. In short, check that you are aiming where you want to aim.

> "You can never put enough emphasis on basic set-up and alignment. This is why choosing a target is so important. In short, check that you are aiming where you want to aim."

Bjorn caught my attention when he started his instruction by talking about getting out of bed in the morning. Now we all can get out on the wrong side of the bed at times and that's what I thought the Dane was going to lead into when he mentioned starting the day on the right side of the bed, but he was not referring to his attitude. He was actually talking about balance. He said he finds his balance changes dramatically from day to day. So when he is playing he is constantly trying to find the position over the ball from where he can swing freely and always maintain his equilibrium.

Of course, his caddie and I smirked at each other as he mentioned physical balance and omitted the mental stability that both he and most of us can at times be accused of letting get out of control on the links.

Effectively, Bjorn was saying very much the same thing as Retief, but with a slightly different emphasis. He talked about whether his weight was on his heels or toes at address, Retief asked where those toes were pointed.

Montgomerie is probably easier for most amateurs to identify with because he has very much an individual style based on a fluid motion.

That was what the Scot was trying to convey to his pupils in Phuket. The golden tip I got from Monty was that he was always hitting the ball all the way through his follow-through. There is no hitting area for him, he is still hitting the ball even though the ball has long since left the club-face. When you watch

Monty swing, that is exactly what it looks like with him.

Given he is not a great fan of the range you are more likely to see him chatting to other golfers during his pre-round warm-up. He explained that naturally he has 14 clubs in his bag and one of them is his putter. So he warms-up with the 13 other clubs at his disposal.

With each of these clubs he hits just two balls. So his warm-up consists of hitting a very small bucket of balls. In fact, his academy in Turnberry supplies balls on the range in rations of 26 balls, two balls with each club, so you can practice just like Monty.

An important observation of Monty's on the mental side of the game was on the need for positive thoughts. He said any negative ideas must not be entertained if you want to be successful. If you have 10 thoughts and nine are positive and only one is negative then of course that negative 10 per cent will overpower the positive 90 per cent.

What Grace Park did rather than what she said was more revealing about how she wanted to prepare for a day's golf. As Monty spoke Grace was readjusting her very well-applied lipstick. Grace's visage is very much a picture of stoic elegance. Beyond the make-up of course lies a very well-prepared golfer.

She told us stretching in her room before she left for the course was something she always does for at least 20 minutes. Despite being naturally flexible, these top golfers do stretch religiously. As Park talked I noticed Monty was readjusting his shirt. We all need to feel physically comfortable before we start competing.

So if you do venture to the range on one of these long evenings, maybe some of the above advice will assist you. Remember quality is better than quantity; Monty's 26 balls with application may well be better than 260 swipes in frustration.

Nelson drawn to Retief's mild manner

MAY 17: In 1983, late in the morning of the final day of the Byron Nelson Classic, Ben Crenshaw joined a couple of other golfers at the players' dining area in the clubhouse at Las Colinas near Dallas, Texas. Crenshaw was leading the tournament and he brought with him to the dining table thoughts of success later that afternoon.

Before he ordered, the legendary Byron Nelson joined him. Crenshaw is well versed in golf history, so for Nelson to present himself at Crenshaw's table armed with a lifetime of anecdotes about his impressive playing days was too appetising to resist. Most players would head to the range about an hour before they were due to tee-off to warm up. Breaking routines, especially when leading the tournament, is not normal.

As the clock ticked and Nelson continued his tales, Crenshaw just couldn't tear himself away from the then 71-year-old raconteur. It was probably the best warm-up a tournament leader with a penchant for history could have had.

Twenty minutes before his tee-time Crenshaw jumped up and said he had better at least hit a few putts before he went to the first tee. Of course, he went on to win the first Nelson to be played at Las Colinas, continuing his own part in golf history along with his other role as historian.

This year is the 60th anniversary of the greatest achievement in golf. Byron Nelson dominated every event he played in from March 1945 till August that year, picking up 11 titles along the way and earning himself a bundle of War Bonds, the prize-fund of the day.

When they went back to earning dollars again after the war, Nelson recalled the security risk of being paid in wads of dollar bills. The top 20 were "in the money" in those days, their reward was a relative cut of the entrance fees which, of course, involved single dollar notes.

From Miami, Florida, to Charlotte, Greensboro and Durham in North Carolina, on over to Atlanta, up to Montreal, back to Philadelphia, across to Chicago and the PGA Championship, the Tam O'Shanter Open and culminating in the Canadian Open early August, Nelson set a record unlikely to be matched or bettered: 11 straight victories.

Getting around was not as easy as it is today, so travel to events could be an ordeal. When my player arrived in a private jet at Dallas Fort Worth airport last Monday, despite having spent about a day in the air indirectly back from South Africa, his journey did not compare with those of the gentleman who had come to the airport in order to greet the world's number five-ranked golfer. Byron Nelson took it upon himself to personally welcome Retief upon his arrival in Dallas to show his appreciation for Retief's decision to play in his event.

As Peggy Nelson, Byron's considerably younger wife of over 18 years, drove the two back to Las Colinas, the extremely lucid if somewhat immobile 93-year-old explained what it was like to travel overland back in the good old days. Despite being able to fly in a DC-3 in those days, the reality was that you had to drive most places, because if your luggage weighed an ounce over 44lb you had to buy another ticket. Unless you wanted to buy a seat specifically for your clubs you were on the road. Even if you did fly, the planes were still very slow. He once flew from Tulsa, Oklahoma, to Seattle, Washington, and it took over 13 hours.

There seems to be a lot of respect in the States for the way Retief plays the game. His serenity, confidence and consistency, without a hint of ego, stands out in a country more accustomed to a more flamboyant manner from top sportsmen. Nelson seemed very aware of the quiet manner of Goosen, which was probably reminiscent of the way that he played and conducted himself.

Despite sitting in a special shaded area overlooking the 18th green and straight down the fairway, Byron was never one to demand attention. There are no elitist nick-names pegged to the great man, such as the King or the Shark.

He is just a humble man grateful for his talent and the life it gave him.

The empathy Nelson feels with Goosen is apparent from his press conference early last week.

"One thing I had to learn to do playing golf and to win tournaments was not to walk too fast. In my day the galleries were not roped off and they walked down the fairway with you.

"You'd hit a shot and all of a sudden people would rush to where they could see the next shot. The next thing you know you'd be rushing with them and you'd be out of breath or tired. Any time your breath got fast, you swung faster and your rhythm changed."

He also went on about how important it was to feel comfortable over the ball. Trademarks reminiscent of Retief: a good set up and rhythm. Perhaps Nelson thought he was revisiting his time as a player though Goosen.

The Dallas event changed to the Byron Nelson in 1968. This year the event hopes to raise over $6 million for a local child behavioural and education programme. It has already raised more than $82 million for charity and prides itself as a leader of fund raising though golf.

The elder statesman Nelson gives as much importance to the fact that his good name is attached to such a good cause as he does to his golfing records.

Having won five majors, had 65 consecutive top-10 finishes and 62 tournament wins, including three when he was officially retired, as much as the honourable Mr Nelson is proud to be associated with Retief Goosen, the South African is equally as flattered by the legend's hospitality at the tournament that carries his message of humility into the modern game.

Alliss lives in the past but sure knows his etiquette

MAY 31: Last Friday was a pretty normal end of the working week for most people and for me, a golf caddie doing the best I could to ensure I actually get to work on the weekend. Being a holiday weekend in the UK, many were making plans to be as far away from work as they could be. For those of us on the golf tour, weekend work is a good thing, it can be well paid overtime.

I got to the course at about 7am for an 8.45 tee time. There are not many mornings that permit you to dine alfresco in Blighty at 7am but I went to the caddie-shack, "Stevenson's Rocket", ordered cereal, tea and toast and sat at an outdoor table surrounded by rhododendrons, and the rich foliage that makes Wentworth such a beautiful place to be in late spring.

The birds on the branches above me sung a tuneful, relaxing melody which, coupled with the pleasant surroundings, made me think caddying was not such an onerous job after all.

I went to the PGA office for a pin sheet so I could mark in my yardage book where the holes were cut for the second round and try to eliminate surprises on the course. I then went next door to the Tour's friendly weather people for the forecasted conditions for the day ahead.

The meteorologists confirmed it was going to get up to 30 degrees with a chance of thunder later in the day. The wind was not going to be strong and would vary from east to south. This is always a concern for a caddie on a course like the West at Wentworth. You see, the wind can be very slippery around the Burma Road. Most of the holes run in different directions and are surrounded by tall trees. So you can never tell for sure which way the wind is blowing. It also swirls viciously in the tunnels which most fairways are, so, even if you think you know where the wind is, chances are by the time your player hits his shot it's not where you thought it was.

I moved on to the locker-room and got the bag ready, stocked it with balls and made sure the rain gear and umbrella were still on board. Even though it shouldn't rain, it is, after all, the British Isles and an unexpected soaking would not go down very well with a player who employs you for your professionalism.

In the upper sanctum of the locker-room, players were receiving pre-round attention from their physiotherapists. There is still an elitist system in operation at Wentworth. Us players and caddies considered to belong to this elite group get to use the upstairs locker-room which is both spacious and unused by anyone else. The rest are downstairs, in a very comfortable room, which is a little more cluttered.

I joined Retief (Goosen) on the range. He had been breakfasting in the players lounge, a marquee just beside the practice area where apparently the bacon was being cut off the bone and the coffee freshly brewed. We began our pre-round routine of Retief warming up by hitting a few wedges to start and working his way through the bag.

Meanwhile, I was behind the bag carrying out menial tasks like cleaning the grips and making sure the balls he was hitting were clean and dry. I was also checking the wind direction – I have a compass reading of the range and always gauge the wind direction over the 45-minute warm-up session. Then when I look at my course yardage book where I have compass readings drawn on each hole, I try to match them up. This is not so simple in Wentworth. I also keep a eye on my boss's alignment to see he is where he wants to be over the ball.

Ken Brown, the TV commentator, sidled over to us; being the diligent announcer he is, he is always trying to dig up anything that may be of interest during the day's broadcast. I never remember seeing Peter Alliss or Alex Hay doing much of this background work, which frequently makes them talk like they are stuck in the past, because they don't seem to have an interest in exploring or trying to understand the present.

We stepped on to the first tee with Darren Clarke and Thomas Levet. Ivor, the official starter, cleared his throat to indicate that we are about to tee off.

Darren had his mind on the illness of his wife. Thomas was his usual clowning self, jovial and animated as only a person from further south in Europe could be. We joked about the expression golfers use when one of their playing partners hits a good shot. Many English players say "lovely shot". There is an expression in French which sounds just like "lovely shot" but means "clean the toilets" when translated.

So the day marched on. I carried the bag, recited numbers to Retief and added my words of wisdom when I felt it appropriate. Unfortunately, he listened to me on the eighth hole when I suggested the wind was hurting therefore he should hit a soft eight-iron instead of a nine. He ended up over 10 yards past the pin. Whoops. Billy Foster, Darren's caddie had a laugh as I received a mild berating of "what are we doing Colin?" as Retief knocked his 30-foot putt eight feet past the hole. If he was a more animated player, there would be far stronger words aimed as his porter. Lucky me.

We arrived back at the clubhouse at two under par. I went back to where I ate breakfast and had lunch, by which time you needed to sit in the shade of an umbrella. I went back to the range to watch Retief hit a few buckets of balls in the glorious afternoon sunshine. I talked to some of my boss's management team about plans. We both chatted to Jeff Hawkes, the ex-tour player, who was telling us about the project he has sunk his life savings into. It sounded like another golf gadget, but who knows what's going to grab people's attentions? I talked to the BMW tournament director, Marco Kaussler, about the set up of the tournament.

> "I take back all I ever said about Mr Alliss. He can stay in his golfing past if his impeccable driving manners remain as they are. He is now my favourite golf announcer."

Philip Parkin, working for the Golf Channel, wanted Retief to describe on air his most memorable four. I jogged his memory about the improbable par he made in the final round of the US Open last year on the 13th.

A little more short-game practice later, I drove my boss's Porsche up to the gym so he could jump straight out of the fitness centre and into his car. There seems to be no limit to a caddie's duties.

I headed out of the course at about 4.45pm and down to a cafe at Virginia Water to meet a colleague for a late-afternoon coffee boost. By the time I left, it was rush hour in Virginia Water. I was trying to turn right on to the main road. I must have waited for five minutes and not one car yielded.

In the sixth minute a swanky-looking black Bentley created some space for me. I noted the registration as I pulled out deferentially, "3 PUT". The traffic was moving slowly enough for me to recognise the driver of the large automobile. It was Peter Alliss. I take back all I ever said about Mr Alliss. He can stay in his golfing past if his impeccable driving manners remain as they are.

He is now my favourite golf announcer. Nostalgia is good when it comes to road etiquette.

A small world is tailor-made for Howth dreamers

JUNE 7: Back in my youth I used to go to play golf at the Deer Park public course in Howth. With a small carry bag on my back I would make the 20-minute walk through some back fields to the course. It is a beautiful walk, past the Gaelic football pitch which overlooks the old fishing cottages of the village and down over the walls of the harbour. Beyond, the heather and gorse bushes with the faded rhododendron of summer would line the west mountain.

A final hop over a fence and there you were at the 12-hole short course, with the most spectacular vista that I would challenge any public facility to match or better. It overlooks Ireland's Eye and Lambay islands, and on up the coast to the Mountains of Mourne on a clear day. The golf was incidental.

These summer trips were to sow the seeds of an unconventional lifestyle for me as a caddie.

About a decade after me, there was a neighbour who used to make the same trips in his summer holidays. Mark Greaney grew up round the corner from me, and his dad, Vincent, used to drive me into school every other week. A few months ago our paths converged again after the usual absence of time, over which you forget old neighbours and move on with different lives.

When I went to the TaylorMade factory in Carlsbad, California, earlier in the year, I made some inquiries about Mark as I had heard that he had recently got a job with the company. From the hundreds of employees based in Carlsbad, I managed to track Mark down. It was on the west coast of America that we met up about two decades after I made my last school run with his father Vincent.

Naturally, back then we had never talked about golf as it is not the most favoured topic of a five-year-old.

Where my career ended up in golf more by accident than design, Mark's route was more thought out. You see, Mark is a club designer, for which there are limited positions in the world. There are similarities with professional caddying, where there are really not that many of us either, so Deer Park definitely spawned two "specialised" employees in very different spectrums of the golf industry.

We also have a strong connection in my boss, Retief Goosen, who plays TaylorMade equipment which Mark helps to design. It is interesting how these links are made.

Before I found out that Mark was with TaylorMade I had never given much thought to those people who put the state-of-the-art clubs in to the hands of player and caddie.

Mark had always wanted to be an engineer first and then a golfer. He figured out that he was not good enough to make a living from hitting shots, which fuelled his desire to be connected with the game he loves as a club designer. When he was 14, he conducted a science project on the aerodynamics of the golf ball. As he began considering his future, he took it upon himself to write to all the golf manufacturers which he had consulted for his project the previous year, to ask them for advice in how best to prepare himself for a career in club design.

TaylorMade were the ones who suggested that he study mechanical engineering, specialising in materials. Mark went on to study engineering at Magill University in Montreal, Canada, and continued with a Masters in sporting goods in UCG.

His first big break, he thought, was going to be designing equipment for the National Hockey League. He started on a project designing a goalie's mask. This didn't get past the drawing board as the funding ran out early. As it happened, it worked out well for the qualified engineer who had always dreamt of designing golf clubs.

His big break came mid 2003 when he landed the position of product development engineer on the metal wood team at TaylorMade. There are fewer than 250 people in the world doing this job, so Mark considers himself extremely fortunate that he got the position.

On the development side, TaylorMade are divided mainly between metal woods and irons. Mark is part of a dozen or so engineers plotting the future design of what we try to go out and hit the short grass with. TaylorMade are in a very strong position with their metal wood products. Mark arrived at a revolutionary time in metal wood history: the r7 and r5 clubs with their adjustable weight ports are ahead of the curve in modern club design.

Even though these designers are scientists and spend most of their time using computer-aided design programmes, they do take great heed of what their stars, the pros, have to say about their creations.

In fact, just a few weeks back in Texas, a large portion of the iron design team were gathered around Retief on the driving range, getting him to hit shots with their test clubs. They were using a machine that was originally designed by the US government in order to track missiles. Now the manufacturers have adapted it to tracking the path a ball takes when it leaves the club-face.

It was interesting to observe the interaction between the test monkey, Retief, and the men in white coats carrying clip-boards. The machine is obviously important, but the hands-on feedback that a top player can give the designers is invaluable.

So two Irish guys who used to ramble around Deer Park public golf course in north Co Dublin have ended up supplying one of the world's top golfers with his equipment. One doing so scientifically, and the other handing over clubs on a seat-of-the-pants basis which, hopefully, the scientists have made caddie-proof.

Classic courses survive the test of time

JUNE 14: It may have been the Booz Allen tournament last week but that was not the main attraction. The venue was the Congressional golf and country club in the state of Maryland but only a stone's throw, relative to the size of the United States, from the pulse of political America, Washington DC. Founded in 1924, there is a sense of tradition and heritage in a club like Congressional.

It is a bit like walking into an ornate old building with wood-panelled chambers and tartan carpets where you sense quality and permanence. It's old world yet like so many of these classic courses they have, with a little tinkering, survived the test of time because their initial design was so good.

It will be the host of the US Open in 2011 and the fact that it is an Open venue attracted the strongest field this tournament has ever had.

The concept of Congressional all began in 1921 as a result of the efforts of Congressmen Oscar Bland and OR Luhring. They felt the need for a club where members of congress could meet socially. The list of founding members is quite impressive, including such luminaries as John D Rockefeller, the DuPonts, Walter Chrysler and William Randolph Hearst.

Given its location just over the Potomac river in the state of Maryland, the club has a rich history of US presidents being members or visiting the club. Presidents Coolridge, Taft, Hoover, Wilson and Harding were lifetime members of the club. Not only was there a wonderful golf course but also facilities for tennis, bowling and swimming. In fact the three outdoor pools were strategically placed between the ninth green and the 10th tee of the Blue course. With temperatures in the high 80s last week coupled with high humidity, it was close to torture having to shuffle by the inviting azure blue pools knowing you had another sweaty nine to go, without a refreshing dip in between.

The tee markers, small replicas of the dome of the capitol building in DC, are probably the most distinctive markers of any course in the world, and add a touch of class to a place with an old money feel about it.

As I wandered around the front nine on the Sunday evening before the event, the quality unfolded in front of me, what you see is what you get. In the sultry heat of the late evening I came across a figure on the back of the eighth green in a beige green-keepers uniform and a floppy wide-brimmed hat protecting him from the harshness of the outdoor sun. I think I heard him singing as he applied a powder to some small ant hills that were developing at the back of the green.

I bade him a good evening and as he replied I detected a southern accent.

The greenkeeper turned out to be from Mitchelstown, Co Cork, paying attention to the finest of course details as they do at such an esteemed club, big tournament or not. It's not the first time I have come across an Irish greenkeeper tending the grasses at some of the more famous courses in America.

Meeting Eoin O'Neill brought to my attention the programme that is operated by another Irishman Mike O'Keeffe. Mike has worked in connection with the Ohio State University bringing potential greenkeepers from all over the world, including Ireland, to America to gain invaluable experience on the better courses.

Eoin will finish his one-and-a-half-year stint of hands-on experience of course care in August and return to Ireland to hopefully continue a degree in agronomy. A self-confessed golf junkie, greenkeeping was the logical way for the Corkman to maintain his association with the game. Having worked on the greens staff in Douglas in Cork, as part of his employment he had to further his education by studying turf management and spraying techniques.

At Congressional last week, Eoin was responsible for three holes. Not just by himself, he said there were up to 90 greens staff working for the week of the event. Eoin talked of the other Irish greenkeepers he had met on his travels, including Liz Crotty who used to work in the Old Head in Kinsale, who has spent time working in Augusta National and will be at Pinehurst this week helping out at the US Open.

It seems greenkeeping is similar to caddying whereby you can ply your trade globally as long as you are happy to travel. There is a camaraderie amongst the 'muck mechanics' but they are also competitive. With big clubs like Congressional on your CV there is always a better chance of landing a top job back home.

If there were 90 greenkeepers involved in last week's event there is bound to be a legion ready to take on the challenge of Pinehurst No 2 this week, where my boss will be defending his US Open title and hopefully the professional greenkeepers will be exercising some restraint over the frequently over-zealous USGA when it comes to preparing the course for their showpiece event.

Goosen gets bitten but he'll be back

JUNE 21: On the 16th hole at Pinehurst No 2 golf course last Sunday, at around six o'clock in the evening, two golfers stood on the tee and asked each other if they wanted to play the last three holes for $10. A few hours earlier they both had expectations of becoming the 105th US Open Champion.

But their chances had disappeared into the dust that the northeast breeze was blowing across the renowned Donald Ross course.

Jason Gore, ranked outside the top 800 in the world and a member of the Nationwide Tour, realistically never expected to become the champion. Twice US Open champion Retief Goosen, leading at the start of the day by three shots, had very realistic expectations of winning for a third time and having his name permanently chiselled into the history books.

We had begun our day as we had every other day, with an hour's warm-up session. He hit balls, chipped and putted in preparation for the round.

Retief had hit the ball only averagely all week by his very high standards. He had statistically played very well on Thursday, hitting 11 fairways and 16 greens in regulation. Despite the statistics he was not really on top of his game. But being a great champion he is able to grind out a score when things are not going the way he would like.

We had worked on his set-up during the week, because Retief did not feel comfortable over the ball and he always believes that his bad swings come from a misaligned address position.

He had been trying to wiggle himself into a comfortable position all week. In fact, in the tournament in Washington the previous week he had spent hours on the range in stifling heat trying to figure things out.

So we began our march towards the first tee on Sunday, up, over, and down a makeshift bridge, through a tunnel under the vast building of the clubhouse and into a corridor with its walls lined with photographs and paintings of legends of the game.

I marched behind Retief, who was flanked by two bodyguards, as he had been all week. I noticed that he looked at Bobby Jones, Ben Hogan and the architect Ross, who had designed the treacherous course that lay between him and the 2005 US Open Championship.

The photograph of Ross was of him as an elderly gentleman, bespectacled and wearing a tweed floppy hat; he had a friendly enough expression and did not look at all vindictive.

Unlike the design of his Pinehurst No 1 course, it has a bark and a bite to match; it is not a course for a golfer to tackle without every facet of his game intact and on high alert.

On the first tee it was audible how much the crowd were pulling for our amiable playing partner, the outsider Gore. There was also a lot of good feeling for Retief. Despite trying to keep your mind on the job, it's impossible to ignore some of the very vocal comments coming from the other side of the ropes.

> "He had been trying to wiggle himself into a comfortable position all week. In fact, in the tournament in Washington the previous week he had spent hours on the range in stifling heat trying to figure things out."

"It breaks more to the right than you think," one guy bellowed as Retief lined up his par putt on the seventh. "It's playing really long today," another shouted on the ninth tee as we decided what club to hit into the unsettled breeze.

If you are not totally focused there is no doubt these comments rattle around in your head as you try to make a decision.

The simple fact for Retief Goosen during the final round on Sunday was that he brought his B game with him that day to a course and event that needed nothing less than A+.

With the pins cut on the edge of the abyss on most greens, being slightly off was highlighted dramatically.

So Retief seemed to find himself staring out of the abyss on many holes towards a not very inviting pin.

He didn't hit the ball well, he chipped poorly, and he never looked like holing a putt. This is not a great combination for good scoring, least of all on a course as uncompromising as the set-up of No 2 at Pinehurst for a US Open.

I am sure there are mutterings of "choking" and not being able to handle the pressure, probably like there were about Ernie Els last year at Shinnecock Hills when he shot a very high last round.

Ernie didn't "choke"; he just played badly on an uncompromising course. I also believe that Retief did the same thing at Pinehurst a couple of days ago; he simply played poor golf which the course exposed very quickly.

There have been days like that before, there will be again, but hopefully they will be on a Tuesday or Wednesday and not during the final round of a major, which he has a realistic chance of winning.

As the ever encouraging golf fans cheered as Gore and Goosen limped up the 18th fairway, the American smiled at me and said the only previous time he had heard his name being called on a golf course before was to announce his departure on the first tee of a Nationwide event. He humbly added with a big grin: "Americans love a big fat guy".

Retief Goosen is a worthy champion. Like all great champions before him, he handles disappointment with the same dignity with which he embraces success. I am sure he is looking forward to the challenge of competing for the next major championship at St Andrews next month.

Cambo and Sponge get the success they richly deserve

JUNE 28: It was the early 1990s and Michael Campbell arrived on the European Tour.

Meanwhile, his present New Zealand caddie, Mike Waite, was by then already well experienced working for Ian Baker-Finch on the US Tour. In fact Waite was probably more recognised as a toter than Campbell was as a rookie player.

It didn't take long for the world to recognise Cambo's immense talent. It wasn't till 1998 that Waite got a chance to work close at hand with that talent. He had caddied for the volatile Robert Allenby and parted company with him and put the word out that he was looking for a good player to caddie for.

Waite got into caddying having been an enthusiastic amateur in Stratford, Taranaki, on the west side of the North Island of New Zealand.

He moved to Brisbane, Australia, like so many of his compatriots, in search of work. He found it on a building site and spent a year and a half in construction.

Then came the lure of the tour. He got the chance to caddie for his compatriot Grant Waite (no relation) in a Queensland event on the Australian Tour. It was the caddie's debut as well as the player's, and they made their first professional cut.

That was back in 1986 and back then most of us caddies looped in the Southern Hemisphere in their summer and the Northern Hemisphere in our summer.

You had to be organised but it was also easier to plan bags because back then there were more players than caddies. Naturally the Antipodeans liked to employ caddies from closer to home if they could.

So Mike arranged to work for the young gun of the time, the ebullient Wayne Riley, and they arrived in Europe full of hope.

It was during a practice round in rain-soaked France between Riley and Ian Roberts that Waite got his nickname.

Roberts took a look at the drenched Waite and said: "Look at you, mate. I never realised you had hair like that – you look like a sponge."

Ever since, he has been known on the tour as Sponge.

It didn't take long for Sponge to earn the reputation as a sound person and a good caddie on tour.

Last week's win in Pinehurst was his 25th as a caddie and his ninth with Campbell. By his own admission, Sponge always rated Cambo.

When Waite began caddying for Campbell, the player had just regained his playing rights on the European Tour after an early hiccup in his career. He finished with Allenby, worked for Stephen Leaney and won with him but then got the chance to join Campbell full time.

Early in the year 2000, the duo won three out of four events they entered, including the Johnnie Walker, the Heineken Open in New Zealand and the Australian Masters in Melbourne.

They are a well-matched pair. Both are very laid back and they know how to treat each other. They are good friends but they know when to give each other space.

They probably have dinner about once a month together; otherwise they give themselves a break off the course, which is the best way when you spend so much time together on the course.

There was a statement of intent by Campbell when he decided to enter the first European US Open qualifying event in Walton Heath 10 days before the tournament, having been persuaded by his former manager Andrew Ramsey (Rambo) to try to qualify. It turned out to be a wise decision.

Such was his commitment to the US Open that he pulled out of the Dutch Open the same week. It was going to be all or nothing, no compromise.

Despite the Campbell team and probably most of the other competitors feeling like they were playing for second place in the US Open, given the lead my man, Retief Goosen, enjoyed going into the final round, it didn't take long for Sponge to realise the lead was very much in sight.

On the fifth hole Cambo made an improbable up and down from the left side of the green. That was possibly the worst place you could have missed that green to a left pin, as it was deep and dark down there. It didn't bother the intrepid Maori; he got up and down for par.

As Sponge glanced at the leaderboard on the sixth green he realised that they were tied for the lead.

There was a list of up-and-downs after the fifth that were obviously to prove decisive during the final round of the US Open, including on nine. Sponge admits his man thinned his chip slightly, which at Pinehurst usually means double bogey. Instead his ball hung on the edge of the green and he holed the putt for birdie. On 15 he made another unlikely save. This is what you have to do to win under the pressures of the last round in majors.

The Campbell camp were aware from an early stage of Sunday's round that they were dealing with some extra energy; there was so much adrenaline pumping around Cambo's body that he had to be careful not to hit his ball over every green.

He was taking a club less than he normally would hit, even into the wind, because they both realised the ball was travelling an exceptional distance on top of what was being factored in for the heat.

Campbell disappeared into the ample comfort zone of his caddie Sponge's torso on the 18th green at Pinehurst a couple of Sundays ago after sinking his winning putt and capturing the 105th US Open title.

Retief and I were standing about 120 yards down the fairway watching his greatest golf achievement to date unfold, and we both raised our arms in recognition of his success.

Retief was genuinely happy that, if he was not going to win, then it should be his good friend Michael Campbell that got to live the experience of being a major champion.

Even the best have to slog it out at times

JULY 12: Not many games are a bag of laughs when things are not going your way. But golf, with its solitary nature, can leave you feeling particularly isolated when you find yourself in a bit of a slump. There are no team-mates to cover for lack of form, there are no substitutes to come on when a change is needed; in professional golf you just have to spell the game backwards and flog all the demons out of your game till you get back somewhere close to your level of excellence.

At the upper echelons of the game, you tend to be constantly under the spotlight, so grinding it out in public is what you are going to have to do; there is nowhere to hide – unless you actually withdraw from the event, and that, of course, spells total defeat and makes a comeback even more of a climb.

All golfers have low points, and the so-called "slumps" are relative. An average player loses form and misses the cut. Better players, at their worst, still make cuts because they are used to having to grind out a score; this is what separates the great from the average. When Tiger Woods was in his "slump", he still won tournaments and only once missed a cut.

Good players have to perform to some degree when they are way under their best and would prefer to go back home and slog out their deficiencies in a secluded area at the back of their home range.

Having played in the pro-am of the Scottish Open last Wednesday with some very pleasant bankers who were average golfers, one of them asked me what I thought Retief's chances were of doing well last week. To him, it seemed like the pro was playing great.

But he had performed poorly in the pro-am by his standards. His playing partners did not really recognise how badly Retief was hitting the ball. The odd booming drive, a deft bunker shot and a putt holed here and there can veil the reality of a top golfer off form to a medium handicapped casual golfer.

In banking terms, Retief was in the red without any immediate signs of generating enough capital to get back into the black in the near future.

But top players never give up. Retief went out in four over par on Thursday and came back in four under. After the round, we went straight to the far end of the range (which meant he could hit into the wind) with three buckets of balls.

Retief does not use a coach, he relies on instinct to figure out what is wrong with his swing. To an amateur, and to most mortals, watching someone like Goosen swinging, it seems impossible to comprehend that he could swing the club badly. With his technique and smooth tempo, his swing always looks as fluid and rhythmical as ballet.

But throw in subtle changes in set-up and, as a result, a slightly altered swing path, and a top golfer can quickly be out of sorts.

Retief knows what needs to be done. He is not a habitual ball-slogger. If he is off form he will hit balls for as long as time permits. If he feels comfortable with his swing he will just hit a modest amount of balls to keep ticking over. This is not due to mood or anything else; this practice routine makes common sense for self-preservation.

Over the past few weeks Retief has been spending a long time on the range, constantly searching for the key to take him out of his minor slump.

After the first bucket of balls had been dispatched in the direction of the yellow flag in the middle of the Loch Lomond range, a green Range Rover pulled up beside the practice ground and Darren Clarke's entourage presented themselves beside us in preparation for a lengthy session with their boss, whose arrival was imminent. Despite being on the leaderboard, the man from Dungannon was also struggling with his swing. Again, his position in the tournament was the sign of a top player performing even though his swing was not in the right slot.

All professionals are different. Darren likes to have a group of confidants about him to absorb some of the stress of this often lonely game. Swing coach Simon Holmes was there, his caddie, Billy Foster, and John Newton, his physio–cum–comedian, were all offering their opinions on the big man's technique.

Beside him the taciturn Mr Goosen was relying on me, his caddie, and definitely not a swing expert, to tease out any obvious flaws in his set-up.

Retief had a club on the ground to make sure he was aligned correctly.

Darren has a special contraption to help him with his set-up which comprises three white, adjustable sticks joined together. He had a brace for his right arm and a Montecristo number four cigar smouldering away beside him, ready to draw on as he gathered his confused swing thoughts between shots.

If his back tightened, even-bigger John gave big Darren a stretch which lasted the golfer another bucket of balls before he seized up again.

This is the reality of the day-to-day behaviour of top golfers and, I assume, top sports people everywhere: hard graft brings success – and success can frequently bring you to a lonely place.

Every day is different in its subtle way, and talent needs to be in harmony regularly with sound technique to provide the desired results.

So when Retief said to me going down the 13th hole at Loch Lomond on Saturday that he was thinking of applying to the South African Cricket Board for a position, he took me by surprise.

I asked him why he would want to do that. He replied (having clocked up a seven on the par four 12th) that anyone who can make a seven off the one ball could be looking at a bright future in the game of cricket and is not suited to golf anymore.

Golf fans may well look at the success of the top players with a certain amount of complacency, but the fact is that a top golfer is trying to prove his worth every time he tees it up and takes nothing for granted.

Only a large dollop of self-belief, combined with obvious talent, pulls great players out of the dark hole of doubt.

Darren Clarke found the secret on the range on Saturday night and ended up finishing second; not bad for a player out of sorts. Retief did not quite find the answer to his problems and hustled around for a low finish at Loch Lomond.

The advantages of grinding a modest score out in these circumstances are hard to see. But a player of Retief's stature always comes out of the murky hole of modest golf stronger than when he went in. Retief left me with the parting quip that his pull shot off the tee will work well around St Andrews; sometimes humour is the only way to combat adversity.

Bring on St Andrews.

Modern golfers are getting all pumped up

JULY 26: Rain delays in the suburbs of Hamburg are great opportunities for idle banter amongst caddies, players and others who are just trying to kill time until a final decision is taken to cancel play and release everyone for the rest of the day.

With hourly announcements of further delays to the Deutsche Bank Players' Championship, the conjecture grew on Thursday last in the Wiking Hotel in

Henstedt-Ulzburg, the official caddie lodgings of the week. It was a convenient location for a rain delay given it was just a five-minute taxi ride to the course. We didn't have to lurk around the clubhouse in wait of an announcement, but could hang out in the comfort of the hotel instead.

As soon as play was officially called off we got on to a discussion about the origin of the fist pump in modern golf.

Most modern sports are given to quite expressive forms of emotion. The days of polite hat-doffing are well and truly from a past era in golf.

There seems to be a direct link between the advent of psychologists and mental coaches and the more expressive celebration of a holed putt. This is not to say there were not scenes of elation in times past.

Chi Chi Rodrigez was probably the most creative of the expressive golfers in the 1950s. He used to handle his putter as if it was a sword, always replacing it promptly in its imaginary scabbard after he sunk a good putt, wiping the blood off it with his handkerchief along the way.

> "Chi Chi Rodrigez was probably the most creative of the expressive golfers in the 1950s. He used to handle his putter as if it was a sword, always replacing it promptly in its imaginary scabbard after he sunk a good putt, wiping the blood off it with his hankerchief along the way."

Nobody has consistently bettered the theatrics of Rodrigez since. There have been some singularly special moments, like the heroic matador scene of Seve Ballesteros on the 18th at St Andrews at the British Open in 1984. He celebrated in true Spanish style after his winning putt had hung on the lip for a moment to add to the drama, celebrating the occasion as if he was a matador killing off a prize bull he had battled hard with for days.

He punched the air, he smiled, he punched again, his smile widened and so as the punches increased in ferocity the smile grew accordingly. True, unrehearsed emotion.

This is what seems to be lacking from modern ceremony of a celebratory moment, the spontaneity, the real feeling of happiness. To me modern celebration looks like a carefully controlled release of tension and aggression.

So many players hiss a seething "Yeesss" as they deliver an uppercut to the air after any putt over six feet finds the bottom of the cup. It seems like their psychologists have given them strict instructions to uncork the pressure valve for a controlled release.

So play was finally called off by early afternoon on Thursday as the dark cloud over Hamburg blackened and dumped even more rain upon the European Tour. It was the first day of the Ashes in London. The caddies interest turned from golf to cricket. Where were the cricket fans going to watch the first day of the Test? The chairman of the bagmen, Martin Rowley, scanned the local telephone book and began dialling in search of a pub that might be screening the cricket match, a tough ask in Germany.

Eventually there was an answer at the Naked Turtle pub. He was told they didn't open till six in the evening as a rule, but if there was going to be enough business they would consider an early start, and yes they did have satellite TV.

Martin described the clientele and tried to explain their passion for the contest between England and Australia. The doors were to be opened by two. The Aussies set up camp on one side of the pub, the English assumed their position on the other side and the Scottish and Irish outwardly sat on their impartial fence in the middle but inwardly took glee in the exploits of the devastating Australian fast bowler Glenn McGrath.

We got back onto the histrionics of the modern golfer. Of course the antics on the modern cricket pitch were glaringly obvious, with post-wicket celebrations falling just short of the melodramatics of soccer players after a goal.

There seems to be no end to the team pile-ups in recognition of a feat that traditionally warranted polite applause from the outfield and a warm hand from the crowd.

The conclusion at the evening drinks break of the first Test at the Oval, was that the etiquette of the refined game of golf seems to be under threat with the modern aggressive fist pump. If you were to look for any one culprit I suppose the main man, golf's now undisputed number one player, would have a lot to answer for in this department. His fist pump would land most opponents out of the ring. Then again, the bar has been raised in golf to new heights, maybe the fist needs to rise with it.

Call me old-fashioned but golf is a game played traditionally in groups of two, three and four. Spontaneous celebration is, of course, most welcome; aggressive air-punching as if there was nobody but the puncher on the golf course, is the start of the inexorable decline in the traditional etiquette of a game that reflects the good things about humanity and competition.

Affable Tiger has Cayeux eating out of his hand

AUGUST 23: For Marc Cayeux from Zimbabwe to get into the NEC Invitational at Firestone last week was a huge result.

For a lesser-ranked player – he was 103rd on the European Order of Merit at the start of last week – this was a chance to gain some valuable funds that will count on Marc's main tour. It also offered a sneak preview of what it would be like to play on the US Tour and an outside chance of taking the $1.3-million first prize. That is a very large truckload of Zimbabwean dollars.

On the European tour, players of similar ability are usually drawn together in the first two rounds, mainly because it is easier for TV to capture the top players' every move that way.

In the limited-field world events there is more chance of a random draw, where lesser players get a little more exposure by being drawn with big names.

So Marc Cayeux was excited about going to Akron, Ohio, home of the World Series of Golf until it changed to the NEC Invitational when the World Golf events were created in the late 1990s.

After he won the Sunshine Tour Championship – a qualifying event for this global tournament – earlier in the year by shooting a final-round 61, he knew he was Ohio-bound in August.

When the draw came out last Tuesday his caddie phoned him with the news of what time he was playing and with whom, emphasising that he was in for a surprise. Of course he could hardly believe it when told he was drawn with the number-one golfer in the world and possibly the greatest golfer in history, Tiger Woods.

Great, brilliant, a dream, thought the 27-year-old Cayeux, or possibly a nightmare.

There was a bigger problem, which didn't simply involve nerves, Marc had a painful welt on his hand as a result of a recent accident. He had spent the previous week with his manager in Austria.

Despite the fact his family still live in Zimbabwe, he cannot fly back there on his weeks off. So he spends them either with relatives in England or with his manager near Salzburg.

They decided to have a barbecue toward the end of the week. Marc went to light the fire, whereupon the box of matches ignited in his hand.

Despite the obvious concern of hand injuries for a professional golfer, he never once considered not making the trip to Akron. The opportunity to play in this event was something he could not miss. He would have presented himself on the first tee no matter what his physical condition.

Marc, like so many serious golfers, committed to playing the game professionally at a young age. He was 18. He had left school at 15 with the intention of turning pro as soon as possible.

I met Marc for the first time when I was caddying for Paul Lawrie at the Dunhill Tournament in Johannesburg in 2003.

He was telling me about his trip from Harare by car. He had been stopped at what he thought was a police road-block, but it turned out to be a car-jack, a frequent occurrence in Zimbabwe.

Under stressful circumstances in the middle of the night Marc managed to escape with his car and ended up in Johannesburg the next day to prepare for the event.

Most players think a delayed flight equates to a travel disaster. Cayeux's adventure was just another part of daily life in Zimbabwe.

Marc had played with Ernie Els in South Africa on previous occasions. He was not really that intimidated by playing with Ernie because he felt they had a lot in common, coming from the same region. He felt they could talk about biltong (salted meat) and braiis (barbecues) and all things African. With Tiger he felt he would have little to talk about apart from how legendary was his opponent, hardly appropriate for a fellow professional.

Tiger approached Marc in the locker room on Wednesday and asked him how his hand was. He didn't have a bandage on it, so it wasn't that obvious; Tiger had somehow found out about his injury. Marc was touched.

On Thursday morning as they headed down the 10th fairway together, Marc was already starting to feel at ease with Woods, whom he describes as humble, very human, friendly, and intensely focused when it came to his shot.

He was also surprised at Woods's willingness to crack jokes. This is how Tiger is. Once he is among colleagues, inside the ropes, he is really just one of the lads.

There is nobody who has played with him that isn't impressed by how Tiger handles himself and respects those around him. It's never a problem playing with him – the problem is often the raucous crowds that follow him.

The obvious problem for Cayeux was that he couldn't grip the club properly.

He tried hitting shots on Wednesday and his hand started bleeding again. So he had to make do with a walk around the course and no practice round. His golf was greatly compromised by his injury. But he did manage to wiggle his ball around in a very respectable plus nine and 49th position for the tournament.

As Tiger blasted his tee shots into the far distance, Marc was disappointed he could not try to give it a whack and see just how far behind Tiger's his best drive would be. Marc at his best can give it a fair wallop.

> "As Tiger blasted his tee shots into the far distance, Marc was disappointed he could not try to give it a whack and see just how far behind Tiger's his best drive would be."

Just as he was getting settled into his round he suffered a further setback. When he picked up his ball on the seventh green after marking it, he noticed it had "practice ball" stamped on it.

He had marked it with his own markings but never really figured out how it got into his bag and how he ended up hitting it without noticing it was a range ball.

As luck would have it, it was exactly the same type of ball he was playing, a Titleist ProV1x. He showed the ball to Tiger, who expressed concern and sympathy. Nobody was too sure what the ruling was going to be.

They called a referee and he confirmed the mistake was a lucky one in that it was exactly the type of ball he had played with for the rest of the round. So there was no penalty.

The world event has given the Zimbabwean some sort of profile in the States. It has also shown the aspiring Cayeux it's not simply brilliant play that earns Woods the respect of the world; it is, more importantly, his humanity and grounding that keep him in touch with the reality of the day-to-day grind on tour for the average player.

Terminal boredom of the jet-set porter

AUGUST 30: Let me tell you about international travel in the month of August in the year 2005. It's not very sophisticated or civilised. I am beginning to feel like a passenger on the pony express back in the Wild West with a broken wheel, very little water, and not much hope.

In terms of flying around the world, the whole month of August is turning out to be worse than a month of Christmas Eves for me.

Let me start with my trip to the US from Germany at the start of the month.

First, an early connection from Hamburg through Frankfurt and a four-hour wait in the plane as it sat on the tarmac with a hydraulic problem. We eventually got off that sick plane and onto a fit replacement. A bad start to an 11-hour flight. But at least we got there in one piece. These things can happen.

Next trip and I found myself in a sweltering Dallas Fort Worth airport in a heatwave aboard my flight to Denver with no air-conditioning and a reputed left-engine problem. We had to wait two hours for a replacement. I was a bit put out but again happy to be getting on to a fit aircraft.

The soldier sitting beside me was at the end of a very long journey back from Iraq for a couple of weeks' leave after a seven-month stint. I ended up feeling very sorry for him – as if seven months in Iraq weren't enough to endure.

I know it sounds like we all travel around in private jets in the States these days. It's true many players and caddies converge at regional airports at the end of tournaments waiting for private craft to whisk them off to their next destination. But even these swanky machines are reliant on the inclement summer weather for uninhibited passage.

After winning the International tournament in Denver, Retief ordered his plane to take us to New Jersey early on Monday after a gruelling 36 holes on Sunday. We took off on time but landed an hour later after circling thunder clouds in the New Jersey area, and ended up landing in upstate New York, a 90-minute drive from our original destination. We would have been quicker on a commercial flight.

At least we got there. When we went to leave from Baltusrol there was an hour's delay – who knows why? – but we got to Akron, Ohio, soon enough.

I finally came a cropper the other night in Cleveland Hopkins International airport, Ohio. I was booked to leave at the conservative time of 7.45pm to make my connection through Chicago and back to London. Retief didn't play as well as usual so we were finished quite early.

I could have got a flight at three in the afternoon if I needed to. No problems. I got a late check-out from my hotel and decided, for a change, to watch the denouement of a golf tournament. Normally we are in transit or actually competing on Sunday evenings. Not this time. I was relaxing. I had buckets of time to catch my 7.45 flight.

I got to the airport refreshed and in ample time for my flight. It was delayed.

But the check-in attendants were very kind in getting me on the earlier flight to Chicago to ensure I made my transatlantic connection. The only problem was that ended up being even more delayed than the later flight. Now if you wanted to witness air rage on the ground, gate B3 at Hopkins International would have been a good place to start a couple of Sunday nights ago.

The majority of the irate passengers were normal people just like you and me. While I was waiting, I began to notice a face that looked familiar in a distant type of way. Someone I recognised but didn't know. He looked like a sort of maverick businessman in a dark, well-cut suit and a slim pair of cowboy boots, the ensemble topped off with a natty hairstyle.

I knew I had seen him before. It finally clicked – it was Sean Penn the actor. He was due to go on the same flight to Chicago.

Sean was taking the setbacks calmly. Even more remarkable, nobody was bothering him, unusual in a nation that doesn't mind invading your space in public, especially if you're a big movie star.

Sean got shifted to the later flight, which went earlier, if you know what I mean, and I got shifted to Washington in an effort to make the last flight from there, which of course failed miserably. I was now due to go on the 6.10 flight the following evening. You won't believe it. I didn't either. We had a technical fault. Yep, it eventually left at midnight. Without me, I might add. I was shifted to the earlier 9.30pm London departure, only because they saw the rage brewing in my reddened eyes from all the hanging about and shuffling of the past 24 hours.

Of course my bag didn't make it. So I got back to Dublin for 23 hours and then headed back to the airport to catch my connecting flight to Beijing on Wednesday.

Now you really won't believe this. The extremely helpful and polite dispatcher at Lufthansa informed me there was an "outage" at British air-traffic control. What this meant was a complete mystery apart from the obvious – I was going to miss yet another connection.

More delays, more pleading and horse trading to get on another flight so I could make it to Beijing at least on the day I was supposed to arrive there.

I am kind of expecting to see Tom Hanks in Beijing International, as the fictional character in the movie Terminal, who ends up living in an airport for years.

I wonder what Sean Penn's next role is? Maybe that was a little dummy run for him at Cleveland International.

All the work and preparation for tournaments pays off

SEPTEMBER 11: Having won in China a couple of weeks ago, flown back home to England for a night and then reassembled himself for another week of competitive golf in Cologne, last week's victory at the German Masters was a testament to Retief Goosen's stamina and diligence.

By his admission he has not hit the ball the way he would like to be hitting it for quite a while. There are two ways to tackle this problem as a professional golfer.

One is to take a step back and try to figure it out in the quiet of the range, away from tournament golf.

The other is to grind it out at the next event, play as well as you can under the circumstances and keep looking for the key on the range after the round. This last option is what Retief decided to do. I must be honest and admit that I was sceptical about this policy. I formerly believed that you must use what you brought to the tournament you are playing in. Swing tampering is difficult when you are pre-occupied with the task of bringing in a score. Retief's recent victories have certainly swayed my opinion on this matter.

Retief had the option of flying on Tuesday morning last with Michael Campbell. But Michael was leaving a little later than Retief would have liked. So he opted for the early rise and a 9am commercial flight from Heathrow instead.

A little over-enthusiastic, some may think, given the previous day's long trip. Retief had played in China with a new set of irons that he had worked closely on with Brett Wahl, TaylorMade's chief iron designer, in creating.

After quite a deliberate amount of refashioning, they finally arrived in their almost finished state a couple of weeks back. Retief was very happy and excited about playing an event with them.

The only problem was that in Beijing there was only one loft and lie machine in the whole city, and it was on the other side of town (a three-hour trip in Beijing), so making the final adjustments was difficult. He battled on with the clubs not set up exactly as he would have liked, and still won by six shots.

He was anxious to adjust the clubs before he played last week. Thus the early rise on Tuesday last. I arrived in Gut Larchenhof golf club last Tuesday to find my man in the TaylorMade repair truck tinkering with his new irons. The club repair men in TaylorMade love it when Retief pays a visit, because he likes to do his own adjustments, so they can take a break and give him the run of the truck.

After some grip changes, a few more layers of tape here and there and some detailed hosel bending to get the right loft and lies on the new irons, Retief was ready to go, looking for the elusive swing key on the range. The repair men took control of their truck again.

Retief could not get into a comfortable position over the ball. So Tuesday last was the start of the search for a comfortable address position. His lower half was misaligned with his upper half, and this was the quest for the week: to try to wiggle himself back into a comfortable and correct position at address. Top players are thoroughbreds, and the minutest of misalignment to them would probably feel to us like we are trying to play left-handed clubs when we are right-handed.

As a caddie on a world trip such as I am at the moment (last week was the sixth event in a row on three different continents), you may not get the time to do your course preparation as conscientiously as you would like. There is a group of my colleagues that have stayed in the same guest house, very close to the course at Gut Larchenhof outside Cologne since the German Masters moved to this location. It is a really pleasant week of barbecues and idle banter over beers on the balcony overlooking the surrounding fields. The house is called the Birds Nest.

One of my house-mates suggested on Wednesday evening that it might be worth getting a few extra yardages before the first round. Still a little disoriented after the China trip, I reluctantly got my laser, put my running shoes on and we took off in the soft September evening light around the course. Golf courses look beautiful late in the day. All undulations are clearly defined by the sinking sun, there is a peaceful air about golf terrain at the end of a nice day.

There was one extra number that my friend, Kevin, wanted to get from the 14th fairway which runs adjacent to the seventh. He figured if your player hit it right off the seventh tee he may have to hit it down the 14th fairway as an escape. I pooh poohed his idea as a waste of time, but went along with his suggestion.

Retief hit his tee-shot right off the seventh tee on Thursday, it came to rest behind a lone tree beside the fairway. He couldn't bend his shot around the tree nor hit it under it. The only option was to go down the 14th fairway. I assured him that I had a good number from down there. He raised an eyebrow as if to say what are you doing with a number from there for? It wasn't the time for explanations. Retief escaped down the 14th fairway and hit his third shot to the par five seventh pin-high for a simple two-putt par. I had to apologise profusely to my colleague later on the Birds Nest's balcony for questioning his logic in acquiring such a yardage.

> "You need to accept poor shots in order to win. You also have to have a clarity of thought to win. His decision to take a penalty drop from the hazard on the final hole in Cologne was an indication of his lucidity under the circumstances."

The search for perfection continued on the Gut Larchenhof range, while the raw Goosen talent brought back yet another under-par card to the scorer's tent each day. He is now 42 under par for his last eight competitive rounds. Despite a punishing double bogey on the second hole in the final round due to an errant drive, Retief was in the mood to win and there is no better man to do so, he knows how to win even with a slightly compromised game.

You need to accept poor shots in order to win. You also have to have a clarity of thought to win. His decision to take a penalty drop from the hazard on the final hole in Cologne was an indication of his lucidity under the circumstances. The more dangerous option would have been to try to play the ball from the hazard. The shot that followed, from the rough, on the side of a slope, to a pin cut eight yards from the water, is what separates winners from runners-up. He hit his 155-yard nine-iron to within five feet of the pin.

We frequently see the stunning end results of top sports people and are left dazed in admiration of their feats. It's what goes on in the design room, the repair truck and the hours of searching on the range, combined with dogged self-belief and an abundance of talent, that leads to shots such as we saw Retief hit last Sunday in Cologne.

Success often comes from unglamorous places.

Pampering makes up for missing Wentworth stars

SEPTEMBER 20: Golf would appear to be a victim of its own success, in this, the early junket season. The HSBC Matchplay event at Wentworth outside London last week is a testament to this. A limited field of 16 players who qualify through an order of merit run over the four majors of the year and a couple of other qualifying categories should ensure that the sponsors have the cream of world golf playing in their exclusive event.

The reality in the leafy environs of stockbroker belt Surrey was that there were very few of golf's perceived stars teeing it up on Thursday last. And I mean no disrespect to the players who eventually qualified to play due to the likes of Tiger Woods, Phil Mickelson and Vijay Singh declining to make the relatively short trip across the Atlantic. Geoff Ogilvy, Steve Elkington and Kenny Ferrie don't conjure up the same enthusiasm to the golf fan's imagination. They are top-class golfers, just not in the league this historic tournament has provided over the recent decades.

There was £1 million on offer as the top prize, points gained counted for the world rankings, the European Order of Merit and the European Ryder Cup standings, and the consolation for losing in the first round was £60,000.

Obviously, a big bank is good at numbers, and they know how to give their guests a warm welcome. Beyond the basic financial details, HSBC bend over backwards to accommodate players, their families and caddies. The only other tournament that has pampered us like they did last week, is at the Million Dollar event in Sun City at the end of the year.

On top of the flights provided for players, family and caddies, they have the option of staying in a house on the estate. There are very few "houses", as most of us would know them, on the Wentworth estate: mansion is more appropriate.

Not only do you get a "house" to yourself, you get a chef to cook for you as well. I was invited for dinner during the week to one such mansion, and the food served that night tasted of a Michelin-rated standard.

The pampering did not stop there. In the clubhouse we had the option to eat in a secluded room beside the locker-room or in the Ryder Cup room downstairs, where a full breakfast and lunch buffet was available each day. William, our waiter upstairs, could not do enough for us, and his warm, friendly and efficient service will be missed when the reality of a normal event hits us again.

For golf events around the world, the recent policy seems to be to try to attract players through pampering and the warmest of hospitality. It seems that no amount of money, whatever the currency, is a guarantee of luring the top players anymore. Which is a disappointment for the sponsors, but a great chance for lesser ranked golfers to seize their opportunity to play for the big prize funds on offer in world golf today.

Like most events there is a pro-am on Wednesday; it is the downside of professional golf that the top players must go through on the day before the tournament starts. It's interesting how many amateurs we play with who understand the distraction of playing with the "golfers like them" while they are preparing for an event, so most playing partners are courteous and get out of the way if they cannot help the team score.

At last week's event there is a system in place sponsored by HSBC to nurture and encourage young golfers called the "Wee Wonders". The little wonders who qualify get the chance to play the par three second hole at Wentworth with the professionals. When my player, Retief, arrived on the second tee, Leona Maguire from the Castle Hume Golf Club in Enniskillen was limbering up for her chance to swipe her fairway wood on to the green in front of the world's number five-ranked golfer. Leona had qualified in the under-10s Britain and Ireland qualifying event in St Andrews the previous week.

Her twin sister, Lisa, was with her, but just missed out on qualifying, so was just there as a spectator. Lisa plays off 10 and Leona off 14. Leona whacked her shot through the green, then confidently holed a 12-foot putt for par to save the team, and Retief remarked that she had a very impressive swing. So hopefully the wee wonders from Cavan will grow into smooth swingers in future years.

When Retief teed off at 7.36 on Thursday morning, the summer had yielded to the murky onset of autumn. It had been raining pretty heavily as Retief warmed up on the range beside his opponent, Kenneth Ferrie. As we headed down the first fairway the rain started to ease.

By the time we got to the green it had almost stopped. Kenny had rolled his putt up to about two and a half feet of the hole, no "gimme" distance. Retief had chipped to about 12 feet, which he needed to hole for par. I was holding the umbrella, as it was still drizzling.

As Kenny went to mark his ball, I asked Retief if he still wanted the umbrella. He replied to me "take it away", which Kenny, due to his proximity to his ball, thought Retief was referring to his ball and not the umbrella. To which Kenny replied "Ta, very much", and promptly put his ball in his pocket, probably a little miffed at Goosen's generosity.

Technically, Retief could have called for a ruling to explain the mis-understanding and have the ball replaced. Instead, he broke into a hearty chuckle, went on to miss his par putt and lost the hole. It was to be the last hole he lost to the amiable Ferry.

Three of the last four players in the matchplay, Goosen, Angel Cabrera and the winner, Michael Campbell, travel to Washington this week as members of the Rest of the World team to take their good form to the Americans in the Presidents Cup.

And it seems patriotism keeps this event from being another victim of golf's success.

Days of etiquette in US are long gone

SEPTEMBER 27: You would want to be fairly thick-skinned to play top competitive golf in America these days against an American team. If there was a modicum of etiquette in the days of dandies and diplomacy many decades ago it has long gone.

We were in the state of Virginia outside Washington DC last week for the Presidents Cup. The American fans seem a bit confused about when a sports event is just that and not another national identity crisis. I speak only about those nasty enthusiasts outside the ropes not the competitors within.

The United States dozen beat the International contingent by three points after a close contest which was swung in the Americans favour by a couple of 20-foot putts from Fred Couples and Chris DiMarco on the last hole.

I stood on the practice range behind my boss Retief Goosen as he warmed up for his duel with the world's best golfer, Tiger Woods, on Sunday. We were beside Trevor Immelman, also from South Africa, and the captain, Gary Player, himself a South African, came along to watch his boys' warm-up session for the singles matches.

He mentioned that when he played against Jack Nicklaus and Arnold Palmer back in the 1960s as the world's best golfers of the era, he got a full pasting from the partisan crowd. He told Goosen and Immelman the crowd would be like wild animals shouting against them. This used to motivate him to beat them even more.

It was a wonderful example of leadership, I thought.

Goosen has had multiple exposure to such hostilities in America over the years as a Major contender. The younger Immelman had been relatively sheltered from such behaviour until last week's bout.

It may have been a little easier to endure in the fourball format alongside a colleague. In singles, out there alone, the hostilities from the other side of the wire may have been a little shocking for the younger player. Player showed great charisma and leadership as captain from early in the week. He was ubiquitous, democratic and undeniably enthusiastic, especially for a man in his 70th year.

If you were to listen to him speak without physically seeing him you would think he was an ambitious young man. He flitted around in an electric cart with his vice-captain Ian Baker-Finch, like a general assessing the mood of the troops before the heat of battle early in the week. He wanted to know what his players were hitting to certain holes, where the tees would be, who felt good playing with whom, he wanted to know what ball they were playing, he wanted to know the bottom line.

I had always envisaged Gary Player as an autocrat. How wrong it can be to make assumptions about people. He was more democratic than Bill Clinton, the official coin tosser to decide who would be the first to hit off the first tee in the first round on Thursday. Gary wanted to know everyone's opinion, he had his own ideas, but he clearly respected his players' ideas. He knew what to expect from the understandably partisan crowd. I had always been led to believe that most of the inappropriate comments come from "those loud mouth New Yorkers", any time we are in the Big Apple's vicinity.

Suggesting that elsewhere in the country you could expect nothing but pleasantries and blueberry pie.

My eye. Player was preparing his captain's pick Immelman for the raucous and disrespectful patrons he was so familiar with, having endured the abuse foreigners can receive his entire career. The survivors learn how to turn the hostility to their advantage. This, of course is what Player did so well.

As Retief walked down the 10th fairway munching an apple one such loudmouth shouted at him: "Watch you don't choke on that apple Goosen – like you did at the US Open".

Each time an International player's ball headed towards trouble, the crowd hissed: "Get in the trap" or "go in the rough". Immelman had a putt to stay in his match on Sunday. He clearly heard "miss, miss," as he settled over the ball.

It is to be expected that a good or even average shot from the stars and stripes would be met with uncontrollable home support, and that a putt holed by an outsider would receive the faintest round of applause.

This is the home advantage. But coming out with such derisive comments as they repeatedly did last week, makes me very satisfied that my player, as ever, let his clubs do the talking and let the inane comments slip idly bye. With four and a half points out of a possible five it would be clear to say that Goosen's clubs answered the hecklers in a more profound way than these morons are capable of understanding.

I fear for the game in America. It is in danger of the inexorable decline into the abyss of cigar smoke, Buds and bedlam on the golf course. It's time for tournaments to re-educate their badly taught patrons. For those of us who have grown up with the game of golf and are familiar with the etiquette of the game, this sort of behaviour is enough to make you want to tackle the malaise of the game in America head on. The rules must be observed because they are the law. This is an easy concept. The undocumented guidelines for good behaviour on the links (etiquette) are either totally ignored or they are completely oblivious to them. Forget finding out about the latest club shaft or high tech golf ball, how about some basic manners on the golf course? The matches themselves were played in the true spirit of the game, competitively and respectfully. It is refreshing to see so many large egos bouncing around the one room harmoniously.

Nowhere was it more apparent than in the International team cottage on Saturday evening where the players, their wives and caddies were enjoying some specially imported Australian beers, amongst other preferred beverages, which had been procured from the Australian embassy in order to make the four Aussies on the team feel at home. The rest of us were extremely grateful too.

Player and Baker Finch were sounding out the team on the thoughts about the singles pairings. Everyone had an opinion, and most of them were different. Load heavily early. Keep the best for last. Stagger the talent.

> "I fear for the game in America. It is in danger of the inexorable decline into the abyss of cigar smoke, Buds and bedlam on the golf course."

Whatever the theory it was a wonderful rare moment of civilised discussion which was all taken in by the captain. All the theory goes out the window when the actual bidding process begins, because when the Americans won the toss to put their first name forward then the Internationals had to jiggle their strategy accordingly. It was a moment of team spirit and camaraderie that I will always remember.

There was a separate caddie area set up for us toters. With couches and catering. The standard had been set early in the week by the International captain and the players saying they would like their caddies to be in the same area as them. The same did not apply in the American camp. Although the caddies were not officially banned from the players' cottage, they were not made welcome. The only caddies who used the caddie hospitality area were the Americans.

Congratulations to the Americans for their well-spirited victory, it would have been an even more enjoyable week of rare team play if the unruly American supporters would follow their players' lead and support with decorum. Golf etiquette is as important as the rules.

Calm descends after the storm of questions

NOVEMBER 1: The Disney tournament was completed on time, despite the misgivings of the weather people and doomsayers that Hurricane Wilma might whip up a tempest during the final day's play.

We were going to be detained in Orlando till Tuesday of last week in order to complete the event, they said. It didn't happen. Lucas Glover holed a 30-yard bunker shot on the last hole for his maiden win on tour and we all bunkered down low and tight in anticipation of a Monday of raging wind and deluge.

I moved east of Orlando to some shelter from the storm and quite frankly it was all a bit of a let-down. The raging waves of the north wind in Hawaii produce spectacular 40-footers on the north shore of Oahu in January. The shamals, or sandstorms, that occur in Dubai in winter are gritty and quite impressive. A tropical storm I witnessed in southeast Asia sent cars floating down the streets after a half-hour deluge. Wilma, my first hurricane experience – and conveniently falling between golf events – was like an Irish snowfall: a bit squishy and anti-climactic.

I know Wilma took her toll and I am not being flippant about it, but the problem in America is that if you pay any heed to the TV you hear so much speculation about impending devastation you begin to expect Armageddon. It's a bit like hearing rave reports about a new film – you know for sure that when you get to see it, no matter how good it is, you will be disappointed.

There was a lot of rain and strong winds and it was the random tornadoes that caused most damage in Brevard county, where I was, but it whipped through in about five hours and left nothing but a load of debris and shattered power lines.

Before the power failed, which was inevitable, I was watching a TV report from the area worst affected by the hurricane in Miami. The wind was over 100 miles per hour and obviously unsafe for man as well as beast. But the intrepid reporter and his assistant were going to make a name for themselves and show just how windy it really was. The assistant was hanging on to his main man's legs as he tried to word the report over the howling of the hurricane. The report ended as both were whisked off screen by the force of the wind, the assistant attempting to give new meaning to the concept of TV anchorman.

Tampa was relatively unharmed by the weather and we were all amazed by how dry the course was on Tuesday last when we came out of our bunkers.

The Copperhead course at Innisbrook was in great condition: a golfers' course where you have to hit accurate shots and are not permitted to golf with impunity like the previous week. Par was of value again, reflected in the nine-under-par score by the popular winner, Carl Pettersson.

We set off on our afternoon first round last Thursday with a considerable group of spectators, maybe a couple of hundred in all, not bad for a first round in an event without Tiger. On one tee I had some time for idle banter with a few enthusiastic young spectators, obviously keen golfers. I gathered from our conversation young golfers are extremely technical these days – or just very good at remembering the finer detail of a professional golfer's club set-up.

One youth quizzed me politely about Retief's putter. A Yes putter, I replied. His eyes demanded I take the cover off and show him the head. He had seen loads of C-groove Yes putters but never this one.

"How old is it," he asked.

"Over four years," I replied.

"Oh, that explains it. Why is the extra lead tape on the sole and back of the putter?" he enquired.

I can't imagine the federal grand jury in Washington interrogating the maverick White House aides Libby and Rove with the intensity to which this guy was subjecting me on the back of the 13th tee at Copperhead, Tampa.

He turned his attention to the woods. Steel head or titanium? What loft? The shaft? Does he have two layers of tape under the grip? How far did he fly it off the par-five 11th? And the second-shot two-iron – how far did that go? Astonishment when I replied the two-iron went over 250 yards.

What kind of shafts has he got in the irons? What's that bit of lead tape doing on the wood shafts? It was a relief to hear Retief ask what club it was off the tee.

Where is this game going? It does seem to be getting very scientific with such curiosity among enthusiastic kids about precise technical details. It makes a welcome change from the mindless hooting and hollering from the standard frat boys, who would never ask such pertinent questions as these young guys did, yet demand nothing but perfection when it comes to shot execution.

It was a day of rare inner harmony for me and my boss. There is no doubt that every day in golf is different in subtle ways, usually because of individual moods.

I knew we were on the same wavelength when I looked over at the Copperhead insignia carved around the 17th tee adjacent to the 12th and asked Retief what he thought the Copperhead stood for.

"You won't believe it," he replied, "but I was just thinking exactly the same thing. It's a snake apparently."

Who's going to argue that mind-reading isn't a major part of the caddie's job specification. That day, before he even asked me, I knew what club he wanted to hit to the next green.

It was only a matter of time before I got off this wavelength though.

Even we caddies have caddies at Sun City gig

DECEMBER 6: It's junket season again, when the world's top golfers go on a global cruise, hauling in as much of the jackpot as they can before Christmas. My man, Retief, had qualified to play in the Grand Slam of Golf the week before in Kaua'i, Hawaii, but declined.

Despite not winning a major this year, he was top of the non-winners' overall major top finishers list, which meant he was the fourth man due to play given Tiger won two majors.

He had played in his hometown event in Pietersberg, in the north of South Africa, the previous week. The prospect of a 30-hour trip to the volcanic isles for a couple of days' play was not the most enticing, given the Sun City event was on the following week. Sixty hours of flying in four days would not be the easiest on the body or the mind.

I know it all sounds very exotic, and indeed it is, but when you actually take those trips and try to perform at your best when you get there, the glamour tends to get lost somewhere, usually at 35,000 feet over the Atlantic. Many of the players in South Africa for last week's Nedbank Golf Challenge were heading off to California on the Sunday night to play in Tiger's event this week. The overnight to London and a quick connection to LA, and there they are in body – but not in spirit. Tim Clark, who played in Sun City, is going to California and heading straight back to play in the South African Open in Fancourt the following week.

On trips like this more experienced players do a cost/benefit analysis on the wear and tear weighed up against the guaranteed and potential earnings. A player in Retief's position is probably more equipped to ease the wear and tear, whereas Clark may feel more obliged to seize the moment and scoop up as much as he can. Junkets can be a bit of a juggling act.

These events are not only splurges for the players. Their bagmen and guests get treated pretty royally as well. I arrived with my guests in Johannesburg's Jan Smuts International airport to the kind of very warm welcome normally bestowed upon dignitaries. Here I was, a bagtoter, whisked through the diplomatic immigration line because I was here to caddie in the Sun City event. Our driver was waiting at the other side to take us on the two-hour trip to the resort. The manager of the hotel was at the reception to greet us and ease our check-in process. The only thing missing was the red carpet.

> "As caddies, we were assigned our own caddies. The scenario those of us who have been looping for a while have always longed for, the caddying lifestyle without actually having to carry the bag."

As caddies, we were assigned our own caddies. The scenario those of us who have been looping for a while have always longed for, the caddying lifestyle without actually having to carry the bag. Albert, my caddie from last year, was allocated to me again this year. There are hundreds of caddies at the resort, so the 12 hand-picked to be the caddies' caddies are the lucky ones.

There is no driving range at the Gary Player course at Sun City, so the 10th fairway is used as the range for the 12 players for the week. So, primarily the caddies' caddies are known as "shag" caddies: they stand down the fairway with a "shag" bag while the players hit balls to them and we caddies pretend we are really important beside our players doing nothing. During the practice rounds and pro-am, the caddies' caddies also carry the bag. We "dignitary" caddies only have to carry the bag during the four rounds of play. Even then it is light, because our caddies take the umbrella, rain gear and any other extras that may overload us and follow us around in a support role.

The off-course activities are pretty enjoyable too. We are invited to all the functions and made to feel very important when we get there. The first function was a dinner which was televised. There were speeches and interviews on stage with the players, including the legendary Player, entertaining as ever, giving his take on one of the sponsors of the US tour, Cialis, a competitor of Viagra. There were plenty of spontaneous laughs for certain jokes which obviously permissible on South African TV earlier in the evening than they are in most countries.

There were no speeches at the following night's function, a beach party at the Valley of the Waves which culminated in a fireworks display. The lack of orations that night was made up for in the last function, a braii, or barbecue, in the bush outside the course – where we nearly ended up again on Sunday afternoon when Retief hooked his tee-shot deep into the undergrowth left of the 14th fairway. I almost stepped in what I could only assume was a large, wild animal's droppings as we tried to find a suitable dropping area of our own for Retief's ball after we located it in an unplayable lie.

One of the speakers at the braii rather stunned his audience when he suggested he understood entirely the dilemma of winners of these big tournaments, when they see their earnings slip straight into the icy grip of their wives or partners, only to be squandered frivolously on clothes and accessories. He didn't receive the most rapturous applause, and I noticed many female guests declined to acknowledge the misguided man's efforts completely.

We all soon forgot our main speaker's faux pas as we tucked into Irish chief Conrad Gallagher's culinary creations. Gallagher is now head chef for the big South African hotel chain, Sun International, and was in Sun City to oversee the delivery of 20,000 meals a day to sponsors and their guests.

As junkets go, the Nedbank Challenge is the junket of all junkets, and if listening to a few misguided speeches is the only downside, then I think I could handle being invited back to this event for many years to come.

Giraffes are just like golfers after all

DECEMBER 13: My first introduction to wildlife on this trip to South Africa was a rather chilling speech by the artist who sculpted the bronze giraffes presented as gifts to the 12 invited players to the Sun City event a couple of weeks ago.

It is a tradition at the event that the players receive a piece of art representing the environment as an appreciation of their making the long trip south.

The artist made what most thought was a tenuous link between the long and loping but extremely elegant giraffe and a professional golfer.

On the one hand the golfer is quiet and graceful with a flowing swing, just like the movement of the giraffe.

But also there is almost a dark side to the golfer. When under pressure he will become aggressive.

Ditto the giraffe, which will "kick out its hind legs and crush the predator's skull causing its eyeballs to explode", according to the sculptor. Apparently the artist had witnessed the dark side of the graceful giraffe's nature.

As a caddie I have never witnessed eyeball explosions during a tight moment in a round, but I have been on the wrong end of some chilling glares that would make your eyeballs pop out if you didn't avert your gaze.

Having a spare week before the South African Open, my boss, Retief Goosen, invited me to join him at his house on a game reserve about two hours north of Johannesburg.

The trip from Sun City was quite an adventure for a driver who is used to negotiating normal, everyday roads with the odd signpost thrown in.

After a couple of hours of bouncing around on dirt tracks, which make your throat itchy and your skin gravelly – and that's with the windows shut – I happened upon a friendly farmer at yet another signless T-junction who knew which direction to point me in.

As I eased onto the tarmac road, it was the first time in many decades of renting cars that I actually felt like they had undercharged me.

If you want to get good value from your hired vehicle, get on a dirt road in South Africa and feel the suspension cringe as you fly through the air.

Retief met me at the entrance to the farm and I followed him to our lodgings. There is obviously a strict architectural code on the property whereby the buildings must have a traditional thatched roof with a designated pitch.

Many homes have a great mix of the traditional and the contemporary: it's not all stuffed buffalo heads sticking out of the living-room walls.

My second introduction to the wild of the veld was the footprints of a sizeable animals about two steps from the front door. Now when you enter a game farm there is a high fence around the property in order to keep the animals in, but my excited mind began to run amok when I saw the hoofprints. My concerned look betrayed me: Retief informed me there was nothing in here that wanted to kill me apart from him – whenever I gave him a club that took him over the back of a green. But that wasn't going to happen this week as there was no golf.

Or maybe there would be. There is a championship golf course on the reserve, which is accessible to all the animals on this side of the fence. Given their freedom to roam, the greens needed to be roped off at night to stop them stomping all over the surprisingly good surface.

As I looked out over the clubhouse, an ostrich pranced, a bit like a drunken old madam trying to move elegantly but failing miserably. When it got to the middle of the putting green it dropped a load almost dead centre. One of the hazards of golf on a game reserve.

I took off for a jog around the course later that evening to find a wildebeest charging in the savannah alongside the fairway. These creatures like to run; any I saw all week long were charging away into the distance with no apparent purpose.

After a couple of days on the reserve I didn't bother to strain my neck to look at yet another antelope. There were so many: impala, eland, waterbuck, bushbuck, nyala, kudu, wildebeest, hartebeest and zebra. They seemed like dogs in the street after a short while.

Of course, after we went out with a ranger who drip-fed us endless facts about the birds and mammals of South Africa, their presence was more meaningful. Our ranger for the five o'clock drive one morning turned out to be a former IT wizard from London who had sacrificed an hourly salary equivalent to what she now earned in a month.

The bush is so thick at this time of year, given that it had rained quite heavily in recent weeks, it is very difficult to see animals once they retreat a few steps from the road.

We came across a giraffe who took about four steps (10 metres for a giraffe) before disappearing from view. Given it's over five metres tall, its hard to imagine such a large creature disappearing so quickly.

We travelled to the other side of the reserve, where there were plenty of animals that would kill you if you got in their way. Hippos were there and we were fortunate enough to see three white rhinos. A male can weigh up to 1,500 kilos and reach speeds up to 40 kilometres an hour. They are massive and powerful mammals and all that from eating grass and the odd mouthful of soil to obtain minerals.

There is an important lesson to be learnt from game watching: the chances are you will not see a whole lot when you expect it – but will chance upon something weird and fascinating when you least expect it.

We headed off the next day to a cheetah and wild-dog reserve in search of a bit of gore. Not only did we not find any hunting cheetah, we couldn't find the entrance to the reserve.

As we headed home we stumbled upon a small herd of giraffes. It was mid-afternoon and the giraffes are not normally active at this time of day. It was cool and the pair that we saw had more than browsing on their minds.

We pulled up, settled back and agreed we might as well take the time to see what giraffes get up to on a Thursday afternoon in December. Two hours later we were still there and the pair of mating giraffes were still at it. Sniffing, necking, shoving, ignoring, a bit of grazing – and finally the act itself, which to the untrained eye looked like a quick jab with a needle.

Given the gestation period of over 15 months and the two-year gap between pregnancies, I suppose we were extremely fortunate to witness the relatively rare act itself.

The artist had made the analogy between golfer and giraffe. After a week on a game reserve I began to see the connection. There is a lot of hanging around; you need to be patient; most of the day nothing really happens, but when you least expect it you might just see something to make your eyeballs pop.

BAGMAN 2
2006
ON TOUR

"He is as fit a 51-year-old as you are likely to come across outside of a California gym. His hair is a little less shockingly blond, age having given it a dusty hue. He wears some deeper lines on his face but his eyes are as piercing as when he was at his predatory best over a decade ago. His athletic frame would look impressive on a 31-year-old man. If you could picture Crocodile Dundee with a more impressive pair of shoulders, that's how the old Shark looked prancing about the range at Castle Pines in full handshaking mode."

Page 118

The Great White Shark photographed in 2006 – his eyes as piercing as ever – and in action during the 1993 Open Championship at Sandwich, the venue for his second Open Championship victory. His first and only other major win was at Turnberry in 1986.

Big country, Big Dipper, big culture shock for old pros

FEBRUARY 14: Western Australia has got a land mass greater than that of southern Europe and a population that would make it sound like a provincial town in most European countries. With fewer than two million inhabitants, and 1.4 million of them living in the capital, Perth, you don't have to wander far to get a feeling of vastness and isolation.

The trip from the city to the Vines Golf Course where the Johnnie Walker Classic was held last week, was just far enough from the metropolis to give a sense of being in the outback.

Perth provided a particularly nice drive in the crisp, dry light of Western Australia. Easing along the Swan Valley wine route, if you let your mind drift over the miles of vines and their ripe grapes ready to be plucked, you could easily fool yourself that you really were on holidays.

After all, most people at home think that this golf tour is just one big holiday anyway.

So the Swan drive at six in the morning, despite the ungodly alarm time, was almost this make-believe, serene scene. The imposing gum trees, with their soft, pink bark that looks like it has been smoothed with fine sandpaper and painted, along-side the well groomed mature palm trees, provide a well guarded avenue, until you reached the open country of the vineyards.

There is a casual nature that pervades in Australia, you meet it at the airport: the immigration officials are actually welcoming. Of course you become an instant "mate".

Once you get to the Vines, if you know where to look you can see kangaroos munching away at the verdant fairways. They seem to have developed a taste for fertilised grass. There was a mob of them on the range and they were very reluctant to stop their grazing, even with a barrage of Titleist raining down upon them.

The only thing to shift that lot was the heat of the day, when they retreated farther into the bush.

Once in the clubhouse, the traditional pie (pronounced poiye) greets you at the snack bar. Despite the efforts of globalisation to eradicate national traits, there is no mistaking where you are when you come to Australia.

As if we had not had enough indication of where we were, Retief was drawn to play with Robert DiPierdomenico, or the Big Dipper, in the pro-am.

The Dipper is, of course, an icon in Australia after his years as a legendary Australian Rules footballer, who has extended his popularity well into his retirement. He's also well known in Ireland due to his involvement with the International Rules series in the 1980s.

He looks like a vast version of Gérard Depardieu. His square jaw looks like it was carved out of rock and his torso is of such a thickness that when you ran into the Big Dipper out on the oval you didn't get up until you woke up in the dressing-room. Retief was amused by playing with the affable Dipper. Robert, in turn, was calling Retief "The Goose" by the third tee. By the fifth he wanted to come to Augusta to watch him win the Masters. It's no wonder he travels the country on a motivational speech trail.

Most golfers' careers, like those of footballers, don't last long, unless you are the tenacious Bernhard Langer. Some top golfers, like Tom Watson and Jay Haas, have managed to step straight from the main tour to the seniors tour without any delay. Others don't quite make such a smooth transition.

The Johnnie Walker in Perth was one such early retirement home for former professionals. I came across a commentary box full of ex-bosses of mine, who have retired from professional playing but, like us all, are institutionalised to a large degree in the only game they know.

The Australian commentary teams included three of my former employers from the old days, and many others who played in Europe through the 1990s or earlier. Ossie Moore, Wayne Riley, Wayne Smyth, Mike Clayton and Greg Turner were all giving their well-informed opinions.

The credits read like a list of "Where are they now", the antipodeans of the European Tour. Of course, there is not such a vibrant golf scene Down Under anymore. It seems impossible to compete with the might of the US Tour and, to a lesser degree, the European Tour.

So there is not enough commentating to sustain such a large team of announcers. So what do ex-pros do to put a loaf of bread on the table? Wayne Riley owns a nine-hole course and driving range in Sydney. Ossie Moore is a full-time commentator. Greg Turner has a course design business and writes for a New Zealand golf magazine.

Mike Clayton also designs and writes, based in Melbourne. Wayne Smyth has a management company in Perth.

There is life after playing, but it is a hard game to leave when it is in your blood and you feel like you have a lot still to offer. The Goosen team backed out of the outback prematurely – golfers are not machines after all.

But the semi-retired golfers in their part-time positions looked comfortable in their new day jobs. With the precarious and stressful nature of the professional game behind them, the trip back to Perth was easier for them to enjoy. The memories of another missed cut and another unpaid week could drift over the vines of the tranquil Swan Valley and out into the vastness that is Western Australia on their trip back to the hotel, from which, as announcers, they were definitely not going to have to check out till Sunday.

Older pros struggle to keep up with belters like Bubba

MARCH 7: It was not the best day to get drawn with a prodigy of the post-Faldo era at the Ford Championship at Doral, Miami, last Saturday.

At the best of times it would have been a challenge to keep up with the long-hitting Bubba Watson. Given Retief's very average ball striking last week, by his own admission, it was going to be an ordeal to keep in the same zip code as the rookie American.

I have come up with a way of categorising this new age of golf when a 350-yard drive is commonplace and 470-yard par fours are reduced to a drive and a mere flick of a sand wedge:post-Faldo.

It all started to happen about 10 years ago when Nick Faldo was perfecting the art of refining the swing so that the ball went very straight, very repetitively.

Unfortunately for the six-time major champion and master of par – and some might argue mundane – golf, the manufacturers were in full creative flow, designing balls that flew ever farther and shafts that flexed at the right point for each individual swinger to maximise distance.

We now live in the epoch of the Crusher – if you are of average length off the tee these new guys will make a mockery of your game, even if you're as talented and successful as Retief Goosen. There is a clear distinction between the pre- and post-Faldo era of professional golf.

"I am sure he could clearly inspect his knuckles at the top of his backswing. To put it in the vernacular, he gives it a fierce clatter."

All that distance advantage is heavily dependent on the way a course is set up. Yet again this year at the Blue Monster at Doral, the sponsors had the best players in the world at their event and they wanted to see them at the top of the leaderboard. Naturally in the long-hitting modern era the big boys end up very close to a lot of greens in one hit.

As I argued in this column last year, they need to rename the Blue Monster to something a little more reflective of its genuine challenge to today's pro. With a winning score of 18 under par the name seems inappropriate. I can only assume the course will be toughened up for the next professional event there, the American Express in March 2007.

There was no rain all week, it was perfect south Florida weather, yet the greens were like puddings and the better ball strikers were not rewarded for their purer ball contact.

Instead, the soft putting surfaces equalised the challenge for all players, whereas only the big hitters with the finishing finesse feature at the majors.

The winner of the event – and most events he tees it up in these days – Tiger, is excluded from this analysis; he is not in the pre- or post-Faldo domain – he is in the superhuman league, beyond comparison or comprehension.

Retief had worked hard on his game all week, but sometimes it just is not there, so to make the cut was quite a result, his short game and relentless quest for improvement getting him through to the weekend.

Despite not being a machine, you still need to search for some form; it doesn't come looking for you. His efforts paid off on Sunday with an impressive

66. The four hours of practice on Saturday afternoon, which left him feeling a little stiff during the final round, stood to him. There is usually a way out of a "slump". Retief's way is by working harder.

There is undoubtedly an infatuation among golf enthusiasts with length. But there is increasing interest among the more established professionals with this post-Faldo group of golfers. As I lurked with my work-mates in the tropical garden with a lush variety of palm trees waiting for my player to present himself for his fourth round, I recounted tales of playing with the biggest hitter of them all on tour today, Bubba Watson.

He was 30 yards short of the seventh green with his drive, I explained. Given the slight dog-leg of 430 yards, this meant his drive went about 390 yards. Not only did he thrash his tee shot but he finished the delicate chip off with the dexterity of a surgeon. "Wow," my colleagues exclaimed genuinely in unison.

The veteran ex-PGA champion Jeff Sluman, now in his late 40s, emerged from the locker-room as I described Bubba's tee shot to the par-three ninth. His sand wedge went over 170 yards; he only meant to tickle it 157 to the pin in a cross-wind.

Disbelief illuminated Sluman's face as he waddled off muttering how happy he was he was almost ready for the Seniors Tour. I teased Jeff a little more as he departed by adding that Watson then went on to chip in for a two from the back of the ninth. He shook his head in disbelief as he headed for a pre-round stretch with his personal trainer.

The most effeminate thing about Watson is the pink shaft he has on his driver; the rest of his game is big and booming and very manly. The size of the man himself only became apparent to me when I saw him move sideways into a portaloo beside the 12th tee. His athletic frame is of such proportions he did not fit easily though an average door.

The international flavour of this US Tour event was spiced up, as so often it is, by the booming introduction of the starter on the first tee.

"From Polokwani, South Africa, Ret-eeef Gooo-sen" came the throaty intro for my man at 9.54am last Saturday.

"From Baghdad (slight pause), Florida, Bub-Ba Wha-hotson."

The only thing more elongated I came across that day was Bubba's backswing. I am sure he could clearly inspect his knuckles at the top of his backswing. To put it in the vernacular, he gives it a fierce clatter.

We were given a reprieve on Sunday: Bubba had left us and we were paired with another veteran very much from the opposite end of the distance spectrum.

Fred Funk was on average about 50 yards behind Retief off the tee, which would have left him 100 yards behind Bubba. It is hard to imagine how the two very different styles of golf can compete in the same event. Such is the nature of the game, they can.

Fred mentioned that when they played a practice round on Tuesday last the player behind them hit his tee shot to the 370-yard par-four 16th as they were on the green and the ball ran between his feet as he putted.

He wasn't offended, he wasn't really surprised, but he was astounded to see that the shot had been hit by an unknown pre-qualifier.

There was a time, probably back in the pre-Faldo era, when if a player hit his tee shot 370 yards you knew exactly who it could be.

In the post-Faldo era there is an abundance of players who are likely to hit their drives this length. Welcome to the new age of golf, where you drive for show and probably have a putt for an eagle.

Fans still have faith in Double D

MARCH 21: Sports fans adore a comeback. The fallen hero who gradually claws their way out of the mire of lost form is always given a bigger reception than the one they got for building their reputation in the first place. We were drawn to play with David Duval and Mark Brooks in the Bay Hill Invitational in Orlando last week.

This was Arnold Palmer's event, the great icon of golf who was fortunate never to suffer such a fall from greatness as Duval did in his career.

In fact, Arnie even got to extend his golfing lifespan with the advent of the seniors tour, thus experiencing a sort of rejuvenation of an already long and rich golfing life. Such longevity is not bestowed upon every player.

David Duval won no fewer than 11 events between 1997 and 1999. He gained access to the US PGA Tour in 1995 due to his success on the then Nationwide secondary US Tour. He shot a record 59 to win the Bob Hope Chrysler Classic in 1999, went on to win the Players Championship in March that year and knocked Tiger out of his position as best golfer in the world after 41 consecutive weeks.

Duval had won four events before the Masters in the same year. He had become a serious contender every time he teed his ball up.

In 2000, Duval was sidelined due to injuries. From wrist to back problems, it was to mark the gradual decline of a blistering career. Despite multiple high finishes, the injuries were obviously starting to take their toll on Duval as he had to miss or pull out of numerous events. In 2001, I saw Duval shoot a stunning third round of 65 in the British Open Championship at Lytham, when I was caddying for Paul Lawrie. He went on to win the British Open that year.

This was the last event that Duval won. He slipped from eighth in the US money rankings to 80th in 2002, 211th in 2003, 210th the next year and 260th last year.

He has gone from being a "big boy" in both weight and status to being a much smaller boy physically and a bigger boy in golfing status back to being a "big boy" again without the status. He has had some major weight fluctuations over the years, which is a complicating factor in a game that is based so fundamentally on balance.

As a major and multiple tournament winner, it is very difficult to throw in the towel at the game that has given you so much joy and success. Because of the exemptions that go with major territory, the system will never tell you when enough is enough. For an average player, the system will shout it loud and clear that you are no longer up to the mark and that it's time to move on.

As a major winner you get a free go at the tour for the following five years. Duval's reprieve clock is ticking away: this is his last year exempt, and next year he can draw on the "all-time money earners" exemption. Before next year is out, his comeback will have to be made.

Given the talent of top golfers it is hard to accept that a once world beater has turned into an also-ran. The overall picture of the scores they produce are what they are judged by, but if you examine the small-print of this fickle game it usually has some hope hidden deep within. Having played with Duval, it seems like there is plenty of game left in him, it is just a question of how much desire there is to bring that talent back to where it once was, and how much the injuries are going to hamper that quest to recapture esteemed status.

Despite missing the cut last week in Bay Hill, he did show all the trademarks of being a serious golfer.

There have been some spectacular demises in golf over the past two decades. Australian Ian Baker-Finch shot a stunning third round 64 on a treacherous Birkdale links in the early 1990s to set up an British Open Championship victory and esteemed golfing status, only to end up in the commentary booth a few years later due to a total lack of form. Bill Rogers faded into the abyss after his Open victory in the early eighties. Ben Curtis, although still competing on tour, has not recaptured any of the stunning form he showed to win the Open in 2003. My ex-boss Lawrie, despite some success in the years after his Open victory, never reached those heights again.

Nick Faldo was playing last week in Bay Hill, hanging on to a place in professional golf very much at a level that he probably knows himself is too low for him to respectfully sustain, although his fall is more to do with age than a premature lack of form.

Golf is a game of habit. There are certain routines we all adhere to that distinguish us from our playing partners. Our pre-shot ritual, the coin we mark our ball with on the green, the height at which we tee up our ball. All these idiosyncrasies separate us from the others.

There is another way to distinguish the great players from the average, and that is through their scoring trend. Just as golf is a game of habit, scoring in that game under the pressure of competition is equally habitual. It is easy to slip into the bad habit of scoring badly, and when you do, as a once world beater, it is even more difficult to recapture those days of golfing "wine and roses". Duval seems to have lost the expectancy of scoring well, but he still has the artistry to do so.

When today's top golfers don their spikes they have an agenda and that is to shoot low. This is how David Duval's script used to be, or "Double D" as the expectant crowd at Bay Hill called the once world number one last week. "It's great to see you back" and "welcome back DD" greeted Duval on many holes. The Americans don't, as a tradition, warm to a loser. But Duval is certainly not a loser, he of course has very much been a winner and there is a strong sense he could well be in the winner's enclosure again and this is why the fans are still encouraging.

David Robert Duval, at the relatively young age of 34, really should not have reached his golfing prime yet, he just needs to get back in the habit of expecting to score in the 60s again.

Judging by what I saw last week there is no reason why he cannot. Every aspect of his former game seems to be present and accounted for. If he can draw on the edge he has over the majority of his fellow competitors, that of being a multiple winner and a mammoth of the modern game, then there is no reason why he cannot regain at least some of the status he commanded back at the turn of the millennium. If the sports fans in America have their vocal way, they will elevate Double D back to his golfing pedestal with just a few more made cuts.

Balancing control and aggression key to winning

MAY 16: The captain of my home club's senior cup team was obviously at a loss in trying to dig up a person to provide some words of inspiration to his team in advance of this year's matches.

How flattering that a bag-man could possibly inspire such skilled golfers. Mind you they haven't heard me speak yet. Given my proximity to golf at the highest level over the years, my words of wisdom to these selected team members is going to be from a psychological perspective, because the mind most definitely rules the body in the fickle game of golf.

I watch great golfers play this incredibly difficult game week in week out. It is sometimes easy to become complacent about how good they actually are.

When you see golfers consistently hit their tee shots over 300 yards, and straight, it becomes mundane. When you witness them frequently nip chip shots off a tight downhill lie onto a bone-hard green to gimme distance, you can forget just how hard it is to do that. It is all very impressive.

But what is most memorable about all these great players and the amazing shots they frequently play, is how they recover from a bad situation, how they dig themselves out of a dark hole.

Given their talent, playing good shots is relatively easy, however the mental fortitude is not always as easy to maintain. It is what separates the good from the great. Golf is a selfish game. Usually there is only one person that can get you out of a tight situation after you tee off.

Low handicap golfers attain their status by playing singles golf, there is no other way of getting your handicap reduced. In team golf, the rules change. You are now playing for the others and if you are a team player that chip off the downhill lie becomes a little more difficult. You are but a small link in what each individual can make a very strong chain. A chain is as strong as its weakest link.

In my experience of observing life in a competitive environment, the constant is that everyday is going to be different. I remember listening to Thomas Bjorn giving a lesson and being intrigued by his basic sound piece of advice.

Balance was the key. He maintains we all get out of bed everyday feeling different. I don't know if he was referring specifically to the physical side, but it is even more true for the mental approach. There is nothing wrong with feeling different, it is perfectly normal, the professional recognises change and deals with it, those less experienced don't know how to deal with it. Searching for both physical and mental equilibrium is vital.

> "The bottom line is you cannot beat thorough preparation. Eliminate as much guess work as you can with sound preparation."

Despite the game at the top end being about routines it is important to recognise when precisely to alter the routine.

In matchplay this is particularly the case, because what your opponent does could have a direct effect on what you do.

This is where preparation is important. You need to have a course strategy.

A plan for the way you think the hole should be played given your opponent has hit a good shot and maybe a more cautious one if he has hit his tee shot in trouble. There is also a third scenario, if you are playing particularly well and you are confident trust your ability and play the hole as you decided in your practice round.

The bottom line is you cannot beat thorough preparation. Eliminate as much guess work as you can with sound preparation. For me as a caddie the most important day of my week is the day I walk the course without my player and familiarise myself with the course. It is not the fancy stuff or the radical ideas that create a winning environment, it is the basic things that induce the winning formula. Retief Goosen, my boss, is very observant, he absorbs everything when he plays his practice rounds. He is very aware of the right thing to do when the wind is a certain way or the pin is in a certain place. Soak up the finest of details as you play your practice round.

All this is basic preparation. That is the simple part. Throw pressure into the equation and the dynamic changes. This is when it is most important to stick to your routine, your normal check-list before you hit your shot. It is when mere mortals are most unlikely to do it. Always remember, golf is a pro-active game. You are in control, you pull the trigger.

If you want to observe how important getting your head around a shot is, watch Jim Furyk's visualisation and pre-shot routine. If he is not in his shot-making zone, he steps out and re-enters that space only when he is ready to hit the perfect shot. The energy is concentrated on the mental rather than the physical. How common was it until quite recently for players to take up to three practice swings. That work has been honed on the range, the key on the course is to hit the perfect shot, you can only do this with an organised mind.

It is also important to recognise we are not machines – it is equally important to relax and not think golf between shots. Being competitive is a vital attribute in performing well in golf.

The balance between control and aggression is the art of being competitive. It comes from understanding yourself and your ability. Know what you are capable of and use your strengths. It's what all great players do.

It is a great privilege to be chosen to play on your club's best team. Given the less egotistical nature of playing golf for a team there is some extra compromise to be made by more habitual singles players.

The most important decision to make is whether you actually want to play in a group and if the decision is that you do then the self discovery of playing the game for others adds more selfless rewards but also includes the more powerful dynamic of compromising for the sake of the club.

Trust your unique ability and enjoy using it for the benefit of the team.

I say, Mr Els, why didn't you leave my Wentworth alone?

MAY 30: Wentworth Golf Club has always drawn mixed emotions from those who visit; its visual splendour of mature foliage certainly does inspire and the course always provokes comment. Those most pass-remarkable are the professionals who revisit annually for the flagship event of the European Tour, the PGA Championship. With the largest purse on offer for a European Tour event and held at Tour headquarters, this is as good as it gets for the European players.

It was decided the course, originally fashioned by the renowned and respected early 20th century course designer Harry Colt, needed a bit of a shake-up to re-establish it as the challenge it once was for the better players.

With the winning scores in the high teens under par in recent years, this seemed to be a logical move. Although with David Howell's 17-under par winning score on Sunday perhaps they need to re-redesign.

I wonder what Mr Colt would make of his course now and so here is a letter I could imagine him writing to the re-designer, South African multi-winner and three-time major champion golfer Ernie Els.

Dear Mr Els,
I am writing to you from way above the clouds, somewhere that I can only assume is the place you go when you live a good and

respectable life. Word has spread up here that you have been tinkering with my masterpiece in the leafy environs of the stockbroker belt in Surrey. I am terribly interested in how you may have altered my work for the better of the modern golfer.

Of course back in my day, I was attempting to combat the march of the new hickory shafts and in later times, the radical steel shaft and that supersonic missile, the Haskell golf ball.

What a lethal combination they were. If you had half a swing at all you could unleash a drive of up to 200 yards. Of course the ball was a lot smaller than nowadays. Naturally, I was concerned my courses were going to be annihilated by the hot shots and their fancy equipment. I was particularly worried that slasher Ted Ray was going to make a complete mockery of the course and reduce it to pitch and putt.

Therefore I wanted some length to the Burma Road but I also wanted to challenge the likes of Ted, who may have been inclined to spray the ball a little bit.

I have gathered from the rather garbled messages I am receiving up here – we don't have internet, and the telepathic vibes I am receiving are naturally open to interpretation – you have lengthened my tricky little sixth hole by about 60 yards, whereby the decision to go for the green or lay up with a shorter club has been taken away from the confused golfer. What a pity.

Of course with the bunkers you have added – up to 30, I believe – you must have done a deal with some middle-eastern group to get such a vast quantity of sand all at once (incidentally what are our relations with those eastern boys – have they taken to the game at all or are they committed to watching their birds fly for entertainment, or do we have any contact with them?).

The first hole, which I designed as a par five, sought, of course, to ease the golfer into the course. Now, as a par four with punishing bunkers left and right off the tee and a cluster of them added by the green, the hole has certainly got some vicious teeth to it, bared while the unsuspecting golfer is probably still trying to get his shoelaces tied.

I heard the new heather-framed bunker on four and to the left of 11 are right up my alley when it comes to the more natural look. I know it's the exclusive Wentworth estate but I always liked the heather to be a little more rugged and not quite as manicured as I hear it is now. I was never looking to contribute to the Chelsea Flower Show.

As you so rightly ascertained, I had a penchant for framing my golf holes. It was heather that took on that role for me, but of course they allowed the members to drag their trolleys over the plant and naturally killed it off. There is no doubt, Mr Els, some of my originals cried out for peripheral adornment.

I must tell you the origins of one of my favourites, the eighth. The water feature to the left of the green had to be kept back from the green because in my day, there was a shortage of golf balls and I was strongly urged to keep the water well back from the putting surface.

The ninth I am a little disappointed about, you see, I felt the camber of the fairway naturally running off into the hazard and trees on the right, was a clever feature. The two bunkers plonked in the landing zone hugely detract from what I was trying to achieve. The game I felt should give the marginally errant golfer the chance to use their skill to recover, the bunkers negate this principle.

Of course, Mr Els, you were a great cricketer and rugby player, they were the sports I was encouraged to play in Cambridge. Golf in my day was not thought highly of so I was something of a maverick getting involved in what was a relatively new game. The game was not seen as promoting the right values, sense of duty, co-operation and honesty. I believe all that has changed now, Mr Els, despite the little rumour going about up here that there was a senior member of your golfing fraternity embroiled in some ball moving scandal in the Far East. Wouldn't have happened in my day.

I would hate to sound sniffy but I either designed, co-designed or reviewed almost one hundred courses in the British Isles alone between the 1880s and the 1920s. I have contributed greatly to the development of courses on continental Europe, I tinkered with courses as far away as the United States of America. I was, like you, Mr Els, a global designer, the most obvious difference was nowadays it doesn't take you a week to get to your destination. But on arrival I do have to admit that I had the pick of some pretty special land.

I heard from a chappie who was recently transferred up here to me there have been some pretty dramatic climate changes in your era.

In fact, he was at the PGA Championship and it had rained heavily for the whole week.

I always liked the West with its healthy soil when the surface was hard and running. Indeed that's when the purpose of design features really come into their own.

I believe the general consensus is that your colleagues are suitably impressed by your handy work, Mr Els. It would be rather foolish to disagree with a man of your stature. I have also been advised that in the modern era not many will give their honest opinion in public; everyone seems to want to be loved by everyone else – what a positively charming place the world must now be.

If you are fortunate enough to get a warm summer in southern

England this year, I would be fascinated to hear the players' opinion about the modern alterations. Because when the ball starts kicking and bouncing into all those treacherous traps, the scores are going to soar, and I am not sure just how enjoyable the Burma Road will be for the average golfer who has to play more than one week of the year.

Must sign off now, old boy, a sterling effort, though given your relatively novice status as a course designer, I always thought a player of your calibre should be concentrating on hitting the shots.

The West at Wentworth is like a fine old tweed suit – it's a bit dank and smelly in the rain but looks its finest when crisp and dry,

Yours sincerely,

Harry S Colt Esq.

Nicklaus manages to rake up a whole new controversy

JUNE 6: The Memorial Tournament falls on the week after the Memorial Day Weekend. This is a national holiday in America that honours those citizens who died in battle for their country.

The tournament was started 31 years ago with the intention of bringing a top-quality event to Jack Nicklaus's home town. The other motivation was to honour those Jack believes have played an important role in the greatest game, golf. This year's inductees were Michael Bonallack, Charlie Coe, Lawson Little, Henry Picard, Paul Runyan and Denny Shute. There was a ceremony on the Tuesday afternoon to induct the chosen golfers into their immortal place in the Memorial Garden below the clubhouse in Muirfield Village.

The official tournament magazine introduced this year's inductees and explained about the changes made to improve and toughen the course. Teeing areas were upgraded and bunkers deepened. What was not mentioned was the rakes they chose to rake these cavernous sand traps.

There are many ways to toughen a course. The obvious ones are, well, pretty obvious. Move the tees back 50 yards, grow jungle thick rough closer to the fairways, add more slope to faster greens and deepen strategic sand traps.

Last week at the Memorial Championship at Muirfield Village in Dublin, Ohio, the rules for toughening up a course all changed. What a surprise it was such a bizarre method reared its ugly head at the Golden Bear's event. Nicklaus is a living legend and has earned the respect of his peers and the golfing world by his golfing exploits over four decades and more recently his ambassadorial role.

I am not too sure if that respect made it through last week's event. An experienced course designer, his obvious changes to his own course were well received, lengthened tees and more, ever deeper traps are a fair addition. The surprise was the rakes used to smooth the sand in the deepened traps. The "new" rakes were the talk of the tour last week.

This is the first time I have heard such concern over something that is usually so mundane. In preparation for this year's event the greenkeepers bought a bundle of old-fashioned wooden rakes and removed each alternate tooth. The effect was it left furrows in the sand and on the players' brows as they were presented with the daunting task of getting their ball out of the creased sand pits in addition to trying to keep it on the green. The chances increased greatly of the ball lying low in a hollowed out crevice, which meant there was little hope of getting spin on the ball.

Professionals with their 60-degree lob wedges have become very skilled at plopping their trap shots in a boringly repetitive fashion close to the pin and spinning it towards the hole. Bunker play is a finely tuned art. Naturally there are those players who are particularly adept at the trap shot.

One of the more menial tasks of a golf caddie is to smooth over our master's scrapings in the bunker. How our masters rummage around in the trap is a way of figuring out just how considerate he actually is. Those who traipse about like it's a beach make a lot more work for us. The more steps, the more raking, which puts us under more pressure to keep up. It's an unwritten rule that you help your colleagues out if their player hits it in a trap.

It was impossible to smooth out the traps at Muirfield Village due to the nature of the rakes, no matter how long you spent manicuring. If you left the traps in the condition we were obliged to at Jack's course any other week we would probably incur a fine. We are meant to leave minimal trace of anyone having been in the sand; it is a major part of basic etiquette. Which makes the whole rake issue of last week so confusing. There is a strong consensus that there is some trickery going on up in the "War Room". It's almost like an advanced method of very bad etiquette. The club had their own bunker rakers assigned to each fairway in order to ensure the traps were raked exactly how they desired.

> "How our masters rummage around in the trap is a way of figuring out just how considerate he actually is. Those who traipse about like it's a beach make a lot more work for us."

The average sand players were really excited about the new concept because basically it reduces the whole field to the same level. It is like a form of handicapping for pros. I always thought golf was a test of skill combined with mental fortitude on a level playing field. This furrowed trap defies this concept.

The theory of the deep-channelled sand apparently relates to Jack's win in the US Open at Cherry Hills – the sand was exactly like it was at Muirfield Village last week. Courses, and particularly bunkers, were never as well maintained back in the 1970s as they are now. It is due to better equipment and an overall push to create a level playing field.

Saying "that's how it was in my day" is not a good enough reason to resort to underhand methods to try to make a course more difficult. If we go along with this policy, why not take it a step further and forget about replacing divots, repairing pitch marks and being respectfully quiet while your playing partners are hitting? The Memorial event has spent three decades building up hard-earned respect.

Continuing with the regressive tactics of tricking up the traps is not in the honourable tradition of the greatest game the greatest living player of all time is responsible for creating last week. He has the chance to redeem himself by admitting it wasn't the right thing to do and return to leaving traps as smooth as possible.

Treading softly for a rough ride

JUNE 13: The Barclays Classic tournament was held at Westchester, just north of Manhattan, last week. But it was too close for comfort to be considered its own event, with the US Open being held just six miles down the Hutchinson Parkway at Winged Foot. The talk may well have been about Westchester, but the minds were truly fixed on the second major of the season.

Preparation is the key for a major and there are many ways to approach a big event. Some do as they always do, arrive on a Monday, play a couple of practice rounds and get ready for competition on Thursday. Others will pay special visits to the venue well in advance and get a sneak preview of what is in store. Phil Mickelson played a round early last week and reported the rough was that thick you would lose your clubs in it if you were not paying attention.

Tiger had his preview to the Tillinghast-designed Winged Foot, venue for the 106th US Open the week before the Memorial event. He apparently was asked what he thought would toughen the course up. His suggestion was to make the 640-yard par-five 12th even more difficult. Naturally this will make it tougher for the shorter hitter, thus eliminating half the field. If the wind blows into you it may be a huge task for those less gifted in long hitting.

AW Tillinghast was a prominent course architect in the US, and particularly in the New York area. He designed the Black at Bethpage on Long Island, where Tiger won the US Open in 2002. He also created Baltusrol in New Jersey, where Phil Mickelson won the PGA last year.

It is hard to see the art of the great Tillinghast design with the way the USGA set up their Open venues. This year will be no different. The fairways are about 25 yards wide on average. There is a couple of yards of a harmless first-cut bordering the short grass. Then you start to tickle your ankles with the next layer of rough, and adjacent to all of that, you are in danger of not only losing your golf ball but also your bag.

The grading of the rough varies depending on the length of the hole. The shorter par fours, which are very clever designs and subsequently will test the US

Open champion's strategy to its limits, have just the first cut and then the calf-deep rough. The longer holes have got the three cuts of rough. The rough is thick and verdant and unless the ball spotters are really paying attention there is a big risk of losing plenty of balls in it, even if you have a fair idea where it was last sighted.

There is an added risk of a player or caddie standing on their ball. It will definitely be a case of treading softly because you may be treading on your ball and any dreams you had of winning the US Open.

Ironically, for those of us from the eastern side of the Atlantic, the weather was not what one would expect of New York in June. Tales of balmy Irish temperatures made many of us feel homesick, especially as it was so wet for so long over here, having endured a soaking in Ohio the previous week.

Some players had decided to arrive at the local White Plains airport mid last week in order to play some quiet practice rounds at Winged Foot. After the rain relented, they finally got to hit some balls off a mat on the range by Friday after-noon – you couldn't think of worse preparation. Half a week away from home in a venue where all you can do is think about the competition and not actually prepare for it. By Saturday the course was still closed. The quiet practice for some never happened.

As a caddie and player your life is reduced to one-venue pockets of seven-day periods. You fly on Monday, practise on Tuesday, play the pro-am on Wednesday and the tournament from Thursday to the seventh day, Sunday, which is hopefully payday. Then you continue the pattern all over again. The big differ-ence this week is that most of us will stay in the same house or hotel for the two weeks. To have 14 days in the one place, to a caddie or player, is tantamount to taking up residence. This is about as permanent and stable as our lives can be in our roaming existence.

Many of those who played Westchester broke the week up by a trip to Manhattan and a change of scenery from the leafy environs of the effective suburbs of New York city. Those with a title on their mind skipped the trip to the metropolis and began their diligent preparation for the national Open even after playing the fourth round of the Barclays event last Sunday.

We all have different ways of tuning up for a big event. There is no doubt the quality of course such as Winged Foot demands even the most astute golfer's full attention. Despite the original designer's intentions being somewhat negated by the modern set-up of rough that can only be escaped from with a shovel, some extra homework around the greens will always stand to the top golfers' ultimate performance.

The relatively big and extremely sloping greens, with their poa annua grass, looked particularly unappealing as I wandered around the course in the evening light last Sunday. It was the same type of grass we had the "pleasure" of putting on at Westchester last week.

So if you were to pick a winner for the 106th US Open, you could do worse than choose a player who had endured the unpredictable nature of the poa annua greens at Westchester. The reason the scoring was not low there was because of the difficulty of holing putts on that surface. It is as much a test of patience as skill. Anyone who has a US Open title has an abundance of both.

All you need is skill and the golfing gods on your side

JUNE 20 WEDNESDAY: I pulled into the caddie parking lot at the idyllic sounding location of Cherry Lawn. A shuttle transported us from the lawn about a mile south of the course to just outside the locker room. The workplace itself, the West at Winged Foot is, however, a daunting ordeal. With single file fairways and jungle thick rough there was no doubt about the winning formula for this year's Open champion. Accuracy.

There was a sense of concern from many players about how best to extract their errant tee shots from the lush rough. The manufacturers wagons were working overtime on building tailor-made seven woods.

Retief toyed with a seven and five wood from the rough on the practice range in an effort to come up with the answer. You were going to miss fairways the way Winged Foot was set up, so practising from the rough was as important as clipping the ball off the short grass.

THURSDAY: Show time and the predictions that we all made earlier in the week are put to the test. Three over is a good score. Ten over will be the cut. You can't expect to hole many putts on these bumpy poa annua greens. We were paired with Stuart Cink and Padraig Harrington. Padraig is a man who has his own theories about the game of golf and will stand by them. When I saw him playing out of the rough I gave a double take. Maybe my eyes were playing tricks on me, but I was sure I saw him lift his left foot completely off the ground as if he was batting at baseball.

I observed closely the next time he found the rough. My eyes were not deceiving me; he was indeed lunging into the ball. He explained his theory later to me on the practice range. He got me to throw a ball. As I raised my arm to launch the ball I realised that my left foot was moving forward to plant itself in resistance to the sling shot from my right arm. I cannot wait to try out the Harrington manoeuvre out of the thick fescue grasses at my home club this week. It certainly worked for Padraig.

FRIDAY: It is quite interesting to walk around the course on the other side of the ropes. It gives us a whole new perspective on the national open. These national championships are institutions, they are not just a major or another event, they are annual outings for some spectators that like the idea of their tradition.

These events are largely supported by fraternity boys. They wear big shorts, trainers, short white socks, polo shirts and baseball caps. They smoke cigars, drink beers from the morning tee times and there is very much a sense of drunken wellbeing by mid-afternoon.

If Jack Nicklaus thinks it's right to fluff up bunkers as a way to ruffle the feathers of the molly-coddled modern pro, why not add on a little abuse from the mouthy crowd to test his nerves even more? As Monty lined up a 15-foot putt on the back nine a knowledgeable member of the crowd whispered loudly to his accomplice that this guy had won 10 or 11 European Order of Merits. After Monty missed the curving putt, the same gentleman continued that no wonder he had never won a major, he couldn't even make a 15-foot putt. The statement probably sums up the major crowd. They are part of a tradition rather than the intelligentsia of the game.

SATURDAY: A sobering start to the day knowing that your chance of competing for the second major of the year is over.

Retief missed the cut having hovered around the mark all day. Halfway around the back nine he resigned himself to the fact that he was not going to hole any putts on these greens. He was not alone in this position. The poa annua grass created the most confusing surfaces for good putters. To those who strike their putts well and are used to watching them hug the putting surface as they track their path towards the cup – these greens are a disappointment.

Lest I get accused of sour grapes, I know some players were holing putts and our playing partners of the first couple of days, Padraig and Stuart Cink, drained their fair share. I can't help but feel that even they were surprised when their balls found the bottom of the cup.

SUNDAY: Golf is of course a very skilful game. At the risk of stating the obvious, no matter how skilful you are you need an element of luck. It seemed like Phil Mickelson was drawing on his fortune just too many times for it to take him all the way to his third major in a row.

Geoff Ogilvy probably could not believe his luck when he got up and down on the last hole to finish on five over par, which was enough to win the 106th US Open. As Phil met his doom on the back nine, Geoff took advantage of his good fortune. His trap shot on the short 13th was a good one, but unless it hit the pin and dropped into the hole it was going to leave him with a 10-foot putt for par. Then on 17 he chipped in for birdie, but like 13, if the ball didn't go in it was likely to be a bogey.

The vicissitudes of the back nine of a major on Sunday were never as apparent as they were in Winged Foot last week. You need the skill to get into a position to win, and then you need the golfing gods to shine favourably upon you in order to win.

Over 72 holes the chances are that equilibrium will determine a worthy champion.

K Club fans get to share errant Goosen's brolly

JULY 11: I couldn't quite figure out what the two spectators behind the sixth green were up to last Saturday on the Smurfit course at the K Club.

You see, my player had hit his approach shot over the green. I know I should not be admitting we hit it long, but I actually think the ball hit the downslope of the trap short of the pin and kicked on. It's what happens when things are not just going your way – that's my excuse anyway.

It had started to rain, the south-west wind that had blown all week long finally bringing precipitation. It all happened as my man had air-mailed the green. Me clutching a gust-busted umbrella, and he contemplating a downhill lie in the rough to a tight pin, was not the occasion for light-hearted banter with some hardy members of the crowd.

I held the shaky parasol and took two steps to the side as Retief prepared for his chip shot. As I did so I realised there were two blokes under our umbrella and neither of them employed me. I had assumed they were seeking temporary shelter from the rain. Not so. Obviously enthusiasts, they were just taking advantage of Goosen's errant approach to snoop in his golf bag. The shelter was just a decoy for a goo in the bag.

They must have seen the dark clouds of the Irish summer roll by earlier in the day which prompted them to gather a bundle of brochures on golfing in Turkey which was not hardy enough for the Irish summer. Retief failed to get up and down, so we battled our way up to the seventh tee as my two umbrella mates considered the benefits of a holiday on the Aegean coast or a new set of TaylorMade irons. With rain pelting sideways I know what I would have advised.

My man arrived in Ireland last Tuesday to play in a select pro-am in Portmarnock organised by Dermot Desmond. It was a balmy summer links day. Short sleeves and very little wind turned the links into a very pleasant walk. Those who do not get much chance to experience seaside terrain are open to the opportunity to play a links course in the run up to the British Open.

I could see Retief musing over his chip shots around the subtle Portmarnock greens with added concentration. The right option around links greens is never that obvious. Particularly when you play homogenized thick rough week in week out. So I could see that Retief was enjoying the special links challenge and I know he viewed it as excellent preparation for Hoylake.

It was an elite gathering and a simple way for the invited guests to raise a generous amount by the time they sat down to a late lunch in the clubhouse. The charity Respect which provides homes for elderly learning disability people were grateful for the efforts of Mr Desmond.

We moved west to Kildare, obviously to an inland course for the European Open, but it was of a different nature to the course we had left two years previously. The Smurfit had matured greatly with thick fescue grasses framing most holes on the surrounding banks. The fairways were firm and fast, the putting surfaces were good, but seemed to have developed some grain in them in the interim. It meant they did not roll as fast as they had before.

By the time we got to the windy weekend many players had paid a visit to the long, twisting fawn grasses that were very much on the periphery of the holes. The forecast for Saturday was such the authorities decided not to cut the greens. Given the severity of the wind, it turned out to be a good decision.

Golf, as most of us know, is an extremely fickle game. You arrive back to a venue where you were victorious, as Retief was here two years ago, and it can be the time to pull out of a bout of bad form. Retief had a two week break, and was looking forward to coming out of his temporary slump. Given the talent of these golfers and the game's nature, it only takes a week to make up for a run of bad ones.

We tinkered with different irons, a putter with which he had won in the States, and had a diligent attitude every day. It didn't happen, no matter how many chances Retief created, the putter just refused to convert them. Retief has won at Loch Lomond, so we will be there this week in search of the week to turn the year around and get back on course.

> "With the amount of events on tour these days and, of course, with all of them being televised it is very difficult to make an event interesting for the live spectator. Free entry may well be the way to go in the future."

The European Open is one of the bigger events on the European Tour. It attracts the Tour's best players. For some reason, it does not seem to attract many spectators. Thanks to one of the events sponsors, Ulster Bank, however, there was an unprecedented atmosphere last Thursday as 29,000 people passed through the gates. The bank had run a promotion for customers to apply for free Thursday tickets. It turned out to be a great idea and certainly made the following days' attendances look sparse in comparison.

In the run up to the Irish Open in May there were those who claimed it had become a "non-event". For those of us who remember the good old days in Portmarnock (it was certainly an "event" then), whereas the European Open in Ireland has struggled to attract a sizeable group of spectators since it started in the K Club.

With the number of events on tour these days and, of course, with all of them being televised it is very difficult to make an event interesting for the live spectator. Free entry may well be the way to go in the future.

My mates behind the sixth green last Saturday were undoubtedly enthused by the proximity gained to the fourth best player in the world, and they gained shelter from his brolly as he was hitting a shot. I wonder if they opted for the clubs or they are looking forward to a golf holiday in Turkey?

Code of the course is what keeps golfers clubbable

JULY 18: There are not many professional sports that are as congenial as the game of golf. Quite frequently I have heard players, even in the heat of intense competition, marvel at playing partners' shots. "Nice shot" and "Good birdie" are pretty simple compliments, but they are meaningful in an age when sports etiquette seems to have taken a serious turn for the worse.

Though golf has had its exponents of gamesmanship and rules transgression, the sport has remained relatively untouched by scandal.

Alongside the written rules that ensure fair play in a sport that probably offers more opportunities to cheat than most – given the vast terrain a golfer may traverse in a round – you have the unwritten laws of etiquette. These have kept the civilised ethos of the game intact over the years. Little mores like keeping quiet when your playing partner is hitting and avoiding walking on a putting line maintain a healthy air of goodwill.

In a much publicised incident in the recent Irish Open at Carton House, Darren Clarke felt morally obliged to play back onto the fairway after his lie in the rough had been improved during the overnight rain delay. He could have played a shot to the green, but being a golfer of integrity he played the chip, for which he was awarded the accolade of "RBS shot of the month".

Darren, feeling he did not deserve the award just for doing what was "the right thing", donated his prize to charity, which is understandable, because he felt like someone being rewarded for not robbing a bank.

Perhaps the RBS assumed golf might be heading down the moral slippery slope taken by so many other sports.

There is a huge amount of leisure time devoted to watching sports, both live and on television. The corporate benefits of bringing clients to watch a game they would probably not have watched without the hospitality frills, have brought new fans to old games.

Most recently the World Cup altered the traditional patterns to the July schedules of many. How enjoyable it all was too. But, at the end of a relatively peaceful tournament, what a sour taste was left by the head butting of an opponent by one of the finest footballers of the modern era.

Most of us learnt at an early age that sticks and stones might break our bones but names would never hurt us.

It is part of playing sports that the opposition try to undermine you by messing with your head.

I could cite as an illustration some first-hand experience of this name-calling involving my man Retief Goosen while playing against America's finest.

When you compete at a high level, naturally you have a heightened sense of awareness. If you are competing in a reactive contact game such as soccer there is a chance you will react to the sledging. Of course this is natural, but the real professional isolates the barrage and gets on with the job in hand.

There is a theory that the reason Colin Montgomerie never converted the chances he had to win majors in the US, was that he could not ignore the abuse coming from the other side of the ropes.

For his part, Retief has listened to dogs' abuse in his quest for majors and chosen to ignore it. I feel he has passed the test in the States insofar as the mud-slinging public actually respect him now. If you can beat Tiger Woods in a Presidents Cup having listened to a spectator say, "mind you don't choke on that apple you're eating like you did in the US Open", the chances are you are mentally fairly resilient.

So for Zinedine Zidane to receive the Golden Ball award having retaliated with such violence to a bit of name-calling, makes it difficult for me to respect soccer as a sport.

I do admire the Frenchman greatly as a genius with his feet – and until lately also with his head. But the lack of etiquette in soccer is at huge odds with what really matters in modern sport. I do not entirely blame the players; this culture comes from a "higher" place.

Soccer is not alone in evincing a dubious morality that seems to trickle down from the top.

The victorious Italians have been humbled by the demotion of three of their Serie A teams for match-fixing. Michael Schumacher's shenanigans in the Monte Carlo Grand Prix were despicable. In horse racing there have been serious allegations of race-fixing and crooked riding. The Tour de France has been the scene of perennial drug scandals.

The sight of Thomas Bjorn and Darren Clarke striding the picturesque fairways of Loch Lomond last weekend, smiling and chatting away amiably while locked in combat for the substantial first prize, was something that must have endeared even the most cynical viewer to the game of golf.

Being competitive does not mean we have to abandon the respect due to our fellow competitors.

Links with past prove tenuous as iron man prevails

JULY 25: MONDAY: It is the unknown quantity, the mystery course here at Hoylake where the only yardstick is the 1967 Open. With the evolution of the game, it might have been 1867 for all it tells us about this year.

Brad Faxon played an amateur event here in 1983 but his memory of it is hazy. So if ever there was a level playing field this is it.

It's pretty flat too. For a links course it has very little undulation, which plays tricks when you try to judge distance. And it is parched from the drought.

Peter Dawson, secretary of the R&A, is out on the 13th green, watching in disbelief as his putt rolls uphill a long way past the hole. He cannot fathom it – which is alarming given he is responsible for the whole show. The holes filled in yesterday are shrinking and dying under a relentless sun. I hope they are going to turn the sprinklers on and leave them on; otherwise there will be no greens left by Thursday.

TUESDAY: The practice ground is on a public course about half a mile away. We are shuttled back and forth in courtesy cars. The players' hospitality marquee is a little bit out of the way so I jump into a courtesy car. The lady driver's face lights up when I inform her I caddie for Retief Goosen – but drops when I tell her he won't be joining me until later.

There seems to be much star-gazing with these volunteer drivers. The prospect of chauffeuring Tiger Woods for a couple of minutes is the lure for many.

We have an entourage at the Open. There are marshals assigned to follow us every day. We also have a bunker raker, a scorer, a standard bearer and, on the weekend, two rules officials. For many, volunteering to work in the Open is an annual tradition.

WEDNESDAY: After late practice rounds the past two days, based on the theory that if you are playing well in a Major you are going to have three late starts, Retief opts for the early time.

We tee it up with a young South African, Thomas Aiken, playing in his first Open. As we get on the tee, Tom Watson, who has won this event five times, appears and asks if he may join us. Retief falls somewhere between the novice and the veteran in terms of experience.

Watson, at 56 years of age, is not here to make up the numbers. Watching him in practice, I understand how he won so many Opens. No grain of dust is left unstudied in his analysis of Hoylake. He hits shots from every conceivable place he might visit over the next four days. He is compiling his own yardage book. He is also the last to leave each green.

THURSDAY: I had walked the course late on Wednesday to get a further impression of Hoylake. The R&A have obviously abandoned hope of sufficient rain, as every green has a keeper flooding it with a big hose. The greens are looking verdant again and the overnight rain has brought the stimpmetre well below 10, from 13 earlier in the week.

Retief dislikes the slower surfaces and proceeds to leave all his bad putts short. I'm sent to the locker room to get the old faithful blade. But after an hour's practice Retief decides to revert to the new model and sends the old one back to the locker.

A half-hour delay because of thunder means it is 3.12pm when we begin our campaign for the 135th Open – a strange time, it strikes me, for the fourth-best player in the world to be given.

The veteran Watson gets to five under. He finishes poorly yet will still make the cut. I can't but feel Watson is looking at Goosen as a version of himself 20 years ago: a similar build, going about his business quietly, confidently and decisively.

FRIDAY : The reinstated putter works for Retief, and the four-iron exceeds all of Tiger Woods's expectations on the 14th hole. The wunderkind is back. Not only does Woods play great golf today he also works his sorcery in typical Woods fashion: a four-iron that most would be just trying to land somewhere on the narrow green ends up in the hole – a wonderful shot that proves an omen for Tiger's eventual victory.

Of course the ball could easily have finished 25 feet beyond the hole, and we all know such shots are one step away from flukes. But it is interesting how many "flukes" great players produce, especially under pressure.

SATURDAY : Dave Musgrove is another veteran on tour. This is his 45th consecutive Open as a caddie. He was here in 1967, when he caddied for Brian Hutchinson. He has also brought in two champions, Seve in 1979 and Sandy Lyle in 1983. He is still looping at 63 years of age.

As ever in the caddie shack, one man's downfall is another's opportunity, Musgrove was actually bagless until he received a call on Saturday from John Bickerton, who had fired his caddie and heard Dave was available.

Accommodation at the Open is always a concern. There are never enough hotels. Most of us rent a house or a room in a house. A retired caddie from the Hoylake area set up three US caddies with a place to stay in West Kirby. You take a chance on what kind of place you end up in, the compromise being location at the expense of comfort.

I ask one of the three about their lodgings – and get the answer in no uncertain terms. The worst ever. It costs a fortune, the three of them are in one room, there are no beds, and Bob, the resident parrot, wakes them up at 4.30 every morning. It's hard enough to get the Americans to travel, and this could dramatically reduce numbers at Carnoustie next year.

SUNDAY: He is the greatest golfer who ever strode the links and he proves his diligent dominance. Tiger had his strategy set from earlier in the week and has stuck rigidly to it. He used his woods simply to hang his towel on and relied on strategic irons off the tees.

Golf would appear to have become increasingly technical, heavily reliant on the latest gadgets. Ninety-five per cent of the field would have used the Graeme Heinrich yardage chart, which has every hump and hollow of the subtle links documented.

The winning caddie, Steve Williams, I notice, is using the more basic, and less detailed, Strokesaver. Maybe it is time to forgo all the confusing detail. And then maybe not – we don't all work for Tiger.

Old pro who kneaded to make ends meet after the Tour

AUGUST 1: Where do all the old golf pros go to? For many, Sky TV gave a new lease of life to those golfers who couldn't quite hack it any more on tour. They re-invented themselves as commentators, maintaining their nomadic existence, but without the uncertainty of where the next cheque was coming from.

Many of the rules officials are now ex-Tour players. One has risen to the position of second in command of the Tour.

For others, the transition from player to non-player has been uncertain. Chubby Chandler is an ex-player who set up a very successful management group. Others failed. Some ex-players coach current ones on tour. The rest are still trying to figure out if there is life after playing.

A few weeks back at the French Open, held outside Paris, a colleague came across an ex-pro in a most unlikely location and profession. Struggling to find accommodation near the course, my friend found himself staying some 20 km south of the venue. It was getting late and he needed a quick meal before he retired for the evening.

A pizzeria caught his eye, so he went in and ordered a quatro stagioni and a glass of beer. The affable waiter obliged. Noting my colleague's broken French, the waiter struck up a conversation in English.

My friend can be aloof if he has had a long day of travelling and looping. He was in one of those moods now, especially now he was located so far from the course. The waiter charmed a smile out of him and eventually got to the root of how he had ended up in his little pizza joint at 9.30 on a slow Tuesday night. He was working at a golf tournament at the French National, he told his host, whom he assumed would know as much about golf as he did about the art of flipping the dough that made the perfect pizza.

The pizza arrived accompanied by another beer and a reluctant conversation ensued. The waiter was familiar with the French National, much to my friend's amazement. He had played it many times, but of course it was not built when he played on the European Tour.

'You mean you actually played on the European Tour?' he asked with wide open eyes. 'Yes, back in the 70s. I didn't last long,' he continued, 'but my brother Fayad is still very much involved with the game – in fact, he coaches Vijay Singh'.

A gobfull of beer exploded over my friend's pizza. Now he really didn't believe his pizza waiter.

The tournament went on, and my friend and the ex-pro golfer continued their evenings together at the restaurant, one explaining to the other how it was then – and the other how it actually is now.

How far removed from the image most would have, of an exotic life travelling and playing golf all around the globe, a lunch-time pizzeria is. The reality for most golfers is they could be frying hamburgers if their games do not live up to youthful expectations.

The next week at the Scottish Open the story spread around the locker room about my associate's chance meeting. It became a chronicle of a career foretold.

The reality for many golfers is a meagre existence full of angst about their careers and whether or not this year is the time to change it all. Without denigrating the art of making a good pizza, the prospect of letting a dream existence in the professional game slip by for a life of dough-flipping must seem harsh.

One player went on and shot a 65 around Loch Lomond the day after hearing the pizza man's tale. My friend approached him, reassuring him that a 65 is no pizza round. It is interesting how the fear of ending up kneading dough for a living puts a whole new perspective on the hardship of trying to break par.

The following week at Hoylake, Fayad came up to my colleague and introduced himself as the brother of the ex-pro who plied him with pizza, beer and tales of a lost era on tour. He is a teaching pro based in Sweden and travels to meet Singh to coach him whenever he requires his tutelage.

There is, of course, life after the Tour. But for those journeymen who have beaten their heads against the unyielding demands of producing under par rounds week in week out the alternatives may seem a little easier. Flipping a flagging golf career around may still seem easier than flipping dough in a lunchtime Parisian pizzeria.

Els and the Shark soar above terrorised stratosphere

AUGUST 15: It's always a relief to land after a long haul across the Atlantic. I walked a crooked mile through Chicago's O'Hare airport trying to get my limbs to work in sync again.

Just as I got into full stride I turned the corner at immigration to discover a long, snaking queue of subcontinental Indian people looking as I was feeling, agitated.

My flight had been delayed in departing and I was now left with under an hour to clear immigration, pick up my bag, recheck it, board the sky train to terminal one, go through the security rigmarole and try to find my gate for the connecting flight to Denver.

The Air India flight is not the one you want to arrive behind; the immigration process seems, naturally enough, to be a daunting task for many of the visiting members of that nation. I remember the first time I arrived in America; it was not the most pleasant experience for a novice. These passengers looked as I recall feeling back then, stunned.

Always a little deferential to US immigration officers, this time I was left in a very rare situation. My guy (a Mexican American who had not lost his accent – I had to ask him to repeat his questions to the point of embarrassment for both of us) wanted to know what I was doing and I told him.

He was in the mood for a chat.

'Oh no, not now. I have to leg it to have half a chance of catching my connecting flight, but the talkative one has the power,' I thought to myself. 'I had better sound interested.'

"You see a two-under-par on a hole is not that normal but it can happen, it is called an eagle. Yes I do know Tiger Woods, he is an absolute gentleman."

"Yes we are in his company a lot, he is really quite normal."

Shock and amazement engulfed the portly officer's face. I heard the bang of the passport stamp echo around the booth and I tried not to snatch my documents back off him as I panicked about my onward flight.

I am sure I grabbed my passport rather abruptly, but my interrogator did not seem to notice as he mused about his new understanding of the game of golf and how he felt closer to Tiger Woods by branding the passport of someone who had been in his company.

My personal airport training stood to me in the end. After scurrying through the sprawling O'Hare at caddie quickstep pace, I begged the check-in person at gate C23 to unclose the flight and let me on board. With a raised eyebrow she snatched my boarding pass out of my quivering hand. I took my seat (or part of it as my very large neighbour had fallen asleep and spilled over on to my part) and the door was slammed shut.

> "You see a two-under-par on a hole is not that normal but it can happen, it is called an eagle. Yes I do know Tiger Woods, he is an absolute gentleman."

The captain announced his regret that they were bound for Denver, Colorado, with 50 spare seats as many international passengers had not made their connections. If I'd had more space and energy I would have explained about Air India and the rest of the saga. My neighbour did not seem to be the chatty type anyway.

My ordeal fell rather short on the inconvenience scale as the word spread that terror went beyond the borders of the United States of Amazement. The news of the thwarted efforts of terrorists to destroy aircraft flying to the US from Britain was met with some concern in Colorado as US international competitors contemplated the rigours of flying back home.

Not all international competitors fly commercially. One such player is the 51-year-old golfing legend Greg Norman, or simply "the Shark" as he was uniquely known back in his "number one golfer in the world" days. He was the world's best for 331 weeks. He plays a limited number of events on the Champions Tour now and accepts just the one invitation on the PGA Tour, to the International.

He was like a politician strutting along the range on Thursday morning last as he greeted all us players and caddies who were around in his golden era. He seemed a little surprised some of us were still there.

He is as fit a 51-year-old as you are likely to come across outside of a California gym. His hair is a little less shockingly blond, age having given it a dusty hue. He wears some deeper lines on his face but his eyes are as piercing as when he was at his predatory best over a decade ago.

His athletic frame would look impressive on a 31-year-old man. If you could picture Crocodile Dundee with a more impressive pair of shoulders, that's how the old Shark looked prancing about the range at Castle Pines in full handshaking mode.

The rest of us contemplated a life of international travel with even more delays than we had got used to post-9/11. There was talk of driving to Chicago on Thursday morning to avoid the inevitable security headache at Denver airport. It was going to be a 15-hour drive. By Sunday most of the terra firma intentions of earlier in the week had yielded to the quicker air option; security couldn't be that bad.

Meanwhile, I was rescued from the airport security nightmare by Ernie Els. He kindly offered me a lift on his jet to Chicago. There was no long line of weary Indians ahead of me, no security scans and no large neighbour spilling over the seat next to me on Els Air.

Sometimes as a caddie you get to move in the rarified air of an unterrorised stratosphere.

Deja vu as Tiger and Sergio and I revisit old glories

AUGUST 22: TUESDAY: I was here in 1999, the year of the famous battle for the PGA title between Tiger and Sergio. Despite Medinah being a wonderful course, probably the most memorable part is the clubhouse itself. In its architecture it looks like a shrine to almost all known religions.

There is the Mosque-style minaret on one wing, the church influence on another, and, the temple-dome look when viewed from a different angle. Either way it gets your attention. It is rumoured that after 9/11 the clubhouse plaque paying respect to Allah was quietly removed from general view.

It was an interesting exercise for me in how my memory works. I had caddied for Greg Turner here seven years ago. I have been to many courses since, so I struggled to recall the holes.

The ones with perilous water carries seemed familiar, but generally the memories were hazy. Then, on the 12th hole, it all came flooding back. It didn't suit Turner's left-to-right shape and we made a mess of it every day. It all became clear when I revisited the scene of the crime.

The 16th, though it had been altered, was also vivid. We were doing well on Sunday and wanted a club that would get up the elevated green. Greg did not get height on his long irons so we opted for the five-wood, which would go long, but long was better than short. There were two TV stands behind the green and a tiny gap between them and the grandstand. We figured it would be highly unlikely to find the gap if the ball went long – and the drop area was okay. The unlikely happened: Greg aimed for the gap and found it, and ended up closer to the 17th green than the 16th. It was the end of our PGA top-10 campaign and scarred my memory of Medinah.

WEDNESDAY: We played a practice round with Sergio. Unlike me, the young Spaniard had vivid memories. He could recall all the holes as if he were in the 1999 PGA once again.

When we got to the now famous 16th, scene of his celebrated shot from the roots of the great oak to the right of the fairway in the final round of the PGA that year, he had to have a closer look at the trunk of the tree.

He took out his six-iron, threw a ball into the base of the tree and re-enacted the spectacular shot he made seven years ago to mark the arrival of El Niño.

The greenkeepers are sick of having to resod the base of 'El Niño's Tree', as all who visit Medinah take a hack to see how they would have done under similar circumstances.

THURSDAY: A sombre, but serene and tasteful start to the tournament. Tom Lehman, the American Ryder Cup captain, held a 6.30am short ceremony in honour of Heather Clarke. Tom was due to play that afternoon, so his sacrifice of sleep was quite a gesture. He spoke of her courage in a long battle with cancer, and noted the relative unimportance of bogey and double bogey when life is at stake. It was an impressive act by Lehman that, as far as I was concerned, put him on something of a pedestal in what is often a self-absorbed sport.

The show got underway and the much hyped heavyweight bout, Tiger Woods and Phil Mickelson, teed off at 8.30. The US Open champion, Geoff Ogilvy, hardly got a mention but it would have been rude to send the boys out in a two-ball.

David Feherty's comment about Phil and Tiger was the wittiest. He said the two are like magnets: they attract pretty much everything around them but repel each other.

FRIDAY: It's not too often the circus that comes to town considers how it impacts on the locals. I got a taste of the non-golfing opinion in a coffee shop during the 88th PGA Championship.

"You can't believe the amount of traffic out there. Where are all the people going to?" an elderly lady enquired of a man nearby.

"Did you see that guy who was leading yesterday until the last hole when he got really nervous, I guess, and made a big mistake and then he wasn't leading anymore?" the man asked.

"Oh yeah, there must be an awful lot of money involved for them to get this agitated," she replied.

"You bet, lady, big bucks."

"Are you going down there?"

"Don't be silly. I couldn't possibly get a ticket."

For locals the most obvious facet of such a global event is the disruption to their daily lives.

SATURDAY AND SUNDAY: Did you see that par that Tiger made on the first hole of the third round? It was outrageous. Three chops across the fairway toward the green and a dead-weight putt down the green for par. It would make the most trusting wonder if the undisputed best golfer of all time is human at all. He is back to the form he had six years ago that made every golfer wonder if he should even consider trying to win any event in which Woods is entered.

It seems we all should fear the Tiger like never before. He is playing for his recently deceased father and nobody is going to get in the way of that.

The trophy Tiger hoisted for the third time in his spectacular career is named after Rodman Wanamaker. He was a man of many interests and I am sure would have found the current holder of his 15-kilo cup fascinating.

Rodman backed early expeditions to the North Pole and built the first multi-engine plane to fly across the Atlantic. In 1916 the businessman from Philadelphia agreed to fund the inaugural PGA Championship, and the trophy that bears his name.

It is traditional for someone to assist the champion to hold the trophy as he poses for the cameras; otherwise he might get tired. I doubt there is any need to check these guys for drug use – as is being suggested in several quarters here in the States. Perhaps though we could perform the Wanamaker test. If the winner doesn't need a helping hand in hoisting it, send a sample to the lab immediately.

My boy keeps his dignity intact at the 'People's Major'

AUGUST 29: Du Page regional airport in the western suburbs of Chicago at 6.30 am last Monday morning was suffering from the hangover of a mass exodus the previous night after the world's best golfer captured his third PGA title. The circus members and their entourages had left town in their private jets by now and there were only a few stragglers left over.

I was meeting Retief to fly with him to Pinehurst, North Carolina, for a two-day event involving him and Gary McCord. The show goes on and despite the intensity of a major there are business commitments to keep.

The first plane to land was a turbo-prop owned by the Home Depot chain of DIY stores that fly their skilled employees about the country to offer their expertise at their various branches nationwide. So a troop of what looked like carpenters descended upon the Du Page terminal with tools hanging out of their work bags. An unusual sight amongst the normally well-heeled looking clientele at the private terminals (apart from a few bedraggled golf caddies).

Dave Pelz, the short game guru, had been at Medinah with his protégé Phil Mickelson. He wandered in, in search of his jet which was due to take him on business east to New York. Guards are down on these casual meetings at private airfields. He spoke to McCord about his star pupil whom he had talked up in the press pre PGA. What I heard this time was the truth which was not meant for the press, so I had better not divulge. The crux of the message was that his best boy was relying way too much on all he had taught him, about getting his ball up and down from seemingly impossible situations.

Retief, Gary, myself and Matt, McCord's bagman, nestled into the chartered Lear Jet and headed south east to the Carolinas for the pre-event pro-am. As you make the final approach to the local airfield, you quickly realize gazing out the window that this is "golfville". It looked like you could play about 800 different holes in a row cut through the sprawling pine forests of North Carolina. With the eight different courses at the Pinehurst golf complex I am only slightly exaggerating.

The "People's Major", known as the "People Against the Pro" event has gone on for the past three years. It is a competition whereby amateurs play three qualifying rounds in the under 50 and over 50 category. The winner of the younger category got to play 18 holes matchplay last Tuesday on the Pinehurst No 8 course against Retief. The older victor went head to head with the Salvadore Daliesque McCord.

John Daly played in the past, but came up against what we call in the trade a "bandit" a couple of years back (an amateur masquerading off a handicap that does not reflect the quality of his play). Daly shot 66 and was beaten three and two by a putative double digit handicapper. The selection procedure of the players and handicaps was more stringent this year.

Retief played against Greg, a Home Depot manager, and sent his man back to the clubhouse after 16 holes. The pro's dignity remained intact at this year's Pinehurst challenge.

It was all played in good spirit even if it was a little hammed up for the television coverage. On our arrival on Monday morning, we got to drop our bags at the colonial-style Carolina Hotel, and moved swiftly to the course for a pro-am with 40 expectant amateurs. A few holes with each group and five and a half hours later we were back at the Carolina hotel for a banquet and some pre-match banter.

We ate breakfast to the suave sound of a pianist tickling the ivories with a soft jazz theme to his repertoire. Golf in America is played in the main on gas carts as not many amateurs walk the course. A stipulation of this event was that the winners walk the course. This was a problem for Retief's opponent as he was a little over-weight. Given the heat of North Carolina in August he was sounding and looking a little the worst for wear after an hour's golfing.

Despite Retief's suggestion that he should use a gas cart after he noticed his discomfort, Greg persisted on foot; he was not going to forfeit the chance to compete and walk with a US Open champion.

Our fleeting visit to Pinehurst brought back some vivid memories of the US

Open last year where we squandered a three-shot lead going into the final round. Thankfully, McCord timed his story well about meeting the legendary Bobby Locke and distracted us from any gloomy reminiscence. He had met the South African golfer at the bar of the Carolina Hotel back in the 1970s. He described a crusty old gentleman sitting at the bar enjoying a suitably crusty old drink. McCord was slugging beer. They had both tucked a few away when McCord realised who he was talking to. Locke was one of the best putters of his era, but he had a unique "hook" action stroke which rendered every putt a right to lefter for him no matter what the slope.

McCord persuaded him to go to the putting green to show him his action, He duly obliged and McCord said sure enough he hit every putt he presented him with a hard right to left spin. By the time he completed his tale we had arrived at the jet which took us to Akron, Ohio, where Retief was competing in the Bridgestone last week and McCord was commentating.

A jumbo jet was parked to the side of the runway as we landed at the relatively small Akron/Canton airport. Compared to the bulk of the Boeing, the plane we arrived in was like a fly landing beside an elephant. As the baggage handlers unloaded our luggage, McCord inquired about the jumbo.

They told him it belonged to Ernest Ainsley. "Oh no, I don't believe it, not Ernest Ainsley," he groaned.

I had no idea who he was.

"He is a preacher," the cringing McCord moaned. "I thought I was doing well until I saw that jumbo, I couldn't afford to taxi that to the runway let alone get it airborne".

McCord had been feeling quite content with his little junket to Pinehurst until Ainsley's jumbo cast a shadow on the runway.

Time to make the tough decisions

SEPTEMBER 12: A week to go to the Ryder Cup and the heat is on the captains of Europe and America to provide the atmosphere to create the winning way for their respective teams.

The preamble to next week's circus has been a long, laborious page of words with much time and space devoted to the worth of both Tom Lehman and Ian Woosnam.

Being in a position of responsibility for others is relatively uncharted territory for most golfers. Their careers have been spent caring for number one; such is the nature of professional golf.

The selection process for choosing a Ryder Cup captain cannot really account for the prospective captains' ability to lead and motivate; neither of them has ever been in that role as a golfer.

They say playing golf is a good way to acquire a grounding for life. There is a strict application of the rules and a strong ethos of etiquette which should guide participants through their playing years. As major winners and multiple tournament victors, both Lehman and Woosnam are proven performers and can obviously handle the pressure of making tough personal decisions on the golf course.

They have hit numerous shots under intense competition and holed slippery putts to keep their scores together. So, what can they do when it comes to making the right pressure decisions for their 12 team members?

To date it would seem that Lehman has taken his new role very seriously and is determined to eradicate what appears to have been the curse of recent US Ryder Cup teams: the lack of unity and sense of belonging to a team; the philosophy of a greater cause other than just "me".

Tom has consulted many team sport coaches and asked for advice about team building. He has had constant communication with his potential players since the team started to take a permanent shape earlier this year. There is no doubt it is a difficult challenge for a self-sufficient golfer to think outside the golfing box and consider the complications of dealing with a large group of even larger egos – egos unused to compromising for anyone other than themselves.

> "Being in a position of responsibility for others is relatively uncharted territory for most golfers. Their careers have been spent caring for number one; such is the nature of professional golf."

We played a practice round recently with the last European captain, the orderly and extremely determined Bernhard Langer. He was telling me he will have no involvement with this year's event; he will merely be a television spectator. He admitted in a surprised way that Lehman had talked to him on numerous occasions about what he had done as captain in Detroit. He was equally amazed that Woosnam had no contact with him at all concerning his captaincy.

Langer and Woosnam were at their golfing peaks at the same time. They have played a lot together over the past couple of decades and have been on many Ryder Cup teams together. A few words of advice from such a well prepared and successful leader as Langer would not have done any harm to the Welshman's preparation.

I am sure Ian has consulted some of Europe's recent successful captains about next week's mission. Tony Jacklin, Sam Torrance, Bernard Gallacher and Seve would all be accessible to this year's captain and would have been happy to impart some of their ideas to Ian.

For Europeans there is a worrying statement of intent from the American team. They are going to be a team such as the US have never been before. This I believe is down to their leader. Lehman has recognised the disparity in the past, and decided early on to harness his players into the concept of team mentality.

The visit of the US team to The K Club a couple of weeks ago was a shot across the bows of the European flagship. Tiger Woods and Phil Mickelson do not disturb their precise schedules and join their Ryder Cup team-mates unless they are serious about their presence as key members of the team.

What they did when they got to Straffan was irrelevant; the fact is they gave their moral support to Tom and their colleagues.

The Europeans have taken their camaraderie and sense of team belonging for granted ever since the other Europeans were called into what was traditionally the Britain and Ireland team. It has taken the Americans a long time to recognise their lack of consensus.

What happened when the European team was announced a couple of weeks ago was a public-relations disaster. There are always going to be players who felt they had done enough to warrant one of the two wild-card picks, and would struggle when learning they had been omitted.

It is a basic captain's duty to talk to those who were realistically in the running and explain his reasoning and generally keep them informed.

For the picks, and more importantly for those left out, it would be fairly basic etiquette to consult them before the team became public knowledge. To fail to do so was a diplomatic faux-pas.

The Europeans' little get-together last Thursday in Kildare was lacklustre given that the entire team was not there, but at least it was a positive effort. Maybe the diplomatic error happened at the perfect time for Europe, in case there was any erroneous assumption of unity.

My own experience of team dealings through the Presidents Cup have shown me the importance of a good captain's influence on performance. Gary Player was the captain and Ian Baker-Finch was the vice-captain last year in Washington.

Gary was more a figurehead and Ian was the effective captain. Baker-Finch came to me weeks before the event to exchange phone numbers in case there was anything I needed to talk to him about. The pairing discussions in the team room were open and democratic; everyone's opinion was taken into account. Gary Player's little speeches before play were inspirational.

The players and caddies on both teams in this year's Ryder Cup are part of something special and I am sure both leaders will treat each and every one of their players with the respect and attention he deserves for the benefit of the team.

Wily Americans would appear to have it in the bag

SEPTEMBER 20: What's in a bag? Well, with 14 clubs and some other golfing essentials the bag simply used to fill a functional role. Not these days, particularly at the biggest golfing team event in the world.

There have been many players who have tried to distinguish themselves through their hair styles or the cut of their trousers. With Ian Poulter not making the European side this year the English trend-setter seems to have passed on his dress sense to the European fashion house.

In fact Poulter set a new trend this year at the US Open when he selected a different bag for each day of competition to complement his daily outfit. A crowd-inciting pink bag was proposed for the final day, as if the New York mob needed any encouragement to pass comment. Not even the style-conscious ladies tour would go to such lengths.

The manufacturers came up with a novel idea for the majors a couple of years back when they designed an appropriate bag for each major, with shades blending with the tournament colours. Green for Augusta, red and white for the US Open and so on.

With team events, however, there is an ever increasing need to distinguish the opposing team's style. So the team bag is another symbol of diversity between the rival groups. The American team arrived at Dublin airport sporting the old country squire look. Their autumnal-coloured, tweed jacket looked like something that Prince Charles would feel comfortable wearing on a grouse shoot. The Europeans looked much more casual in their zip down shirts and suede jackets.

The American looked stylish in their golf gear yesterday. The Europeans were donning a band leader-style stripe down their collective trousers, very Poulteresque.

Finding it hard to make a distinction between the two teams from a golfing perspective during the first official practice round, I started to notice some subtle differences in the team golf bags.

The Americans have a very stylish Club Glove, a mainly red bag with a little splash of navy. It has a similar shape to the bag that the 1977 team would have used in the Ryder Cup at Lytham. The top of the bag around the handle has got the stars and stripes on it. The shoulder strap is dotted with stars. Effectively it is a subtle version of the national flag. The oval shaped simple retro-looking United States Ryder Cup team badge is the main feature, and the gold trim and rounded pockets all contribute to possibly the most understated American golf bag since the event became as mega as it is today.

The European bag is a standard Burton brand. With a predominantly blue colour and its adorning golden 12 stars and bars, it looks like the Swedes would feel very much as if they had their national flag draped over their clubs. For Robert Karlsson and Henrik Stenson, it must remind them of home every time they look at their new bags.

There is nothing subtle about the Europeans bag with "EUROPE" in big letters being its main feature. The base of the bag has got the original "Europe" splayed across it too.

With the predicted forecast of westerly gales and an accompanying deluge, the true functional value of the respective bags will almost surely be put to the test. Questions like "does it double as a canoe" may be as important as how aesthetically pleasing it is – and what the subtleties of the design do to the opposition.

With the support teams charging about the Palmer course at The K-Club, there should be no shortage in the supply of dry towels, so extra capacity will not be paramount.

If the bags were to decide this year's Ryder Cup there is no doubt who would be the winners. The American's pièce de résistance is obviously a result of some very clever planning. When the caddie lays down the American bag, a green shamrock is revealed. It's going to be hard to pull against these opponents with such a strong symbol of Ireland winking at the home spectators from the bottom of their golf bags.

After Tuesday's practice round the US are one up.

K Club feels the lash of autumn gales

SEPTEMBER 21: There will be days like this, but hopefully not as many as the weatherman is predicting.

There was a wind that would blow a dog off a chain and many limbs off the mature trees on the K Club estate yesterday. Those of us approaching from the north were well protected from flying debris in the secure environment of the Weston Aerodrome.

Nobody was allowed on the property early yesterday and those had made it there before this decision was taken had to evacuate soon after.

I have witnessed many tents and hoardings taking off at the rate of knots in previous tournaments over the years – and believe you me you do *not* want to be in their tumbling path.

I was happy to do some safe plane spotting instead. A line of helicopters were wobbling in the gale force westerly that buffeted the airfield.

The small jets beside them looked secure, but the light aircraft beyond looked like airfix models about to lift off in the relentless wind.

When we finally got the all-clear for entry to the course, we all shuffled up to the snaking bus queue and listened to a bit of diddly-eye music as we idled though the ticket check line and onto the K Club shuttle buses.

Not being a fan of the mega event and its inconvenience, I couldn't help but marvel at the infrastructure and overwhelming size of this spectacle in little old Ireland. This thing is bigger than Christmas. Presidents Cups, Masters, US Opens are all massive events where there are makeshift structures like temporary train stations built specially for the event. This was the case in Shinnecock Hills on Long Island a couple of years back. If you went there now there would be no sign of the six carriage long platform that had been erected for the 2004 US Open.

So when we return here for the European Open next year it will be interesting to see if the undergrowth has reclaimed the North Bus Terminal that used to be an over-grown field.

The concern on the golf course, given the amount of rain that has fallen in Kildare in the past few days, is that there will be a lot of mud splattered over the players' golf balls. Motorists too may face a severe case of plugged automobiles in one of the many already-sodden designated parking sites. The golf ball caked with mud is an added variable for both player and caddie to try to come to terms with when making a club decision. There is a general rule, which is hard to rely on 100 per cent, that when there is mud on the left of the ball, it should fly hard to the right. Similarly the lump of mud on the right should steer the ball towards the left.

When the mud is on top of the ball it frequently falls out of the sky a lot quicker than normal.

Sometimes it does none of the above.

Such is the concern of the players that already they are talking about the lift, clean and place policy being enforced for the matches on Friday.

> "There is a general rule, which is hard to rely on 100 per cent, that when there is mud on the left of the ball, it should fly hard to the right. Similarly the lump of mud on the right should steer the ball towards the left."

As the Ryder Cup is marketed as the greatest event in golf, it is hard to believe we will see players sticking a peg by their golf ball, picking it up, scraping the rich Kildare soil off it and then propping it up in a preferential lie.

Most tournaments will do everything within their power to avoid that spectacle. I have never been to a major in the past two decades that has had a placing policy in operation. The decision will finally be made by the chief referee, Andy McFee from the European Tour.

He will consult with the two captains. That is the theory. By the sounds of the rumblings from the team members, particularly the most influential ones on both sides, this is the one event where the players' wishes will be granted. It is in no professional's advantage to second guess the careerings of a mud-ball.

The sight of the Ryder Cup being decided by balls nose-diving into the river Liffey like wounded ducks because of mud does not seem at all appropriate.

The spectators would not want such a capricious way of deciding the event any more than they would want to watch a tractor extracting their car from a quagmire of a parking lot.

Time for the US to rethink Ryder Cup approach

OCTOBER 3: As the sludge that had become The K Club by two Sundays ago began to get back to a squidgy, at-best-yielding terrain, the show had moved on to North London for the American Express World Championship.

If this is not the ultimate form of professional golf, it is as close as it gets – given that it is a hybrid event that offers exemptions to players from the world tours of Australasia, Asia, Japan, Africa, Europe and of course the USA to travel and compete against each other.

Now the world's best tend to be American.

If they do not come from America they spend a hell of a lot of their time golfing there. So lest we forget where you establish yourself and secure your future as a recognised professional, it is on the US Tour. If you do not perform there you rarely get a global mention. Tiger Woods blitzed a world-class field last weekend. The Ryder Cup euphoria has settled.

This is not to detract from the heroic efforts of the European Ryder Cup team, but the reality is that these thoroughbreds perform their best in individual competition.

In attempting to analyse why this is so, my guess is that somehow those putts that the best players in the world hole under the pressure of a regular strokeplay event do not motivate them enough to actually go ahead and make them in a mere team matchplay.

I do not think it is a conscious process, rather a subconscious lack of intensity.

What pushes the best to excellence that eludes the average is their desire to win. If that desire is not strong enough then the chances are you will not win.

So if you were to ask Tiger Woods or Phil Mickelson over a cold glass of beer what are their golfing goals, it would be interesting to hear if the Ryder Cup featured highly on their shopping list of titles.

These players are products of the system that has afforded them private jets and more homes than they could possibly live in even if they had extended families of mid-20th-century Irish proportions.

The prize funds on the US Tour are top heavy. Last weekend it was $1.3 million for the winner and $750,000 for the runner-up. There is no doubt it is worth stepping up a little higher in order to reach into that top drawer stuffed with dollars.

In Europe the distribution of prize funds seems to follow more of a socialist model.

Of course, the winners in the US don't quite take it all; top-10 finishes are well rewarded too.

Therein lies a further problem for the US Ryder Cup team. Their selection procedure doesn't really recognise those who finish outside the top 10. If it did, maybe those who fell outside this category would be more motivated by the Ryder Cup than the individual predators that are seemingly thrilled only by the lone kill.

Tom Lehman did all he could to unite this US team. He left no stone unturned but still they failed miserably. Many critics felt it was their lack of cohesion that worked against them. I am absolutely certain this was not their problem in Straffan; they were most definitely a team.

Perhaps the root of the Americans' problem is a chronic lack of recognition of the team event.

You may say who could blame them. If you are taking care of business as a professional golfer, it means you are making money. They are all doing that.

Getting selected for the Ryder Cup team is not what is getting them out on the range every day of their lives.

There is no doubt that the wonderful golfing jamboree that arrived here a few weeks back has become embedded in the popular psyche over the past decade.

It is largely a result of the change of system from Great Britain and Ireland team to a team encompassing the whole of Europe, which made the event more competitive and turned the tide of American dominance.

The problem is that many new golf fans may be fooled by the strong marketing of the event into thinking that this is the biggest prize in golf.

The event represents one week of a golfer's two-year cycle. To compete and win it is a great accolade, but it is not gaining the player world ranking points.

Our own star of a couple of weeks back Paul McGinley did not qualify to play in last weekend's World Championship, which comprises the world's best golfers.

There is a further theory that some of my American friends threw at me last week as they conducted the Straffan post mortem. Seemingly, America the superpower is under attack from "insurgents" on all sides. I know it sounds paranoid, but they feel every other nation is so up to beating the US because they sit so high on their pedestals. And so it is almost impossible for the Americans to win.

It seems to be the way in baseball and basketball, where it is undisputed that the best players in the world at both these sports are most definitely Americans.

A further argument I heard last week was that the US players have no affinity with the PGA of America. This body makes all the loot out of the Ryder Cup. Somehow, the argument goes, the players feel they are playing for an alien body that is reaping the rewards of their talent.

One reporter cynically mentioned last week that it is no surprise that Tiger made his post-Ryder Cup comeback in the American Express event, where the slogan is "My life, my card".

Conversely, a colleague of mine suggested to Sergio Garcia – an inspiration to the European team in Kildare but conspicuously below his best in Watford – that he should have been a soccer player. In strokeplay he was not quite up to Tiger's level but in the team environment he thrived.

It's time for the US to rethink their selection policy and focus on who wants to play and who is there because he feels obliged.

One member of the victorious European Ryder Cup team finished in the top 10 at the WGC on Sunday. That was Luke Donald, and he plays on the US Tour.

As the dust settles on The K Club after arguably the most spectacular event in the history of Irish sport, it is easier to see that the weekly routine of four-round tournaments makes the US Tour the real melting pot for professional golfers.

Big-name players enjoy Asia Tour's military precision

OCTOBER 10: We have reached the time of year when you frequently get asked what your schedule is like for the last couple of months of 2006. However predictable your plans may be up to now, it is guess work after mid-October and it is hard to apply much logic to anyone's arrangements. With events in Australia, Asia, America and Africa it is tricky to pin most guys down to a continent let alone a specific tour.

The reason for this has a lot to do with both the success of the golfer and the overall prosperity of golf worldwide. This is Retief's (Goosen) second visit to Asia in four weeks, he was in Seoul, Korea, for their national open three weeks ago; this week we are on Hainan Island off the southern coast of China for the Volkswagen Masters; we come back for the HSBC event in Shanghai early November; and finish off in Asia with the Hong Kong Open the week after.

That's not all, we have Sun City and the South African Open in December and then we get to celebrate Christmas in our respective homes. Provided there are no US wins between now and the year end, we will have the first week in January free and maybe start again in Honolulu in the second week of January.

It is becoming very difficult to actually split the years and have a clear break between seasons.

When I caddied in Europe in the late 1980s, I seem to remember the European Masters in Switzerland been held at the end of September as marking the end of the year. That was a time when you played in whatever you were exempt from because it was likely you were going to have a long winter's break anyway.

It is the complete opposite for most players today. With the European Tour starting their year in November in Asia and continuing on in South Africa there is added pressure on players to begin next year's schedule before this year is over.

It is easy to get sucked into playing too much simply because the choice is there. You find those who have a disciplined and sensible plan that allows enough time to rest between events perform better overall. Otherwise you need a lot of resilience.

The trips to Asia with a top player are usually a bit of a junket. That has been frequently, but not always, the case. I remember caddying for Anders Forsbrand in the Philippines Open which was played on the very outskirts of Manila in the early 1990s. We stayed in a swanky hotel downtown. In the morning a chauffeur came to pick us up, not to drive us to the course. He was just giving us a jaunt to the shell of a downtown skyscraper that was being built by the owner of the golf course. Each day a helicopter chopped its way on to the lower roof of the building, we would jump in and made the 15-minute journey over the capital to the course.

At the course a couple of buggies used to transport us over the final 300 yards to the clubhouse.

This was all very embarrassing especially when you happened to arrive as the regular Asia Tour players were peeling themselves out of the official bus which had taken one and a half hours from their hotel, and they happened to see you jump out of the chopper.

I suppose that is what makes the game so competitive. The sight of some named players (and their bagmen) falling out of choppers would probably be an incentive to get invited back as a star to play in Asia instead of as a full-time competitor enduring three-hour daily trips to and from the course every week.

I also recall the earlier days in Asia when the European Tour ground to a halt in September. Me and a colleague started our own global tour.

We used to both caddie and make yardage books on the eight to 10-week Asian Tour at the time. This was no junket. We were not doing the books for some extra profit, we made books in order to try to break even on the trip.

At the army-owned club in Bangkok, Thailand, we were the unfortunate victims of some military might. There had been a simple misunderstanding which nearly turned into an international incident.

It involved the printing rights to the very basic hand-made yardage books we were providing the pros with. The upshot was that our documents were ripped up and tossed into a nearby bin and we were frog-marched at gun-point out of the Bangkok Army Country Club in timing with the squeak of our overheated caddie trainers.

There were some disappointed customers and a couple of rattled entrepreneurial caddies who changed their strategy after the incident and decided to stick to the day job for the rest of the Asian Tour.

I arrived on the holiday island of Hainan yesterday, completing the final leg of a long and winding trip eastwards. There were some Asian tour players on the flight, most of them had come from last week's event in Taipei. I was greeted at the airport by a chauffeur in keeping with Asian junket tradition.

The regular players made their own ways to their hotels. The yardage books this week, I am assured, will not attract any military intervention.

The art of winning is what makes the best players special

OCTOBER 24: Retief Goosen's recent victory in the Volkswagen Masters in China is a milestone in his successful career. For the first time in his career he successfully defended a title.

No big deal, many would think, for a man who has won two US Opens and a range of other prestigious events, but a win, no matter where it happens, is very important to any golfer.

Winning is what drives the best, I have always marvelled at the hunger of some of the golfers who may play for a nominal amount in a practice round. The chances are the money wagered will never change hands (some of these golfers are like royalty they don't do cash) but their will to beat their opponent is a remarkable drive which the most successful golfers all possess.

There are winners and there are those who are simply going to work. The trouble with trying to win is the thought of it can be scary and thus it can persuade you to change the way you play, especially in the last round when you have a five-shot lead. Despite sounding like a dream scenario for a pro, the big lead can lead to a change in strategy. When you start the final day with the comfort of a five-shot lead it is difficult to argue against a more conservative tack, but the chances are you were playing well in the first three rounds and that really is the way you should continue to play, regardless of the margin.

I suppose Retief got caught in the defensive mode in China in his last round, but given his experience he still has not lost the art of winning.

Theoretically, he had not won this year, his last win in the South African Open was on this year's schedule but was actually played in December 2005. Given a lack of recent form it is easy to slip into the clock-in mode. It is even easier to start to believe that you cannot win given a 10-month lack of ultimate success.

> "There are winners and there are those who are simply going to work. The trouble with trying to win is the thought of it can be scary and thus it can persuade you to change the way you play, especially in the last round when you have a five-shot lead."

Many of us begin to expect a lot from the top guys, on tap. Despite Tiger's recent blitzing form it is not possible for most players to dominate week in week out. Sure there are runs of form and, in particular, confidence and heightened expectation where players think they are unbeatable. Enjoy it while it lasts; it can evaporate more quickly than it could ever take it to form.

There is usually a decisive period in a tournament that determines the ultimate outcome. At the time it happens it may not always be that obvious. Retief's moment came in the middle of the back nine during Saturday's round. Lu Wen Teh from Tapei was putting some pressure on us in the front nine and he drew level with Retief after the 11th.

On the 13th hole, a downwind par five with water all down the left side from tee to green, Retief instinctively wanted to hit a three-wood off the tee towards the right traps. If he was brave and hit driver he could carry the corner of the water and leave himself a medium iron to the green. We deliberated on the tee for longer than normal, I could sense what Retief was thinking of the conservative play but the persuasion of the astute golfing brain and, in particular, the winner's way of thinking, which was to hit the driver, dictated that now was the time to push.

He hit six-iron to the green and holed the putt for an eagle, went on to birdie the next hole and had suddenly created a three-shot gap between himself and the Chinese Tapei player. It was obviously a psychological blow, and really proved to be the decisive moment that ultimately determined the overall result of the tournament.

Retief's VW Masters victory marked his 33rd in his 15th year as a professional. It is a rather large trophy cabinet by anyone's standards. Despite his gradual progression up the world rankings over the past three years he hit a bit of turbulence this year.

He had not been happy with his swing since the end of last year. This year his lack of form continued and the malaise crept into the rest of his game. This was particularly true of his putting.

We figured that in 2004 he three-putted twice all year long. This year he was three-putting twice a day. That's what happens when you keep hitting it so far from the pin.

His chipping and general decision-making were poor. In the fickle game of golf, it does not take too much time for a minor problem to become a crisis, and the head can easily exacerbate what are the normal tribulations of playing golf for a living most days of your life.

It was an important victory in China a couple of weeks back and with six tournaments left for us this year there is plenty of opportunity to realise some more of the potential of the very talented Goose.

Creature discomforts

NOVEMBER 28: The speed and frequency with which a golfer can find himself on a different continent week after week at this time of the year, means sometimes you can genuinely lose all perspective as to where you are.

It was undeniably Africa when I woke up yesterday and looked out of my bedroom window. Flowering bougainvillea, frangipani, jacarandas and ornate coral trees framed my view of the bushveld that surrounds the Sun City resort. I spotted a monkey squatting among the foliage, and there was the exotic melody of birds singing that is very different to the sound of sunrise in the Northern Hemisphere.

Even though the Gary Player course here is well manicured for the Nedbank Challenge, you do not have to train your eyes too far from the finely clipped fairways to realise that, without much attention, nature would quickly reclaim this land.

I went for an early morning stroll, only to hear the greens staff who had beaten me to the course. There was a distant hum of lawn mowers. As I meandered down one fairway, I was reminded of exactly where in the world I was. A freshly decapitated snake lay wriggling on the freshly cut fifth fairway; civilisation had got the better of this unsuspecting serpent.

A fence surrounds the complex, and it is not there to keep us two-legged creatures in. A leopard was sighted on the course two weeks ago. If you hit an errant tee-shot you come across droppings of all shapes and sizes in the surrounding bush. There are elephant and rhinos beyond the perimeter of the back nine. Troops of baboons wander across the fairways during the tournament. You get the sense we are very much the animals' guests.

The early ramble on a course cut out of the bush got me thinking about what animal you may encounter on a course like this. There is an area to the right of the 15th fairway the local caddies will not go near. It is the natural habitat of cobras, puff adders and black mambas.

A television cameraman thought he had got lucky when he came across a hissing cobra there about five years ago. It would have made great footage for those dead moments on camera if he could get a close-up of a riled snake, he thought. His sound man shook a stick at the snake, and as he brought his camera up to his eye ready to film, the sun reflected off his lens, spooked the cobra and it spat its venom right into the cameraman's eye.

A spectator who happened to know about snakes walked by soon after and explained that the only antidote available at the relatively remote part of the course that would save his eye was urine. There would not be many occasions when you would be happy to let someone urinate in your eye. This cameramen was happy that he did, and his eye was saved.

It would be fair to say the cameraman got what he deserved.

There was an English golfer who came to South Africa about 15 years ago to play the Sunshine Tour. He arrived in southern Africa for the first time in high summer. The tournament was held in a hotspot in the northeast of the country at the Hanse-Merensky Golf Club near Phalaborna, where it gets up to 40 degrees during the day.

The tour had been used to the non-native golfers dragging their heels due to the intense heat, so they had tried to keep on top of slow play. The tour official who was stationed on the seventh hole radioed through to say that no player had been sighted for over half an hour, maybe someone could go back a few holes and try to find out what the problem was.

When he finally tracked back to the third hole he found three distraught players and their caddies. The tardy golfer, who was by now completely dehydrated, had managed to snap hook his tee-shot towards the dam to the left of the hole. Unfortunately for the unsuspecting Englishman, there was a pod of hippopotami living in the same area where his tee-shot came to rest. Worse still, there was a hippo cow with her young who surfaced as the Englishman approached his stray shot.

Hippos are very territorial, and of course mothers are very protective of their young, so the hippo cow chased the entire group to a safe distance from her young. They reckoned they were two kilometres into the bush before she backed off. The rules official took pity on the group and decided not to penalise them for slow play. The Englishman was not deterred by being thrust into the roots of southern Africa and actually settled in the country as a club professional.

I am most definitely in Africa and thankfully, globalisation is not going to dilute that sensation for a long time.

A career put on the long finger

DECEMBER 19: Brazil is a great place to go for a bit of plastic surgery, they say. The Brazilians don't mind a bit of a nip and tuck; a buttock enhancement is particularly popular with the locals.

The English golfer Andrew Raitt, with whom we had the pleasure of playing last weekend at the Humewood Links outside Port Elizabeth, is feeling great after his extended trip to Sao Paulo for a bit of surgical enhancement. In fact I have never seen him looking so well.

Andrew is tall, athletic and well proportioned. Hard to see why he needed any adjustment. It is only when you look at the little finger on his left hand that you realise why he spent so much time visiting a surgeon in Brazil.

Andrew's little-finger story began 12 years ago about three weeks after he turned professional. He was at his local club, approached a member's Alsatian dog and ended up having to pick up the end of his finger from the ground and rush to hospital. The dog had bitten it off, but thankfully didn't have a taste for it.

Of course it was an awful start to a hopeful young pro's career. Over a decade later he is still dealing with the effects of the severed digit.

He hasn't played golf for the past two years and he is ecstatic to be back in contention at his chosen profession after such a long and painful absence. He had to give up watching golf on television because it was too frustrating for him.

In August of this year he visited his surgeon for the last of four months of daily visits to have the screws turned in the finger after his third operation. This time they had taken some of his hip bone and inserted it in the finger.

When the court case following the Alsatian assault went against him, he lost his house and his car in the legal battle that ensued. He separated from his wife and probably would be entitled to be just a little bit bitter about the whole incident, but he is not.

He smirked when he said he is happy not to have his house to deal with anymore. While others haggle over the property, Andrew is back doing what he loves best: competing on the links.

He played on the European Tour intermittently from 1999 to 2004 with a sore pinky. It wasn't so much the finger as the left arm that seemed to cause most of his discomfort. If he made the swing he wanted, his left arm would pop out of its shoulder socket. As he was going through the court case he managed to shoot 21 under par at the Tour School in Spain, thereby seriously impairing his argument that he had been disabled by the bite.

You right-handed golfers may be aware that trying to grip the club firmly without a little finger entails serious compromise. This is what Raitt was trying to argue in court.

He finally got the ex-golfer Andrew Murray to testify about the vital necessity of a fully operational little finger to a right-handed golfer. Murray could not persuade the courts either.

In 2001 Andrew went to Brazil to play some events. He was practising his putting on the Wednesday before the tournament with Kenny Ferrie. The tournament director approached the young pros and asked them if they could play in the pro-am as two others had pulled out.

This is seen as a privilege for a young pro (until they realise what a chore the weekly pro-am can be). They both agreed and Kenny was overjoyed when he found out one of his partners was Ronaldo the footballer. Andrew, in contrast, thought he had drawn the short straw again; he was to play alongside some medical doctor.

The doctor turned out to be the surgeon Jose Luis Pistelo, who has a particular expertise and daring in difficult hand surgery.

He took a look at the problem finger and told Raitt to come back to Brazil and stay in his house and he would perform the necessary surgery.

Three operations later he is finally getting back to where he needs to be as a golfer.

Raitt had his hand in a clasp for four months last year, making it virtually impossible to do anything. He had intended to practise tai-chi during his four-month convalescence in Sao Paulo but realised he was incapable of any such physical activity after the operation.

When the clasp finally came off in August he went to the buffet at a restaurant, picked up a plate and balanced it in his left hand like he had never been able to do for 12 years. He knew then the final operation was really going to help him.

Andrew finished tied-fifth at the South African Open at Port Elizabeth last week.

We have all heard of the heroic efforts of golfers battling their demons in order to conquer the game. Not many have gone to the lengths to which Andrew has gone, against his own surgeon's advice that the risks of operating were very high, and come out with such good prospects.

Pistelo has given Pele successful surgery on a damaged wrist. He has performed miracles on a leading businessman's young child who was born with no thumbs; the doctor managed to rejig the child's tendons so that his index fingers function like thumbs.

Now he has given some promise back to a golfer who has had his career on hold for the past decade with an enhancement that one does not normally associate with average Brazilian makeover.

BAGMAN 2
2007
ON TOUR

"Padraig adopted the mentally resilient attitude after he hit his ball in the burn by the fairway and by the green. His were not mental errors or strategic blips, just things that happen under the strain of winning your first major on an extremely testing run-in. He stressed after his victory that he kept focused on the fact he still had a chance to win – as opposed to lingering on the fact he might have blown it. This is what separates the best from the rest: mental resilience."

Page 164

Padraig Harrington in focus around the green during the third round of the 136th Open Championship at Carnoustie, 2007. The following day Harrington would capture the first of his three major titles in a play-off with Spain's Sergio Garcia. Top left: Padraig and caddie Ronan Flood moments after his victory. Below: Padraig and his wife Caroline savour the moment and the Claret Jug.

Game turns loopy on a Sunday

JANUARY 30: How did Retief Goosen win the 2007 Qatar Masters? He sank a "looong" putt on the last hole to beat Nick O'Hern by one shot. Professional golf is a game played very much by routine. From the swing weight of the players' clubs to the firmness of the cover of their golf ball, given the influence of technology, the game is all about careful selection and control.

But of course the game of golf is not played in a laboratory, it is played in a big open area where there are strict rules but where the elements and the capricious nature of competition are likely to take over, especially on a Sunday evening when the tournament in which the pros are competing reaches its denouement.

Everything seems to change on a Sunday afternoon in professional golf. The going gets tough and what appears to be a perfectly civilised and predictable game can frequently turn a little loopy.

We were in the Middle East again last week for the 10th Qatar Masters. It is the middle week of the Middle East swing and a week when all of us westerners were getting accustomed to the timing of the mullahs' call for prayer.

Qatar, the country that is shaped a bit like an elongated ear lobe and juts up into the Arabian gulf, is about a 40-minute flight from our previous tour stop of Abu Dhabi. The tour descended into Doha last Monday to celebrate a decade of golf in this country which has only one course on which to hold its professional event.

The Doha Golf Club's tale is pretty similar to the history of the other clubs in the region; an oasis in the desert which was originally built in the outskirts of the city and almost a decade later becomes very much part of the sprawling city. I first came to Qatar in 1998 when the course was isolated. The only spectators were the volunteers.

15,000 was the attendance figure at last week's event. Given that it was the strongest field in the event's history, I will have to assume that the named players were worth the invitation to the desert. Not that their performance is guaranteed, but the leaderboard would suggest that the invited guests rose to the occasion.

The first year we came here it was very much local rules. Alcohol was hard to come across in the city, but the accommodating organisers set up a Bedouin-style tent alongside the ninth fairway for us foreigners that had an ample supply of drinks for us to choose from. Ten years later, we are of course served drink in the clubhouse, the tents have been replaced by swanky hospitality constructions and beyond the imam's cry for prayer, you would be hard pressed to figure out that you were in the Middle East.

These Gulf countries put our own rampant development in Ireland to shame. In my absence of four years, about 50 skyscrapers have erupted and thousands of mansions have been built. Doha is definitely developed.

The pro-am, as always played on the Wednesday before the event starts, can be a bit of a chore. Last week we got to play with one of Retief's sponsors from Rolex, a local bank manager (who had not yet been found out by the handicapping committee) who was the best 22 handicapper I have ever seen play the game, and Ronald de Boer, the Dutch international footballer who has gone out to graze in the Middle East in the twilight years of his successful career.

It is always fascinating to play with top sports people, because so often they show exactly the same traits as other high achievers in other professions. Ronald was an engaging character who played hard and played to win.

Not being a big soccer fan, I made the mistake of asking Ronald if he had played for his country. Sixty-seven times was his curt reply. His brother, Frank, played over a 100 times for Holland.

He was feisty, inquisitive and overall a great companion on the frequently tedious tournament on Wednesday.

And, having come from Rangers, his form of expression on the course would not have been out of place in Glasgow.

When I provided him with yardages he, as is the case with many high achievers, questioned the veracity of my information on more than one occasion. In previous times I would have limited my information after the first expression of doubt. Ronald had disarmed me in addition to which, not much amazes me anymore with superstars.

As we strode down the 10th fairway on Sunday I heard someone shout my name from the top of the hospitality area beside the 18th green. I looked up and there was Ronald waving enthusiastically. With about 300 spectators turning up for a soccer game in Doha, I can't help but feel that De Boer is somewhat starved of atmosphere at live events in his adopted country.

Saturday saw the start of the loopy end of the control game. Retief was five shots behind the lead with four holes to play and ended up tied for the lead. Two shots behind on Sunday with two holes to play and he ended up winning by a shot. The look on O'Hern's face betrayed the bizarre nature of the final scene in a very tragic act for the Australian.

Retief's three-wood to the par-five 18th ended up on the fringe of the green about 40 feet from the pin. O'Hern's shoulders collapsed as Retief's ball charged into the hole at high speed for an eagle three. It is, of course, how champions finish off a tournament.

It is what separates them from the throng. It lends weight to the cliché about fat ladies and never give up. How did Retief win? He made the dream become reality when the pressure was at its most intense. Sometimes knowing what you have to do as a finely tuned golfer makes the task more attainable. Perhaps this dynamism is part of the winner's routine on Sunday afternoons.

To the rest it may well appear like nothing more than good fortune. The skill of capturing a title is certainly an art and not a science. Those who prevail under these conditions of competition would probably contest this belief. If they could explain it, well, naturally we would all be at it. It is this secret which distinguishes a consistent champion.

Coming to a screen near you

FEBRUARY 20: As you descend over the winter scene of snow-capped mountains at Lake Tahoe and into the summer scene that glistens over the urban sprawl of Los Angeles, it is easy to see why southern California is such a popular place to live – sun, sea, sand and snow, and of course Hollywood.

LA is agog with aspiring actors parking cars and working bars, temporarily, until the right part in a movie presents itself.

I, naturally, was not in LA for a movie part, more a bit-part in the Nissan Open at the historic Riviera Club north of the Santa Monica district of LA. As it happened, Retief (Goosen) was making a TV commercial for his sponsor Taylor-Made. They were shooting the piece last Monday, and somehow it was decided that instead of having a professional actor play my role as caddie I should play myself.

On the 11-hour flight from Dublin, I had plenty of time to let my mind wander into a fictional movie set. I was, after all, heading to LA and felt entitled to dream of the big screen.

The director's assistant phoned on Sunday night to say the chauffeur would be at my hotel by 6.45 the next morning to take me to the set. Wide awake at 4am – due not to excitement but jet lag – I was still waiting anxiously outside my hotel at 7am. No town car driven by a man in a black hat was to be seen.

There had been a mistake. The driver had picked up the leading man, Retief, and forgot about the supporting actor, the bagman. One of the production team was staying close to my hotel and would pick me up in his rental car. The reality of my role in this "movie" was becoming apparent.

Mike, from the financial side of the production company, collected me and off we went at full LA speed, 40mph maximum on the San Diego freeway any time outside 3-5am. We cruised past Santa Monica Boulevard, Sunset Boulevard and Mulholland Drive. My imagination took me back to the movies; I had got over the missing town car.

We arrived at the country club where the ad was being shot. I had expected a handful of people to be on the production team. Not so. This ad had the infrastructure of a movie set. There were articulated trucks, trailers, three catering vans, dressing-rooms, toilets and, of course, film equipment everywhere.

Annie from make-up and hair greeted me, Julia from wardrobe suggested what shirt I should wear, and Raul from catering brought me an excellent cup of coffee to sip as I was being dressed for my part. There were up to 70 people involved in this crew, from camera technicians to caterers; this really was big-time.

Once made up, Retief and I were escorted to the elevated set, the seventh tee. The tee was surrounded by professional extras. There were about 60 men and women representing the average group of spectators at a tournament. This is what these people do for a living. Some of them had worked with the assistant director for over 10 years.

The director introduced himself. A tall, well-built middle-aged man with the look of an American Indian, shook my hand and began to explain through gesticulations the "plot" of the commercial.

The gist of it was that this new TaylorMade Burner driver was going to take the *wimp* out of Retief's game and inspire him to whack his tee-shot on to the dog-leg par-four green with this supersonic driver.

As supporting actor, I was to then rip the head-cover off and hand my heroic boss his new Corza putter after his tee-shot comes to rest on the green. Simple.

Kenka propped himself in his director's chair and, surrounded by six assistants at his screen, called "roll" and "action", and off we went. The whole scene was to take about 20 seconds. We had started at 8am. By mid morning we were still "acting". That was only for the wide scenes, the close-ups were to follow.

Southern California can be quite fresh in the morning. Between takes, Julia was on hand to drape a jacket over my shoulders to protect me from the morning chill. I was dreaming of Hollywood again, so I let myself enjoy the pampering. The yogurt parfait they served was raspberry and not strawberry as requested. I decided it might have seemed a tad fussy to send it back, so I made the most of the raspberry-flavoured one.

The Riviera Club has hosted most of the golfing Hollywood stars over the years. The clubhouse walls are lined with black-and-white photographs of Spencer Tracy, Audrey Hepburn, Bing Crosby and Dean Martin, to name but a few. I glanced at the spectators beside the 18th on Friday last and noticed Dennis Hopper. In the pro-am we were fortunate to be paired with the charming Jerry Weintraub, one of Hollywood's biggest producers.

I returned to my real bit-part on the other side of Retief's bag last Tuesday, where there was no Julia to carry my jacket and a parfait of any flavour would have been graciously accepted.

Star gazing par for course

MARCH 27: Groupies, hangers-on, obsessives, call them what you want but when you get a gathering of famous people, you get plenty of punters who want a piece of them.

Frequently I walk past autograph hunters and hear what they really think of the star whose signature they just got. "Who was that?" is probably the most common question I hear. "He's much smaller than he looks on television". "He's so cute", "so polite" or "so rude", there is always a comment. I have seen fans gaping and staring at the ground where the star just vacated.

Whatever the attraction, there is a fascination lingering on the obsessive when it comes to professional golfers on the US Tour.

Of course the fascination does not limit itself to America. In Europe there have been plenty of golf enthusiasts who showed up most weeks of the year no matter how distant the venue. The "sweetie" people used to travel across Europe, usually by car so that they could transport their stash of hard boiled sweets which they distributed to the golfers and caddies on the course.

Most of the tour took their mother's advice from childhood about never taking sweets from strangers until the "sweeties" became familiar by being such a fixture on tour that they became part of it. There were serious sugar withdrawals when there was foot-and-mouth scare in the UK and the sugar dispensers had their sweets confiscated by customs and excise as they examined the content of their syrupy insides.

> "There was The Duchess, a middle-aged north European lady who followed the tour as a golf enthusiast for months until it finally became clear that she actually wanted to caddie. She did caddie and ended up winning an event."

There was The Duchess, a middle-aged north European lady who followed the tour as a golf enthusiast for months until it finally became clear that she actually wanted to caddie. She did caddie and ended up winning an event.

There was The Exocet, who always turned up at the German events. She was so christened because of her uncanny knack of always being on that narrow pathway where you could not possibly side-step her. Thus the sobriquet of the missile; you could see her coming but you just couldn't get out of her way.

Not to make light of professional star gazing. I know on reflection how I found myself stunned by the sight of the odd movie star I happened to have come across in an airport over the years. I have definitely been left mouth agape and extremely embarrassed. For those of us closely connected to golfers, the idea of having to spend another minute of divot duty with a golf pro than is absolutely necessary, is anathema. But for a golf enthusiast the chance to get a word with a famous pro when recognised in public is seemingly too exciting a prospect to let pass.

Golfers are assaulted by many of the same autograph hunters at revisited venues each year. There are some events where you recognise the parents pushing their children forward to seek an autograph at the appropriate moment. It is said that these are actually professional autograph seekers. If you ever look on e-bay you will see how many signed photographs and balls there are for sale over the internet.

There is a relatively famous aging golfer who appears at Augusta every year with outrageously loud clothes for a gentleman in his 70s and spends the practice days loading up on signatures. The fascination in America for a player's scrawl is limitless. Despite a healthy interest in it in Europe, we have a long way to go to reach the enthusiasm of the Americans.

Public attention for professional golfers is part of the price of success and most of them deal with it graciously if the timing is appropriate. Last week in Miami the attention for one player got a little too intimidating. I suppose for most young women keen on getting close to a single professional golfer, the young, athletic and handsome Australian, Adam Scott, would certainly be high on their list. For anyone who knows Adam, his pleasant demeanour is even more reason to want to get close to him.

Adam started to notice that there was a Korean woman taking a very keen interest in him at the matchplay event in Arizona last month. At every event that he has been to since in the States the same lady has made herself very visible.

She was so apparent that every time he stepped out of his hotel room there was the same woman miraculously near his doorway. The Marriott Hotel at Doral last week was as convenient as you can get for a tournament player. The rooms surround the main area of the clubhouse. The players were assigned their lodgings on site for the week and obviously the sponsors had the pick of the other rooms available.

So when Adam stepped out of his room on Tuesday last week he was once again greeted by the same woman who had being laying in wait for him at every other room he stepped out of in the last month.

He made some inquiries with the tour's security. It turned out that the woman was making bookings through her false association with the Korean player YE Yang. Adam asked Yang if he knew the woman, which of course he didn't. She had been making bookings through the tour, for player and family allocated rooms, on the pretence of them being for YE's parents.

The trials of a golfers day usually are limited to bogeys and birdies, but now it appears that bogus women have been thrown into the mix. If she is the stalker that she appears to be, then Adam may have to buy himself a big yacht like Tiger to ensure total privacy at coastal tournaments.

Ten out of ten for Augusta's 10-shot rule

APRIL 10: The Masters for Retief Goosen began in earnest on Friday afternoon amid the towering pines and leafy magnolias to the right of the 18th fairway. My boss had holed a 12-foot putt for birdie on the 17th to get back to plus six for the 71st Masters.

Gauging the cut mark is always difficult in a major because of the 10-shot rule. The authorities figure anyone within 10 of the leader after two rounds has a chance.

Possible of course, but highly unlikely.

The havoc a bone-hard Augusta National was wreaking on the world's best must have been sobering for the average chopper to witness. Zach Johnson's three-putt from as many feet on the 16th did all of us on the borderline a huge favour. It brought the eventual winner back to two under after two rounds, and with the wind stiffening, it was unlikely anyone would better that.

I explained to my colleagues in the caddie shack over a tilapia-and-salad lunch that we had lost a ball on the 18th.

"Never!" they responded in reference to what must have been a first in Masters history. With so many spectators, marshals and officials around, someone always at least sees where errant balls finish, whether in an azalea bush or a hazard.

The tee shot on the 18th required a fade with the northwest wind. Retief let it take too much of the wind. As the balls drifts right off the tee you notice players and caddies training ears to hear if it hits a tree. Sure enough, there was a very loud thonk off a sturdy Georgia pine. Many saw it hit the tree but never saw it come to rest. History had been made again in Augusta: the only 30-metre pine tree to swallow a ball. Either that or a patron went home with a Goosen souvenir.

Retief went on to make a four from his second ball, walked to the locker-room and packed his bag for the journey home. In such circumstances, golfers always pessimistically assume they have shot one too many to make the cut.

But this was the 71st Masters, where the course has been fattened on chemicals in the preceding months and carefully starved of sustenance, particularly water, once April came.

There had been serious rainfall the week of the Masters in recent years, and that has been the only natural ally of the players. There was just a sprinkle early last week, barely enough to keep the dust down. The organisers, left to their own devices, wanted the course to be like porcelain. The greens were so firm on Friday your feet hurt when you trod on them; I felt like I was wearing hobnailed boots and walking on glass. The last time I saw such rock-hard greens was in Shinnecock Hills at the US Open 2004.

Anyway, thanks to some bizarre occurrences, we somehow made it to the weekend. We got drawn with a past champion, Fuzzy Zoeller.

Fuzzy is 55 and a unique, old-style golfer who gets on the tee, pauses whatever conversation he happens to be having, hits his shot and resumes talking. Playing with him in the Masters is the most relaxing experience you could wish for on a course not otherwise designed for relaxation. As we waited for the pair ahead to putt out on 16, Fuzzy clipped his nails and smoked a cigarette.

Retief shot 70, which may not sound brilliant but turned out to be the round of the day. I went back to my lodgings to watch the oil-smeared, hairpin bend, otherwise known as Augusta National, on television. From the comfort of an easy chair, I watched almost the entire field go into free-fall while we catapulted from 60th to eighth by close of play.

From missing the cut to having a realistic chance of winning – there was a seismic shift in attitude in the Goosen camp by Saturday night.

Golf, despite its sometimes mind-numbing repetition, is played on momentum. Especially during the final round of a major.

Retief had his trusted old putter, with which he has won his US Opens and many other titles, in the bag again for the first time this year. He holed out heroically on Saturday. His form held up on Sunday; he had an eight-foot putt to go to five under for his front nine.

He hit a good putt, but missed his chance on the high side. Every putt he hit on Sunday was a good putt. If he missed from a makeable distance the putts all missed on the high side and always looked like they had a chance to go in.

There is a comfort in playing the final round and giving yourself an abundance of chances. In this sense Retief's round was less stressful than it might have been. As the leaderboard took shape, two over looked for a time like a winning score.

We took a defensive line around Amen Corner. You need an element of fortune to win. Our tee shot to the par-three 16th pitched exactly where you would want it to – or so we thought – four metres past the pin and six to the right.

Maybe 999 out of 1,000 balls would feed down to the pin from there; for the ball to stop where it did seemingly defied physics.

You need nerve, belief and talent to win a major. You also need to make the cut. Making it on the mark and easing around Amen Corner with a legitimate chance on Sunday would suggest the 10-shot rule is a worthy tradition.

Men in green ensure Augusta is the toughest Master

APRIL 17: A few days of post-major wind down gave me time to reflect on what was the toughest Masters I have experienced. You would not last long if you had to endure those conditions each week. All of my colleagues felt the same way too.

There has been a tradition at the Masters that double figures under par wins the Green Jacket. This respectable score was shattered by Tiger Woods in 1997 (18-under) and ever since the "tradition" has become less traditional.

Rough was introduced to the previously widest fairways in golf, then the course architects were called in to lengthen all of the holes. Trees have been added in the interim to narrow the driving area for the world's longest hitters.

Phil Mickelson won his second Green Jacket with a seven-under-par total last year and two weeks ago Zach Johnson won with a one-over-par total. So the question must be asked. Is the course too tough for the best in the world and have the organisers gone too far in their punitive course set-up?

At the end of our second practice round my boss, Retief Goosen, suggested level par would win the 71st Masters. On a new golf course nobody is too sure what the winning score may be. On a track like Augusta National, which is familiar to annual contestants like Goosen, there is an innate awareness of how the course played in previous years, and how that has been altered since. Given the analytical nature of my boss, I knew he knew what he was talking about. He had based his judgment on the firmness of the greens and the weather that was forecast for the remainder of the week; it was going to be dry, windy and cold. The forecast was very accurate with only a light sprinkle of rain barely covering the course on the Wednesday evening.

Although Augusta at almost 7,500 yards is not lacking distance there is only one effective way to challenge a top golfer and that is by presenting a hard and fast course. Given Augusta's undulating greens, this presented an even greater challenge than at any other major course.

Nothing happens by chance at Augusta, and the likelihood is that the green-jacketed gentlemen that run the Masters decided it was time for these constant par-breakers to learn a little humility. In recent years the problem has been that of extracting moisture from the greens, which has been aided though the sophisticated drainage system. The sprinklers were seemingly set at off until Saturday night when the severity of the putting surfaces was most apparent after the highest average round was recorded at 77 during the third round.

Professional golf, of course, should entertain its spectators.

The Masters has in the past been an amphitheatre of drama, met with the vocal appreciation of its patrons. Nowhere in the golfing world is the stage set more dramatically than at the aptly named Amen Corner of the 11th, 12th and 13th holes. There is a greater distance between the crowd and the players at Amen Corner than at any other course yet the intensity is unparalleled.

The volume had been turned down considerably this year. There were a lot of expectant "ooohs" followed mostly by disappointed "aaahs". Augusta had been muted, not by a sudden lack of skill by the golfers but by a less exciting reward system set up by the organisers. Pars were the new birdies in Augusta.

I do not think this is such a bad thing. However, on speaking with people in the crowd and those watching on television the consensus was that it was not really that entertaining to watch. The majority preferred birdie golf or at least realistic birdie chances being created. The average golfer knows all about putting for par. They don't really want to see the true exponents struggle to do the same.

Majors are a media feast. There are millions of words written about them, with traditionally non-golfing scribes adding a welcome outside view to what can sometimes be a mundane sport. I got to read some professional opinions, trying to make their sense of what must have seemed like a goalless draw in a cup final with six attempted shots at goal in the 90 minutes and extra-time.

Some pined for the glory days of Nicklaus, Palmer and Watson of the 1960s and 1970s, or in recent decades the finesse of Ballesteros, Langer or Faldo. Of course it is pure nostalgia.

Despite the equipment changes and improved standard of living and therefore play today, none of the above would have broken par on such speedy greens and inaccessible pins as played a couple of weeks ago. The speed of the greens has increased dramatically in recent years.

There is also an indirect gripe that such an "unknown" in Zach Johnson won the Green Jacket. Perhaps we are all programmed to expect the superstars to win the big ones. There is a suggestion given the size of the average purse the competitors have lost their winning edge. Holing a putt under pressure is still more difficult than making a print deadline. I have seen the fear in golfers' eyes and heard the tremble of their voice too many times to be complacent about how difficult it is to win.

There is a depth of talent on the US Tour in particular that provides way more potential winners each week than in the Golden Bear era. Golf is different now but top golfers are no less talented than 25 years ago. The organisers present the weekly challenge, the players make the most of the circumstances.

> "Holing a putt under pressure is still more difficult than making a print deadline. I have seen the fear in golfers' eyes and heard the tremble of their voice too many times to be complacent about how difficult it is to win."

The contenders wilted quicker than azalea petals in a cold-snap on the back nine at Augusta. This was not due to lack of talent or commitment. It was purely that the demands presented by the course and its guardians are daunting – even to the best.

Balancing progress with practicality

MAY 1: With the recent bout of spring weather it is hard not to contemplate just what is happening with the world's climate. I played on my home links course last week, wearing shorts and a T-shirt and a liberal coating of sun-block. Last time I played in spring I seem to remember wearing my thermal underwear and a woolly hat. I also found myself in some thick rough on numerous occasions normally associated with summer conditions. Equally, some of the lies I got around the greens were bare enough to cause my knees to collapse under the strain of a delicate chip, where the slightest contact with the ground before the ball would be disastrous.

I watched some of the coverage from the much delayed Spanish Open played in Madrid last week. The players, when they eventually got out on the rain-sodden course, were wearing sweaters and rain gear. In Augusta Georgia earlier in the month, the temperatures dropped low enough for morning frost on the weekend of the Masters tournament. Meanwhile, back home the nation was enjoying warm walks on the beach.

Of course golf in Ireland did not contribute greatly to global warming in years past. We were almost totally unexposed to the gas-cart of the 1970s and 1980s which became part and parcel of American golf and which has now been replaced with the environmentally friendly electric cart.

Today there tends to be a huge maintenance budget using a lot of machinery and chemicals to enhance the visual aesthetics of the modern golf course. I remember going to tournaments in Germany in the late 1980s and hearing from green keepers about the difficulty they had in presenting a manicured course because of the active green lobby. We are slowly catching up with our more progressive European partners in all matters concerning the environment. My own club has got to wait until the change of season before it can continue work on the flood protection bank it is building down the north side of the links on the Bull Island, given its importance as a bird sanctuary.

There are plenty of complications entailed with the ecological system of a golf course in today's climate which challenge the acumen of course superintendents. I paid a visit to the Cariglas estate in Longford during the week to see the course which is being designed by Jeff Howes, with my player Retief Goosen helping as signature designer. The mild spring has helped the development of the course. It has also got the superintendent thinking about what kind of grass he should plant for the fairways and greens.

There is now an abundance of choice available to those with a relatively generous budget. They are getting advice and suggestions from the leaders in agronomy in the United States. Despite the Irish climate being of a similar nature to parts of America there are of course still some contrasting extremes which still make it a guessing game for those wishing to use a suitable new grass for a new course in this country. Having seen how quickly greens can deteriorate for a variety of unforeseen reasons I do not envy the decision maker in Longford trying to balance progress with practicality.

The recent trend is to create courses that provide positive environmental effects. Another course that my player has a consultancy involvement with in South Africa has been delayed greatly by the environmentalists in the Eastern Cape who are concerned about the water supply in the area of the proposed 36-hole development.

Golf courses are places where environmental science and recreation can co-exist; one hundred acres of turf produces enough oxygen for a family of four for four years. Ponds with shallow slopes create an environment for flora and fauna. Shoreline greases stabilise banks and prevent erosion. Using partially treated waste water conserves drinking water. You can recycle grass clippings, wood debris, water, petroleum products and scrap metal. Organic products can replace synthetic fertilisers, water additives and soil supplements.

At the rate that temperatures are increasing and sea-levels rising, there is a chance we will not have to worry too much about the plethora of courses built close to sea level, such as in Florida, as they are gradually reclaimed by the sea.

There are huge efforts going into eco-friendly golf, including the use of bio-degradable tees and electric lawn mowers. I still do not see too many Toyota Prius dual battery and fuel operated cars sitting in the members car parks of most clubs no matter how environmentally conscious their committees may be.

Good players make good caddies

MAY 29: I have been frequently asked the question "what makes a good caddie?". There are certain things that all good bagmen do and they tend to be the basics. Realistically a very good player makes a very good caddie. It is a similar situation with swing coaches. Few golfers have been turned into talented players by a swing coach – the coach simply brings their innate ability to the fore.

The same can be said of us caddies; we try not to get in the way of good players, providing them with the space and information they need to perform at their best.

The best caddies in the world have a style of their own. Take the likes of Steve Williams. He has a strong build and he certainly takes his space in a crowded area. He walks as if someone has just offended him and is catching up with them as quickly as possible in order to give them a piece of his mind. He has an aggressive movement, almost like he is pumping iron as he strides. The 15kg bag seems part of his person.

There is very much a part of the player in each caddie. Despite carrying out the same basics in our daily toting routine, there are certain things we do for one player that would not suit another.

Our first-round three-ball in Wentworth last week was made up of three diverse characters; Colin Montgomerie, Retief Goosen and Johan Edfors. Their bagmen have learned to blend with their player's requirements. When we got to the sixth green last Thursday afternoon I noticed that Edfors caddie, Mike, had a gash on his leg which was bleeding profusely.

Given that he had tacked his way across the previous six fairways I supposed both of them had seen more of the Burma Road's undergrowth than the closely mown areas. When I pointed out that his leg was bleeding he replied: "Yes I know, I have been off-roading".

Mike is very much a hands-on caddie who will literally get stuck into a situation very quickly.

When Edfors hit his tee-shot into the trees on the 13th his ball came to rest among debris. When I looked over at Mike, he was stretched out face down by Johan's ball removing the loose impediments surrounding it. Many players would not like you getting this intimate, but obviously Edfors is quiet happy with Mike's extremely attentive approach.

When Edfors hit his ball into the water beside the eight green the next day the rest of us were peering into the murky swamp trying to identify his ball.

Meanwhile Mike was clutching onto the bank with one hand while poking around with a club in his other, the water just short of his neck as he desperately tried to scoop the ball up from the sludgy bed. There is no questioning this caddie's commitment.

Of course the same caddie's behaviour would not be appropriate for Edfors' playing partners given their different dispositions. It is part of Alistair's duty as Monty's bagman to have peripheral vision.

Monty could spot a horsefly on a rhododendron petal 150 yards down the fairway and the chances are he would not want him flying while he was preparing to hit his shot.

So you can imagine the crowd – and nature-policing – that Monty's man has to exercise throughout the course of a normal round. Throw a few bad shots into the mix and Monty's hyper-sensitivity demands even more control.

My guy Retief, on the other hand, is as nonchalant as a human being could be on the course. If there is someone moving or making noise he either blocks it out very discretely or genuinely does not notice. Asking the crowd to be quiet or keep still would only be highlighting it to my boss, so it's best to say nothing.

As caddies, we learn that there is usually plenty of emotion flowing from the player during the course of a round. Normally it's best for us to keep as level as possible emotionally on the course. A birdie is sometimes greeted with the same expression as a bogey.

I caught a few holes on the TV at the end of play on Saturday. Marcus Brier from Austria was standing over a six-foot birdie putt on the 18th green.

His caddie, Max, was also in the shot and as Marcus' ball trickled towards the right edge of the hole the burly Max stood on his tippy-toes and contorted his big frame enticing the ball to catch the lip of the cup and fall in.

What a pleasure to see a grown man bend his body in such an animated fashion to influence the path of the ball.

What makes a good caddie?

Doing what your player expects from you as discretely as is appropriate.

Daly's troubled life hits all-time low even by his standards

JUNE 12: There is something of the rock-and-roll lifestyle of the golf tour that appeals to young hopeful professionals. If you win a tournament in America you are an instant millionaire and are afforded a status that could make impression-able players a little heady with success.

For some, dealing with success is as difficult as achieving it. John Daly was sleeping soundly in his Southwind country club home in Memphis, Tennessee, early last Friday morning when, apparently, his wife woke him. However, she was not getting him up for his early tee-time. There was something on her troubled mind and her husband was going to bear the brunt of that burden. This was how it was told to the county sheriff anyway.

Mrs Daly, the story goes, attacked her husband with a steak knife while he was sleeping. When the two-time major champion and colourful figure presented himself on the first tee surrounded by body guards (seemingly too late), he looked like he had been mauled by a wild animal.

There is a thin line between sanity and eccentricity with many talented people. Having been around very talented golfers for decades, I have no doubt that if they were not eccentric before they played golf for a living, then that pursuit pushed them closer to the edge.

I have always thought that skilled golfers are often burdened with a special talent, just like artists, and if that talent is not realised in the manner that they believe it should be, then it causes them a lot of anguish.

Daly's life has been a litany of highs and lows that have never escaped public attention. From his initial elevation to revered status as the unlikely US PGA Champion of 1991 to the abject images of him with the delirium tremors as he tried to compete during an event some years later, there have always been extremes in Daly's life.

> "Sherrie Daly, John's fourth wife, spent five months in jail in 2006 having pleaded guilty to a federal money laundering charge. There were investigations involving drug trafficking, illegal gambling and corruption to boot. A shopping spree would have been less damaging."

There were rumours that the only reason he played a tournament in Perth, Western Australia, was that he had left such a huge debt at the local Burswood Casino that he had to return in order to repay it with his presence at the tournament the following year.

There seemed to be a heavy dependence on many substances that were, of course, detrimental to his health and ultimately his golf.

I remember a player telling me about an incident in the clubhouse of the Players Championship where there was a spread of fine food laid on for the players at lunch time. Daly took one look at the gourmet selection and immediately asked the waiter to phone the local McDonald's for a take away, including a very large diet coke.

The worst thing a modern golf pro usually has to worry about on tour is the damage that his wife could do on a shopping spree.

Sherrie Daly, John's fourth wife, spent five months in jail in 2006 having pleaded guilty to a federal money laundering charge. There were investigations involving drug trafficking, illegal gambling and corruption. A shopping spree would have been less damaging.

With time on her hands, Sherrie got to think about what she really wanted. She filed for divorce: John followed her a day later.

As anyone living the nomadic life that we on tour all lead will tell you, its hard to maintain a relationship. It takes a very understanding partner to accept the vicissitudes of life on the road. Throw in a few addictions to the already compromised lifestyle and you have a litany of failed relationships and personal disasters behind you, like Daly has.

JD is such a likeable person. He is always friendly, warm and respectful on the course. He has his own quick way of playing but he doesn't try to upset his playing partners in the process. He has held an endless fascination for the golfing public for a number of reasons.

All amateurs love to see a player beat the cover off the golf ball and launch it 330 yards down the fairway. To do it with such a long and powerful swing as Daly does is even more enthralling. He is the darling of the German golfing public and plays two events there each year. As much as he is the polar opposite of the standard German amateur, who is staid, conservative and in no danger of hitting it 330 yards, they love him. It is probably as much the stories of his drinking, gambling and failed marriages that attracts the German golfing public to him as much as his golf game.

At Augusta and other events throughout the year, John's travelling shop flogs his branded clothing, named Wild Thing. The appropriate nickname was tagged on to him after his wild swing became so recognised in the mid-90s. His style is his own and I cannot imagine that Brown Thomas's will be looking to stock it in its present state of fashion.

When he arrived on the first tee last Friday with his traditional Maxfli hat adorned by red flames on the peak, there was a suggestion he was taking his advertising a little too seriously with matching stripes on his cheeks.

It might have been a relief for Daly to get on the course last Friday and away from the steak-knife story. With survival instincts on high alert, he went on to shoot four over par and make the cut.

Daly was the first of the maverick rock and rollers of the modern golf era. With his fast pace of life it is hard to see how he can keep re-inventing himself and sustaining such a destructive lifestyle.

There's something divine about Angel

JUNE 19: Friday evening in Allegheny county and 18 professional golfers lingered around the Oakmont country club locker room, trying to figure out if they were going to play the final two rounds of the 107th US Open.

There was one player left on the course that could scupper their weekend plans. He was the burly Argentine, Angel Cabrera. We had been fortunate enough to have played with him for the first two rounds. There is a flair about the Argentine golfers that is almost a South American preserve and does not pervade any other nation so collectively.

If you look at the way Angel's countryman, confidant and best buddy Eduardo Romero swings the golf club, you instantly recognise a natural style based on fluency, elegance, elan and power. There is no entourage of swing coaches, mental gurus and fitness fanatics in tow; the Argentine way is the natural way. Angel smokes a cigarette instead of consulting a psychologist. It would be facile to say that they grip it and rip it, but there is very little pomp and ceremony to their shot-making.

There is a trait amongst all of them and how they swing their golf club; Jose Coceres, Ricardo Gonzalez and, more recently, Andres Romero, display free-flowing, non-mechanical swings that generate enormous power at the hitting zone.

Cabrera stood on the ninth tee on Friday last at one over par for the championship. Those on the projected cut mark felt reasonably confident that if Angel made a par on the extremely difficult par four that they would all be playing at the weekend. He crushed his drive, starting it just inside the flag-pole by the clubhouse supporting the Stars and Stripes, Oakmont and USGA flags, and it drifted towards the left gable end of the clubhouse which was the line that we had all identified on the blind tee shot as being the edge of the hazard that runs just off the left side of the fairway.

As with many tee shots at Oakmont you are never quite sure if you have hit a good one or not. It is hard to let yourself say good shot with confidence. Cabrera looked at his caddie Eduardo for reaffirmation, and he glanced in my direction with an inquisitive look on his face.

He shrugged his big shoulders, turned his lips down and suggested his ball's fate was out of his hands. As we reached the top of the hill on the ninth we saw that his ball was in a perfect position on the left side of the fairway, about 30 yards past my player Retief Goosen who had hit his best drive of the day.

The prospective cut makers took a collective gulp as Cabrera held his pose steady as he stared his sand wedge approach shot down as it headed towards the tight right pin. Most of the field had hit medium irons into this hole all day. Angel stuck his shot to within two feet of the hole and almost guaranteed his birdie.

There was a flurry of activity in the locker room as many of the 18 players on 11 over par started packing their bags. Not only did Cabrera become the first Argentine to eventually win the US Open, he also knocked 18 other competitors out of what they had assumed would be an 11-over-par cut.

As we mounted the stairs to the clubhouse I had to side-step some of those 18 coming the other way with all their belongings and a bitterly disappointed look on their faces. Luke Donald, our other playing partner, jokingly asked of Cabrera as we shook hands after the round, "what have you done to us Angel?".

There is a boyish charm about the 37-year-old from Cordoba; with his head sunk into his ample shoulders, his cap tight on his head revealing the tops of his ears, his impish grin after he hits yet another good shot and his ungainly gait which looks like he is not really too sure about where he is going. You could be forgiven for not taking him too seriously.

His golf, which I witnessed first hand for two rounds last week, was pure art. He hit fairways and greens with boring repetition and his deft touch around the greens confirmed what a complete player he is. The only chink in the Argentine's armour to date has been his volatile nature on the course. I knew he was playing great golf but I didn't think he had the patience to overcome the ultimate endurance test in golf, the US Open.

As with any major in America, there is such an ingrained fascination with American players that if the leader is a non-American, the chances of him getting any airtime or press is minimal, until the point is reached where they can ignore him no longer.

Saturday's local paper had a shot of Phil Mickelson on their front page despite the fact that he was 11 shots behind the leader and still sleeping at home in California, having been edged out of the cut by the eventual winner.

I sense the remarkable talent of Cabrera will be conveniently overlooked in the star-obsessed world that is sports coverage in the US. Tiger looking at his yardage book was more important than Angel settling over his birdie putt on the final hole.

Cabrera gave me a big smile as we walked off the 16th tee on Friday. Being ignored by the US media mob is not something that would unduly bother the affable Argentine.

Birdies an endangered species as major changes kick in

JUNE 26: Golf may not be the usual pastime of philosophers or deep thinkers; they are more likely to prefer a game of chess or a spot of sculpting as recreation.

And yet, as time-consuming as a round of golf is today, the irony is that professionals have about four hours per round to think about whatever enters their heads. Really, it should be an ideal pursuit for philosophers.

I had plenty of time to do some thinking about what it is the USGA were trying to achieve when they set up their annual professional showpiece, the US Open. With the realistic par of 74 on a notional par-70 Oakmont course, we had extra moments for contemplation in Pittsburgh, Pennsylvania, a couple of weeks ago. My man Retief Goosen opted to play his first practice round at 6.45am on Monday in order to have an uninterrupted look at what everyone had been warning us about. Many of the private-jet brigade had dropped by Pittsburgh at various times before the big event and returned with tales of woe about what lay ahead.

Oakmont was the brainchild of HC Fownes, a Pittsburgh businessman who had been wrongly diagnosed with a terminal illness. When he realised he wasn't terminally ill he decided to buy the Oakmont land and personally design the original course, which was completed in 1904.

It was a one-off for the revitalised amateur designer, and as I tottered down the first fairway in the thick morning light on the Monday of the US Open, it looked like nothing I had seen before on a golf course.

There was a unique feel to what had originally been a tree-lined course. Now that the trees (some 5,000) have been "taken away", and with a grand vista over almost the entire course from the first fairway, it has the look of an inland links about it: obviously inland but with a vast expanse of virtually treeless terrain broken only by tall, swaying fescues.

One of the goals in the USGA's manifesto for their national Open is to offer everyone who attends, the finest experience possible, whether inside or outside the ropes. This seems like a pretty laudable objective. The trouble is I find it hard to believe.

There seems to be a general policy among the major organisers this year to "out-tough" each other. Of course there is nothing wrong with a stringent challenge for these ever-improving and extremely talented professionals. That is the endurance test we inside the ropes have all come to expect from a major in the 21st century. But having rambled outside as well as inside the ropes, I am not sure the USGA are meeting their goal for the punters who pay handsomely to come and watch the endurance test.

There are some stands that provide good viewing for a small minority of the patrons, but if you want to follow a group then the opportunities to get involved in the round are minimal.

> "It was virtually impossible for enthusiasts to comprehend the skill entailed in simply two-putting from 30 feet above the hole at Oakmont. Unless you had walked on the greens you were unlikely to gain adequate perspective. It is understandably far easier for the layman to appreciate a holed birdie putt than a well managed two-putt."

The main problem for the public at Oakmont is the Pennsylvania Turnpike, which bisects the course. The one spectator bridge spanning the freeway reminded me of the Howrah Bridge, which they say supports hundreds of thousands of Indians at rush hour in Calcutta. It was no place for a claustrophobic golf enthusiast, especially if you are further unnerved by the sound of cars hissing below at full throttle.

Some venues, I understand, just cannot support the tens of thousands of spectators that want to participate in a modern major. I get the feeling the USGA should be paying the spectators for providing a vibrant live atmosphere at an event that is undoubtedly more accessible from in front of your TV screen, in your uncluttered living room.

A spectator mutation began at Augusta this year, the dearth of birdies at the Masters muffling the expectant crowd to relieved applause, whenever the most skilful exponents of the game somehow coaxed a ball into the cup for a par or bogey.

Perhaps it is time for spectators to reassess their expectation of their star players and turn up the volume for a par at majors.

It was virtually impossible for enthusiasts to comprehend the skill entailed in simply two-putting from 30 feet above the hole at Oakmont. Unless you had walked on the greens you were unlikely to gain adequate perspective. It is understandably far easier for the layman to appreciate a holed birdie putt than a well managed two-putt.

The USGA's philosophy would seem to be ultimately based upon control. They seemed determined nothing should be left to chance when it came to asking questions of the best golfers at their event. From fairway width and bunker preparation, to height of rough and firmness of the putting surfaces, everything was factored in.

With the density of the rough and the speed of the severely undulating greens, there seemed little room for creativity; the only question asked of the players was whether they could hit their golf balls straight.

Despite there being a "risk/reward" clause in the USGA list of important criteria in course set-up, the severity of the rough and narrowness of the landing area on the shorter par fours at Oakmont negated the lure of taking the holes on.

Simple accuracy of course, negates the original course design. Where HC Fownes wanted you to embrace the challenge of hitting a certain shape from the tee on each hole, the present set-up simply requires a straight one.

It may not be entirely coincidental that modern equipment seems to have taken the shaping of tee shots out of the equation too.

Where the designer originally wanted to punish the errant tee shot with a wispy "flying" rough from which your ball came rocketing out with top spin, the present set-up simply requires you to chop your ball back onto the fairway with a wedge.

Extremely sophisticated ball and club technology in the hands of very talented golfers has led the guardians of the game to seriously tamper with the philosophy of some of the world's best course designers.

Just whose philosophy is more important is obvious when you see what those in control do to some of the world's best golf courses.

Tiger Woods maintained that a 10-handicapper would not have broken 100 in the third round of the US Open.

If the set-up of Oakmont a couple of weeks ago is "for the good of the game" then I need to reassess my philosophy on golf.

The little brother will still be a stern test

JULY 3: The Smurfit course in Kildare has been reinstated as a golf course, instead of the hospitality area it was reduced to last year for the Ryder Cup. It is a course that could easily disappear from sight given the volume of new courses that been

"My new employer for the next three weeks is a young and extremely talented Swede, Alexander Noren. I do not really know Alex, apart from some brief phone conversations. We were paired with him a couple of years ago and I do remember being impressed with his ball-striking." **See page 242.**

Colin and Alex Noren on their first outing together – the first round of the Abu Dhabi Golf Championship, January 2009.

Alex at full tilt during the third round of the Dubai Desert Classic on the Majilis course at the Emirates Golf Club in late January, 2009.

"Like most young professionals, Alex has had a strict work ethic instilled in him from the outset. As much as hours on the driving range can be beneficial it can also be detrimental if you over do it. There is no point in hitting your best shots on the range, the game is about hitting them with a card in your back pocket." **See page 294.**

"I remember trying to savour the dream of my first year caddying for Retief and telling myself that nothing lasts forever. It has been a life-changing run for me to be the wing-man for one of the best golfers in the world. Not only did he treat me well, but he also played well."

See page 229.

Retief Goosen and Colin during the third round of the 2008 Masters Tournament at Augusta National Golf Club – their fifth and final Masters as a team. Goosen's record at the Masters with Colin on the bag was 13th (2004), 3rd (2005), 3rd (2006), 2nd (2007), 17th (2008).

"Villegas had lines representing not just north and
south, he had north east
and south east and so on.
He was particular about the
elevations between shots.
He added numbers to his
yardage to include how cold
it was, how up – or downhill
the shot was, how much
wind was involved. So it
wasn't as simple as 150
yards and 10 to the pin. It
was plus two for the hill,
three for the temperature
and four for the wind."
See page 283.

Colombia's Camilo Villegas with Colin
during the second round of the 138th Open
Championship on the Ailsa Course, Turnberry, July 2009. Villegas's preparation was
meticulous. He finished 13th in the championship.

"All amateurs love to see a player beat the cover off the golf ball and launch it 330 yards down the fairway. To do it with such a long and powerful swing as Daly does is even more enthralling." **See page 154.**

See page 154.

Is there anyone out there who swings it this long – and so successfully? The legend that is John Daly during the 2009 Open Championship at Turnberry.

Offaly's Shane Lowry celebrates winning The 3 Irish Open at County Louth Golf Club in May, 2009. Shane defeated Robert Rock on the third hole in their sudden death playoff.

"The Offaly gang brought as much if not more oomph to the event than any named player on advertising hoarding could have done."

See page 271.

"I looked at Tiger as he weaved through Amen Corner last Friday evening and despite his wealth of experience and success around Augusta, the look of intensity was deeper and much longer than in any other event of equal importance throughout the year."

See page 196.

Tiger Woods hits his tee shot on the 18th hole during the final round of the 2008 Masters at Augusta. He finished second, three shots behind South Africa's Trevor Immelman.

"There is a boyish charm about the 37-year-old from Cordoba; with his head sunk into his ample shoulders, his cap tight on his head revealing the tops of his ears, his impish grin after he hits yet another good shot and his ungainly gait which looks like he is not really too sure about where he is going. You could be forgiven for not taking him too seriously."

See page 156.

Argentina's Angel Cabrera celebrates with his caddie Ruben Yorio, after defeating Kenny Perry on the second hole of sudden death, to win the 2009 Masters.

"Although it seemed outrageous that Watson should dare to present himself on top of the leader board on Thursday morning last and stay there until the very end, the silence in the locker-room as players and caddies hushed for his nine-foot putt on the last hole on Sunday to try and capture his sixth Open betrayed how those at the very heart of the modern era truly believed an ageing legend was going to win at almost 60 years of age."
See page 285.

Tom Watson tees off on the 7th hole during the final round of the 138th Open Championship at Turnberry, 2009. He had us enthralled right up to the end which effectively came when his nine-footer at the 72nd hole (above) slid by, forcing him into a play-off with Stewart Cink.

"This is how Tiger is. Once he is among colleagues, inside the ropes, he is really just one of the lads."
See page 74.

Tiger Woods reacts to his putt during the second round of the 2008 Masters.

built in Ireland over the past decade. Given the attention its older brother has been receiving in the run-up to the Ryder Cup, it could be forgiven for having an inferiority complex. It is a good course which is probably less favoured due to the mature surroundings of the main course and its own relatively barren environs. Strategically, it is a very demanding course which will challenge Europe's best this week, hopefully more than the weather will.

A number of key holes will force those in contention to make a decision, particularly over the closing holes which question more the commitment of the golfer than the club selection off the tee.

Starting on the front side, there is almost a very clever hole in the short, dog-legged par four fourth. With the contours of the fairway leading the ball towards the green and the surrounding water, it is close to being a classic risk/reward hole. But a bold suggestion of taking out the bunker situated in the landing area for a drive would tease players into thinking about driving the green. With its present set-up nobody is tempted to hit the driver.

The designer has almost made the decision for the golfer. The best design asks the question of the undecided and demands that they both think and subse-quently execute the shot to perfection. The fourth is nonetheless a testing hole, but a bunker away from being one of the classic risk/reward shorter drivable par fours.

Holes six and seven will challenge your accuracy rather than decision-making. The sixth is a tight driving hole and the seventh a perilous drive due to the fact there is a man-made, water-filled quarry alongside the right of the fairway. Thankfully, the faux rock that adorned the centre of the fairway when the event was first held in 2004 has been taken away.

The seventh hole, as an aside, was the scene of one of the most bizarre caddie incidents in all my years of looping. There is a considerable walk from the sixth green to the seventh tee, so many caddies hand their player the driver, march forward and congregate down the left flank of the seventh for a bit of idle banter or a whinge about the fortunes of their man.

One group walked forward in the opening round last year and stood chatting as they saw the incoming ball of one of their players heading in their direction in a low, dipping flight. Instead of following its flight path, they decided to try to avoid decapitation and dived for cover. One of the bagmen both heard and felt the ball brush by him. His act of self-preservation did not take job security into account, survival was more in mind.

The group spent their allotted five minutes looking for the misdirected ball in the tall, thick grass where they assumed the ball had come to rest. They didn't find it, and the player made the long walk back to the tee to re-load.

It had been a bit cold, but with the events of the seventh hole the tempera-ture began to rise and by the time they got to the ninth hole the caddie who had almost been decapitated by a ball decided to take his jacket off.

For caddies, disrobing is a little more cumbersome than for most, because we have to deal with the appendages of an awkward caddie bib. You need to plan the shedding of layers well. As the caddie lifted his bib over his head, a ball dropped out of one of the two front pockets. He picked it up and realised it was the ball that had come screeching towards him to the left of the seventh fairway at high velocity half an hour earlier and ended up, not in the long fescue grass but nestled snugly in his caddie bib. The stitching on Smurfit bibs is obviously of the highest quality.

Assuming you don't snap hook your tee-shot off seven into a clutch of caddies and you are on target for a good tournament, there are numerous holes on the back nine that will get your attention. The 13th is a demanding tee-shot and approach which will question your club selection off the tee and your accuracy in approaching the green, with water waiting to claim bad shots at both ends.

The Smurfit is a challenging course from both a strategic and shot-making perspective. As with all good courses, the closing holes should test a worthy champion and this is the case at The K Club. Sixteen will test your commitment from the tee, the ambitious will be rewarded and the conservative golfer will make it a very long par four, where cutting the left corner of the sharp dog-leg reduces the distance to the green considerably. Seventeen is a par three which demands a stoical attitude when the pin is front or left. Eighteen has got a prominent life-belt hanging by the lake that engulfs the reachable par five for the longer hitters.

If you can keep your ball out of your caddie's bib and stick to a disciplined strategy, the Smurfit is a rewarding course for those who respect it.

Where archaic traditions can dim path of progress

JULY 17: There is a build-up to a major which may not be the type of preamble that would befit such a prestigious event. Schedules are chosen carefully throughout the year so that the week fits in at a potential peak time for performance. The players try to be fresh and some come and play a sneak preview practice round; others spend an intensive week with their swing coaches. Each to their own when it comes to British Open preparation.

It is on a much more practical level that we loopers approach the event; where are we going to stay for the 136th British Open Championship at Carnoustie, a place that is not known for its surplus of hotels? Despite Loch Lomond being a prestigious event, the weekend at the Scottish Open sees some serious posturing for last-minute house deals among the bagmen.

As caddies we have been reared not only on flexible scheduling but also on a shoestring. So the idea of spending £4,000 on a modest three-bedroomed sandstone semi-detached house on the outskirts of town is not the most appealing option. Experience has told us that the weekend before the event sees many cancellations and subsequent panicking from residents.

The upshot of my group holding out for an exorbitant weekly rental, instead of an outrageous one, was that we all converged in the 19th Pub on Kinloch street on Sunday evening waiting to meet our Arthur Daly-like character with keys and contracts for a three-bedroomed box at 10 times its weekly rate.

The tradition continues at the Open and, as ever, no one is left out in the rain at night.

Another tradition is the notoriously poor organisation when it comes to gaining initial access. I have been at every Open since 1985 and despite the mammoth advances in technology, medicine, health, education and general well-being, the ticket system for this great event is lagging way behind the average progress curve.

Here is how I approached the Open at Carnoustie: from the first security guard whom I encountered at a car-park near the clubhouse, I received a shake of the head and a reluctant conversation informing me I would have to go to public parking a bus ride away. I found a spot on the street.

I greeted the next security guard with my European Tour credential, which has a photo of me and looks very official. I asked politely, "May I go in and get my credentials please?" to which he replied you need a badge to get in. To which I responded, just like I did in 1986 in Turnberry, "The badge is inside and I need to get in to get it."

That is the way it was and, two decades later, that is the way it is.

At which point I shuffled off in a huff and appealed to another security guard if I could gain access to get my ticket and find my player who was at this stage waiting impatiently for me.

I took off at caddie pace, found a gap in a fence, vaulted a wall and regained my balance by the 18th fairway close to the Barrie Burn.

I looked over my shoulder and there was no security guard in sight. I skulked across the 18th fairway and got distracted from my security alert by the strong tidal flow of water through the Barrie Burn. I had broken into work.

That burn is like one of those sites that have been the scene of some horrible disaster. I had a vivid image of Jean Van de Velde standing in the burn with his trousers rolled up as his mind unravelled on the last hole on the last day of the 1999 Open.

How awful, and all I was worried about was getting chased out of the Open for not having the right credentials, which were impossible to get because of the archaic system that had been upheld by the tournament organisers. This is one part of the tradition I really wish would change.

Traversing the 18th fairway was enough to suggest that the organisers have very much got it right in the set-up of the stunning Carnoustie Links.

In 1999 caddies were afraid to place their players' bags in the rough in case they lost them. The sight of experienced professionals staggering off the 18th green looking like they had encountered a mismatch in a heavyweight boxing bout suggested things were not as they should have been on the links.

Carnoustie was renamed "Carnasty" when the Open was held here last.

This year the R&A look like they understand and respect the competitors as well as the course.

With the impeccable condition and sensible set-up of the course, with normal-width fairways and rough that makes you think and not immediately reach for the lob wedge, the Open is once again an exciting challenge. Carnasty no more; let's call it Carnicey.

Getting accommodation – well, we are used to the waiting game on that front and experience guides us.

But if only I could walk though the entrance gate in a civilised fashion instead of stealing into work, I might actually feel I was acting in a professional manner where tradition can embrace progress.

Harrington feels burn but stands heat

JULY 24: Padraig Harrington said, quite believably, that if he had not won the 136th Open Championship, he was not sure he would have wanted to play golf again.

Just in case you were thinking the carnage at Carnoustie over the closing holes on Sunday was not really that intense because a certain T. Woods was not involved, think again.

This was the biggest moment of Harrington's career. For the former "Kid from Castellon", Sergio Garcia – or El Niño, as he was affectionately know until he started growing a beard – last Sunday was the biggest moment in a life that has been dominated by golf from a very early age. He did not fail (though to him right now it will probably seem he did); he just didn't win.

Just as the putts have not dropped for Padraig at crucial moments in many close misses in the past, they refused to drop for the young Spaniard last Sunday.

There will be a number of post-major discussions about the strategy adopted by the challengers over the final holes.

There are many major venues where you tell yourself if you adopt a strategy whereby you par the last four holes under pressure you can win.

Not that Jean Van de Velde needs to be trawled up again, but he stuck to his strategy on the 18th back in 1999. Then, suddenly, an unexpected situation presented itself – the rebound off the stand.

Padraig stuck to his strategy on 18 until it came to the play-off, where he had a two-shot lead standing on the final hole. Here, on the assumption Garcia would not birdie the hole, he turned the par four into a par five by hitting a rescue club from the tee.

Padraig is as astute a golfer as any; he adopts a strategy suited to his game. It resulted in a double bogey on the final hole of real play. Some strategy, you might say. Some hole, I say.

When your knees are twitching, as are everyone's when faced with the opportunity to make a complete hames of things with the world and its wife watching, a hole like the 18th at Carnoustie will test strategy, resolve and leg power.

Having finished my round with Retief, I was to drive to Glasgow airport but stayed around to watch the end of real play. I had kidded myself I would walk around the final few holes with Garcia until the difficulty of outside-the-ropes viewing came home to me. I opted for the television screen in the caddie shack.

When it was time for me to go, I tuned into the extensive coverage of Five Live radio's Open coverage, lost the signal just past Dundee and found Radio Gael, which had a stronger signal if not the most knowledgeable commentators.

Garcia had decided to hit a three iron off the first of the treacherous final holes, the 480-yard 15th. This is a very conservative option for an excellent driver of the ball. His reasoning must have been that if he hit driver with an assisting wind it would leave him with no room for error; there is gorse on either side of the fairway to collect an errant ball and bunkers well placed to the right side.

He left himself over 230 yards to the green. His approach shot came up short and he ended up with a sloppy bogey.

He also adopted a similar, long-iron, long-iron approach to 18 and ended up bogeying that.

> "The three ingredients required for major success are talent, technique and temperament. Padraig has all of these in abundance, and thankfully Carnoustie didn't end with him contemplating the end of the road."

He played the last two holes in two over, just as Padraig did. Without the pressure of trying to win a major, parring the last four at Carnoustie is an ordeal.

The tee shot on 18 leaves no room for error on either side of the fairway; the Barry Burn sucks up the slice and the boundary fence looms large for the hook.

An added problem is that you cannot see the landing area off the back tees, so there is always an element of doubt even after you have hit your tee shot.

The hole measures 499 yards in our yardage book, so hitting an iron from the tee is bringing the burn, which meanders back again about 10 yards in front of the green, into play. So you have the burn to negotiate twice.

The answer to the 18th and the three previous holes – much like the rest of the course – is that you just have to hit a good shot regardless of strategy.

Padraig adopted the mentally resilient attitude after he hit his ball in the burn by the fairway and by the green. His were not mental errors or strategic blips, just things that happen under the strain of winning your first major on an extremely testing run-in.

He stressed after his victory that he kept focused on the fact he still had a chance to win – as opposed to lingering on the fact he might have blown it.

This is what separates the best from the rest: mental resilience. That is why these golfers have their mental coaches on hand all week long. Bob Rotella was never far from Padraig's side throughout the week.

The three ingredients required for major success are talent, technique and temperament. Padraig has all of these in abundance, and thankfully Carnoustie didn't end with him contemplating the end of the road. Instead, as 136th Open Champion, he starts a new phase of an already illustrious career.

Harrington must deal with major decisions

JULY 31: So you win a major and the long hours of relentless practice begin to make sense. For as many times as a player has had the nightmare of having to play an impossible shot from inside a phone box, he has hopefully had as many dreams of hoisting one of the coveted trophies which are presented to a major winner.

For the very few has the dream become a reality. Not that Padraig Harrington was not a serious contender for major titles but there has to be a series of events that go against your fellow competitors, and a few things that go your way to make the dream become a reality; the freakish bad luck of the young Argentine Andres Romero on the 17th hole when he hit the wall of the Barry Burn and bounced out of bounds. The battling up and down that Padraig made on the last to get into a play-off. If he had made seven on 18 he may well have been thrown in the Van De Velde bin of also-rans.

Of course this didn't happen, rather Padraig made it happen for himself. You make your own luck in the fickle game of golf and despite others smoothing your path to victory you still have to bring in the lowest score.

The rewards for success in an event like the British Open Championship are vast. As a player with a wily management company you should be set for life. Eight years ago the dream came true for Paul Lawrie, the local boy from up the road in Aberdeen. A short while after his victory he bought his first "sponsor's" house and the big car that went with such an abode. It was a dream that he did not expect to become a reality so soon in his career – if at all.

Incidentally it was observed by some of my colleagues that Paul won with a Wilson golf bag and the Kartel name stitched on the front of his clothing. Funny that Padraig also plays Wilson and wears Kartel. Next time the Open is back at Carnoustie it might be wise to predict your winner based on bag and the branded clothes.

Depending on who you talk to and what their accounting principles are, the Open champion stands to earn €20 million on the back of the victory. The snag is that it is not put straight into his bank account. As a serious contender winning a major can become a major distraction if you are not selective and fairly ruthless in how you deal with the aftermath of that success.

As a caddie, the idea of receiving a bigger percentage of a win is that you somehow share not only in the victory of the event but you also get a little extra reward for all the other spin-offs that the player receives from sponsors, and any other bonus deals that go with winning. Of course everyone's deal is a personal matter and there are no set rules for how a caddie is paid.

On Sunday, July 22nd, at about 7.30pm local time on the Angus coast Harrington began his reign as 136th Open champion. He immediately assumed the role of ambassador with a speech that said all the right things about all the right people. It is of course no surprise to Padraig that he won the Open and, knowing his attention to detail, he did not just think up those words after he sunk his winning putt.

His words now are more important and of course more sought after by the world's media. For a man who has been so generous with the media since he turned himself into a world-class player, they are probably going to make even more demands of him. For a professional who is devoted to his practice regimes this means that without a strong discipline he will have to eat into his practice time or just spend even longer at the golf course taking care of on- and off-course business.

In tour-speak Harrington had a free week last week. As those of you listened to the radio or watched television or played in the boys Tilestyle competition at his local club at Stackstown will be aware, it sounded like anything but a free week.

Although it sounds a little mean, management companies will have set times for how long their client is obliged to spend at functions in events at which they have been contracted to play. This may not always be necessary but it is frequently problematic when they have to attend a dinner served at 10pm and they have to perform as a golfer the next day at 7am. Legal restrictions are a wise safety net. Golf is after all not just a game at this level, it is very much a business.

Padraig's aspiration to win more majors has probably increased in the past weeks. Therefore it is important he keeps working on the aspects of his game that got him to where he is today. Padraig will be invited to play in events here, there and everywhere, and this is part of the calculation of the €20 million potential earnings from the win.

These events are draining on a player, but it takes a strong will and a realistic sense of your potential as a player to refuse some, if not all, of these offers.

The challenge now is to balance the guaranteed financial rewards against the belief in his ability to earn even more by competing effectively in the big events in the future. This is the toughest decision for a successful golfer. Do you take the guaranteed money or do you try to win more big titles?

Knowing when and how to say goodbye

AUGUST 7: Paul Simon sings about 50 ways to leave your lover. I wonder how many ways he would come up with for a caddie to leave a player? This caddying business is as nondescript a job as you are likely to come across, and its life cycle is unsteady even by modern short-term contract norms.

The fact is, with virtually all caddie and player employment arrangements, you can hire and fire at will; there are no contracts stopping you from walking.

It is a precarious existence whereby planning a family and taking out a mortgage can put you under a lot of pressure to get along with a working relationship that otherwise may not be that workable. Probably the average time-frame for a caddie and player to stick together is about three years, but it can be as short as three weeks. There is no job description but if you do the wrong thing too often you will find out soon enough what is required of you as a bag toter, by which time it may well be too late.

I woke up early last Tuesday, as you do making the trip west over the Atlantic, and headed up to the Firestone Country Club to enjoy the relative cool of the morning in Akron, Ohio, given a forecast for a temperature peak of the mid-90s for later in the day.

Akron was the tyre centre of the world in its day. I drove past the Goodyear plant which looked like a behemoth of the good old days of industrialised America; a massive red-bricked factory which looked idle now apart from the clock on its tower that seemed to tell the correct time still.

I turned on my car radio and was instantly tuned into the PGA Tour station with 24-hour golf news. They were relaying a story from the previous week's Canadian Open where a player dumped his caddie during the back nine of their first round. Apart from being intrigued at how you could talk about golf all day long, I was fascinated by the on-course mutiny in Canada. There are frequent "jockey" chances as we say on tour but rarely do they happen mid-round.

The story as told on the radio station was that there had been an altercation between player Jay Williamson and his caddie, Mike Mollet, which resulted in the player sending the caddie back to the caddie shack mid-round and pulling a random spectator from the crowd to continue as a replacement toter.

The stand-in had actually competed in the Canadian Open many years previously when it was a caddies' market and players were not quite so flippant with their comments to their bagmen for fear of having to carry the load themselves. The story continues that Williamson wasn't too keen on the replacement "Mike" so the scoreboard carrier got to have a go at caddying as well.

I arrived at Firestone and went into the air-conditioned caddie marquee where breakfast was being served and some of my colleagues who had been at the Canadian Open were sitting around preparing themselves for the day ahead.

Of course now I was going to get the unedited version of the on-course dismissal and just who fired who, with only the slightest of caddie shack bravado and embellishment.

Williamson, my colleague continued, pull-hooked a nine iron to a par three on the back nine on a hole where the wind was unsettled and hard to tell just from what direction it was coming. When you pull-hook a ball the chances are it will go at least 10 yards further that required. Williamson let his caddie know that he wasn't impressed with his club advice. To which the caddie replied he could carry the bag himself, took a fist full of his golf balls out of the bag, ripped his caddie vest off and flung the balls into the nearby pond, strode off towards the clubhouse, and told his now ex-boss he would be waiting for him when he finished and not to forget his cheque book.

There are many occasions when this is just how we, as often obsequious advisers, would love to react to an ear-bashing from our players but mortgages and general cautiousness stop us from doing so.

It probably doesn't do the resigned caddie much favours for future employment when players hear of the caddie-shack tale of events at the Canadian Open: the official version is better for potential future job opportunities.

Caddies have been fired for all sorts of reasons apart from what is usually the most likely one – that the player is just sick of the sight and sound of him and it's time for a change.

We do spend increasing amounts of time with our players because, in addition to the hours on the course there are the lengthy practice sessions, possibly long flights together and sometimes evening meals. It is a wonder that some of us last so long. It can be an unhealthy amount of time for two grown men to spend together.

So you can jump on a plane, catch the next bus, send him a text or simply flick the bag off your shoulder on the course if you are unsatisfied with your player's attitude. But with today's abundance of information and lack of available players it is probably wiser to part company in a more civilised fashion if you plan to work again as a travelling porter.

Heat and Bible Belt fail to make Tiger buckle

AUGUST 14: We arrived in Tulsa, Oklahoma, for the 89th PGA Championship amid rumours that the hot spell had arrived and was due to plant itself in the state for the foreseeable future. If there is something that is predictable in the United States of Amazement it is the weather. Weather forecasters, especially inland, tend to speak the truth. We jumped out of the plane and it felt like we had opened the oven door while the fan was blowing. It was a burning wind and a temperature that felt like 150 degrees.

So when I watched a seven-day forecast on the local news station that had big orange sun-balls for the entire week and upper 90s to low 100s predicted as highs with the lows not much lower, I realised why they call it a sweat-box down there.

There is one thing you have to be in such heat when you have to go outdoors to make a living, and that is, sensible. Not always the easiest way to be, for a major-pumped golf pro. But limiting your time outdoors was the order of the week. My boss, Retief, played just nine holes on Tuesday and nine on Wednesday in his effort to conserve energy. Adopting a normal routine, and particularly for majors, we would have at least two 18-hole practice rounds completed before the tournament starts, so easing off on preparation was a big compromise for many diligent golfers.

John Daly took the cautious approach to the extreme by not coming to the course until Thursday in preparation for his first-round tee time. He had been going through his preparations in a nearby casino, stating that he knew the course well having gone to college not far away in Arkansas. In keeping with the brain-numbing heat, Daly went on to shoot the best round of his year, a three-under-par 67. So for those trying to cite preparation and routine as a means of achieving success, last week may not have been the best example.

I am not sure how many bottles of water I drank on average during each round, but I consumed at least 10 litres each day.

> "The word was that Big John was guzzling more Diet Cokes than usual and maybe smoking slightly fewer cigarettes, but he likes to stick to his consumption routine no matter what the temperature."

The word was that Big John was guzzling more Diet Cokes than usual and maybe smoking slightly fewer cigarettes, but he likes to stick to his consumption routine no matter what the temperature. I heard his caddie suggesting he might want to try a couple of Gatorades instead of the Cokes.

Not only does the liquid come out quicker from your body at these soaring temperatures but the golf ball comes off the clubface a lot quicker too. To give an indication of just how much the heat affects the distance the ball goes, without any wind the ball was going at least two clubs farther than at the last major in Carnoustie.

Bermuda grass deals well with the heat but bent grass does not. So we knew during the practice rounds that the big electric fans that moved the stifling heat around the putting surfaces were so placed to keep the greens alive, rather than keep us humans cool.

We all took advantage of the big blowers, directing our players toward the rush of cold air by placing our imaginary hole-placement discs near the fans, so we could linger in the relative cool a little longer.

I think Oklahoma must have been the state where they invented mall walking, the practice whereby people go specifically to the mall not to shop but to take their daily exercise in the cool of the air-conditioned complex. Walking from your car to the entrance of the mall could result in a mild outbreak of heat stroke.

The tournament officials have a rule that when the heat index goes the other side of 100 degrees we loopers can go topless, so to speak; we are not obliged to wear our caddie bibs.

I am sure it is a legal requirement rather than a compassionate gesture. Anyway, most of us took advantage of "biblessness" – though I have to admit that you become fairly used to using the little pouches in the bibs for throwing your bits and bobs into, and when you go without them you realise how handy they are in normal weather.

I went to the mall to do the cultural thing and participate in consuming on a grand scale. The people of Oklahoma are extremely friendly and are quick to pick up on a foreign accent. So as I was paying for my purchases the shop assistant struck up a conversation.

I explained what I was doing in Tulsa and she immediately asked if I knew Tiger Woods. She had a theory about why he had not won an event in Oklahoma, apart from the fact that this was only the second event he had played in Tulsa since he turned professional. The lady went on to explain that we were in the Bible Belt and given that Tiger is a Buddhist, she continued, he had no chance of winning in Oklahoma.

I will be looking out for the Buddhist temples when next I return to Tulsa because there was a change of religion last Sunday at the Southern Hills Country Club.

Despite some outrageous attempts by Big Buddha Woods's main rivals, Ernie Els and Woody Austin, to steal his thunder, the eastern philosophy was never really in danger of yielding to any other religion in the final major of the year.

Sightseeing in the fall between two stools

SEPTEMBER 4: It was not the usual mad dash to a back-to-back tournament last week on the east coast of the USA. We could enjoy a gentle saunter from New York to Massachusetts for the Deutsche Bank event. With the Labour Day holiday weekend, and a Monday finish, we had an extra day to get to our destination, so some of us took the rare opportunity to enjoy some sightseeing in Manhattan.

We are so programmed on tour nowadays to move on swiftly to the next event, or so anxious to get home if we have a free week, the idea of actually looking around at the cultural attractions of such a metropolis is seldom entertained.

It was the end of the first week of the new regime on the US Tour, so the 24 of the initial 144 players who did not make it into the top 120 on the FedEx Cup playoff list could spend as long as they liked absorbing the rich culture of the city, or head home to reconsider their golfing plans for the rest of the year.

I have always found the extremities of America – the cities on the outer rims – the most fascinating. So spending back-to-back weeks on the northeast coast proved a welcome break from what can become a monotonous trail around the central part of the tour. Making a few detours along the route through New England, through towns with either British or native American names, you get a true sense of how refreshingly different that part of the country really is.

The Westchester Country Club in upstate New York represents old money. The course would not look out of place in Surrey, and the members are probably the American equivalent of Surrey folk.

The TPC in Boston is a new club with a cleverly contrived old look. It reminded me of a heathland course in the south of England with its rugged bunkers and fescue borders.

On the one hand the tournament represents this very American idea of a playoff; on the other hand it represents the new, global concept of a modern event. Seldom has such an American idea been sponsored by so many non-US companies; two weeks ago it was Barclays, last week it was Deutsche Bank, and this week it is BMW, whose brand is ubiquitous around the neatly trimmed fairways.

Despite the fact that strokeplay is about getting around in as few shots as possible, this FedEx thing can be a bit of a distraction.

Just what are we chasing – dollars, points, retirement funds or birdies? No matter what we are chasing the sponsors are hot on the heels of viewers, but the television ratings were disappointing in Westchester a few weeks back.

Football, the very sport with which the new system was trying to avoid competing, had more viewers for a final pre-season game. A mini-league baseball event for 11- and 12-year-olds attracted more couch potatoes than did the denouement to the Barclays Classic.

Despite the fascinating duel between KJ Choi and the revitalised Steve Stricker, after which the gracious Korean admitted golf had won in the end, there is seemingly no show without Tiger Woods.

This is both good news and bad news for golf. As long as Woods is happy to chase his ball around big events, those of us who make a living competing in the same arena are benefiting. As soon as he decides he has had enough of this pursuit the arena is going to shrink dramatically.

There is an unhealthy dependence on the main man. This of course is not his or the tour's fault; it is more a reflection of the tendency toward obsession with superstardom in the States. Most US golf fans would prefer to see Tiger replace a divot than see Phil Mickelson or Padraig Harrington hit a three iron to within 15 feet of the pin.

For those of us who have been weeded out of the second "cut" in this FedEx Cup system, there are decisions to be made about where to play for the rest of the year. For my player, Retief Goosen, the Deutsche Bank event determined if we went west or east.

Aware our current lack of form is due mainly to a cold putter, we headed east on the weekend. The autumn of our golfing year will be spent in Europe and Asia.

This is an indication of the many tiers in the pecking order of world golf.

The elite US golfers will curtail their involvement in the fall finish to the US

Tour. Cutting back there will offer opportunity and incentive for foreign travel if they so desire. The tendency may well trigger more invitations to Asia and particularly China.

For those who have been eliminated early from the FedEx there is still the opportunity to play in tournaments all the way to early November.

Despite these events being less prestigious they offer great opportunities for players of modest profile to take a tour title, because there will be fewer truly elite players competing.

Woods is the Manhattan of golfers, and despite the beauty and charm of Chicago and San Francisco, New York city will always be more alluring for the majority of golf buffs. Television ratings soar when he plays.

Let's hope, however, he does not beat Jack Nicklaus's record in majors any time soon – or we all may have to take a pay cut.

Enjoying the game outside the ropes

SEPTEMBER 11: Impelled partly by a fascination with the biggest team competition in men's amateur golf, and partly by curiosity about the progression of the infrastructure in the north-eastern part of the country I decided to take a day trip to the coastal town of Newcastle, Co Down, to watch the first day's play of the Walker Cup last Saturday.

With the 100km trip from north Dublin, to arguably the best links course on the island taking less time than the 10km trip into the city centre at rush hour, it was a pleasure to keep in fifth gear for most of the trip.

Apart from playing in a regular competition in my home club I have never been to an amateur event here or anywhere else in the world. Despite it resembling a busman's holiday, I was looking forward to experiencing a world of golf without money as the lure.

On a relatively balmy day for a time of year when you might have expected to be wearing thermals, the heralded links looked stunning, having been groomed to perfection by the greens staff under the guidance of the R&A.

Not having paid much attention to amateur golf in the past I had no idea how many spectators to expect. Would there be public catering, scoreboards, stands?

On arrival I got the impression of a mini-Open Championship set-up. The ticket booth at the entrance was the same as that at the Open; the marquees and the Bollinger tent were scaled-down versions of those at the Open.

As I wandered out on the course and caught up with a few matches, I began to recognise the referees accompanying the players. I even bumped into the secretary of the R&A, Peter Dawson, rambling down the links looking more casual than I ever remember seeing him at Open Championships.

Spectating at a golf event for someone who is more accustomed to being on the other side of the ropes was uncharted territory for me. What do you do? Do you stand or sit at the one chosen vantage point, or do you march around with the one group? I ended up doing a bit of both and neither very effectively. I was drawn quickly into what live golf spectating is all about: socialising. What a great way to wander around outdoors having a chat, watching the odd shot and applauding at the appropriate moment.

I also became aware of the number of experts there are at these events. As Lloyd Saltman took a bit of a slash at his tee shot off the 10th a local sage remarked, "That boy's swing is gone; that match won't last long."

How right he was; Saltman went on to lose. Who needs professional pundits?

I made it to the 10th fairway and found myself drawn back to the dune beside the ninth green, which to those who have a fondness for links land is probably the closest place to heaven you will get here on earth: the verdant basin that is the ninth fairway stretches below to the north and up to the massive bank that leads to the tee and beyond east to Dundrum Bay. Across to the left lies the 10th green surrounded by craggy banks and rugged bunkers.

Directly below is the gently, sloping ninth green and beyond is the undulating practice chipping green, which leads onto the roofs and steeples of the town nestling under the dominant gaze of Slieve Donard.

One even got to see the members sipping their afternoon malt whiskeys in their perfectly appointed lounge in the clubhouse.

Having torn myself away from the ultimate golfer's view I wandered out on the links and happened upon the Rhys Davies and Dustin Johnson game on the 11th fairway.

Of course being on the manicured fairway was the privileged treat of amateur golf. The marshals contained what looked like a healthy-sized crowd by using ropes to keep us at a respectful distance from the players.

I am not sure if it was a coincidence that I came across a couple of management agents out scouting, and getting a rare view of fresh young talent from directly behind the hitting line.

Given any knowledge of the swing, it is a great way of viewing prospective clients from a technical perspective.

With about half of these very talented amateurs about to relinquish the relative comfort of golf for pride rather than money, the agents were taking full advantage of this final opportunity to sign a potential big name.

I scampered up to the top of the hill left of the 12th green and looked west over the other side to see the march of the diehard amateur golf fans of the nation coming down the 16th fairway. It was the lead group of the superstar of European amateur golf, the local wunderkind Rory McIlroy, and his opponent Billy Horschel.

I have not seen such an enthusiastic mob since the last time I saw the throng of thousands follow Tiger Woods. It was McIlroy mania.

The marshals needed stout ropes to keep this eager crowd from a flat-out stampede. For old-fashioned golf aficionados, the Walker Cup at Royal Co Down was the game at its best, played on the links land in all its splendour.

Even the local pub I visited later had tiger lilies adorning the toilet. How civilised.

Better to break par than clubs

SEPTEMBER 18: There are sports that are sometimes best played when you are a little fired up or angry. Some team sports may entail a rousing speech from the captain or manager before competition. From team ball-games to athletics there are a bundle of games where you can vent some anger successfully during competition.

This tends not to be the case with golf where tranquil, monotonous Zen-like behaviour is required for the optimum performance. If you get aggressive the chances are you are going to get even more upset as you hit more errant shots. The best advice you could give a golfer under pressure is to stay cool and take your time.

Thus lies the great conundrum of the peaceful and ballet-like serenity of golf; what do you do when you get really hacked off with how your round is going? As pedestrian a sport as golf may appear, it has the potential to ignite a raging inferno in the most unlikely of candidates.

The game has the capability of turning mice into monsters once they put on their golf shoes. The constant challenge for us all, is how to contain this emotion and somehow channel it as a positive force. For a professional who is put to the test four times a week the chances for blowing a fuse are greatly increased.

"Another player took to a golf bag which he thought was his and as he was busy demolishing it was interrupted by his playing partner, the actual owner, who had the same brand of bag."

I am not suggesting adopting any of the methods I am about to mention to those level-headed golfers amongst you, who are overwhelmed by the joy of being free from the office, and out in the open air chasing your golf ball round the links. But having observed some of the world's best golfers and the world's most notorious ragers, I can recommend a few valves of release when you next feel the tension rising on the track.

Caddying can be a perilous job; there is very little job security and you are very much relying on your player's talent for your living. On a day-to-day basis it can be particularly dangerous. One of the first players I caddied for told me the only rule he suggested to which I pay particular attention, was to keep my hands away from the golf bag after he had hit a bad shot – because the club was liable to come flying back in the direction of the bag or be hurled back into the bag at full force. It was an invaluable piece of advice given his litany of bad shots, followed by the bag and club thrashing he had warned me about.

This was in the days before the abundance of television cameras and a dearth of spectators at most European events, so the chances of being seen or offending spectators was slim.

Of course bad behaviour should not be encouraged. With the advent of sports psychologists and the excess of them now, it's widely agreed it is best not to drag your anger around the 18 holes with you, it should be released as promptly as possible. Many top players have mastered the art of cursing with their back to the camera or whacking some innocent object out of view of the spectators. There is no doubt some release is required and part of your professionalism is knowing how to do so without getting caught.

The bag and the caddie are probably first in line for abuse after a bad shot. Tee markers are also in a precarious place. Last week in Cologne, the markers were big wooden blocks with the Mercedes-Benz logo adorning them. I don't know the details, but one of the markers on the 16th tee had been disfigured to the extent you could almost identify which iron had been embedded in it.

The unofficial tales in the caddie shack of "head-offs" are endless and if the recipient of the assault is a tee marker then the story cannot be contained for long. I have heard of players biting themselves in anger so deeply they drew blood. You could tell one player's putting round by the red lines on his forehead where he whacked himself for missing putts he thought he should have holed. I have helped an embarrassed Australian golfer search in a rice-field for a driver he hurled surprisingly far in anger.

A colleague had his camera, which was in the golf bag, broken by a vexed player's club. Another had to dive into the bag to pull out a coke can which had been pierced in a blow from a six iron, causing it to burst. Another player took to a golf bag which he thought was his and as he was busy demolishing it was interrupted by his playing partner, the actual owner, who had the same brand of bag. The original rager of the modern game, Tommy Bolt, ended one round with only one usable club in his bag.

A South African threw his whole bag into a pond after a poor round. As he strode to his car he realised he had left his keys in the bag. So he fished it out, retrieved the keys and threw the bag back in.

An American reversed his car over his offending clubs after he missed the cut. He pulled forward and reversed over them a second time in case he didn't break them all in the initial crunch, and pulled out of the car-park leaving a wake of dust.

One American golfer started to demolish his Ping bag and, as he finished, his disapproving caddie pointed out that due to him leaving a hole where the "n" had been, Ping now spelt Pig.

A good friend of mine, in his usual calm style of caddying, once placed his player's bag in front of his player's ball on one fairway during a tournament and said he would not move the bag until the player calmed down. The fuming player responded: "Do you not think I can get my ball through the bag?."

The same player begged the same caddie to reveal where he had hidden his clubs after a bad round. As he calmed down he pleaded to let him have just one of the clubs to break.

Caddying can be a perilous job and gauging whether or not to respond to a raging player only comes with experience.

When one seasoned looper was asked by his player, "Give me something to break", he tersely replied, "How about par."

Heritage a fine venue for battle

SEPTEMBER 25: In the absence this year of the biggest distraction to aspiring golfers, the Ryder Cup, we will have the opportunity this week to enjoy some international team golf without the hype of the greatest marketing achievement of the professional game.

I have just arrived in the suave and sophisticated city of Montreal in preparation for the Presidents Cup, in which the US (including Tiger Woods) takes on the Rest of the World at Royal Montreal Golf Club. It is always difficult to bond a team of traditionally egotistical players into an enthusiastic unit for a long weekend of matchplay, even when they come from the same country. So the idea of such a disparate group as the Rest of the World gelling is hard to envisage.

Yet somehow it seems to happen. There is a theory that nothing is as unifying to a contrived team as the thought of beating the mighty US. I am not sure how valid this argument is, but having been around top golfers at varying stages of their playing weeks, I do know that there is one consistent trait: they do not like to lose, even in a practice-round side bet.

So despite the Presidents Cup being effectively a non-earning week for the pros, where they are given a certain amount of money to donate to their chosen charity, it is usually not much of a talking point before the event. But come curtain call there is no doubt the players from both sides desperately want to win their individual matches.

In fact, the competition starts in the team rooms. Last time in Washington, each team cabin had a table-tennis table on which players began their warm-up routines by trying to beat the best opponent presented by players and caddies. So despite these "silly season" events being somewhat contrived, do not question the desire of the participants to win.

The Seve Trophy, which has somehow established itself as a permanent alternate-yearly fixture on the European Tour, kicks off this week at the Heritage Club outside Portlaoise. Despite some difficulties with the relatively new club over the years, this is a great opportunity to get what is a very fine golf course, designed by the creative and meticulous Jeff Howes, on the map.

It is, of course, no surprise that the Heritage was chosen as this year's venue, given Seve's attachment to the club. I believe it will be a deserving venue no matter what the weather may bring. Given the abundance of new, quality courses in the country in the past decade, it is hard for one to raise its head above the rest I would imagine the players will give the course the credit it deserves.

The Presidents Cup has had its ambassadorial heads in Jack Nicklaus and Gary Player as non-playing captains since its inception. The Seve Trophy has had Seve Ballesteros at the helm of the European team, and until now Monty has led the British and Irish team.

There is a new departure this year as Nick Faldo begins his foray into leadership. I assume this is to give him a test run ahead of his Ryder Cup-captaining debut in America next year. As thorough as Faldo is, I am sure he was keen to test his steering skills early. Having observed the formidable golf of Faldo in his prime, I would have said he would never have made a good captain. His single-mindedness and isolationist attitude in his heyday, when he moved among us as a muted giant letting his clubs speak loudest, suggested that he was not a communicator.

What a difference a decade makes. Nick has turned into an expert communicator in his golf commentary, which is witty and insightful and gives his viewers a sense of how his brilliant golfing brain worked when he performed at his best. Those of us inside the ropes were always aware of his dry, if diffident, wit on the course.

In not choosing an Irishman as a wild-card for this year's team the captain has already shown that performance and not politics is what motivates his selection procedure. Most of us thought Paul McGinley, despite his relative lack of form, would get the captain's nod for obvious reasons, especially given Padraig had decided not to play.

This was not the case with the RoW team. Captain Player went for the political choice in the home favourite Canadian Mike Weir. Given that these are largely "fun" events, there is a strong argument from a local-fan perspective of trying to get a homeboy on the team. I wonder will our fans' allegiance be more European than British given the Irish have been temporarily dropped from this year's billing.

It is a great opportunity to watch the rare form of team matchplay with some of the European Tour's finest competing on a quality course and with two legends of European golf applying their acumen and statesmanship to leadership.

My money is on Faldo.

Winter breaks just get better

OCTOBER 23: The scene at the Victoria Golf Club on the Algarve in southern Portugal was one the Portuguese tourist board would have hoped for in mid-October.

I stood on the verdant putting green last Wednesday before the pro-am and looked back up towards the purple bougainvillea breaking the monotony of the brilliant white-washed walls beneath the clubhouse and the azure blue sky beyond and realised this was not going to be such a bad office to work in for the week.

Caddying is at its best when you do so in almost perfect weather conditions. Not only is it a pleasant working environment but, more importantly, the golf bag is as light as its bulky frame permits. For some unknown reason, the marginal weight of an umbrella and a couple of sets of waterproofs are way heavier than their actual weight suggests.

So when the daily forecasts last week predicted 26 degrees with a light southerly wind and no rain, the bag was emptied of excess equipment and the locker was packed to capacity.

With some 30 courses dotted along the Algarve it is very much golf central for a large proportion of the visitors to this region for the idyllic south European autumn.

With almost half the courses concentrated in the area just west of Faro it is no surprise you are surrounded by fourballs in the evening time as well as during the day. It is obviously a traditional trip for a lot of the golf tourists that I encountered.

Through a golfing friend at home I was put in touch with the owner of the Fairways restaurant, which is situated on the marina at Vilamoura beside the 19th Hole bar, to mention a few of the golf-related evening hang outs.

I was met at the airport by my "tour guide" and "nutritionist" for the week and whisked away at full Portuguese driving speed to the Fairways.

In true caddie style I made my entrance via the back door and through the kitchen with my suitcase.

There are some of us who live by the rule of if you find somewhere good to eat early in the week you should stick with it. So I dined there most nights using the front door the rest of week.

The charming owner, Julio, had an affinity with golfers in general and caddies in particular. He grew up caddying and caddied for Seve Ballesteros' uncle Ramon Sota in the Portuguese Open back in 1961.

He had caddied in a golf club outside Lisbon as a young lad and he explained to us how that club had such a high proportion of hole-in-ones relative to any other club in the world.

It was a rule that, if a member had the fortune to make a hole-in-one, the caddies would benefit by being given a bonus and a big drink.

The green-staff were in cahoots with the caddies, whereby, if a ball looked like it was going close to the hole on the blind par three, a timely kick in the direction of the flag would be followed by a load roar from the green, back slapping up on the tee, and generous tipping at the end of the round, as yet another hole-in-one was celebrated.

With the advent of the electric cart, the abundance of hole-in-ones has been greatly reduced in the Lisbon area.

Julio has changed careers and now is very good at making his guests feel welcome. It seems he has plenty of Irish regulars to whom he is an understanding host.

Last Friday his restaurant was taken over by a large group of Irish golfers who brought their own after-dinner entertainment to the restaurant, in the form of a banjo and fiddle.

> "Those veterans amongst us remember when many caddies used to winter in the Costa del Sol where there were enough amateurs with used bank notes to keep them going for the off-season."

Of course the golfing year is technically drawing to a close. It is the time of year where both players and caddies are thinking about their off-time and how they will spend it.

Those veterans amongst us remember when many caddies used to winter in the Costa del Sol where there were enough amateurs with used bank notes to keep them going for the off-season. It seemed like a pretty alternative way to spend the winter back then. Some progressive caddies even ventured further west to the emerging golf scene on the Algarve. With next year's schedule having been released this week it gives us a chance to plan our winters. They do not include the south of Spain for the modern global caddie.

With 14 events on the "European" Tour to be staged in Asia next year there is a strong case for those of us with a yen for somewhere a little more exotic to while away the winter months by basing ourselves in south east Asia; Thailand would appear to be the modern caddies destination for off-season hibernation.

Meanwhile, as a foretaste to the end of season, a week of mixing work with a reasonable amount of pleasure on the Algarve is a perfect way to prepare for real down-time.

How I easily won the 'Eejit of the Year' award

NOVEMBER 13: Now I am in Hong Kong, which has been associated with mainland China for a decade, I feel already very familiar with my surroundings. You see I was here just last week. It was an impromptu side trip on my journey to Shanghai, which is of course very much at the heart of the Republic of China.

It is a rare occurrence but I left Shanghai twice in the one week and arrived in Hong Kong a couple of times too. Having had a few free weeks before the HSBC Champions event I decided to leave for Shanghai a day early in order to acclimatise. The trouble was that I left Dublin on Sunday and didn't arrive at my ultimate destination till Tuesday.

I landed in Pudong International airport on the east side of the sprawling metropolis feeling groggy, wobbly and disoriented. On the trip I had watched movies I had already forgotten I had watched, dozed in and out of restless sleep as you do on these long trips and found myself in a state of semi-consciousness shuffling with the rest of the BA passengers toward immigration.

As I stood in line I was planning my day ahead based upon the best activities in which to partake, so as to avoid falling asleep and hopefully combat the jet-lag that overcomes you with an eight-hour time change: check in, unpack, go to the golf course, get a yardage book and walk the course, followed by a light work-out in the gym and dinner, all of which should take me up to bedtime.

I walked forward having been pulled out of my day-dream by the voice of the immigration officer. Distinguishing facial features among Westerners must be as difficult for the Chinese as it is for Westerners when it comes to the Chinese.

With the squinting and head jerking ritual the official was carrying out, it seemed he was finding it hard to reconcile my passport photo of a year ago with how I appeared to him after a long flight from Europe.

My identity was to be the least of my problems, I soon realised. Another officer was beckoned, there was a rapid exchange of dialogue in the vernacular, which I took to amount to, "Mr Byrne, your papers are not in order. Follow me."

I was to be assigned my own personal immigration officer for the next three hours. He was like my shadow and got me to the top of every queue I could possibly have stood in during my "status" ordeal.

As I got to the next immigration office in Pudong airport it became clear my visa had expired. As someone without much of an eye for bureaucratic detail I did not think too much of the finer print on my expired visa and assumed it would be easily rectified.

An hour later, in another immigration bureau, having signed an official form, I fathomed through an airline representative that my easiest option in this unfortunate case would be to make the two-and-a-half-hour flight south to Hong Kong and obtain the necessary papers there.

"Oh dear," or words to that effect, I recall uttering to myself as my plans for staying awake for my first day in north-east Asia had been abruptly disrupted.

Despite Shanghai and Hong Kong being effectively in the same country, it is easy to forget the system under which China still conveniently operates. There are no exceptions, so I could have flown back on the plane I flew out on from London or taken the shuttle down the road, relatively, to Hong Kong.

Despite the inquisitive looks from fellow passengers, especially Westerners, having your own immigration officer shadowing you through the airport is liberating on the one hand because you glide though each queue without delay. On the other hand you begin to feel uncomfortably like a fugitive when you have to ask permission to use the toilet and can hear your "escort" pacing patiently in the background as you use it.

Thankfully the travel services in Hong Kong are well practised in dealing with undocumented immigrants like me. Despite my having to wait overnight, the process of obtaining a visa was painless, though not free. Which made me wonder why I had to go through the inconvenience in the first place.

I arrived back to Shanghai with my papers in order and checked into my hotel a day and a half later than anticipated.

Word spreads quicker than an epidemic on the golf tour. I was greeted with the quips and jibes that I had expected from my colleagues: "Illegal immigrant! Refugee!"

I could not have picked a worse event for which to be disorganised. HSBC held the second annual caddie awards this year with a light-hearted roll of honour for us world porters.

There were eight categories. seven in jest. The "caddie of the year" award was of course more serious. Unfortunately for me the first award went to the most "prepared" caddie for the Champions event in Shanghai. I was naturally the favourite for this ignominious award and the secret ballot confirmed my suspicion. "Eejit of the Year" was awarded to me last Friday night.

Three Irish caddies were recognised that night. Dave McNeilly received the "most dedicated caddie" title and accepted it with a flowery speech in which he compared the European Tour to a form of cookery in which the various parties involved in the make-up of an event are the ingredients. Analysts are still trying to make sense of his speech.

Ronan Flood received the "caddie of the year" award as Padraig Harrington's bagman.

Meanwhile, my knowledge of the Shanghai-Hong Kong route and its relationship with the mainland is building almost as quickly as my new-found respect for having my papers in order.

Confusing but not because of the vino

DECEMBER 18: The last event of the year or the sixth event of the year, I am not too sure which. It is the confusing time of the year on the European tour when you don't really know if you are at the end of it or just the beginning. The calendar year is a mere guide to where you stand in the Order Of Merit with Christmas an interruption to the golf.

We congregated in the Western Cape last week to compete for the second oldest national championship in golf. It was played on one of the newest courses in the country, the Pearl Valley GC, situated on the vine lands outside Paarl about an hour north east of Cape Town. It is in the heart of the Cape wine lands and is set against the stunning backdrop of the Drakenstein Mountains.

Ernie Els has his winery about 25 minutes away just outside Stellenbosch. David Frost grows his vines close by in Paarl and my own boss, Retief Goosen, has his vineyard four hours up the coast near George. With vines stretching around the foothills of the surrounding mountains there was no mistaking the theme of the week.

Not that we should assume that everyone has the luxury of a great golfing talent and a refined pallet with which to create a profitable hobby. Lest we forget the reality that lies beyond the luxurious nature of the course (and modern country club living worldwide) and the streamlined second homes that line the manicured fairways, not everyone has a links view on the Cape.

There are a number of local South African caddies that show up each year in the hope of securing work. Caddying for one of the more recognisable players there is a good chance you will have at least two self-appointed caddies to carry your bag. I was wondering why the local caddies were so enthusiastic with their welcomes earlier in the week. As I took off to the range on Tuesday I realised that I had two guys on my shoulder.

If I went to get a bottle of water, a bottle of water was handed to me by both. If I went to bin the empty bottle, it was snatched from me. I had to sort out the employment arrangements for the week and through my best attempts at diplomacy, I ended up with just one caddie shadowing me.

It is tradition on the Sunshine Tour, and something that takes the shine off the gleaming way of life for those living on the complex, when you see others battling to survive. There was a protest scheduled for Friday last by the local caddies which was just about averted.

This seems to be a common occurrence on a tour that is not flush with funds unless staging one of their co-sanctioned events with the European Tour. Despite the fact that we are permitted in the locker-room and in most clubhouses on the European Tour, we aren't when we come to South Africa.

Caddies are strictly not allowed in to the clubhouse at any event on the Sunshine Tour. For those of us who have fought a long battle to ensure some dignity in our daily duties in Europe, this is a big setback. There are seemingly two tiers of caddies in South Africa; those who have caddied in Europe and around the world and those who have not had to use their passports. The guys who loop in Europe needed a helping hand when they first left home and now are self-sufficient. It would be great if their experience rubbed off on their colleagues who have not travelled.

The weather delay last Sunday sorted out my dilemma over the end or beginning of the year. The freak rain delay in a month where the locals say it never rains on the Cape meant that some of us teeing off later in the final round were going to miss our flights back home. This could only happen at the end of a very long year.

BAGMAN 2
2008
ON TOUR

"So Darren went out in the final round and flushed his ball and flashed at his putts. He missed everything all day long until it came to the unlikely 35 footer heading towards the final hole in overdrive which somehow went in the hole to give the almost sheepish looking Northern Irishman his first significant victory for five years and his 16th in his professional career."

Page 200

Darren Clarke celebrating after his 35 footer rattled into the back of the hole to win the BMW Asian Open at the Tomson Shanghai Pudong Golf Club.

Gunslinger really has that big screen quality

FEBRUARY 26: Most of you will recall a defining moment in your golfing career when you surpassed yourself. When you went beyond what you thought you were capable of, which culminated in you beating your opponent, your own record or simply hitting a shot you never thought you could possibly hit.

Those who are not fortunate enough to have had this experience, be patient; one day it may happen. It will reaffirm why you bother going back out to play the game.

There is a golfer in America who does this virtually every time he plays. If he doesn't it is the exception, not the rule. Top golfers consistently make good decisions and tend to perform no matter what hardships are thrown at them, in good times and bad. They make the right decisions, they do the right thing, they make it happen.

We were in the spectacular and vast state of Arizona last week for the Accenture WGC Matchplay Championship. The scenery beyond the traditional stands, draped in advertising framing the holes, was like the landscape from *The Good, the Bad and the Ugly*. If you shut your eyes you could hear the menacing whistling in the background.

Matchplay is an unusual form of golf for the modern professional who is almost mechanically prepared for four-round strokeplay golf. It is like a lottery trying to pick winners over 18 holes head-to-head, where the top seeds play against the lesser seeds; Tiger Woods played the 64th-seeded player JB Holmes, number two played the 63rd ranked golfer, and so on.

The question "how?" sprung to my mind as I watched incredulously as Tiger Woods dug himself yet again out of the depths of a desert canyon that for most mortals was too steep to escape. Three down with five to play is never a great position to be in. The crowd thinned over the closing holes as they sensed a vanquished Woods. To those who don't know any better he may have been down. He didn't think he was out, though. He never does.

JB Holmes played excellent golf but he didn't "get it done", as they would say in the vernacular over here. We are frequently told about what separates the great from the good; quality of ball striking, length, sand play, chipping, putting, plane of the golf swing (if you ask a swing coach). The fact is at the level that was represented at Dove Mountain last week, virtually all the players possess the above mentioned attributes. What really separates them is the intangible, unquantifiable, almost supernatural qualities that only Harrison Ford or Sylvester Stallone possess in the fantasy world of the big screen.

We seem to have our own fantasy man on tour in the shape of the greatest golfer that ever lived. (Apologies to those who still cling to nostalgic memory of Jack or Arnie as the greatest; Tiger is only half-way there and already he has accomplished so much.)

To indicate the great man's humility, a journalist with a good relationship with Tiger whispered "lucky" to him as he made his way to the press room. To which he responded with a big grin on his face, "I know".

Sitting in the caddie shack having been beaten in the first round by the accomplished young Argentine Andres Romero, and watching Woods' escapade amongst colleagues who live in the real world of professional golf, was sobering.

To experience their sense of expectation as they looked at Tiger crawl back to victory in a miraculous fashion is an indication of just how even my hardened fellow bagmen expect Tiger to succeed – even from the most difficult of positions.

Despite Tiger's intimacy with the desert during the week of matchplay, in territory where the snakes play amongst the sagebrush and the saguaro cacti, he prevailed.

Was it karma, talent, good fortune, the position of the moon, timing or destiny? I don't know and I don't think anyone else does, no matter how much they might try to persuade you with impressive rhetoric that they do.

With putts of 14, 17, 22 and 36 feet from the 14th culminating in three consecutive birdies and an eagle, the world's best golfer went from three-down to one-up and his unfortunate opponent didn't get the option to make a mistake in the denouement to the first round.

You can ask any expert from psychologists to coaches to make sense of what happened in the desert on Wednesday of last week, and not one of them will convince me that it is anything other than the unquantifiable nature of humanity – to look at a desperate situation and relish the thought of escaping from it, or shudder at the prospect of the challenge and capitulate.

A friend of mine once asked Tiger about his ideal round of golf. How would it go? He had asked other top players the same question and got a fairly standard reply about good shots and birdie putts amounting to a 62.

With Tiger his vision was dramatically different. He would hit long drives and hole his approach shots. If it was remotely *possible*, he would consider it *probable*. He is an exceptionally talented dreamer whose dreams are realised more often than not and always at the most opportune moment. Dreams have always been open to interpretation.

What I am saying is that Tiger would have prospered in the desert with nothing but a bag full of rattlesnakes and a state full of saguaro. How? Well I am going to ask all the experts I know this week to explain it and I am not antici-pating any of them to have a feasible answer other than "Tiger".

Dodging the wildlife and the dodgy nightlife

MARCH 4: West Palm Beach in southeast Florida is a region of America where you are most likely to encounter a rather dense population of high-waistband, flared pants, 1970s bouffant-style hairdos, big old roly-poly Cadillacs and old-timers with leathery skin ravaged by decades under the gruelling, tropical sun.

We were back on the east coast last week for the start of the Florida swing of the PGA Tour. The PGA National golf club hosted the 2008 Honda Classic, and as is usual in these older-style country clubs the starters on the first and 10th tees were of the Cadillac and high-waistband variety. If the player has a tricky name or residence to pronounce they will often sound out the caddie for advice on the syllables to accentuate.

Last week I had the most unusual request – in all my time looping – from a starter. I was asked, in the most polite fashion, to shoo with my hand only and not with a club, any of the birds that might encroach upon our space near the greens.

With an abundance of lakes and ponds, the course is a natural habitat for an array of birds, and despite being well accustomed to club-wielding humans tramping around their neighbourhood, they are understandably unversed in golf etiquette.

> "The breeze did not, however, help the hapless caddie of Ben Crane on the same hole. He had set Ben's bag down on a slope beside the green but leading toward the water. When he looked around the bag had managed to lose its footing and slide down the slope and into the drink."

It would obviously be a little unsettling for bird-loving viewers to observe caddies lashing out at tame cormorants or egrets as they got a little too close to their players' balls, hence the first-tee announcement.

The trick to getting your ball around the Nicklaus-redesigned water-lined course, was to avoid those wild-life habitats. On the 11th tee last Friday a blue heron glided across the flight path of the tee shot of our playing partner, Robert Allenby, and barely rose high enough to avoid what had looked like a mid-air collision that would have resulted in disaster for both parties, if fatal only to one of them.

The sixth hole ran parallel to a waterway that looked and smelt like an aviary; it had herons, egrets, cormorants, pelicans and flamingos perched all over the foliage which was burgeoning out of the wetlands.

The wind was heavy with the odour of birdlife. The only advantage of the same fetid wind for a golfer was that it blew your ball away from the water on what was one of the toughest holes on the course.

The breeze did not, however, help Ben Crane's hapless caddie on the same hole. He had set Ben's bag down on a slope beside the green leading toward the water. When he looked around the bag had managed to come adrift and tipped into the drink.

We have had some stories of colleagues accidentally dropping individual clubs into hazards – but never the whole set.

Thanks to its mild weather, Florida is a popular winter golf destination.

There tends to be plenty of work for caddies who loop for amateurs. Many of them try the old-fashioned way of "getting a bag" in the car-park of the professional tournament venue. It is not uncommon to see 10 or more old time cads with their faded visors and threadbare towels lining up on the chance of a loose bag.

The amateurs who play in the pro-am on Wednesday must take a caddie with them; the rules here forbid electric carts.

As we took off down the first last week, I realised one of the caddies with us had won two majors in the late 1990s with Mark O'Meara, and now finds himself back in the local scene having reached the pinnacle of the professional game in the not-too-distant past.

When you are not familiar with an area it is easy to get stuck in a hotel that you really do not want to be stuck in for a night, let alone a week. I had never been to the Palm Beach area before, and had assumed that the lodging recommended to me, given its proximity to the exclusive golf course, was situated in a reasonable neighbourhood.

The price was three-star, but the stars soon became clouded over in a murky scene of dubious night-time activities.

As I left for an early tee time I was panhandled on my way to the car. When I inquired about the hotel some locals advised me it was not far from the crack neighbourhood. Indeed, the night-time goings-on seemed distinctly shady.

I survived the ordeal, and it took those of us caddies who stuck it out for the week in the no-star hotel, back to our roots of looping on a shoestring when such frugal accommodation was the norm.

Next time I am in the neighbourhood I think I will try to move closer to the high-waistband crew instead of the high-wasters district I inadvertently found myself in last week.

Weather monitor a key on pro tour

MARCH 11: We had an impromptu meeting last Friday evening, in a cafe just south of the Copperhead course at the Innisbrook golf resort in the Tampa Bay region of Florida.

A thunderstorm loomed over the state for much of the afternoon and it had been the topic of conversation all day. What time we were going to be hauled off the course?

In the modern era of caddying, much like everyone else, we all have instant access to information and in our business the weather is a relevant talking point and not just a convenient introduction to conversation.

Darkness had descended on the golf course by mid-afternoon. It was dull enough to warrant the suspension of play in cricket, but given the forecast, the golfers were only too happy to squint their way along the fairways.

Some of us caddies met quite by chance, gathered around a table, and started to think out loud about the half rounds we had just completed in extremely difficult windy conditions. The wind was such that as the ball was on its journey towards the green you would see a look of angst and hope on the bagman's face until the ball came safely to rest in the vicinity of the green.

It had been a balmy and blustery day with a south wind blasting the course.

The objective for those of us who had teed off on the back nine first, was at least to get through the par-five first hole before play was suspended.

The wind was due to change to the north on Saturday which meant that you wouldn't reach the green in two shots. Psychologically it was a one-shot advantage.

We blew the froth off our coffees and engaged in the sort of post-game analysis that, in all my years of caddying, I have rarely experienced.

"How difficult was it out there? I mean, you couldn't tell if the ball was going to come up 20 yards long or 20 yards short of its target," one of my colleagues said.

In this era of lasers, altimeters and compasses it didn't say much for our levels of accuracy if we were guessing within 40 yards.

Another said: "I drove up to the course this morning and could barely keep the car on the road. What chance have the golfers of keeping the ball on the fairway?"

An elderly couple came in and engaged in conversation as only Americans would; uninvited and without encouragement. The couple had been working as volunteers at the tournament and were golf enthusiasts. We explained what we did and who we worked for.

We had come off the course standing at level par. The gentleman was certain that my man would make the cut: "After all he is a two-times US Open champion, of course he will make the cut."

How far from reality can avid amateur golfers be at times, we wondered as the two battled out to their car through a lighter moment of the deluge.

It really doesn't matter what you have done in the past – as a golfer you need to continuously prove yourself by bringing in the scores. The young modern professional may well be respectful but rarely nostalgic.

We missed the cut.

"My guy's got the wrong set-up in his bag for this wind," another of the coffee fourball continued.

"He's got a rescue club in the bag and he can't hit it into the strong wind. He needs a three iron instead but it's impossible to tell him. It cost us two shots a day."

The caddie who had trouble keeping his car on the road continued: "My guy hasn't made a cut all year and as he came out of the locker room this morning I could sense he was a different person, I could tell that he was going to play well."

His player went on to make the cut and finished the tournament in the top ten.

Even the law of averages applies to Tiger Woods

MARCH 25: The dark clouds built up to the west of the Doral Country Club, Miami, Florida, last Thursday evening, and the caddies to the top players in the world started to delve deep into their golf bags in search of the rain cover, anticipating a deluge.

The conversation in our little three-ball of relative minnows in today's golfing world of Jeev Milka Singh, Seán O'Hair and my man, Retief Goosen, was about when it was going to rain. Were we going to make it back to the clubhouse dry?

I can safely assume there were similar conversations going on in other low-key threeballs on the Blue Monster course as it is known in the region. There is a conspiracy theory on tour that if there are any breaks to be had during a day's golfing then you had better be around the invincible Tiger Woods, because if there is any good luck going then he is going to get it, they say.

As Tiger Woods was walking off the 18th green at about 5.25pm last Thursday, the heavens opened over the Miami area. Our group was huddling under umbrellas on the 16th green as Tiger was signing his card in the dry, scorers room. I was beginning to believe the theorists as the rain seeped through my trainers and trickled down the back of my neck. With the humidity and temperature still high, it is too uncomfortable to wear rain gear even in a deluge in this climate.

I remember back in the days when Tiger was in a relative slump and we were trying to figure out what the cut was going to be in the Masters. Tiger was on the cut number and as he finished there was a unanimous agreement in the caddie shack that the cut would drop to Tiger's score. Naturally it did.

Luck plays a big part in golf, as in most sports. The idea of playing four-round professional events is that hopefully the vagaries will balance out for all players. You don't get lucky in golf for four rounds in a row, that is for sure. We have all hit putts and chips at the wrong pace and somehow they have ended up in the hole. We recognise this as good luck just as we whinge and moan about ending up in a bad lie in a bunker or the ball defying physics of bouncing right off a left-sloping hump.

I am beginning to believe the conspiracy theorists who believe that Tiger always gets the right side of the draw or the best lies in the rough. Of course it's only a light-hearted theory, as we are all prone to remember the bad and let the good slip by unannounced. This is where the mind mechanics come into force.

Tiger was on a quest for eight events won in a row. For any one player to dominate in a game such as golf where you play the field is outstanding. But just as the mood gripped in favour of Tiger winning his seventh event on the trot in Bay Hill last week, the odds of continuing to hole putts of reasonable length at the crucial denouement of a tournament seem to have lengthened.

Whether the experts tell us it is a technical issue or not, there is of course an element of chance when it comes to holing putts over 15 feet in length. It is highly unlikely that you are going to continue do so repetitively even if you are Tiger Woods.

The mood in Doral was that Tiger's phenomenal streak is coming to an end.

This does not mean failure for the "chosen one". The fact that he has won seven in a row is exceptional and it is not reasonable of even the most expectant fan to expect such form to continue.

So we all lingered in Doral on Sunday as thunder clouds surrounded us, threatened to burst, and then decided to move on. We were on and off the golf course five times and still we did not complete the final round.

For a player who was nervous then there is no doubt that the final Monday finish would have calmed them considerably. It was more relaxed than a casual Monday practice round, there were virtually no spectators as we teed off.

The Tiger streak ground to a halt yesterday on an understated finish to the CA World Golf event. There was a sense around the caddie shack and the locker-room that Tiger could not maintain his incredible run.

In fact even the sports editorial of this newspaper sensed the end of the Woods rampage. Not that he played any different, or the field played any outstanding golf in the final round, the run just ran its course like most things do in life.

Even the law of averages applies to Mr Woods. His consecutive wins have been enthralling to experience and of course none of us would be surprised if he got on the right side of the draw at Augusta in a couple of weeks' time and started another winning streak.

TV moguls have too great a say

APRIL 1: I remember the days when you went out in a tournament and you were pretty certain of the endgame; shoot as low as you could and hope that someone didn't outshoot you. Of course there were exceptional events when the weather was so bad that a round had to be cancelled and a player was deemed the winner after three rounds.

Whatever happened the players always knew what the circumstances were before they went out to play. I recall going to the US in the early 90s and marvelling at how decisive they were at making decisions when it came to inclement weather. Rarely were you kept hanging around the golf course all day.

There seems to be a new dynamic on tour in the US when it comes to dealing with bad weather. There is not a lot we can do about the weather in the short term but we really need to reconsider our lifestyles when it comes to the bigger climatic picture. Indeed, it is no different for golf which of course is at the behest of mother nature.

With an abundance of meteorologists heavily armed with Doppler radars and other sophisticated weather readers on hand at a golf tournament today somebody calling the shots is not listening to their advice or is being guided by a more influential force.

The PGA Tour is driven largely by its popularity on television, especially when the world's number one is in the event. Of course last year saw the advent of the FedEx Cup and a brand new departure for the US Tour in a conscious effort to maintain its television ratings. Naturally when the main man doesn't play the punters use the remote control more often.

There is a strong suspicion on the tour's corridors that the decision two Sundays ago in Miami, resulting in a large part of the field sitting back in their hotel rooms for the best part of the day, having completed the third round earlier that morning, was driven by the demands of the TV producers. Most of the players seemed to favour continuing on with the same pairing that they started with that morning. This, they felt, would give them a far greater chance of finding a winner by Sunday night instead of late Monday morning.

On hindsight, and having monitored the available weather reports, this would have been the most convenient move for all concerned. Perhaps the TV moguls were betting on having Tiger in the last group, just in case he looked out of place playing in any grouping earlier than that.

There was a general consensus that the Monday finish could have been avoided, a finish that did no favours to those of us who were committed to the Tavistock Cup which was held in Orlando on the Monday and Tuesday.

Having hung around all day on Sunday, Monday was a contrast where the only delay was waiting for the rotor blades to slow down to avoid decapitation by the helicopters laid on to take us from the private planes, on which they had flown us all up on from Miami, in order to make our tee times at the Isleworth club that afternoon.

After our whirlwind trip to Orlando where the hosts, Isleworth, beat the visiting team, Lake Nona, in the world's most exclusive club competition myself and Retief made our way last Tuesday night to the Big Easy, New Orleans for the Zurich Classic. It was a golf marathon that we had got involved with, and the previous Sunday's delay was beginning to take its toll.

Retief rallied on the back nine on Friday to make the cut on the mark. It was a cut with 81 players qualifying to play at the weekend. There is a new rule on the PGA Tour which comes into effect when more than 78 players make the Friday cut. It means that there is another cut on Saturday back to 70 players. As if the professional golf existence isn't precarious enough already, the double cut has thrown another element of uncertainty into the mix.

Retief shot two over on Saturday and having hung around for an hour after play to try to gauge if we would make the Saturday cut or not, the odds suggested that we would be fairly safe in heading home that afternoon. One of the advantages of your player having his own plane means that you can make a quick getaway if needed. We were on the way back to Orlando at four in the afternoon when a storm hit the New Orleans area. Play was suspended at the tournament. 1With the suspension of play it meant that they could not enforce the third-round cut. As I was walking towards the gate to catch my flight back to Europe I got a phone call from Retief telling me that he was heading back to New Orleans to play the fourth round at 7.48 the next morning.

He was as baffled as I was with the convoluted new weekend system that had been devised by the tour. He wasn't the only player who had to turn back to New Orleans last Saturday evening. Fortunately for me Retief understood that I could not retrace my steps so he drafted his pilot in as my replacement.

I hope he is not expecting the same favour if the pilot is indisposed in the future.

Pushing too many buttons can damage your game

APRIL 8: One of the greatest privileges of an advanced civilisation is the freedom of choice. Our own progressive little plot in Ireland has witnessed the offer of an abundance of choices from medical to material in recent times. Choice is no less abundant on the golf tours of the world. There are numerous opportunities to change technique, equipment and teachers, all of which is an indication of how far the modern golfer has come down the technical road in the last decade.

From my weekly observations in tournaments worldwide, and in particular in America, it has become increasingly clear how much influence the scientists have over a game that is a true art. It makes me wonder just what is the ultimate objective in playing the game of golf; bringing in a score or perfecting a technique?

There is a simple answer to this and for a change I will use Tiger Woods as a shining example of what a player should do (in order to win the tournament) during a competitive week. One word – compete.

There is an old-fashioned theory which goes back way beyond the arrival of the high-tech driving range: you use what you have brought with you to a golf tournament. It is very difficult, if not impossible, to find a swing by beating balls all day long on the venue driving range. Because if you do find something the chances are that you have exhausted yourself in the process and will not have the resolve or mental awareness left in order to take your form successfully through the back nine on Sunday.

Woods arrives to an event, usually with the 14 clubs he is going to compete with, and puts in a minimal show on the range and consequently a maximised performance on the course. The only time I have seen him engage in lengthy practice sessions, especially during a major, is if he is totally at odds with his swing.

Otherwise the range is for warm-ups and wind-downs only. All his hard graft is done on his weeks away from tournaments. His focus is strictly on the four days of five-hour rounds and beyond that on non-golf-related fitness or relaxation. For those with a strong work ethic the idea of leaving the range when there are buckets of balls waiting to be bashed is anathema. Those with no other distractions start to feel guilty and following the lead of leading ball bashers which creeps into the professional psyche; the thought being, "everyone else is doing it so I had better keep up with them."

I got to the range a couple of weeks back in New Orleans. Beyond the banquet table full of gleaming golf balls from every manufacturer known to golf nuts, and past the coaches presiding over their machine-like pupils diligently thrashing balls down the range, and past the representatives with their bags filled with the latest booty for the aficionados to wile away the day in distraction, lay the most recent addition to our world of techno-toys – the TrackMan.

The TrackMan is a device invented by military scientists in order to track missiles as they fly through the air. As the golf industry expanded, these devices were adopted by the manufacturers in order to assist them with streamlining their ever-changing product range.

The launch monitor basically measures the launch angle, spin rate, club-head speed and smash factor the player gets, among other terribly interesting statistics. There are so many of these machines now on tour driving ranges, that there is confusion as to who owns what. Some players even travel with their own machines.

> "What the scientists, and more importantly the golfers themselves, need to remember is that most players are innately talented and sometimes, particularly during competition, it is enough just to remember that instead of paralysing the talent through analysis."

Of course this scientific approach is relevant to top golfers who are after all on a quest for the elusive edge, the narrow margin between success and mediocrity. But what the machines do not tell or lead the golfer to, is strength and character on the back nine when you need to hit a great shot and hole a putt under the most stressful of conditions.

I forgot to mention the hordes of mind gurus in the long line of support teams that litter the tournament range. This is their job. Naturally they have a range of their own mind games designed to improve the golfer's ability to deal with the stress of competition.

What the scientists, and more importantly the golfers themselves, need to remember is that most players are innately talented and sometimes, particularly during competition, it is enough just to remember that, instead of paralysing the talent through analysis. When good golfers play well they actually become well-oiled and free-flowing machines and not labouring technicians looking for the next button to push.

It is hard to halt the wonderful advances the technologists have made to enhance our lives. But there is a huge danger in science centre-stage over the beautifully skilful and innate art of a wonderful golfer letting his or her natural talent weave in and out of a complex array of birdies and pars en route to a tournament victory. The most sought-after skill is the frequently elusive art of bringing in a score when the launch monitor would have long abandoned you as a failure with your ball striking.

As we warm up for the 73rd US Masters, the golfers get a unique opportunity in the modern game to play uninhibited by the technology-pushing manufacturers, who are not permitted to bring their laboratories inside the hallowed gates of Augusta National. They are banished to the environs of the course. The privilege of a truly advanced society is not just having access to information and technology, but understanding when to discard it and simply trust your talent.

Worth making a song and dance about Amen Corner

APRIL 15: No sooner had the commentator Nick Faldo given the background to why we were looking at Justin Rose perform at such a high level in Augusta, Georgia, on Friday evening during the second round, than doubt and confusion crept into Rose's carefully planned strategy.

Faldo had been explaining how Rose, in order to reach an elite status in world golf, had employed a chef over the festive season to ensure he was getting a balanced diet.

If this doesn't smack of having too much money or a debilitating eye for detail then I don't know what does. The young Englishman proceeded to make a cobblers of the 15th with a triple bogey, followed quickly by a three-putt bogey on the next, something we all could have done on a fast-food diet.

In the Butler Cabin, Gary Player was ranting on about the perils of obesity, the daily consumption of processed food, and an excessive intake of sugar as he suggested he was fitter than most 30-year-olds and was worthy of his 52nd appearance at the Masters next year despite having shot a totally-uncompetitive 18 over par.

There was a strong suggestion from the scores of the old-timers that Augusta really was no country for old men inside the ropes.

The appetite for nostalgia in the haven of central control is insatiable. We read about the past to understand the future but lingering in the past makes it impossible to move into the future. Move over lads and let the competitors compete.

Perhaps you were sheltered from the hourly trip down memory lane in Europe. Over here, watching the Masters' carefully-controlled coverage, there was an hourly nostalgia trip; the weepy music droned and the heroic tales of Arnie, Jack and Gary were repeated ad nauseam. Despite a constant reminder in the local newspaper about the legends of Augusta, they seemed to have a healthy balance of information.

In fact on Thursday last, I fumbled with my *Augusta Chronicle* before my first cup of coffee of the day, thinking that my eyesight had deteriorated badly over-night. It turned out I was looking at the 3-D section which had a full supplement of photos from last year which all looked out of focus until you looked at them through the rose-tinted glasses that were provided by the paper.

The event is trying to move into the future; last year we caddies were provided for the first time with a tour-standard yardage book.

This year a very sophisticated pin sheet was presented to us each day.

There are 3-D newspapers and a website dedicated to the wishes of the contemporary patron in today's Masters. Unfortunately, we still have boiler suits and questionable rules.

The place is a bundle of contradictions; the most sophisticated aeration system under the putting surfaces (the first course in the world to have such a system) and the caddie wears a boiler suit (as far as I am aware, the last course in the world to enforce the wearing of such uncomfortable and demeaning attire).

With the temperatures in the 80s the painter and decorator outfits were particularly uncomfortable earlier in the week.

Golf at Augusta is a game of inches and when things don't turn out as planned you could declare that the inches won. For those experienced Masters campaigners you could say the more trips you have around the place the luckier you get.

I looked at Tiger as he weaved through Amen Corner last Friday evening and despite his wealth of experience and success around Augusta, the look of inten-sity was deeper and much longer than in any other event of equal importance throughout the year.

Such are the demands of the most subtle course in the world. With the devious pin positions even the experienced campaigner will face near impossible two-putt situations where he is putting to a hole while standing at a 90 degree angle to it.

You most definitely would not want to put yourself through this every week, it is way too mentally draining.

The theme at this year's Masters was the 50th anniversary of the coining of the phrase "Amen Corner", which refers to the 11th green, and 12th and 13th holes. Herbert Warren Wind, a celebrated sports writer, wanted to capture the unique atmosphere he experienced at that part of the course. He was a jazz enthusiast and was referencing a song the Chicago band led by Milton Mezzrow recorded called *35th And Calumet*, which had *Shoutin' In That Amen Corner* on the flip side.

The only part of the course isolated from the gallery had been christened in 1958 by Wind. A retired executive from the sports management group IMG has since researched the song and contested that Mezzrow never recorded *Shoutin' in that Amen Corner*.

Regardless of the detail, it is an appropriate name for these sphincter-twitching three holes at Augusta.

I have been a regular visitor to the Masters over the past seven years and the one tradition I really do appreciate is their credentials system.

When you present yourself at the gate on Monday morning in order to gain access to the course they direct you to the credentials office. There, your photo identification awaits you with a photo dating back to the first year you came to the Masters.

You can keep the rest of the old retrospection they indulge in throughout Masters week apart from the old photo identity system which really does make you feel so young.

Far away... fairway... KJ... pay day... runway... g'day

APRIL 22: Those of you who travel long distances on business will be familiar with the feeling of not having any idea where you are when you wake up in strange surroundings and wondering how you got there. A day or two of meetings and you find yourself back at home feeling as if you had been in a virtual dream in some faraway place.

We frequently move like ghosts through a location without knowing a word of the local tongue, whether we are in the north or south of the city and if, indeed, the country we are in is coastal or land-locked. This is the downside of moving around the globe too easily and way too quickly: often there is no sense of location.

Well, last week in South Korea I had an extreme version of this sensation; a 13½-hour direct flight from New York and a 13-hour time change later, I shuffled around my hotel room in Seoul last week as if I had just landed from another world.

My lodgings were effectively a transit hotel in Incheon airport outside Seoul. The staff were in shock that I kept on reappearing each day for breakfast. The golf course was on the other side of the airport, and apart from its location it was inextricably linked to the North East Asian hub south of Seoul.

Some ten years previously there had been a mountain beside some mud-flats. The government decided to blow up the mountain, fill in the mud-flats and build a brand new airport on reclaimed land, while creating the appropriately named Sky 72 public golf complex on what was left of the flattened mountain.

When curious people ask me about my peculiar job I have in the past tried to play down the exotic nature of global looping by saying that most weeks on tour entail airport, golf club and hotel. Well, last week I had all three rolled into one by staying at the airport which was built out of the golf club land which now overlooks it. I couldn't get away from any of my weekly compulsory haunts.

We made the long haul from the exclusivity of the 72nd Masters to Korea for the SK Telecom tournament which in its infancy, is one of the showpieces of the Korean Tour.

There were two star guests at the event; my player, Retief Goosen, and the local hero KJ Choi.

Sky 72 is a four course public golf facility and upon our arrival on Tuesday last, it looked like we had interrupted a ladies' golf outing where the dress code was strictly prim but loud and gaudy. I thought perhaps roles were reversed in this corner of Asia where the women played golf and the men stayed at home and looked after the household.

It must have been an exception as the next day it was back to an all-male affair in the pro-am and the only women I saw on the golf course were caddying.

There is one caddie assigned to three amateurs in the pro-am. Their bags are loaded on to an electric cart, the caddie has a remote control with which she manoeuvres the cart along a magnetic strip on the cart path in order to speed up the procedure of looping for three. I hope the idea does not catch on in the professional game or two out of three of us will be looking for alternative employment.

So much for being at a low-key event. We played a practice round with Choi on

> "They were presidential bodyguards who were experts in martial arts and surreptitious conversation. The martial arts were not required, given that ours was an understated grouping."

Tuesday afternoon, which was the most chaotic nine holes I have ever witnessed at a tournament. There were three movie crews each vying for the best angle of KJ's every shot. On top of countless TV cameras, there was a gaggle of stills photographers, all of them willing to test the limits of just how straight a jet-lagged superstar will hit the ball on a Tuesday afternoon, in their quest for a winning shot.

Both star players were assigned their personal bodyguards. The necessity for security seemed a little excessive. This was certainly the case for Retief who, if it wasn't for the bodyguards and the management representative, would have had nobody following him for our 7am tee time on Friday. They were presidential bodyguards who were experts in martial arts and surreptitious conversation. The martial arts were not required, given that ours was an understated grouping.

During the entire week the two minders never spoke an audible word. Instead they muttered into their miniature mouthpieces and obviously communicated only in such a fashion.

They carried stun-guns as you are not permitted to bear arms in Korea. Their ability to shadow you was unflappable. I tried unsuccessfully to give them the slip a couple of times during the week but each time I returned one of the shadows was standing to attention watching me reappear.

Despite our global desire for homogeneity, there are, thankfully, plenty of cultural traits to remind you are somewhere very different. The driving range was a separate entity, a five-minute trip away. It prided itself on being the largest driving range in the world. If you can imagine an oversized football pitch enclosed by a single story stand then you can picture the Korean range. Everyone hit into the middle of the range.

There was elevator music droning out of speakers set by the practice putting greens. If there was a rules issue the minders got on the phone to a translator in order to explain the situation. Unless a foreigner was on the leaderboard it was difficult to figure out who was leading and who you had to beat when it came to the crunch on the back nine.

KJ won the SK Telecom Open and Retief finished third. The beauty of the proximity of the professional golfers three most visited places at a tournament; airport, hotel and golf course, was we didn't have far to go to escape from the virtual reality of life on a faraway golf tour once our duty was done on Sunday last.

Simply winning or losing is not a random occurrence

MAY 6: There is an often held expectation about how a top golfer should perform each week when he or she tees up in competition. Almost like the major brands we expect a certain quality and performance from names that we normally associate with success.

When Tiger Woods, the ultimate brand in professional golf, only finishes second, those very demanding amongst us scratch their heads and wonder where it all went wrong. The fact that top golfers compete and win on such a regular basis is a phenomenon that I, at close quarters to the action, cannot even comprehend.

There are so many things that can happen on the back nine of a golf tournament that are out of the player's control which make winning even more elusive than it already is. If you seriously contemplate winning it becomes even harder to reach that goal.

When you have been at the very top of the sport and through personal circumstances and a general decline in the level of your golf sees you slide down the greasy pole of success into the relative abyss of average performance, then winning can seem even more intangible than it did that first time before you really knew what failure was.

A couple of weeks ago in the brave new world of modern golf in Shanghai, while a 35-foot putt was travelling at high speed towards the hole on the 18th green at the Tomson Golf Club, the golfing gods decided to exercise their mystical magic once more as Darren Clarke was in search for redemption from the abyss of world golf.

He had played well all week long from tee to green, holed a few putts in the first three rounds, and then missed everything on Sunday as you tend to do when you are a little on edge and when you question if you belong in that position – one in which the rest of the golfing public assume you will languish forever. There have been plenty of great golfers who prematurely ended their careers in the past. They won majors and then disappeared off the face of the golfing world; Bill Rogers, Ian Baker-Finch and David Duval amongst others who have never really fulfilled their potential.

So when the gradual decline occurs it is only the most determined and resilient who will continue to seemingly bash their head against the clubhouse wall in search of former glory.

Darren, as we all know, suffered the torture of watching his wife fight cancer for a couple of seasons. Retief Goosen and I, were drawn to play with him on the Saturday of the PGA Championship at Wentworth a few years back when he came to us on the range about 20 minutes before we were due to tee off, to say he could not play as his wife was about to receive emergency surgery. It is a wonder he could continue to make cuts in events as he did when all this was going on in the background. The ultimate heroic performance came at the Ryder Cup shortly after Heather passed away when Darren not only agreed to play on the team but contributed greatly to the resounding European victory.

I suppose the reality of his new life sunk in after the Ryder Cup distraction and without hitting the ball that badly he lost the art of scoring, simply getting the ball in the hole from tough situations became very difficult for Darren.

He tumbled down the world rankings and his long-time and highly-regarded caddie, Billy Foster, decided, with Darren's consent, to move on. Darren tried out a few different bagmen in the interim and finally settled for another veteran Philip "Wobbly" Morby.

The consensus in China was that given his pursuers going into the final round, Clarke was in a very good position to capture his first win. This is what leading an event is all about, pressure and expectation.

So Darren went out in the final round and flushed his ball and flashed at his putts. He missed everything all day long until it came to the unlikely 35 footer heading towards the final hole in overdrive, which somehow went in the hole to give the almost sheepish looking Northern Irishman his first significant victory for five years and his 16th in his professional career.

You are not supposed to hole those putts, least of all when you have missed the really short ones that you should make. The golfing gods decided it was time for Clarke to rejuvenate himself at 39 years of age, shake off the memory of the hard times and get back where he belongs, in contention.

We flew back to London on Monday last, Darren was sitting close to me and I looked around at him as we sipped our pre-dinner drinks and raised my glass to toast the most elusive victory of his long and successful career.

He looked back at me with that inimitable cheeky grin of his and gave a satis-fied sigh as if the whole ordeal had sunk in and he was finally realising the enormity of it all.

Even as a great golfer and with the realistic or misguided expectation of those who expect great things on tap, there is no telling when that tap will run dry for good. With his usual strong work ethic, diligence and desire for success, culminating in the Chinese victory, Clarke has moved into the outside lane ready to ease back to his rightful position in world golf.

El Nino and grizzled Goydos dazzle even without Tiger

MAY 13: There is something about The Players championship, the fifth major, that is unquantifiable. Of all the past winners there is no one quality you can attribute to any of them. Long, straight, tall short, it doesn't seem to matter what type of professional you are, The Players Stadium Course at Sawgrass is a good golfer's course with no preference for your ability – assuming you have some.

Sunday saw journeyman Paul Goydos, veteran Kenny Perry, the uncloaked prince, Sergio Garcia, and senior player Bernhard Langer all vying for the biggest purse in golf.

There are a number of theories about the diverse make-up of the challengers at the PGA Tour headquarters in Ponte Vedra, Jacksonville.

The primary explanation was the main man, Tiger, was sitting this one out, therefore everyone else had a chance of finishing one spot higher than normal.

> "Sergio had been hanging out back stage in golf for quite some time and if you had followed his progress, and particularly his statistics, you would have noticed he was playing well tee to green but once he reached the short grass, things hadn't been going so well for 'El Nino'."

Despite the fact that this was not really mentioned in the vast new clubhouse at Sawgrass, there was a tacit consensus that Tiger's absence has a huge impact on the tournament.

If you looked into the crowd it was obvious that without the main man the attendance had thinned greatly. The gathering around the showpiece 17th hole had a lot of gaps. It may be an indication of the slow down in the American economy, or simply of the lack of public interest in an event that does not include the world's most dominant player.

There is an undocumented link between Tiger and ticket sales.

The reality of The Players Stadium is it is truly a tough course that tests all aspects of a golfer's skill. The final denouement saw two very different styles of golfer battle out for the title; Goydos the older, grey-haired, sagging-shouldered, un-sexy member of the US Tour and Garcia, the youthful, athletic, slick-backed and sexy star of the same tour.

A good course is playable for all types of golfers and where Garcia hit powering fairway woods off the tees and penetrating shorter irons, Goydos was caressing drivers and following them with soft medium irons. The picture was different but the results were remarkably similar.

I had a rare opportunity to stay around for the end of a golf tournament; normally there is a mass exodus on a Sunday evening, frequently on the back nine, players and caddies are planning to be "anywhere but here", especially if things are not going so well on the course. There were plenty of these cases in the final round.

Most of us on tour travel in selected groups. Last week I was invited to join "team Sergio", which was something different for me. Most weeks we stay in a hotel but given the logistics in Ponte Vedra, renting a house was the best option for those of us one-week visitors.

I was staying with the caddies of Sergio, Camilo Villegas, Miguel Angel Jimenez, Trevor Immelman (not for long as Trevor never made it to the first tee on Thursday due to illness) and Sergio's manager. They have a special camaraderie of all the groups I have been around on tour. It is one for all and all for one in their household.

Short of having a menu for the evening meal slipped under your door by Camilo's caddie who was the chef for the week, every day there is a full schedule in which everyone is included. Sergio and Camilo were staying close by, and came around each evening to exercise, eat and hang out. These guys generate a family atmosphere which makes displaced caddies and golfers feel like we are in some sort of home.

So when you get the chance to actually watch the extensive coverage of the tournament in which you have played, and where you have such an affinity with the challenges of the course that day and one of your "family" for the week, ends up winning, it is something to savour.

Sergio had been hanging out back stage in golf for quite some time and if you had followed his progress, and particularly his statistics, you would have noticed he was playing well tee to green but once he reached the short grass, things weren't been going so well for 'El Niño'.

As usual, Sergio struck the ball purely, which is a great help when the wind is gusting up to 45 miles per hour, with water and alligators surrounding many of the exceptionally small greens. Finally he got his previously unpredictable putter working when it really mattered.

Despite the fact that only a handful of players ended up under par and that it was the opposite spectrum of the modern professional world that played off for The Players championship, much credit must be given to the authorities for the quality and set up of the course.

They were acutely aware of the weather forecasts for strong winds, set the pins sensibly, and kept the greens at a reasonable pace to fairly challenge the players.

Maybe the great golfing public will recognise that watching top golfers chase a coveted title around a spectacular golf course is hugely entertaining even without Tiger Woods. The show that the crown prince of modern golf, Sergio Garcia, put on against the talented and less flamboyant journeyman, but extremely gracious Paul Goydos, is proof that watching players with different types of talent is always entertaining on the appropriate Stadium Course at Sawgrass.

Grass is not always greener on other side

MAY 27: There is an unofficial theory on tour that is widely entertained in the caddie shack: as soon as a long-standing caddie/player relationship ends you should get a substantial bet down on the player to win the very next week.

Mike Kerr had worked for the charismatic Spaniard Miguel-Ángel Jiménez for over four years. They were a successful partnership over those years, and they enjoyed each other's company on the course and on various voyages around the golfing world. If you observed the two together you would almost certainly surmise they were very comfortable in each other's company.

Mike is in his 30s and Miguel in his 40s. Age is more relevant for players than caddies. Despite being a serious contender on the European Tour over a couple of decades, Miguel is at the age when you are not too sure how long this form may last. There is no hard-and-fast rule for the age of decline but in terms of average peak-performance trends, Jiménez has extended his life cycle already.

Despite his typically Spanish attitude to camaraderie and good living, I did in recent years frequently notice Jiménez's distinctive ponytail bouncing about on treadmills as I passed hotel gyms. His relative maturity had not taken away his hunger, and despite maintaining the lifestyle of the bon vivant, he was including gym visits in his daily regime.

Nevertheless, Kerr decided that despite Jiménez's determination to stretch the glory years a little further it was time to move on with a younger player.

Nick Dougherty had just split up with his caddie of many years and became available. Obviously the talented young Englishman's bag would be much sought after. It wasn't a matter of Kerr just making the decision; there were others to be considered too.

The Players Championship at Sawgrass was to be Jiménez's and Kerr's last appearance together. They faded rather than burned out by making the cut but not making an impression on the leaderboard.

So when Kerr went to the locker-room after the final round he had to break the news to the amiable Spaniard of his decision to move on. Kerr had been preparing his resignation speech all week.

He was dreading it, as Jiménez had done nothing wrong and they still had a good relationship. It is always easier to part when the relationship has been fragile.

Kerr told me Jiménez made it very easy for him to break the news of his departure. He was gracious, understanding and encouraging and wished him much success with his new player.

This is in stark contrast to some other player/caddie partings, one or other party learning of the divorce via text messages or curt phone calls from an agent followed by frosty glances on the range or in the locker-room over the following months.

Just as life is a balancing act of swings and roundabouts so is a round of golf.

As unlikely as it was for the winner of the 2008 BMW PGA Championship to hole his 205-yard tee shot on the par-three fifth hole on Sunday, it was even more unlikely he would miss a 15-inch putt on the 15th green, which re-established equilibrium and meant that ultimately he had to endure a two hole play-off with Oliver Wilson.

The dedicated and ever-improving Wilson is a prominent feature on the European Tour leaderboard and is in danger of taking on Padraig Harrington's old mantle of most consistent second-place finisher with more than a handful of runner-up prizes on tour in the past couple of years. But as with Padraig a few years back, it is only a matter of time before Wilson sets the record straight.

Of course, in hindsight, one caddie's slightly hasty decision to change positions is another bagman's benefit. Paul Smith, who has caddied for Jiménez in the past and more recently was with Paul Broadhurst, took timely advantage of Kerr's decision to move on, went back with Miguel and ushered him past the winning post.

With Smith having suffered some health issues in recent years, it was an extremely popular win in the caddie shack. Kerr indeed was one of the first to extend his congratulations to the winning team.

From a personal perspective, the Retief Goosen pendulum was taking a long time to swing back to positive after a string of poor performances over the Burma Road, at Wentworth, in his long association with the European Tour.

Given it is the flagship event on tour, Retief has felt an obligation to support the PGA. It is the most convenient event he could possibly play in given that he lives less than five minutes from the course. But it is a case of horses for courses in professional golf, and this course has never suited this horse.

It was with an element of loyalty and a vow to make this the last effort to try to get to grips with the West course, which until last weekend had always been a good walk spoiled, that Retief returned last week.

The mature foliage and tasteful mansions that adorn the West at Wentworth make for what should be one of the most relaxing walks in golf. But if you don't putt well on poa annua greens then the tranquillity can turn quickly to turmoil.

Having been six over par standing on the 12th tee last Friday and weighed down with a bad history at Wentworth, we knew the odds of Retief making the cut were very high.

With five birdies over the last seven holes, including an eight-foot putt on the last for par, he made the cut on the mark. By the 17th tee on Sunday, standing at seven under par, he looked to have an outside chance to win.

Besides the aptness to this game of the cliché about never giving up, I cannot explain the change in his performance apart from finally hitting a lot of good shots and holing some putts.

Sometimes it not that easy to simply see the shots ahead of you; they tend to blur with images and memories of previous encounters, be they good or bad.

I assume what happened last week was that Retief got his focus just right. And I suppose, given the success of last weekend, we will be back again next year.

Woods fits horses for courses bill

JUNE 10: There is no such thing as a dead cert in sport as all of us sports fans can attest, but in the case of this week's US Open it would be safe to make an exception. Those of us who have been exposed to sport in America over the past couple of months will be inherently aware that the big bay colt Big Brown was such a certainty to win the Belmont Stakes and capture the Triple Crown over the weekend. It was hardly worth the effort of actually running the race.

It was 30 years ago since Affirmed won the Kentucky Derby, the Preakness and the Belmont Stakes which make up the Triple Crown. The racing world was in such denial about the loss last Saturday in New York that the cameras followed the last place finisher Big Brown back to his stable instead of the 38 to 1 outsider Da'Tara back to the winner's enclosure.

Well, the Grand Slam of golf is only possible for one player this year and that is the winner of the first of this year's majors, the Masters champion Trevor Immelman.

A bit like the Belmont Stakes winner, Immelman will not be the first name that springs to mind when predicting a winner at Torrey Pines next Sunday but of course the world's number one golfer will be very much in mind when thinking of the 108th US Open champion.

There is a regular tour event, the Buick Invitational, which is played over both the north and the south course at Torrey Pines in very different conditions in January. Torrey South will be the longest course on which the US national championship will be played at 7,643 yards.

The number one- and number two-ranked players in the world have won respectively, six and three times around this course. Tiger Woods won for the first time when he was a scrawny 15-year-old, the last victory was by eight shots five months ago as a well developed 32-year-old.

So despite his long lay-off from competitive golf since his knee surgery after the Masters in April, you would still fancy Woods, though only 75 per cent fit, over a course where he has dominated in tournament golf.

When it comes to horses for courses, a lame Woods is still likely to be the best runner over four days at this course. This is in contrast to the veteran Kenny Perry who won the Memorial a couple of weeks ago and who has decided not to play this year's US Open. He would have had to pre-qualify and given his record of three previous appearances at Torrey Pines without making the cut, he wisely opted to sit this one out.

It is of course one of the advantages of experience that over decades of beating your head against the wall at a course that clearly does not suit you, empirical evidence suggests that sitting it out is the best option for retaining one's sanity.

The question of exempt players opting not to exercise their right to play in a major is an age-old talking point. Perry clearly has designs at 48-years-of-age to play in the US Ryder Cup team and making that team is more of a realistic priority than winning a US Open on a course where he does not feel like he can realise his golfing potential.

It leads to the question of why professionals play. Is it simply to pay bills or romantically to compete and possibly win a place in golfing history? It's the dreamer versus the realist and given the large portions of realism you need to keep sane playing the constantly challenging and often inexplicable game of golf professionally, I would support Perry's decision.

The expectation, the demands of a challenging course manicured and often taken to the limits of fair play when prepared for the event, and the demands made off course at these big events begin long before Thursday morning, make Majors a fairly daunting task.

Many players engage in lengthy interviews and promotional campaigns weeks before the event thus adding to the premature expectation. Some, like Phil Mickelson, camp out at the venue a week in advance.

Despite the challenge of a very tough course and the need for extra preparation to meet those demands, I can't help but feel it would be better for some players to show up for a practice round on Wednesday morning and see how their game copes without any expectation, thus avoiding all the hassle.

There is nothing left to chance at these majors when it comes to course preparation. For the past seven years Torrey Pines has been readied for this week. The fairways are three-eights inches high, 23 to 33 yards wide; the intermediate rough is 1¾ inches high and six feet wide; the primary rough is 2½ inches high, 15 feet wide; the second cut of primary rough is 3½ inches high; the fairways will be firm and the poa annua greens will run at 13 on the stimpmetre. All is carefully controlled and monitored.

The officials of the Southern California Golf Association rated the course at 79.7. This means Torrey South is one of the most difficult courses in the world. Hopefully it won't humiliate the world's best golfers and repeat the upset that the racing world suffered last weekend as they watched their hero limp over the finish line in last place.

When it comes to horses for courses, a lame Woods is still likely to be the best runner over four days at this course.

Rich talent, wise head – Kaymer is the real deal

JUNE 24: There was a victory of monumental German proportions in Munich last Sunday. The Germans have waited a long time for a home winner of their BMW Championship; it has been two decades since the inaugural event, and even the great Bernhard Langer has never managed to capture the title during a long career as a serious contender in world golf.

The wunderkind Martin Kaymer overcame an abundance of emotional upset and one serious mental error on the 65th hole, where a three-shot lead was wiped out as he splashed his way to a triple-bogey eight. This probably brought him even closer to the patriotic crowd that lined each fairway heavily armed with the national flag and ever eager to encourage their young hero.

Triple bogeys are something with which many German amateurs can identify. Despite the size and affluence of the nation, and a quite sophisticated system for introducing amateurs to the game, golf does not seem to thrive in Germany.

Langer was an exception. He grew up in southern Germany not far from where the physics genius Albert Einstein was born. In golfing terms Langer was himself a genius and despite his relatively good form as he approaches his 51st year it is time for the nation to pin hopes of further success on the 23-year-old from Dusseldorf.

> "Kaymer is the modern version of Langer. He is big but not brash, clever and never cocky. He clearly respects his fellow competitors but is also quietly confident about his own ability."

Kaymer is the modern version of Langer. He is big but not brash, clever and never cocky. He clearly respects his fellow competitors but is also quietly confident about his own ability.

Martin made a low-key if promising entrance to the European Tour. He qualified through the Challenge Tour in 2006 and attracted everyone's attention last year as he appeared frequently on leaderboards, posting some eye-catching low rounds on tough courses.

It wasn't just the scores that impressed; it was also what he said when interviewed – he was modest and made sense.

Although the equipment manufacturers and management groups were schmoozing the bright new star, the Kaymer camp was patient and disciplined in making its choices.

A hundred loopers must have given Martin their number last year when he announced he would be choosing a new tour caddie this year, instead of using his brother and local caddies, as he did last year.

There is no doubt he was a prize catch for a manufacturer, manager and caddie.

Martin has had a strong association with the Swedish caddie, Fanny Sunesson, since his early days on the German amateur team.

Fanny has created a niche for herself as advisor and consultant to several golf groups, the German Golf Association being one of them. In fact the relationship Kaymer has with Sunesson is ground-breaking from a professional golf perspective. It is an indication of the original thinking in the Kaymer camp.

Most new players search out established management groups in their early quest to find their way on tour.

Realistically, an experienced caddie should be well placed to give objective advice to a young player without vested interests determining the strategy. It was quite likely Fanny's advice that led to the patient approach to building a support team for Kaymer.

He chose as his management team the Swedish-based Sportsyard group, who work mainly with European players. They offer a comparatively low-key service with a very personal approach.

Kaymer signed club and ball deals with Titleist. The final piece in the jigsaw, the caddie, was chosen by Sunesson, which of course is very unusual; normally it is the player who recognises a caddie he feels will suit him,

That he let her nominate a caddie for him shows how much Martin trusts Fanny. She chose Justin Grenfell-Hoyle, an Australian who has worked for many players these past 15 years. He was selected for his quiet, conscientious and professional approach, which fits snugly with the Kaymer way.

Despite frequent visits to the leaderboard last year, Kaymer did not register his first Tour victory till earlier this year in the Middle East. He had a strong lead going into the final day at Abu Dhabi and, probably feeling the pressure, scraped his way through the last round to win eventually by a narrow margin.

In Munich last weekend it seemed like Abu Dhabi revisited. Martin took a six-shot lead and the expectation of an entire nation onto the Nord-Eichenried course, which was draped in German flags. Most golfers will admit that pleasing an excited home crowd is among the most difficult challenges in golf.

A six-shot lead sounds insurmountable in professional golf, but of course with the skills of those ahead of you on the course, your six shots can disappear quicker than your ball in a murky greenside pond.

Kaymer's lead did indeed dwindle. With back-pedalling, the crowd's expectations, and the constant worry over his mother, who was ill in hospital, the young German showed Langer-like tenacity and grit to birdie the last hole and set up a play-off with Anders Hansen from Denmark.

His five-iron second shot on the first play-off hole came to rest about 12 feet from the hole and the eagle sealed his second tour victory and left nobody in doubt about what Martin Kaymer is made of.

There is indeed a new order in German professional golf and it comes in the shape of a 23-year-old from Dusseldorf.

Martin Kaymer has catapulted up the world rankings thanks to a combination of great talent and wise planning.

The Germans should keep their national flags to hand because there will be plenty of opportunity in the years ahead to wave them around the fairways of the world in support of a man with a very bright future.

You 'can' because you think you 'can'

JULY 1: "If you think you can or can't you are probably right." This is not a quote from a famous philosopher, as far as I am aware. I heard it from the Yes putter representative during a recent idle moment he had from pushing putters beside a practice green at a tournament in the States. Representatives, like caddies, get a lot of time to contemplate life's complexities.

Then, when one of the other 20 putter pushers is foisting their brand upon an unsuspecting player with a high putting average, we are left watching our 500th divot sailing down the practice range subconsciously admiring the trajectory of its flight and wondering when our player will become as bored as we are and pack it in.

It is actually a wonderfully terse and accurate quote which could apply to most aspects of life, sport, business and relationships. No more so than the ultimate mind game, golf, where opposition is not required to apply pressure on the individual – we are quite capable of exerting pressure on ourselves without any outside influence. In other words we can think we "can't" when we really need to assert that we "can", all in our own little heads.

I suppose I need to qualify this theory a little bit by saying I am referring to the talented ones; those with tour cards in golf, tennis players who are in the final stages of Wimbledon this week, and all those soccer players who competed over the past three weeks in Switzerland and Austria, I am assuming, are all of a similarly high standard in their chosen sports.

Now of course the best exponent of this theory in our game of golf is the guy who is sitting out the rest of the year in an effort to restore equilibrium into the distorted world of men's professional golf – Tiger Woods.

It is important not to get misled into thinking Tiger hits his golf ball any better than half the other guys he is playing against each week because he doesn't. His clubs are as good and pretty similar to the next pro he is competing against as is his ball, his bag, his caddie, his coach and whatever else he has in his competition armoury.

Tiger simply thinks he "can" day and night, in the rough or on the fairway, behind a tree or on the green. "Can't" does not exist for him. The trouble for the rest of us on tour is we all think he "can" too, which hints at the logical conclusion that not everyone "can", so therefore we believe "can't".

There seems to have been more challengers to the ultimate exponent of "can", Tiger Woods, recently. Rocco Mediate will be the last man of the 2008 season to have had this privilege. But which one of us watching the play-off in the US Open actually believed the ageing Mediate would overcome the best golfer in the world no matter how handicapped he was with his sore knee? I hear silence. No matter how many down Tiger was in the play-off, I never thought he "can't".

So where did he get the "can" mentality from and how did he convert all of us to that theory at our own expense? Tiger was born with it but he also was trained to compound it from an early age by his parents.

The rest of us bought into it more gradually as we witnessed him run roughshod through every competition he played in since he came on tour. Belief – unless questioned – is largely what we learn from a young age. We all felt much younger on tour until TW came along.

I was intrigued to listen to the very entertaining punditry on RTÉ over the past few weeks after the European Championship games. I know it makes for good viewing to have a "devil's advocate" on the post-match panel and I am sure they are encouraged by the producer to be argumentative.

So when I was listening to Eamon Dunphy's dismissive attitude towards a technically and talent-wise, inferior German side, I was bemused by his simplistic attitude when it came to the power of belief. I know it from having been in the heat of battle with top golfers that if you drill into them that they are playing well, they might just let their talent take over, let it all happen and realise their high potential – no matter how well the competition is playing.

Of course Liam Brady and John Giles were, in visual disbelief that Dunphy was suggesting Germany were too poor a team to ultimately succeed in the European Championship. In my limited knowledge of soccer I agreed, though what I had seen they did not look like a great side despite being all individually talented. But for someone to deny the power of belief in top sportsmen is to deny the very nature of competition. Again I say this assuming a certain amount of talent in those competing, which of course the Germans have.

It seemed like the rest of Europe wanted Spain to win the final, I got the feeling that it was because they recognised that the Spanish side were the best team of the competition. This didn't matter on Sunday last. Germany, despite their technical inferiority, believed they "can".

They made Spain feel they could, too, when they started the second half. Spain's talent eventually took control.

However, to dismiss the power of "can" at any top level of sport is to deny that Tiger Woods exists and more importantly, that the philosophy hatched out of the humdrum daily duties of us labourers on the golf tour is simply idle banter.

Champion whips up his own storm in the end

JULY 22: So you have just won the Irish PGA Championship for the umpteenth time and instead of going out on the town to celebrate you go to the gym and start whacking an impact bag. Is that normal? No, but then again elite sportspeople are not carved out of the same stone as the rest of us.

There is a dedication and determination about the best performers in their line of business that is difficult to describe. It is a relentless quest for perfection and search for the answers to the winning questions.

Of course winning the Irish PGA by a wide margin is a great accomplishment but for a world player it is a mere aside in the greater scheme of things.

So of course a visit to the gym after a resounding victory is more appropriate with one of the biggest tournaments in the world coming up the following week.

How could Padraig Harrington get better? Seemingly by battering the back of his right hand against an impact bag, that's how.

The trouble is that in looking for the answers to these winning questions you are in danger of pushing yourself over the edge. And when news broke that the reigning British Open champion was in danger of not being able to tee it up to defend the Open title, it was a big story.

Instead of the Irish PGA champion dealing with nothing more than a celebratory hangover he was left in serious doubt, because of that wrist injury, about playing at all last week.

With the main man, Tiger Woods, convalescing at home in Florida the usual sound-bites were going to have to change. What a wonderful alternative: practice-round speculation about the defending champ's right hand.

As caddie to one of those due to play alongside Harrington in the first two rounds, I had to take the attitude that whether he played or not was quite irrelevant – apart from the fact there would be fewer people following the group and likely fewer distractions.

Despite my player, Retief Goosen, carding arguably the best round of the opening day, one over par, having been out in the worst weather, it was obvious that the defending champion was of far more interest to the media.

Padraig had arrived on the first tee last Thursday having warmed up for an hour under the scrutiny of as many people as could gather around the Royal Birkdale driving range. Did he grimace with pain as he hit his longer irons? Was he committed through the ball? Did he look like a man in any condition to be competing in the championship?

I did sneak a look at him as well and it looked like it was business as normal: whack, whack in the inimitable Harrington style, totally committed.

My first intuition Padraig might not be quite up to it came when he arrived on the first tee at about 7.50am and the legendary starter, Ivor Robson, was offered Padraig's left hand to shake; the right hand was being saved for swinging the club.

There is a theory among purists that modern equipment has taken much of the skill out of the game. This may well be true until you get a 30mph wind, accompanied by driving rain, over a primed championship links. Then the theory is cast aside and the old-school battle of wits and skills is what really counts. Can you really hack it under the most arduous conditions?

I recall saying to myself the gruesome weather was only temporary and would probably blow through by the next day. It was a time to give yourself a boost by looking at the bigger picture for a change. Golf is normally best played in the present. Hang in and things will surely change.

Well, the rain stopped as we played the 17th hole; for many parts of the preceding 16 holes it had felt like being on the deck of a trawler in a storm. Our third player, Justin Leonard, played out of turn (he was 50 yards ahead of Padraig when he did so) not out of bad etiquette; he was simply unable to discern anything apart from his own battered world.

Padraig looked defensive and uncommitted in his first five holes and it took him this length of time to trust his right hand and fully release the club at impact.

The first day's weather was so severe it was simply a battle for survival in which competitors sought the refuge of the clubhouse with some sort of presentable score intact.

The hardy members of the crowd without umbrellas were the only gauge for the players as to how shots had worked out; you could just about hear their applause depending on the direction of the wind. If the wind was no help you looked for their hand movements in the distance as an indication of the quality of the shot. If you hit a green, the crowd were generous in their appreciation, recognising the difficulty of simply holding the short stuff.

> "The gruelling conditions suited a gritty golfer, even one with a sore hand. I did not see Pádraig grimace once even if he hit a wayward shot. At no stage did he look like he was suffering with his weakened wrist."

In many ways the weather made the task of bringing in a good first-round score in a major easier because you could simply focus on somehow wiggling your ball into the hole instead of being unnerved by the size of the occasion. Padraig was supreme in getting up and down from 80 yards, a feat only a seasoned campaigner would have the audacity to do. He made some crucial par putts to hold his opening round together.

The gruelling conditions suited a gritty golfer, even one with a sore hand. I did not see Padraig grimace once even if he hit a wayward shot. At no stage did he look like he was suffering with his weakened wrist.

Whatever about the tenacity of the Open champion in eking out a score in a storm it was the quality of shots he produced in the final denouement to the championship that separated him from the rest of the field.

From 15 to 18 on the final round, when you are most likely to be at your twitchiest as a tournament leader, Padraig produced a succession of shots befitting a supreme champion.

He took control of the Open over the closing holes, leaving his nearest challengers in a wake of outstanding approach shots.

I doubt the 137th Open champion was punching his impact bag on Sunday night after raising the Claret Jug for the second time in two years.

Perhaps Sunday night is his night off from the gym.

Curious incident in bunker takes the biscuit

JULY 29: There was a curious incident at the Canadian Open at the Glen Abbey Country Club in Oakville, west of Toronto, last week. This occurred in between the torrential rain and thunderstorms that lingered over Ontario for the entire week of the tournament.

To those of you who are not particularly interested in golf, the incident involved the minutiae of the rules and therefore you might want to move on to something a little more stimulating at this point.

For the rest of you, who have some sense of justice and equality in a game that arguably has the most rigid and often inane rules of any sport, this will certainly get your attention.

The rules of golf are strict and fastidious because with the isolation of the game, played over a vast terrain for four hours and more, it would be very easy for competitors to overlook a few guidelines when nobody was looking. For this reason the rules are uncompromising, if somewhat bizarre when examined more closely.

Given the aptitude for modern sports people to stretch the strictures of their chosen sport often beyond the limits, from doping in athletics to blatant child-like dishonesty in soccer, I am in favour of the preservation of the strict rules of golf.

However, there are always exceptions, where the application of the rules makes me wonder if one should not be playing professional golf with a lawyer present at all times, given the consequences of mistakes can be so severe, from penalties and disqualification to dismissal.

In most cases, basic common sense will lead the player and caddie in golf to make the correct judgment about what is right and wrong, but in the grey areas of the rules of golf almost 100 per cent of the time the penalised player gets punished for an error when there was zero intent of getting an advantage and never a notion of cheating.

Last Friday in Toronto we finally started our second round at 4.55pm, having hung around for six hours the previous day to finish off our last hole of the first round. Such are the boring breaks of nature, the thunder clouds just wouldn't shift, so basically, everyone had to hang around on standby, and an unhealthy amount of sugar was consumed out of boredom in the environs of the Glen Abbey clubhouse.

The Canadian Open cookie was what overloaded most of us. It is a sweet delicacy that is baked exclusively during the week of the tournament.

So when we finally did get back on the course I couldn't figure out whether it was the sugar rush from the excess of cookies, or the thought of actually completing our round and not having to get up at 5am the following morning for more of the same that fuelled the players to shift around the course at high speed.

It is fascinating to monitor the speed of play at professional events on the first three days compared to Sunday when players are eager to get home. Maybe it is just a coincidence, but Sundays are always quicker.

Anyway, we got back out on Friday evening and we knew we had no chance of completing our round. My boss Retief (Goosen) hit his second shot to the par-five fifth, our 14th hole, and ended up in the greenside bunker. The sun was sinking low behind the spruce and beech trees that lined the fairway and the light became very dim. Retief was struggling to see clearly. The siren had not sounded for the suspension of play for the day so he had to make an effort to play his trap-shot.

Retief had walked into the bunker to assess his shot. As he did the klaxon sounded which signified that the players may elect to stop playing or complete the hole they have already started; the choice is theirs. Our group chose to stop. But the group behind decided to play on without us knowing.

So as we walked back to get transported to the clubhouse I realised the group behind were playing and thus there was a chance one of them could have hit into the bunker we were in, which was still unraked.

It is not a rule of golf that you rake a bunker, but etiquette demands you leave the sand as you would wish to find it, relatively smooth. A tour rule also ensures a fine for those who do not rake a bunker after playing out of it. Retief had marked his ball with a tee and was going to wait to resume play the following morning.

I ran back to the trap, quickly asked an official who just happened to be there if I could rake the bunker, and he said I could. As it happened, one of the players behind hit his approach about a yard from where I had raked.

"Big deal", I hear you say. The next morning the same official informed us I had, in fact, breached a rule and would have incurred a two-shot penalty for Retief if the official had not given me permission to rake the bunker.

By his consent, despite the fact a rule was broken, he takes the responsibility and not me. If he had not, I would have been deemed to have tested the surface, which is a breach of the rules.

The trouble with this is that the rule has actually promoted bad etiquette. How would I and the player who ended up in the unraked part of the bunker have felt if this had happened?

It was very close to happening. If you didn't have a good relationship with your player there is a good chance of getting fired over such an incident, all done in the interest of respect for fellow competitors.

A rule of a similar nature was amended after a similar bunker incident in New Orleans earlier this year. The player involved was disqualified, the caddie humiliated and the next week the guardians of the game got together and changed the rule.

My curious incident in Canada last week will also be reviewed by the authorities this week. From a professional perspective, my dilemma now is whether to overlook etiquette in order to observe a nonsensical rule.

This is a worry because etiquette in this era of selfishness is a word that many modern golfers would have to look up in a dictionary.

"It is not a rule of golf that you rake a bunker, but etiquette demands you leave the sand as you would wish to find it, relatively smooth. A tour rule also ensures a fine for those who do not rake a bunker..."

Absence of Tiger makes Tour a safer place for all

AUGUST 5: The final World Golf Championship of the year was held at the Firestone Country Club in Akron, Ohio, last weekend. The Bridgestone Invitational had as strong a field as this week's PGA Championship but it seemed something – or rather someone – was missing.

I noticed the New York Times correspondent didn't bother to show up till midweek. If the "main man" had been about he would have been in Ohio with a thick notepad at the ready by early Monday morning.

If a hint of apathy has seeped under the door of the press room then the opposite could be said of the attitude in the locker-room. Knowing the "great one" is not playing has sharpened the competitive edge of players who had tacitly submitted to the Woods winning spell.

There is a new mindset from the early part of the week: "Tiger is not here so we have a better chance of winning."

The idea is to get into a position to win come the back nine on Sunday, when of course the obvious absence of Tiger has a huge impact. Not to discredit the rest of the field, but when the most fearsome of competitors is not there it does inevitably remove a serious obstacle to title-chasers on those closing holes.

There is no doubt that in Woods's absence the numbers are down in all areas. The television ratings have dropped and the number of live spectators has dwindled.

But there is a benefit. Overall it is a more pleasant experience to be at an event without the uncivilised mob that usually stomp all over the course in pursuit of the world number one.

I talked to some regular spectators on tour in the States, and they agreed it was much more enjoyable to be at an event without Tiger playing.

Last week was seemingly the busiest week in professional golf worldwide. With the US Seniors Open in Colorado; the alternative PGA Tour event in Reno with a controversial lady playing; the regular Nationwide event in Nebraska; and the Women's British Open in Sunningdale all going on at the same time, it had to be a feast for fans, who could potentially watch the game all day long on television.

At some events we visit around the globe we are presented with brochures about the resident flora and fauna. We have been at events in Germany where the presence of a rare and endangered frog in a pond has led to the redesign of an adjacent hole for conservation purposes.

Well, the sight of a very large black bear looking even more bemused than some competitors on the 13th hole at the Broadmoor golf club in Colorado Springs during the second round at the US Seniors was a little more alarming than the sound of a toad going "ribbet" from his protected swamp in Bavaria.

The big black bear wandered out of the wilderness and onto the East Course, crossing the fairway between ESPN's on-course analyst Dottie Pepper and Bernhard Langer and his caddie Terry Holt, before trying to mingle with spectators. Neither the bear nor the spectators were harmed; apparently the animal had already dined.

After assessing the situation the bear eventually wandered home of his own accord.

The authorities thought they had all angles of on-course security covered, with bodyguards accompanying marquee groups. They had to call in the wildlife experts for the weekend in case the bear decided to come back with his family for another look at the closing stages of the tournament.

Two other big names obliged the sponsors in Ohio by coming in first and second in the weekend denouement. Vijay Singh and Phil Mickelson were the final pairing on Saturday, which softened the no-Tiger blow for the media.

There are some dubious tactics being used by the sponsors to up their television ratings. Not that the black bear in Colorado was a carefully orchestrated stunt to gain attention. But inviting the talented if somewhat badly advised Michelle Wie to play in the Reno/Tahoe Open – a PGA Tour event – was an act of blatant opportunism.

Young Michelle's first involvement in a men's tournament came when she was invited to play in the Sony Open in her native Hawaii. That was understandable as a one-off.

Of course tournaments need to be promoted. But for the tour to continually support her failed attempts to perform (last week was her eighth failure to make the cut in a men's event), when she is obviously out of her depth, is hard to understand.

Michelle seems a pleasant young lady who has been manipulated and misdirected by mature adults who should know better. The poor girl has been gifted with a talent to play golf but greed and mismanagement are hampering her true enjoyment and expression of that gift.

Of course the main man is absent again this week in Detroit. But watching the rest deal with the pressures of trying to win a Major is always fascinating. It should be another enthralling few days.

Thriving again on hostile terrain

AUGUST 12: The 90th US PGA Championship came around with a considerable amount of nostalgia for those who had played the Ryder Cup at the same venue outside Detroit, Michigan, on the famed Oakland Hills Country Club in 2004. The previous jamboree at the South Course was the US Open back in 1996.

There have been a lot of changes since both events; the distance the modern professional hits with technically superior equipment is really the most significant advance in golf.

The bodies who run these major championships, such as the PGA, are constantly looking for ways to improve, while at the same time testing competitors seemingly to the limit and beyond.

Rees Jones has been responsible for much of the tinkering the USGA have asked him to do on more recent US Open venues. The ingredients tend to be the same: push tees back as far as the perimeters of the course will allow and scoop out a sand trap in the landing zone for the long-hitting pro.

The stuff of genius or just a fundamental solution to current paranoia among the authorities about under-par scores winning major championships?

As ever the modern game is driven by the people with clipboards paying too much attention to statistics and less to the art of playing a challenging golf course while actually enjoying it. The numbers reveal an area the pros regularly hit to and the "creative" designer plops a bunker there. Simple.

Not only was Oakland Hills lengthy at just under 7,400 yards but the surrounding rough was, as the commentator Ian Baker-Finch suggested, on steroids, it was so dense.

Padraig Harrington seems to be the best pupil this semester, adapting to the harsh circumstances thrown at the major competitors.

Just as my boss, Retief Goosen, figured out how to win US Opens earlier this decade, Padraig has mastered the British Open and in an unusually difficult PGA he battled his way through to his first American major in truly gritty fashion.

The nature of Oakland Hills changed so dramatically overnight last week that practice rounds were irrelevant in terms of preparation for what was presented to the players on Thursday. The greens were much harder and faster and the rough seemed to have been fluffed up and thickened.

The weather changed through a series of thunderstorms from summer to winter over the weekend, and we finally got to restart the third round at 7.15am on Sunday with a sharp, icy north-westerly blowing over the course. They were knuckle-down conditions, very much like what we had seen at the Open Championship in Birkdale.

Grinding out a score on the seemingly impossible par holes and taking your opportunity on the relatively easier ones was the key to playing Oakland Hills and Birkdale. Padraig succeeded at both venues with similar determination and similarly wonderful shot-making.

It is not the classic shots that win you major tournaments, rather the dogged pars in the most unlikely of circumstances – like Padraig's on 18 last Sunday. This comes less from technical perfection than from sheer mental fortitude.

They called Oakland Hills the "Monster" after Ben Hogan tamed it to win the US Open in 1951. With the recent changes and last week's set-up it was more a monstrosity.

Our Padraig may be Irish but he's a man apart

AUGUST 19: With little to celebrate from an Irish point of view in Beijing in the opening week of the Olympics, Padraig Harrington saved our sagging sporting egos by capturing the 90th US PGA Championship in Detroit.

His victory is, of course, seen as something the entire nation can celebrate. The fact is professional golfers represent their countries less than they ever did, with singles stroke play the yardstick for judging how good a golfer is.

The closest the golfer gets to playing for a team (apart from Ryder and Presidents Cup distractions) is by representing his support team of caddie, coach, manager, psychologist and physiotherapist. Aside from the increasingly less popular World Cup of golf they virtually never play for their country anymore unless they are American.

Naturally, due to the egocentric nature of the game professional golfers are islands moving through a sea of other islands; you could call it one big archipelago if you like, particularly in the upper echelons of the game.

With the nation latching on to Padraig's wonderful achievement of winning not only the British Open but backing it up three weeks later with the US PGA, victory would suggest strongly that we Irish should be pushing for golf to be an Olympic sport – and quickly – while the world's number three golfer is Irish and at his peak.

As I was listening to the story of the Irish runner Pauline Curley who was extremely happy to finish 63rd in the marathon, I was a reminded of a humorous interaction between the former cricketer Geoffrey Boycott and a Swedish golfer who was introducing himself to Boycott on the first tee for a pro-am.

The golfer greeted the cricketer and went on to say he had finished 50th in the European Order of Merit the previous year, in case he hadn't heard of him.

To which the candid batsman replied, "If I finished 50th in anything I wouldn't be telling anyone about it."

The golfer had been proud of his achievement, with his limited talent he had over-achieved. For one of the best batsmen of his day naturally such a lowly status would be an embarrassment, not something to publicise.

Realistically it must be a daunting task for our Olympic minnows to haul themselves to China and into the cauldron of their chosen sport knowing that qualifying for a further stage is probably the best they can do, winning a medal simply being an unrealistic dream.

Therein lies the conundrum for any sports person; where do I belong – or indeed do I belong in the final group on the Sunday of a major or in an Olympic final in the Bird's Nest in Beijing?

It was a position Padraig found himself in having secured his European Tour Card in 1996 and, surprisingly for himself, winning his first event in Madrid later that year. He decided he could become better and made serious changes both to his swing and his whole professional approach, from diet and exercise to the most telling aspect of top golf, the mental game.

Padraig had finished second too many times it seemed, perhaps he just wasn't a winner – maybe he had reached his level just like the Swedish golfer and it was time to settle for second.

> "Pádraig had finished second too many times it seemed, perhaps he just wasn't a winner – maybe he had reached his level just like the Swedish golfer and it was time to settle for second."

Of course he never thought this. It was simply a learning curve, albeit an agonisingly slow one for Harrington. It seemed to take him longer to feel like he belonged at the very top instead of being just a player who might have the odd shot at a title.

He really has so much in common with Sergio Garcia, who looks like he has been going though his own painful learning process over the past couple of years in how to win a major. His bitter experiences of Carnoustie and Oakland Hills will stand to him when he finally realises his major potential over the coming years. Harrington, on reflection, must have had a lot of empathy with Sergio recently.

Compared to the Olympians, golfers get more opportunities to compete and test themselves under the pressure of big competitions. Their big test comes but once every four years and besides world championships and European events they are not consistently on the big stage. I would imagine the "gag" factor takes over, not being able to experience the feelings of being in a major championship too often.

At the top of the game of golf there is virtually no room for national identity, golfers are playing for themselves and being self-reliant is what has got them to where they are.

The Irish Olympians who are of course self-motivated, are doing it for themselves but clearly in their country's colours and with the nation's financial backing.

So despite Padraig being Irish, patriotic and proud, he really has very little connection to the governing bodies of the game in this country; he decides who he needs on his team, he pays them and he moves forward in the lonely world of professional golf at his own pace, at his own expense.

It is interesting to see who jumps on the Paddy wagon of success, individual sponsors who have nothing to cheer about in the corporate world are delighted a golfer with whom they are aligned, has hit form at an ideal moment for the flagging business world.

So it's "Up the Dubs" and "Go on Paudie" because we seem to have little to cheer about as a nation on the world stage in any other sport. Let's make golf an Olympic sport and bolster our national sporting pride.

Making the cut this year means rich rewards

AUGUST 26: The first of the much fabled FedEx play-offs of the season took off at the Ridgewood Country Club in Paramus, New Jersey, last week. What it all meant was the subject of much locker-room and caddie- shack chatter.

The play-off is an established denouement to any major sporting season in the USA. The main sports here – football, basketball and baseball – all have their end-of-season play-offs in search of the best team of the year.

The PGA tour felt that the golf season was lacking finality, an endgame to find the best player of the year. So the FedEx play-offs were devised and had their inaugural year last year without producing anything out of the ordinary. Tiger won.

Of course this year we have a sidelined Woods and a rejigged points system devised to give more weight to the performance of qualifying players in the four play-off events. The complaint last year was that those who had qualified for the first two of the four events could do little to improve their rankings to gain entry to the final two, which was where all the points were.

Ridgewood Country Club was a one-off venue set in the old world of golf on the east coast of the US. It is a classic, mature and elegant AW Tillinghast layout with a clever mix of long, tough par fours and shorter, risk-reward holes that tempt the long-hitting modern golfer into taking on punishing par fours.

Interesting then that such a new form of professional golf should have been tested on a course that was designed over 100 years ago.

Despite The Barclays marking the start of the end of the season, in golfing terms it really just felt like a normal event. There was some uncertainty for those at the lower end of the rankings as to where they were going this week. Boston or bust?

As caddies, most of us make our own travel arrangements. Many caddies have latched onto a website called priceline.com that allows you to bid for a hotel room by naming the lowest price you think it will accept.

The result last week was that the Hyatt Place hotel in Paramus looked as if it was playing host to a caddy convention.

Those of us in the top 120 made our plans for the Deutsche Bank Championship in Massachusetts. Others were hanging on to get a closer look at how this new points system was going to affect their FedEx rankings.

We got stuck in a group that was infected with bad putting. In these events you are paired with players of a similar ranking; we were all around the high 50s before the start of last week.

The greens defied the putting skills of each member of the group, and with the early leader posting an outrageous 62 it is no wonder that most players felt intimidated by the very low score on a seemingly difficult course.

Tim Clark made the cut on three under, holing two putts in the final two holes for birdies. Retief Goosen and the other member of our group, Peter Lonard, missed the cut by four shots. Some putt better than others on poa annua greens.

I handed the bag over to Retief early on Friday afternoon and he promptly packed up and headed home for the weekend. He parted with the uncertainty this new points system has introduced to the tour showdown very much in mind. "I'll see you on Wednesday in Boston, if we qualify for it," were his parting words.

The tour reward system is very top heavy. The top 15 is where most of the money is. There is little difference in prize money once you fall outside the top 25. Not so in this year's play-offs, where making the cut seems to be well rewarded.

Our playing partner Tim Clark finished 38th in The Barclays and moved up 20 spots in the rankings to 40th. Outside the play-offs you would normally have to win to make such a dramatic jump. Some argued that the rankings had been reduced to a game of hop-scotch.

Drama ensued as the first of the play-offs resulted in a play-off and the main protagonists, Vijay Singh and Sergio Garcia, going head to head for the title alongside the lesser-known Kevin Sutherland.

Singh birdied both play-off holes on the way to snaring the title. The Fijian matched Garcia's birdie on the first play-off hole (18th) while Sutherland was eliminated. The 45-year-old Singh then birdied the par-five 17th to close out the world number four Garcia.

The FedEx formulators must have been gratified by the proof there can be life in a golf tournament even without Tiger.

To top it all it was a dream finish to test out their new, improved points formula. Vijay moved up seven spots, Sergio 10 and Sutherland 57.

For those who missed the cut the slide was equally dramatic. Our other playing partner, Peter Lonard, dropped 25 places and Retief fell 24.

There is no room for nostalgia in these play-offs either; Padraig dropped 19 spots by missing the cut in New Jersey.

In this uncertain life on tour, where you are as good as your last performance, at least we know one thing from this week in Boston: if we miss the cut we definitely will not make the third play-off event in Missouri.

The other important lesson from last week is that despite the alarmingly low rounds of 62 and 64 carded by the early leaders, eight under par played off for the title. It's the play-offs. Stick in there if you can.

Nantucket still possesses that old world charm

SEPTEMBER 9: For those of us who didn't earn enough points to make it to the third showdown of the FedEx Cup in St Louis, Missouri, it provided a rare opportunity to take a vacation in New England.

I took a short hop in a tiny plane to the small island of Nantucket, just south of Cape Cod off the Massachusetts coast. It is like taking a step back in time, to an age where neon lights had not yet been invented and one distinct type of architecture was enough to keep visitors to the island content in a very understated way.

Nantucket, apart from being a low-key getaway for wealthy east-coasters, was originally a whaling centre. It is very much a seafarer's island which attracts fishermen who are ready to tussle with big fish. The elaborate fighting chairs on most of the fishing boats in the wharf suggest that they would be equipped to haul in Moby Dick.

The terrain on the island is very much like the north coast of Europe, reminiscent of the coastal towns in Belgium or Holland.

Naturally this sandy land is ideal terrain for golf.

Without golf in mind, I stumbled upon a course that is as close as you are going to get to a links course at home: bunkerless, rolling sandy fairways, the club flag flapping high above the course in the frisky sea breeze, and golfers out walking the course instead of using the electric cart that is now the tradition in America.

I wandered towards the modest clubhouse to see what sort of club I had found. A very different one, if the poster on the secretary manager's wall was an indication. Over his desk there was a picture of the Dalai Lama. This is a first in all the golf clubs I have visited around the globe (I must confess I have not been to Tibet).

Not only had I come across a course that you would expect to find in a sleepy fishing village on the coast off Brittany, but the extremely welcoming manager informed me that the club hosts a very elaborate caddie programme unparalleled anywhere in the world.

I was redirected to the Caddie Camp at Sankaty Head Golf Club, which was situated between the 11th and 13th holes on the links.

I rattled along the sandy track to the camp, passing fourballs of elderly men and women pulling their caddie-cars, dressed in long-sleeved shirts and flannels. I could have taken a step back in time to a British upper-class continental summer retreat. All that was missing was the plaid rug and the wicker picnic basket.

Having crossed the 12th tee, I pulled up to the deserted Caddie Camp, which looked like a small army barracks.

I was greeted by the camp director, Peter Montesano, who was in the process of closing up the camp for the season, hence the members pulling their own bags. The campers had packed up for another year the previous week, so it had the look of an abandoned outpost.

The camp originated in 1930 shortly after the club was founded. Traditionally there have been boys from California to Canada at the camp, and more recently representatives from Ireland and France.

For boys aged 14 to 20, the residential camp combines varied competitive sports and recreational activities with "healthful" work. The essence of the camp is to develop such values as honesty, integrity, industry and money management.

During the summer camp experience the lads should become acquainted not only with fun and comradeship but also with some of life's adversities and challenges, and how to cope with them.

Wandering around the empty camp you get a sense of a form of life training and discipline from which, I am sure, all kids would benefit. For those of us who did not have obligatory military service, the Sankaty camp would probably be as close as you would get to it.

Through daily caddying duties the lads get the opportunity to save quite a bit of cash. The director figured that in the 10 weeks they are in camp their savings range from €2,000 to just under €8,000.

This, coupled with the concepts and philosophy in the camp, makes the experience more about these ideals, rather than the basic militaristic accommodation.

The Sankaty Head Caddie Camp is a wonderful tradition in a truly mystical place that gives the impression that time has forgotten it.

Which I am sure would please those elders who have gone to great lengths to maintain Nantucket's old world and understated atmosphere.

Koran of the caddie shack is in danger of being ousted

SEPTEMBER 16: Just as a sailor has his nautical charts or an adventurer has maps, we caddies have yardage books to accurately guide our masters around the links. The book is our satellite navigation, used to get us back to the clubhouse without giving our players any mystery numbers.

Those of us loopers who go back a couple of decades remember the trials of making our own yardage books on a weekly basis. That was back in the days before the laser and odometer, the era of primitive pacing and other basic methods of calculating distance.

Eighteen years ago an Australian caddie who had taken great pride in making an advanced book in his day decided that there was a market on tour for the quality of book he produced. He was right.

Others made books for general consumption in competition but for their own reasons dropped out of the book race. Graeme Heinrich moved off the bag and onto the drawing board.

And so the Graeme Heinrich yardage chart was born and it evolved over the years to be a well recognised document, without which no European golfer worth his salt would be seen at a tournament.

At Dublin airport there is a big advertisement, just before you descend the final steps to baggage claim, with a picture of Tiger Woods consulting one of Graeme Heinrich's yardage books.

You could not have a more influential golfer endorsing of your product.

Heinrich has produced the book for the European Ryder Cup team this week in Kentucky, as he has for six previous Ryder Cups.

Team USA have their own American numbers expert commissioned to guide them strategically around Valhalla this week. The yardage chart is undoubtedly a vital document for caddie and player.

Strange then that the said Koran of the caddie shack is in jeopardy of being ousted from its permanent perch as "the" yardage book of the European Tour. It is the current topic of much debate in both the caddie shack and the locker-rooms of Europe.

I suppose you could say the revolt came about because of the change of price. The price of the Heinrich book went up to €25 in May and then a short time later jumped again to €30.

Having a yardage book on which a player and caddie can rely comes at a price. Good decisions on the course are based upon good numbers. Knowing you can depend upon a yardage book when you show up at an event is a great comfort and a huge time-saver.

The majority of caddies have only known life with a guaranteed book each week. Only a few of us remember the hassle of having to hand-make one. The price hike pushed the majority over the edge.

The caddies association actively sought a direct competitor. The sentiment was that the guy who had provided the reliable service every week for 18 years was not worth the price he was charging: a matter of pure economics. The word was that "we" wanted competition.

There were discussions between the caddies' association and Graeme Heinrich. Nothing was resolved so the association decided to call up Dion Stevens – coincidentally, also an Australian – who provides the books on the Ladies Tour. He now produces a book for both tours, which ultimately is going to be difficult to sustain.

Interestingly, the newcomer has pledged €1.26 a book to the caddies' association when he becomes established. This strikes me as not a true form of competition but another type of monopoly.

I found myself in a slightly awkward situation last Tuesday, as Graeme's salesperson and Dion were in situ outside the Gut Larchenhof clubhouse near Cologne selling their wares. After 18 years of monopoly, now there was a choice to make.

The state of play at present is that we have the choice of two yardage books on tour each week. The Heinrich for €30 and the newcomer's version at €20.

We all know the value of our currency. Naturally the cheaper one has made a huge impression on the market share.

The European Tour seem to have sat on the fence when it came to supporting the person who had effectively provided an outsourced service to the tour for so many years. The tour has traditionally sprayed paint on the fairways to indicate yardages. This goes back to the days when we made our own books. The paint was supposed to make gauging yardage easier.

> "Spraying the paint controls the bookmaking process. This tour policy must surely end in tears as dubious tactics have reportedly been already used by the paint sprayers."

Without endorsing Heinrich, there was tacit consent to his spraying of the fairways each week in return for use of the printing facilities. It was a cosy if rather loose arrangement from which, given Heinrich's reliability, the tour benefited greatly.

When this recent dissent manifested itself the tour didn't take sides but their curious response was that both parties had their permission to spray dots on the course and whoever got to the venue earliest got to spray.

Spraying the paint controls the bookmaking process. This tour policy must surely end in tears as dubious tactics have reportedly been already used by the paint sprayers.

Nothing lasts forever (that is for sure) and choices are the advantages of democracy. We choose different products often based on price, sometimes because of quality or simply because we are free to choose and we feel like changing.

There is a real fight for market share among the numbers providers and by the end of the year one of them will be squeezed out by price, preference, or simply the desire for a change.

'Hooting and a hollerin', the Americans did it their way

SEPTEMBER 23: The American crowd loves a catchy name to latch onto when they are strolling the fairways of a golf tournament, beer in one hand, stogie in the other and the attitude of bonhomie that exudes only from a group of friends getting together for a few days at a major sporting event, especially when there is patriotism involved.

Retief Goosen was very popular among such chanters in recent years. There was something uniquely simple and accessible no matter how many beers had been consumed in hooting "Goooooooose" in harmony into a cloud of cigar smoke from beyond the ropes.

He is not a home boy so there was only so far you could go with the "Goose". The American mob was extremely grateful that Boo Weekley arrived on the scene. Not only does the B get a more manly baritone sound into the chant but naturally he is more American than the quintessential, beer bellied, sneaker wearing, logo shirt bedecked American golf spectator and that takes some beating.

Boo captured the European imagination last year when he played the British Open for the first time and a mixture of myth and poetic licence led to tails of alligator wrestling and hunting trips of Ernest Hemingway proportions. Boo is a southern boy who is a very talented golfer.

He is charming if somewhat indecipherable when he is conversing with his caddie, Joe; they both speak the same southern dialect.

Boo was a first timer to the Ryder Cup last week and it seemed like he was a little over energised by the experience. I am sure if you play the game with a passion it is difficult not to be. Even on the BBC highlights at one in the morning I was stirred by the players, fans and particularly the commentators partisan emotion. I was surprised to see that Padraig appeared to be the only one receiving physio attention and that more players didn't dislocate their shoulders with the ferocity of the elated fist pumps which have reached new vigour.

The punch now involves a squat and uppercut worthy of a heavyweight boxer. There are, synergistically, more than 24 volts running through the European and American teams.

I have never caddied in the Ryder Cup and find it hard to appreciate the emotion and camaraderie that it generates. It is only when I talk to caddies and players who have been there, even long after the euphoria has simmered and their faces fill with energy recalling memories from the week, that I realise how different it must be from the hum-drum emotions of regular tournament play.

Such excitement and almost childish enthusiasm is exactly what is missing in regular tournament play and it is a key factor in the declining interest which the golfing public have for the current four-round strokeplay.

The PGAs of the world have been instrumental in popularising the game of golf, which with the dwindling numbers of amateurs playing the game, is a marvellous achievement. The charged and energised attitude that huge financial reward does not seem to give to golfers anymore was what this team's altruism has recreated.

I don't know whether there was a spin-doctor in both locker-rooms reminding the players to highlight the team and not the self in any interview but that was the message they all sent out; rather the cup than a personal-point tally.

The attention of the world's media on the event, and the subsequent opinions from columnists who spend the rest of their words on world events that really matter is another indication of the importance this Ryder Cup business has become beyond the fairway.

Opinions are of course like bottoms, everyone has got one. Some of the current affair experts' views on the cup were like listening to an opinionated taxi-driver solving the nation's problems from the cocoon of the driver's seat.

The captain, the somewhat odd but hugely successful golfer Nick Faldo, got a pasting from the golfing and part-time golfing press. I don't think he did much wrong apart from coming up against opposition who hit shots with deadly accuracy and holed more putts when it mattered.

A key factor in making this Ryder Cup so interesting to a larger public was the way the course was set up. The greens were receptive, not overly quick, the rough was extremely tame and the pins seemed quite accessible for the singles matches. There is nothing more exciting for the occasional spectator than seeing a ball dancing around a pin like the player has remote control over it.

The Boo factor was huge. The 13th man on the team, screaming like teenage girls at a boy-band concert, gave an edge to the home team. That captain Azinger advised his team applauding (screaming and shouting in the States) was acceptable behaviour, was unacceptable.

The Ryder Cup is nouveau golf. Just like the essence of the Olympic Games has moved so far from the wishes of the founders centuries ago, the Ryder Cup is a long way off the standard of gentlemanly behaviour that Samuel Ryder had in mind back in the 1920s.

For those who are familiar with live golf in America it is a vocal and often participatory game where those who pay to see the live act see no harm in voicing their opinions instantly and very loudly.

We all have traits that set us apart as members of different nations. Hooting and hollering is an American idiosyncrasy that will not change. Despite it overstepping the line of decency from a European perspective it will never change.

So "Boo SA" is here to stay. Have tickets will holler. It's the American way, they did it their way and when this fascinating challenge returns to Europe next, we will do it our way.

No regrets at end of wonderful experience

SEPTEMBER 30: Almost five years ago I was in a similar position to the situation I am in at the moment – between bags. With a life expectancy of three years in a good caddie/player relationship, stretching my partnership with Retief Goosen to almost half a decade is acceptable.

Back then I had just finished with Paul Lawrie, and I had managed a three-year stint with him. Our working relationships on tour are largely based on success: good golf will tend to sustain a relationship. The majority of us do not have contracts, so the option is always there for both parties to opt out if they feel like a change.

It is, of course, a precarious existence this global looping, the lack of certainty would not suit everyone. But a non-contractual relationship is actually the most efficient system, as strained relations are impossible to sustain in a competitive environment. It is best for both parties that they are free to move.

Many of us can hear the "axe being ground" at the end of a bad run, the mood and gestures betray a decay in communication. It is not the easiest conversation to broach: "Eh, we need to have a chat about things."

Often the caddie is the first to go in an attempt to turn a career around. There is nothing like a fresh voice to give a player a shot in the arm, the same old lines of encouragement have a limited shelf-life. I know mine was a tired voice droning out the numbers to my man over the past year.

When I got the call up from Retief about three weeks after finishing with Paul Lawrie at the end of 2003 it was unexpected, exciting and flattering. For those of us caddies who have had relatively sustained partnerships, being between bags is a little unnerving.

It is then that you become aware of how the bush telegraph works on tour. I didn't tell that many people about our parting of the ways, but within no time I was deluged by calls, texts and e-mails asking me about the split.

So how do you go about getting a new bag? You become aware of the efficiency of players' managers. If you are on tour, the caddie shack, of course, is where the rumours, both true and false, begin. If not, then you are reliant on the phone to ring, or the message box to catch your eye on the lap-top.

So the question was posed to me by Retief's manager back in 2003 if I would be interested in caddying for the world-beating South African. I naturally replied positively with as much delay as I could reasonably muster – one doesn't wish to appear too eager!

This was the promotion all of us toters hope for: some get the chance, others don't, and I still do not really understand how it works.

Retief changed my life. I was given the opportunity to work for one of the Big Four of that era: Tiger, Mickelson, Ernie and Retief. It is not like I had not served my time, but who knows if "the" opportunity will arise and if you will be available to accept it if it does? It had finally happened for me.

All vessels are raised on a rising tide and this particularly applies to a caddie for a top player. My first impression in those first few weeks with Goosen was that not only did everyone want a piece of the boss, they were also tugging at the bagman.

With my previous players, I had always tried to avoid socialising with them for the simple reason that we spend enough time together on the course: I have always felt it was best to keep our free time to ourselves and have something to discuss on the course the next day. Retief enjoys spending time with his caddie. It was very different for me and it took me some time to get used to his hospitality without seeming ungrateful.

"From winning the US Open in our first year together and nine other events in our lengthy partnership, our union has run its course."

I would go back to spend time with him and his family in America when we had spare time. More recently, I was invited to fly with him on many of the longer trips we took. I was always included in dinners and social functions at the tournaments that he was invited to play world wide. I got to places that caddies were not really used to going to; dinner with the daughter of the former leader of China, sports events where tickets only seemed to become available to top sports stars. It was an opportunity that Retief's status and inclusive nature afforded me.

I had never been in a situation before where I felt that every week my player teed up in a tournament, he had a chance of winning. But as intangibly as that mood pervades when confidence is high, it is equally as elusive when form disappears.

From winning the US Open in our first year together and nine other events in our lengthy partnership, our union has run its course. Working for Retief was a rare opportunity to observe and participate in life at the very pinnacle of world golf.

I remember trying to savour the dream of my first year caddying for Retief and telling myself that nothing lasts forever. It has been a life-changing run for me to be the wing-man for one of the best golfers in the world. Not only did he treat me well, but he also played well.

It is a new departure for both of us to try to find, in his case, a voice to suit his ears and, in mine, a pair of ears suited to my voice. We will officially sign off after the Grand Slam in Bermuda in a couple of weeks.

It has been a wonderful experience and a wonderful privilege to have assisted one of the best players in the world in his search for greatness.

Tall tale of Hale's flail regales in Scots gales

OCTOBER 7: As much as those with a sense of history regarding the game of golf always enjoy returning to the cradle of the game in St Andrews, there is a serious compromise involved for those who tread in Old Tom Morris's footsteps at the Dunhill Links Challenge, which was held there last week.

With a north-east wind cutting across the hallowed links and playing in fourballs with two amateurs, plus the downside of playing the unique links with its shared greens and criss-crossing holes, meant that it took up to six-and-a-half hours last Friday for the groups to get back to the clubhouse.

If you were playing badly it was a logistical nightmare; if you were playing well it was a particularly arduous test of tenacity to remember what swing thought you had started with that morning and how to keep doing it, despite being frozen stiff, six hours later.

There were images of jowls jutting underneath woolly hats as players and caddies made the most of their long days on the links with some idle banter. My link to the tour these days is through colleagues who keep me informed by e-mail about the latest caddie-shack banter.

One of the tales was about Gonzalo Fernandez-Castano's caddie, who happens to be a Scot. He is known familiarly as "By the way, Jeff" for the simple reason he starts 90 per cent of his conversations, "By the way..."

Jeff caddied on the women's tour before moving over to the men's a couple of years back. He was at an event one week and a TV crew approached him about partaking in a documentary they were making about caddies.

A number of caddies contributed to the programme, all speaking in English, as it was an English production. Jeff gave them a juicy interview and he admitted he was particularly critical about the reality of caddying for the top European lady golfers.

A couple of months after his interview, he received a DVD in the post, as promised, from the production company. Impressed by their efficiency, he settled down to view the finished product.

He watched his colleagues' contributions, all of them with their differing English accents and then finally got to his part and was shocked: "I was ****ing subtitled," he told us indignantly, "It went, 'By the way...'"

For those of you unfamiliar with our Scottish neighbours, travelling seems to thicken their accent and not soften it as you might expect.

The next tale from the shack during the many idle moments last week goes back to the Seniors PGA in Colorado with Bernhard Langer, Tom Watson and Hale Irwin playing together in the first round.

In a seniors event this is the equivalent of Tiger, Mickelson and whoever the hometown boy may be on the main tour. Irwin went to college in Colorado and still has a huge following there, and naturally Langer and Watson are star attractions to the mature crowd.

They had a tee time of 9am in the first round and Irwin was first up. Things are very punctual at these events and clocks are synchronised. The crowd was 10 deep around the tee as Hale shuffled over his opening tee shot, the crowd having settled down after giving him a hero's welcome.

Irwin got to the top of his backswing and the deadly silence was broken by the chimes of the monument beside the first tee which was built to commemorate a legendary cowboy famous in these parts when horsemen roamed the West. The chimes sounded traditionally at the top of the hour, and quarterly thereafter.

Now a younger man like Tiger Woods could have – and frequently has – aborted his swing at that point. Irwin tried, but didn't quite have the reflexes to halt, producing a virtual whiffed shot that spluttered across the tee and came to rest behind a temporarily installed Rolex.

The crowd gasped, as Irwin stood tangled on the tee in disbelief at what had happened. Not only that, how was he going to get out of this one? Professional golfers will try anything to get relief out of a bad situation, but this seemed to most – and particularly to his playing partners the stoic Langer and the uncompromising Watson – almost unbelievable.

Irwin called for a referee and asked if he could play the shot again, arguing the chimes of the lonesome cowboy as he made his swing, constituted an act that had interfered with his shot enough to warrant a second serve, so to speak.

Well, thankfully, he didn't get to play the shot again but fortunately, the temporary Rolex was impeding his pathetic tee shot sufficiently to get him relief, and thus a clear shot back to the fairway.

It was a generous ruling and resulted in Irwin holing a lengthy putt for a miraculous par on the first.

It also resulted in the tee times being altered so as they didn't fall at the top, bottom or any quarter of the hour.

Those times were dedicated to the chimes of the Lone Ranger.

Bermuda the ideal setting to celebrate

OCTOBER 21: The mid-ocean amphitheatre was the scene of the Champions reception of the 26th Grand Slam of Golf held in the idyllic old-world island of Bermuda early last week. The distinguished guests, caddies included, gathered to celebrate the 92nd year of the existence of the PGA of America.

A vibrant introduction video pulsed around the room from giant screens indicating the passion that the association and its members have for the game of golf. A long list of past champions from Bobby Jones to Padraig Harrington featured in footage from their finest defining moments as winners of major championships.

The two current major championship holders, Trevor Immelman and our own Padraig with his two titles, alongside their wives and caddies, were introduced to the audience, as were past US Open Champions Retief Goosen and Jim Furyk, who made up the quota of four for this year's Slam.

Brian Whitcomb, the president of the PGA, spoke passionately about his association and the game of golf and encouraged us to enjoy the warm and generous hospitality of Bermuda and the PGA. For all guests, of which there were many, this was a great way to celebrate in the success of the association.

The PGA encouraged us to "have a little fun" during the Grand Slam week, courtesy of them. It is without doubt the most generous week of the year for us caddies, all due to the inclusive nature of the PGA of America.

Jim Huber, the highly-respected American sports commentator sat in an easy chair on stage in a comfortable lounge set-up and gave his view of this year's majors. His style is reminiscent of the stately Alistair Cooke's quiet anecdotal tone in his legendary radio show Letter from America.

Huber has a timeless, soothing voice that could console a fund manager that the recent financial crisis was nothing more than an unfortunate triple bogey amid a fine round of golf.

First to join Huber in "his front room" was the Masters champion, Immelman. The message that the South African relayed was that winning the Masters, even last week, did not seem real.

To me Immelman seemed too in awe of the tournament he had won and not convinced he belonged alongside the legends who have donned the coveted Green jacket in the past.

Next came Padraig and in his own inimitable fashion looked perhaps like he shouldn't belong but of course he most definitely does belong to the triple Major Champions Club. Padraig eased into Huber's salon and continued to beam out his infectious grin across the Mid-Ocean room as he explained the run up to the first of his two major wins this year.

It was all about the punch bag incident on the Saturday night before the British Open and after his Irish PGA victory. Padraig explained through Huber about his right-handed practice routine which he felt left the left hand with no attention in his strict practice regime.

So the Open champion chuckled self-effacingly and said he was adopting the same procedure for his left hand in order to give it and its owner "something to do".

Both the candid nature of such a champion and his good nature had the assembled guests chuckling heartily. I overheard a lady sitting behind me declaring "Isn't he just the nicest guy ever".

The other two invitees reminisced about their past victories with the affable announcer and then we all retired to the ballroom for a selection of fine foods prepared by the local master chefs.

Of course we were there ultimately to compete for the Grand Slam title, however distracted we had become with the relaxed nature of the Bermudian atmosphere. Once we arrived on the first tee it was the competitors who presented themselves – albeit with a holiday like demeanour.

The Masters champion Immelman did not play well. My man, Retief Goosen, played well but failed to convert the numerous birdie chances he created. Padraig played solidly and putted like a demon. However, the eventual winner, Furyk, plodded along in his traditional steady manner capturing the 26th Grand Slam trophy in the first play-off hole against Padraig.

In case you got the impression that this was just a junket you would be mistaken. I chatted with Padraig as we descended from the 18th tee during the first round. The walk from the tee was the only place you could get a clear view of the pin on the last hole. As we talked Padraig excused himself as he shimmied off track so that he could eye up his approach shot in advance, which would have been impossible from beside his ball down on the fairway. Harrington's diligence and focus are never in doubt, no matter where he is playing.

On a personal note, I extended my stay on Bermuda along with Retief and his family for a few days after the event.

Retief invited me along on the final night for a farewell dinner after five years of service. The location for our final feast together was appropriately named "Elbow Beach".

The young master of Castellon thrives

OCTOBER 28: There was something very different about the European Tour event which was held on the Costa Azahar, about 60 kilometres north of Valencia last week. It had become known familiarly as Sergio's event, not because he was the eventual winner, but because it was held in his front garden, outside the small town of Borriol in the province of Castello, in eastern Spain.

You climb inland, high above the coastal town of Castellon, and into a volcanic plateau to find Club Mediterraneo. It is a typical Spanish country club with a golf course, tennis and paddle tennis courts, football pitches and a swimming pool. It's a family-oriented scene where golf is simply part of a bigger social scene formed around sport.

To enter the clubhouse you have to sidestep an elephant-sized sculpture of a reclining, portly woman adorned with artistic distortions. You quickly realise that art is a fundamental part of Club Mediterraneo, as there are many more sculptures around the clubhouse.

It is the work of a local artist Juan Ripolles, who can be seen in the vicinity dressed in anything but golf gear.

This is the home of Sergio Garcia, the Boy Wonder from Spain who became a phenomenon as a teenager, earning his playing rights on the US Tour while he was still in school. There is a shrine-like photograph of the young Garcia positioned in the café area of the club holding a trophy. The young Sergio, or El

Niño, is fresh-faced, and his image is surrounded by plaques with his achievements indelibly carved into the Mediterraneo history books.

El Niño's wall space is discreet, unlike the huge charisma that he exudes when you meet him. He is a warm and engaging Spaniard whose face lights up when he greets you. He plays golf, frequently with a running commentary about his shot as the ball is in mid-air. In true Spanish fashion he is animated, and he speaks mainly in English, so you always know what he thinks of his shot.

It's not just Sergio who has a presence in the club. His father, Victor, is still the professional there and his mother, Consuelo, runs the pro shop. The club is very much a Garcia family affair, Victor rambling about the place with a traditional club under his arm like he always does when he follows his son about the course anywhere else in the world.

Sergio's elder brother, Victor, and his younger sister, Mar, were wandering around the club last week like they usually would I suppose, just last week there were more people than normal with whom to engage in idle banter.

The Garcia children took part in all the sports programmes that were run in the club. They were given a chance to figure out which sports they preferred. Sergio is a natural sportsman who is adept in all the sports he played as a kid. Golf was not forced upon him. To pursue it as a profession was, of course, an easy choice.

> "It was easy to see what shaped such a world-class player as Sergio. The course winds its crooked path through olive and palm trees and small terraced stone walls."

Naturally because of Sergio's association with the club, the Castellon Masters attracted a relatively star-studded field. I am not insinuating that there were not some sort of sweeteners to get such players as Angel Cabrera, Justin Rose and Paul Casey to compete. Sergio's good friend from the US Tour, the Colombian Camilo Villegas, played because of his friendship with Sergio.

It would restore my faith in human nature if it really was as a gesture of camaraderie that these players showed up in a remote part of Spain for an obscure European Tour event which, in the past, has been nothing more than the lifeline for tour players trying to secure their rights for next year, as it is the final full-field event of the year.

Another mini-event within the tournament was for those around the top 60 in the Order of Merit trying to secure a spot in the Volvo Masters this week. The course is the complete opposite both in style and nature to the majority of courses that Sergio plays in the US and around the world. Mediterraneo is very much a "members" course.

Despite its long par threes, if it had not rained heavily during the week the course would have been a drive and a flick for the modern, big-hitting pro.

It was easy to see what shaped such a world-class player as Sergio. The course winds its crooked path through olive and palm trees and small terraced stone walls. The holes demand different shaped tee-shots, most of them to narrowing landing areas, which means that accuracy is paramount.

Garcia is probably the best driver of the ball in the world, certainly among the top players. If you compare his driving accuracy to Woods et al, Sergio comes out well ahead.

The difference last week, was that the event really had the Garcia stamp on it; delicately balancing the high profile of Sergio with the modest, low-key family approach.

Naturally the Kid from Castellon had a lot going for him last week; unbounded talent, acute local knowledge, huge local and familial support, the passion to perform in a relatively small event and the killer instinct to add the Castellon Masters plaque to his photo in the clubhouse, which is already enveloped in accolades.

Eastern promise marks the end of an era

NOVEMBER 4: There was something poignant about the end of an era of European Tour tradition in the south of Spain in late October. The 21st and final Volvo Masters, the denouement to the European golfing year and the flagship event for over two decades which has been held on the Costa Del Sol, has finally succumbed to the Eastern lure.

The Volvo Masters was a prestige event, with the top-60 golfers of the year playing their final exhibition of four-round tournament strokeplay at the much talked about Valderrama golf club in the exclusive Sotogrande development close to "The Rock", or Gibraltar, depending on your mother tongue.

Valderrama is the brainchild of Don Jaime Ortiz-Patino, or "Jimmy" as he likes to be called by his acquaintants. A wealthy miner from Bolivia, the Economist suggested in an article about Don Jimmy that there is more to him than meets the eye.

He and his family were great collectors of art and impressionist paintings in particular. Having lost out in a bid for one particular work of art that would have completed his collection, the story goes that Patino turned his artistic attention to golf and in particular the creation of Valderrama.

In a part of the world that is very much of the modern persuasion, it is no surprise that Valderrama's "est.1985" sign, is relatively historical in the region. Designed by Robert Trent Jones senior, it is surprising that in places it verges on the unplayable for the mere mortal golfer. But, curiously, it holds a place way beyond its realistic position in the hearts of those with a sense of "golf history" on the Costa. Consequently it is very much elevated in the minds of those who have heard about it. Marketing is a very effective tool in convincing the masses about the importance of the required message, regardless of the consensus of more qualified opinion.

On tour, the Valderrama debate is always provocative because it does generate serious conversation amongst the players. Some like it, others hate it and those in between accept that it is an unique form of golf much like Augusta National and it must be taken as that. I have yet to hear anyone say they would love to play the course on a regular basis.

Apart from the end-of-season finale being played on a controversial golf course the contents of the clubhouse go a long way to making up for the capricious nature of the course.

Without going into too much detail, the main criticism of the course is that it does not reward good shots and that there is a huge element of luck involved in etching out a good score amongst the rare cork trees. Mr Patino has got one of the most important collection of golf artifacts in the world on display inside the clubhouse. He obviously has a keen eye for art, which does not seem to have transferred to his supposed masterpiece of a golf course.

Valderrama is from tee to the greens' edge in wonderful condition. Given the extensive rainfall last week on the southern coast the course constructors have got to be commended for its excellent drainage. The greens unfortunately are only good if you ban anyone, including the competitors, from walking on them unless they are wearing calf-leather slippers. The putting surfaces are as delicate as fine china and need to come with warning signs not dissimilar to an art gallery – "please don't touch".

With the elaborate lighting system on the course I suspect the view of the course from above at night is aesthetically pleasing to the eye.

The European Tour's grand finale got under way amid strong northerly winds which were to abate for the rest of the week and be replaced with deluges of tropical proportions.

Anyone with a nose for wet weather, access to a weather forecast or the practical nature to stick their head out the door and make a logical assessment of the climatic situation could tell Friday was obviously going to be a washout. Everyone but the authorities it appeared knew that.

For the earlier starters, who had endured the most horrific conditions on Friday morning, play was finally brought to a halt at about midday. This was a good, if somewhat stalled decision as some vociferous players let it be known, especially those who had waded around the front nine, clocking up bogeys quicker than the bunkers filled with water.

It is the luck of the draw, as is always going to be the case with golf played out over the course of a day. There were a number of legitimate complaints from many competitors. The leaders got to play their entire second round in perfect conditions. The early players on the course were playing in conditions that were arguably unplayable. Three over was not a bad score for the front nine. Furthermore, the players were kept hanging around a sodden golf course all afternoon when the extent of the rain clearly indicated that play would not be possible at all that day.

To compound the inconvenience of the big wait, when we did finally complete our second rounds on Saturday, the authorities did not seem to think it was worthwhile sending the players straight back out to play the third round when the weather was perfect.

Instead a new draw for the third round was made and almost unbelievably commenced just as the rain started to fall heavily again.

The standard reasons given for such decisions are; satisfying the sponsors and more importantly appeasing the TV people.

I would have thought everyone concerned would have preferred to show golfers playing in Andalucia in clement weather and not in a deluge.

The final Volvo Masters held in the south of Spain marks the end of an era. It is very much a sign of the direction that golf is going when the flagship event of the European Tour is destined to be held on another continent next year. Golf in Spain is passé, bring on the new, the Middle East.

First race to Dubai is a marathon

NOVEMBER 11: The HSBC Champions event held at the Sheshan golf club outside Shanghai is the starting block of tournaments for the "Race to Dubai", which is taking over from the south of Spain as the grand finale to the season.

With the inclement weather in the south of Spain a few weeks back the race began at a heady pace, with players and caddies plotting alternate routes to get them to China early enough to overcome the travel fatigue that such a long trip brings with it. Monday evening saw the earliest arrivals in the Meridian Hotel, about a kilometre from the golf course. The latest arrival was the winning caddie from Valderamma, who set a record of only making his first appearance at the course on Thursday morning – Soren Kjelsden's win got him into last week's event and getting a visa for China doesn't happen over a weekend night.

It is a unique week on tour where virtually everyone connected to the event stays in the same hotel. With the trials brought about by the second week in a row of torrential rain and constant delays, the hotel was beginning to take on the appearance of a very luxurious prison. Such was the daily routine of 5.15am starts, all congregating for breakfast, transferring to the course, waiting till darkness fell just before 5pm and reassembling in the large dining area for the evening buffet before retiring before the 5.15am start again. This was the dreary routine all week long.

It was a rare opportunity for all different categories of Tour life from players, agents, organisation staff, PGA officials, sponsors and caddies to mix in a social gathering more than they have ever done throughout the year. How harmonious it all was, particularly given the frayed nerves by the weekend as the rain forced the tour to opt for a Monday finish.

We are creatures of habit on tour, sub-consciously guided by a seven-day location clock. Not only do we run out of clean clothes by Monday but also tolerance for what was by day seven, becoming the place that we could never leave. With pressure being put upon the Tour to hold the prestigious HSBC Champions event over 72 holes, like all majors are, the tour, after consulting their players, decided to yield to the sponsors' wishes and extend the first race to Dubai from a sprint to a marathon.

There have, of course, been many delays over the years which have resulted in Monday finishes and sometimes the odd caddie has decided to opt for his original planned departure. I have never seen so many tour caddies heading home leaving their players in the delicate hands of the local female club caddies complete in red uniform and visored helmets, for the completion of the final round yesterday.

There was going to be no deviation from their Dubai race plans. There was also no denying the reality of the strain of a long year on the road no matter how much the tournament represented the beginning of the 2009 season, the hearts and minds of these bagmen were very much at the end of the 2008 season.

Indeed, had the fourth annual caddie of the year awards been held next week, I am certain those loopers who were part of the early exodus from Shanghai would have featured prominently as nominees in the "mystery" of the year and "best excuse" categories of the year. In the less flexible modern world of air travel changing plans is not a viable option for those on a controlled budget.

The caddie awards have quickly become a tradition of the Champions event. It is the brainchild of Giles Morgan, the head of sponsorship for HSBC, and it is he who had been instrumental in promoting the event. So despite the ungodly scheduled 6.45am starting times for Saturday due to the persistent rain, Giles continued the tradition by opening and closing the free bar an hour earlier on Friday night than originally scheduled.

The awards are strictly for those with thick skin. Poor Ross Fisher's caddie won two awards on the back of his man ending up in the swilken burn, at St Andrews, in the play-off for the Dunhill Links Championship.

The caddie of the year trophy went to the hugely-popular Gareth Lord, who naturally enough admitted he could not have won it without the exemplary golfing of his very talented boss, Robert Karlsson.

BAGMAN 2
2009
ON TOUR

"This was not just a matter of skill, this was the test of a very young and extremely talented golfer who needed to show his mettle. Anyone who may have doubted his resolve under pressure in the two previous occasions in his embryonic career, when he stared down the barrel of victory, have surely now quelled their scepticism."

Page 247

Rory McIlroy celebrates on the 18th green after winning the 2009 Dubai Desert Classic on the Majilis Course at the Emirates Golf Club. "Just as I hope he keeps his unique look I hope everyone's expectations of the boy wonder do not change his self-effacing manner."

With a new season comes the new challenges

JANUARY 13: With impeccable but purely coincidental timing, I began my new working year last Sunday with a trip east to Abu Dhabi. The crisp, cold, clear air of winter and the stunning light it casts upon our landscape had warmed up and the rise in temperature brought with it the grey, wet, windy and damp weather that originally got me on the move with global caddying in search of the 12-month summer.

After a long winter break of six weeks (it was closer to a six-month winter recess in the old days), I had the sensation of the definitive end of one year and the clear start to the next. More recently, with the extent of global golf, you could easily pass from one season to the next without noticing the change of year.

Having spent almost five years with my previous boss, Retief Goosen, the change of status has marked a rejuvenation of my looping career. With a top golfer your schedule tends to be well planned and filled in advance, there are few surprises from a continuity point of view.

Having split from Goosen, I found myself in the less secure position of not really knowing with whom or where I was going to work next.

In that sense I have some empathy with those who are experiencing such a position for the first time in their lives given the economic downturn and resulting rising unemployment.

In fact, it will be interesting to see how full the car-park is today in Abu Dhabi with expectant caddies in search of new bags for the new year. It is always a fair indication of the global economy on tour when you measure the excess of touring caddies over available players. I suspect there will be some who have made the trip in vain.

Heading off last weekend brought back the memories of the 1980s, when I had began travelling as a caddie with a wanderlust about the world beyond home. I did not view emigrating to work as a bad thing, it was a great opportunity to break free and find out what made the rest of the world tick.

So despite some people being forced to travel to find work for the first time in well over a decade, it is important for them to remember that it can be a fulfilling experience.

As I prepared to meet my new employer for the Middle East section of the European Tour, taking in three events in the desert, I got the feeling once again of the sense of adventure that I had felt in my early days of caddying.

Compounding this sensation was the fact that some trade fair in the Emirate has made finding a hotel for the week virtually impossible. This is a throwback to the old days when we rarely, if ever, made an advance hotel booking. I was going right back to my roots.

My new employer for the next three weeks is a young and extremely talented Swede, Alexander Noren. I do not really know Alex, apart from some brief phone conversations. We were paired with him a couple of years ago and I do remember being impressed with his ball-striking.

Having had the wonderful experience of caddying for a top golfer in his prime with Retief, it is now a completely different challenge to spend a few weeks with a young, hopeful golfer who has it all to prove.

So probably stumbling off an overnight flight from Dublin and onto the range for Monday morning duty with a brand new player was not the best of preparation, but we will have three days to acclimatise to each other's idiosyncrasies in preparation for Thursday's first round.

It was back on tour with a bang yesterday as half a dozen flights landed in Abu Dhabi's international airport. These flights had transported players and caddies from all corners of both hemispheres: Buenos Aires and New York, Paris, London, Dublin and Johannesburg.

It was like a European Tour convention at the baggage carousels, the terminal was alive with the chatter of friends who had bumped into one another by chance.

There was a series of belated New Year's greetings. As luck would have it, a colleague had a spare room booked which he passed on to me.

For those who had arrived from the north, there was a rare bout of enthusiasm to get out for a Monday morning practice round in over 20 degrees of heat and just a calm breeze to cool any over-heating limbs.

The memories of Jack Frost and Christmas carols faded as most of us Europeans recalled just why it was we followed the circus out of town all those winters ago. Pass the sun-block.

Hail of a time in Abu Dhabi desert

JANUARY 20: The European Tour stretched its borders in recent times in order both to extend its calendar and to take advantage of the weather in countries situated nearer the equator. This globalisation has given a new lease of life to the slightly misleading description of the European Tour, with over 30 per cent of the tour's events taking place well outside Europe's boundaries.

It has changed the nature of our golf and the extent of our travel and made it possible for us to play when most of Europe, as we know it, is cracking ice or so heavily muffled in clothing that swinging a golf club would involve an act of unhealthy contortion.

The 2009 season kicked off in earnest last week in Abu Dhabi, where the temperatures were more conducive to golf than back home. That was until the heavens opened on the Tour early on Thursday morning as many caddies and players alike had been lured into thinking that it doesn't rain in the desert. It shouldn't, it couldn't, it wouldn't – but it did.

It was not just a downpour, the precipitation came in the form of skin-stinging hails such as no local can remember in the Middle East. Many bagmen regretted leaving the rain gear and umbrellas in their lockers as the hail bounced up around their bare shanks. The courses in the desert do not have to worry about rain as a rule, so their drainage is not built to deal with sudden outbursts of rain. The result was that play was delayed by two hours while they mopped up the flash flood.

Despite the Tour having found new playing fields for its boys in faraway places, the demands on the schedule have tended to force us into playing these destinations either just a month too early or a few weeks too late. Whether it's dealing with deluges in the desert or downpours in Andalucia, it seems difficult to find the appropriate weather slot.

So last Thursday marked the first hail delay in the desert's golfing history and thus the first event to entail an early morning restart for half the field on Friday.

Restarts are a little bit messy, with 60 players and their caddies putting immediate demands on the catering facilities, the locker-room, the range and the transport system to get them all back to the holes which they vacated at dusk the previous night. Logistically, it is difficult for the organisers to deal with such a surge early in the morning.

The players go through their usual routines and allow some extra time to get back to the hole they left on the previous evening. Depending on what part of the course you had to get to, you either took a golf cart from behind the range or a courtesy car from in front of the clubhouse. We were allocated a car to take us to the fifth tee.

At 7.35am on Friday last, after much prodding of the driver, we finally exited the car-park in search of gate seven near the fifth tee. There was myself and my player, Alex Noren, Alistair Forsyth and his caddie, all full of the early morning banter that the camaraderie of group inconvenience sometimes brings.

By the time we noticed that we were heading at high speed towards Dubai, the only option was to divert across the desert in what looked like the "crow-would-fly" direction of the front nine of the Abu Dhabi golf course. There were fresh jeep tracks ahead of us, we were confident at 7.39 that we were following the trail of another courtesy jeep going the right way.

The sand became less compacted and more uneven as we turned a corner and realised that there was a well-constructed fence between us and the golf course with no opening in sight. The banter gave way to urgent questioning of our location and how, with less than five minutes to go till the klaxon was due to sound for the restart of the first round of the Abu Dhabi Championship, were we possibly going to get there on time.

It was a four-wheel drive jeep of some sort and our driver was being encouraged, quite easily, to test the limits of its off-road handling. With a mud splattered wind-shield and four bemused passengers, the vehicle pulled into gate seven at 7.49. Two caddies thrust balls and drivers into their players' hands and told them to run in the direction of the fifth tee. Our other playing partner had already hit but was confused as to why both his playing partners had not bothered to show up to finish off their rounds; he had come out with a driver with a better sense of direction.

There were no penalties incurred by our players for their late arrival on the tee. The chief referee approached us on the sixth hole to find out what had happened. In all my years of caddying it is fascinating to experience yet another slightly freakish occurrence in a tightly monitored professional sport. The responsibility in the case of delays is for the player to get himself back into position on the course, and the tardy arrival could have resulted in disqualification.

The seasoned travellers among us have long since learned that getting in a taxi in the Middle East requires confirmation of directions from the driver unless you want a long, circuitous trip to your destination. It seems that the same applies to courtesy car drivers: check your directions back onto the golf course after a rain delay.

Sod's law as the old meets with the new

JANUARY 27: Player/caddie relationships will ultimately end, that is a given. When they do there is a good chance of the player very quickly going on to win a tournament, this is sod's law. There also seems to be an increased likelihood of the ex-player and caddie getting drawn to play together with their new "partners" within a very short time of their split, this is the golfing gods working in their unfathomable way.

As many of you will know I parted company with Retief Goosen late last year after almost five successful years together. A couple of weeks after our separation my ex-boss went on to win a tournament in Malaysia, with a local caddie on the bag.

Of course this does not do the "invaluable" reputation of us tour caddies any favours, his win was noted with humour in the European caddie-shack. You need a thick skin in the world of professional golf, so the ridicule I received from my colleagues was no surprise.

By the time he won again in South Africa a couple of weeks ago the quips directed at me had lost the sting of the Far East win. I had enjoyed less success since our parting.

That was until my Middle-East swing employer Alexander Noren from Sweden shot a 66 last Saturday at the Doha Golf Club in Qatar. My ex-boss, Retief, shot a 67 a few groups behind us to end up on the same three-round total.

The golfing gods odds were pretty low of us being drawn together. Naturally we were.

The fact that we parted company on very good terms made the pairing something to look forward to rather than dread, as many of those who parted on bad terms in the past have had to deal with.

The tour is a small little travelling circus in which each act has been well scrutinised by the next, there is very little that slips by the unofficial tour news.

So by Saturday night last I was getting the message from my colleagues that I would be able to catch up on the past months since our separation. Retief was surrounded by his ex-caddies. My predecessor was in the group behind us with Johan Edfors, and Retief's looper before him, was a few matches behind with Sergio Garcia.

There are no restraint of trade orders in caddying, we are all free agents who can offer our advice to any player who is willing to listen just days after the cessation of employment with another.

As I nibbled on my morning toast on Sunday last in the clubhouse library in Doha which had been turned into the caddie dining room for the tournament, my colleagues reminded me of the long list of similar occurrences in previous player/caddie separations. "Oh yeah, no sooner had I finished with Hennie Otto last year and hooked up with Charl Schwartzel did we get paired together," Hennie's previous caddie informed me just as Peter Hedblom's man piped up about the time he got Niclas Fasth's bag and ended up being paired with his disgruntled previous bagman the very next week.

> "Of course there is no way to rig the drawn but there has long been a conspiracy theorists belief that the Tour are on the look out for inconvenient pairings."

Of course there is no way to rig the draw but there has long been a conspiracy theorists' belief that the Tour are on the look out for inconvenient pairings.

I ate breakfast with Retief's current caddie and chatted as we all normally do over breakfast. Then we ended up on the practice chipping green together Alex, my current employer, and Retief, my past paymaster, chipping balls to the same hole with me now looking at Retief's practice session in a whole new light.

There was not much said on the practice chipping green between any of the four parties involved. This is normal, it is a professional situation with the players preparing themselves both mentally and physically for the final round.

There is one sure thing with us humans, despite the fact that we are all very similar in most ways, when it comes to the detail we all differ greatly. This is particularly so with top sports people, their individual idiosyncrasies are what we caddies are employed to recognise and feed, or starve, as we see fit.

I had a set routine with Retief, which he was accustomed to, and I believe enjoyed, whereas Alex could take or leave all of these little touches.

Of course, when you get on the course it is all about business and no one's better at this than the two-time US Open Champion.

As anyone who has been around him will testify he uses his words sparingly and when he does converse it is quietly and tersely. That is his way.

Retief has adopted the hands-on approach to his new working relationship and seems to be doing everything apart from carrying the bag for himself. In my new position I have figured out that my player likes a considerable amount more information than Retief required from me. I am still getting used to the more hands-on guidance that Alex enjoys.

It is, of course, the art of caddying and advising in most jobs; figuring out what your boss wants and needs and furnishing him with both in required helpings.

Neither my current or past employer played particularly well, both putted averagely. It was appropriate then that we both ended up on the modest total of eight under par.

Retief headed home promptly on his private plane and myself and Alex hung around for a beer and a bit of down-time before our commercial flight to Dubai.

The same result from two players of a different nature, similar talent but at very different stages of their career. It is interesting to observe a superstar touch the life of a budding star – one with the accolades that drive the other, divided by a golfing lifetime that is sometimes connected in the rare pairings that remind one of where they have come from and the other of where they would like to go.

McIlroy has learned well from the master

FEBRUARY 3: Ten years ago the club was merely a big square of grass surrounded by sand. A decade ago Rory McIlroy was a kid playing with his mates on street corners in Holywood. Last week he ran with the big boys and came to the front after a nervous finish in the concrete-clad desert.

McIlroy came to the Middle East three years ago on an invitation to play the Dubai Desert Classic. He narrowly missed the cut but followed Tiger Woods on the weekend, scurrying around inside the ropes with the photographers, trying to capture his own images of how the best player in the world plies his trade.

He learnt well. Because, despite playing world-class golf and reaching 22 under par after 68 holes, the reality of leading a golf tournament gripped him. It was time to abandon the birdie golf and knuckle down to getting the job done and win his first European Tour title.

This is what the master Woods and other multiple winners are so good at and it is, of course, the art of four-round professional golf, winning without necessarily hitting quality shots.

McIlroy had obviously learned well from the grandmaster because Woods did not play great golf in the final round in 2006. He worked the ball around the Emirates course and somehow got it in the hole.

McIlroy made a veteran's par on the par-five 18th last Sunday with water and disaster looming for two of the shots he played under the most pressure he must have felt in his short life to date. His up and down from the back trap to a pin cut on the end of a severe downslope with water just five paces beyond, was a sand-save that only a player with guts could pull off.

This was not just a matter of skill, this was the test of a very young and extremely talented golfer who needed to show his mettle. Anyone who may have doubted his resolve under pressure in the two previous occasions in his embryonic career, when he stared down the barrel of victory, have surely now quelled their scepticism.

A six-shot lead at one stage of the final round can lead to complacency. It is an isolated place in which you might think a golfer would love to find himself.

It's not always the case, mainly because it is difficult to keep up the pressure of aggressive golf. When you have such a lead there is a tendency to try to steer your lead back to the winner's podium. Of course the very thought of winning is a fatal distraction.

McIlroy is head of a new era of golfers who all seem to be cut out of the same quality cloth.

Ross Fisher, Martin Kaymer, Oliver Fisher and Alex Noren are all young, talented and extremely well-mannered relative newcomers to the European Tour who have been very well groomed in etiquette, behaviour and respect for those around them.

I certainly notice a refreshing attitude from these superstars who could quite easily have assumed a right of passage and entitlement which some of their predecessors have been guilty of in the past.

I was the victim of an untimely collision with a cement truck while travelling in a taxi in Abu Dhabi a few weeks ago and was visibly carrying a neck injury. I don't know Rory that well but his genuine concern for me was heart-warming. Any day I have seen him since he has enquired about my progress. I was touched by the concern of an acquaintance who took the time to worry about a relative stranger's welfare.

It is probably over 30 years since Europe has had such a prodigy in its domain. Seve Ballesteros was the youngest player to win in Europe and, of course, went on to be the most dominant and entertaining player to walk European fairways for decades. His flair and bravado matched his fiery Iberian temperament.

Rory McIlroy is the modern Seve. He is a toned-down version with the quiet confidence of a winner rather than of the bulldozing manner of Ballesteros.

He has a fine head of hair which should be his trademark; there are enough clones in the game. Just as I hope he keeps his unique look I hope everyone's expectations of the boy wonder do not change his self-effacing manner.

Just as Seve was the talisman for European golf throughout the 1980s, let's hope that Rory keeps entertaining us on European soil over the next two decades as well as taking his enormous and exciting talent to America.

Noren's given me a shot in the arm

FEBRUARY 10: I read a newspaper headline last weekend, before Ireland's skilful display against France, that Brian O'Driscoll is "still hungry" at the ripe old age of 30. I would imagine he still is, how else could he face the fearsome task of modern top-class rugby.

There is, of course, no age limit for the modern golfer to be considered fairway unworthy although many do fade somewhat as they advance into their fourth decade. There are always exceptions like Bernhard Langer and Jay Haas who still performed on the main tours at a very high level in their late 40s. Of course the seniors' tours around the globe, but particularly in America, have rejuvenated many the flagging old pro both psychologically and financially.

As a rule, though, there is a fading chance that you are going to win majors as you advance into your 40s in golf. So despite golf being one of the professional games with the longest lifespan, there is naturally a limit to the realistic expectation for major success.

The same cannot be said of a caddie. Having lugged bags worldwide for several decades there is no doubt that the appetite to continue wanes the further you go, this is particularly true in today's limitless worldwide golf seasons. Golfers are of course reliant on their own talent. Caddies, however, are reliant on their player's talent on top of their own caddying expertise. The player's talent being way more significant than the caddie's, I must add. The old adage of "the best way to be a good caddie is to carry the bag of a very good player" will never be untrue.

One of the great advantages of being a caddie is that you can transport your skill from player to player: as one relationship loses steam there is always the prospect of regenerating interest with another golfer.

I have recently enjoyed almost half a decade with the one player whose talent certainly made me look like a great caddie. As time passed and the air miles mounted, our partnership lost its dynamic. It was tired.

So when I got the opportunity this year to link up with a young, enthusiastic and very talented Alexander Noren, my own flagging career was given a shot in the arm.

It raises the question of what is the ideal age partnership with a player and a caddie? I remember going to the States for the first time and being slightly shocked at how elderly the average caddie was on the US Tour.

In Europe it had been a young man's game, so I was amazed by the amount of greying temples on tour over there.

As a player I am sure there would be a comforting air in having an experienced hand at your side. Then again there is an age group of the opinion that older is not necessarily wiser.

A bit like we all felt at a certain stage of our youth; our parents seemed stupid and uncool for many of our formative years.

It is the same for young golfers. Do they appreciate the reassurance from a weather-beaten caddie with decades of experience and a face betraying a lifetime of afternoons spent in intense sunshine? Or do they prefer the plucky advice from a smooth- skinned young advisor, whose enthusiasm is matched by his stride, and whose positive nature could easily be mistaken for the final word?

Much of a caddie's lifespan depends on how well he or she has taken care of themselves. I have noticed some European caddies who have been around for a long time getting sidelined due to physical incapability at a relatively young age. One of our colleagues got stranded in Asia last year due to deep vein thrombosis. Many of us have experienced back and limb trouble with years of contorting our spines to accommodate the unnatural act of humping a heavy golf bag around the fairways of the world.

Apart from the physical demands of the job, the lifestyle of globetrotting has curtailed some bagmen. Dealing with family life is not always the easiest on a caddie's budget. A compromise in recent years has been for some older loopers to get involved in sharing a players bag over the year with another caddie, thus getting more time at home with the family.

There is a general consensus that a caddie with decades of experience can be an invaluable asset to a young ambitious player. The problem can be that the age gap makes it difficult for a young golfer to relate to an older caddie in matters other than golf. So the balance of wisdom and age difference is a delicate one. Who wants a caddie that looks like his daddy?

There is a sentiment that the older caddie can contribute greatly to the keen-to-learn younger pro, particularly one who has worked for a top golfer in the past. Many are hoping to gain some of their employees knowledge which has been effectively gleaned through their former superstar bosses.

It makes sense.

It is both invigorating and flattering to feel the inquisitive eyes of a young hopeful golfer absorbing the stories of your old boss and sensing that they are taking a short-cut to the position that they yearn to hold in world golf.

So like O'Driscoll in his 89th game in an Irish jersey, of course he has desire, but it has been reignited by the ambitious talent that surrounds him in the green jerseys. And the same can be said for some of us ageing bagmen with our enthusiastic and hungry young bosses.

Clammy conditions go against the grain

FEBRUARY 17: A man has simply got to rub his hand across his face at midday in Malaysia to realise how quickly things grow when you are so close to the equator. Your five o'clock shadow appears a lot earlier in this hot and extremely moist land.

As a drenched bag-toter standing idly by on a green, scratching your chin in contemplation of your player's plight as he drips over another putt that he cannot envisage being able to hit hard enough to get it to the hole, you begin to fathom why the greens are so very slow.

Grain is something that us Irish golfers have usually only to consider while choosing our morning cereal. In Asia and most hot countries grain is an added complication when it comes to deciding on what line to hit your putt. As the temperatures soar throughout the day the grain stands up like the stubble on a hot caddie's chin, causing all sorts of deviations to the course of the ball along its crooked, slow and uncertain path towards the cup.

The common consensus in the air-conditioned locker-room last week was that the greens were the slowest that most players in the modern era could remember. Some players felt like they were swinging their putter harder than their driver in order to get their putts uphill into the grain.

I remember playing golf in southern Africa for the first time and looking in disbelief as I was advised by a local that my putt on a right to left slope was actually going to break left to right because of the strength of the grain. It is an alien concept for most of us from Britain and Ireland and one that favours the local players when it comes to the shorter grass end of the game.

The incessant heat is not conveyed clearly on television as it is close at hand when the slightest exertion from the fittest of golfers results in pools of sweat forming in unusual places, like on their knees or around their bottoms. Your umbrella is used strictly as a true Spanish parasol, a hint of rain would be as welcome and refreshing as a freak gust of cool breeze. You seem to get neither here. Moisture simply oozes and seeps around you; from the permanently lush grass beneath you to the damp air about you there is no escaping the humidity.

> "The common consensus in the air-conditioned locker-room last week was that the greens were the slowest that most players in the modern era could remember. Some players felt like they were swinging their putter harder than their driver in order to get their putts uphill into the grain."

We were at the Saujana Golf and Country Club outside Kuala Lumpur for the Maybank Malaysian Open, one of the co-sanctioned events between the flagging Asian Tour and the more robust European Tour. It gives us Europeans a chance to experience the exotic Far-East and all its eastern promise. Simply looking down the starting list with names like Periasamy Gunasegaran, Amandeep V Johl, Akhmal Tarmizee and Somkist Srisa-Nga, there is no doubt Europe has temporarily extended its borders.

I had previously thought that Robert Dinwiddie was an ear-catching name before I perused last weeks draw sheet.

As the capital of Malaysia extends further into the surrounding undergrowth the local wildlife has sought refuge in the remaining foliage of suburban golf courses. The tournament was played on the Cobra course and the king Cobra himself lives between the eight and ninth holes.

There were prominent and plentiful signs about the presence of snakes in the area. There are monkeys all over the Saujana country club and they are keen to show the course is most definitely theirs and is only to be used by humans at their peril.

There are signs behind most greens advising golfers to leave no valuables far from sight as the monkeys are highly likely to take them. A player has had his yardage laser pinched by them in the past. As I shuffled through some dense trees towards the next tee a small bit of debris bounced at the foot of a spectator on the path in front of me. I looked up and a monkey was brazenly gaping down, letting us know what committee set the rules on this part of the course.

Things are very different on the Asian Tour. On the surface the tournament is set up like any other big event worldwide; roped-off fairways and some modest spectator viewing areas. The temporary barriers had a different meaning however, they were there to be ignored. Being in the last group during the final two rounds we had the majority of the galleries with us. In fact driving into the complex was an indication of the Malaysian system; cars were blatantly abandoned along the roadway to the golf course.

I overheard some unruly spectators discussing their viewing strategy on one hole, suggesting that they take the left route up the fairway, which was prohibited to spectators, as they had a better chance of being seen on television from that side. The rules officials were reduced to "sheep-dogs" at the weekend with the impossible task of reining in a mob that had a "free to roam" policy.

Kuala Lumpur was soupy, soggy and so different from any European climate we experience. The last time I felt that hot was in a sauna with a towel around me and not outdoors, fully clothed with a heavy bag on my back in the soaring midday sun.

We have all got the crisp dry heat of Western Australia in the relatively low forecasted high-30s to look forward to this week. There are snakes on the course but the local kangaroos do not have the tendency for petty on-course theft like the Malaysian monkeys did in Saujana last week and the afternoon stubble remains less pronounced in the dry heat.

New kid on the block

FEBRUARY 24: There are not many people who are prepared to tell golfers exactly how things are. The professional game has got more than its fair share of sycophants who massage players' egos with what they think their player would like to hear.

We were in the one country in the world last week where gaining favour through flattery is most definitely not part of the culture. The Johnnie Walker

Classic returned to Western Australia and the Vines Resort set in the Swan Valley vineyards east of Perth.

The tournament was what is reported to be the final professional appearance in West Australia of "The Shark", Greg Norman. The iconic Norman, in his 50s, still commanded more attention early in the week at the Vines than any of the promising whipper-snappers in the field.

That was until he missed the cut and the race began for the trophy, with the relatively young and less famous contenders battling over the benign back nine last Sunday.

The usual conditions did not pertain, with soft fairways and greens making the strategic Graham Marsh-designed course very tame.

The weather had been extremely hot for the past month which meant the greenkeeper could not risk firming the greens up in the run up to the event. This was coupled with the notable absence of the "Freemantle Doctor", the cooling south-west afternoon wind that soothes overheating bodies but plays havoc with golfer's minds.

The Australians demand a lot from their sports stars, probably a symptom of the fact they tend to punch well above their weight given the size of the population.

Despite "The Shark" losing his teeth, so to speak, in golfing terms he still has the charismatic presence of a superstar. He seems to have defied ageing in the last decade, he is physically as fit as he was 20 years ago, and his athletic figure would be more fitting on a 30-year-old.

So as the Shark bemoaned his bad putting as the main problem with his game, some local residents figured they would let everyone who walked down the left flank of the 11th fairway know how they felt about the national icon. They draped a sign outside the master bedroom window simply stating "Norman Ain't Performin".

In case "The Shark" didn't notice the message, the residents had perched themselves on their hot-tin roof and vocalised their thoughts as the Norman entourage stormed by.

The media and golfing public in Australia have never been lenient on any "tall poppies", as high achievers are called in the land of Oz. I remember being here back in Norman's prime at a time when he had finished second in quite a few events, snatching defeat from the jaws of victory. As the television commentators were filling in some idle moments they started chatting about the sponsors of the event in question, "The Holden Australian Open". They mentioned the car company had named a class of car after the great man. "The Greg Norman Holden". To which the other commentator replied, "Is that the one with the automatic choke?"

Humorous, if somewhat cruel. If a commentator had suggested that in America he would lose his job. In Australia political correctness will never get in the way of a witty jibe at a national icon.

Many of the contestants and their bagmen stayed at the dune-dotted beach at Scarborough, north of Perth, a scenic location that meant a long bus trip out to the Vines each day. The 6am bus wound its way through the parched land towards the vineyards and at 6.40am last Thursday pulled into the Resort.

The driver took a wrong turn but was abruptly alerted by an Australian colleague. He pulled down Henley Brook Close in order to rectify his mistake.

My mouthy colleague unnecessarily riled the under-pressure driver by suggesting he was going to get us stuck down a cul-de-sac. The driver was determined not to make any more mistakes and in his haste he gave a lamp post a bit of a nudge while reversing. It was listing slightly and the street sign was hanging off its last screw.

Somehow the resident who benefited most from the particular street lamp was suddenly outside in his front garden scratching his head and berating the bus driver, who was now picking up speed on the right road for the clubhouse with an impatient bus load and the listing lamp post a distant vision in his rear view mirror.

Plain speaking in Australia is not just a male preserve. We played with a Queenslander, Tony Carolan, who had his wife caddying for him.

Having been in four bunkers in the first four holes and watching his tee-shot descend into another trap right of the pin on the short fifth, Carolan's wife said, "I have had a gut-full of raking traps for you, you can do this one yourself."

Her husband splashed out to three feet, marked his ball and went back to rake the trap. He knew she wasn't joking.

Listening to the commentary of the final round last Sunday I did not hear any suggestion of the eventual winner "choking" or backing off. Probably because the 18-year-old amateur winner, Danny Lee, a naturalised New Zealander and Korean by birth, was doing anything but backing off over the closing holes of the Johnnie Walker Classic.

While those around the hottest young prospect in world golf were in the commentators words "facing ugly par putts", or "having their rounds going south quickly", he was birdieing the final two holes to capture his first professional event as a teenage amateur. In doing so he became the youngest winner on the European Tour and only the second to win as an amateur.

Norman may not be performing but the Koreans are and there are plenty more promising golfers where Lee comes from. It's time for the Australians to let "The Shark" go and embrace this new young talent that has been nurtured on Antipodean soil. Danny Lee is the real thing and that's the truth.

Cool when the heat is on

MARCH 3: If Thongchai Jaidee is walking around the New Kuta Golf Club with a towel covering his head for most of the final round of the Enjoy Jakarta Indonesian Open (held in Bali) then you know it is hot. Jaidee, not surprisingly the eventual winner of this year's event, grew up playing in similar conditions in Thailand.

The dilemma for golfers in hot and humid countries is that when there is no wind the course is easier, but what you gain on the swings you definitely lose on the heat index roundabouts. It was sauna time again in Bali last week.

The Indonesian Open marked the end of the European Tour's Middle and Far East swing of the season and for many the idea of returning to the end of winter in Europe seemed like a reasonable prospect.

You would want to be geographically aware or you could have ended up on the wrong island last week with the slightly confusing name enticing you to enjoy the capital city on the island of Java.

As a serious professional who plots and plans his career from practice routines and daily gym sessions to physio and nutrition there has to be a serious question mark over the rationale behind competing in such a stressful heat.

You just have to look at a player walk to the first tee after a gentle warm-up on the range and he already has the appearance of someone who has spent the entire day toiling manually in the relentless heat.

The objective of playing a professional round of golf is ultimately to get around in as few shots as possible. In southeast Asia the objective seems to be one of survival. In order to survive you need to fill every idle moment on the course drinking. At times is seems like you do not have enough time to drink the amount you need to stop you dehydrating.

New Kuta, being a new resort course, has been designed for cart play and not walking. So there are considerable distances between greens and tees. Thankfully we were shuttled between many holes getting some much needed airflow over the face and opportunities to drink even more water.

Of course these Asian events are co-sanctioned between the Asian and European Tours, so not all players get the chance to play in these limited field events. But for those Europeans who are exempt, I would seriously question the decision to put yourself through the physical challenge of the heat endurance test within the Indonesian Open; Bali is a perfect holiday island, its much better to take a break here and play golf in a more temperate climate.

Of course there is a contrary argument; given the weakness of the field, it is a good opportunity to take advantage of a slightly easier standard of play.

My man, Alexander Noren from Sweden, and Steve Webster and Simon Dyson, both English, who all tied for second place are examples that turn my argument on its head. There is no doubt that the grain on the greens (without banging on again about it) is a contributing factor in giving local players the edge with the flat stick.

We played with Jaidee in the final round. Not only did he putt very well, he also holed a chip shot that required a detailed knowledge of the grain on the green, to which he paid particular attention in his added preparation for his chip-in from behind the fifth green. What a charming place to end a long stretch on tour. Bali is known as the Island of Gods. The idyllic island in the Indonesian Ocean is predominantly under the Hindu influence unlike the rest of the country which is largely Muslim.

It is very much a ceremonial land with different gods being celebrated throughout the year from Galungan in January and February symbolising the victory of Good (Dharma) over Evil (Adharma) to Pagerwesi (Iron Fence) in November, when they pray for strong mental and spiritual defence.

It is a very ornate island with many buildings adorned with stone and wood carvings. Temples are ever present and near the course which is known locally as Dreamland.

The course complex is owned by the deceased Dictator General Suharto's son, Tommy. It is, of course, a haven of nouveau, cut though the small holdings of local people.

You do not have to stray too far from the fairways to see how real people live their traditional life amongst the latest in Callaway drivers or TaylorMade irons.

Before we went out on Sunday I consulted the local priest attending the temple positioned to spiritually look over the golf course. The temple was situated behind the practice putting green. As I entered I noticed that the priest was stoking up a big fire in front of one of his altars.

He said he was throwing a few extra logs on in order to keep the rain away. Unfamiliar with the workings of this unique form of Balinese Hinduism and looking at the big black rollers out beyond Jimbaran Bay, I decided to keep the umbrella in the bag. It didn't rain a drop all day and we are still in the rainy season.

The tournament ended in true Balinese tradition with a Legong Dance. The beautifully adorned girls rolled their arms and crooked their necks to the drone of the hypnotic Balinese music. Jaidee took the trophy, the winner's cheque and the local painting which was also presented to the Thai Asian specialist. The aesthetics of the Balinese paintings is a reflection of their beautiful surroundings and art is a big part of Balinese life.

Next time I return to the Island of Gods I will leave my umbrella in the locker if I see smoke billowing out of the golf course temple in deference to the Hindu gods and their powerful, if somewhat mystical influence.

Flying below the radar is helpful route to success

MARCH 17: So you are leading a golf tournament by five shots with the final round to go and you need to sleep soundly for one more night on that promising but not insurmountable lead.

How do you do it? Well, the first thing you don't do is read a newspaper or listen to any form of media coverage, or the chances are your professional brain will get so muddled you will forget what you were supposed to be doing in order to secure the title.

Expectation is probably the most difficult emotion for professional sports-people to deal with and it takes the most talented and experienced handler to deal with the likelihood of ultimate success.

It is a standard line that professional golfers churn out in post-round inter-views, "I just tried to stay in the present, hit each shot as it comes and let go of any errors I made in the past."

Living the moment – sure, weren't us Irish experts at it before our recent dalliance with rampant capitalism?

Today we are regretting the past, trying to put up with the moment and really looking forward to a brighter future in six years, by all accounts.

I have been involved with numerous players who have had agitated Saturday night slumbers, resting on the lead of a tournament.

> "Expectation is probably the most difficult emotion for professional sportspeople to deal with and it takes the most talented and experi-enced handler to deal with the likelihood of ultimate success."

Most slept worse than others on tournament leads.

It takes a lot of emotion to cope with the fear of failure and even more to deal with the image of success. Of course knowing how to deal with it is the DNA of superstars: on top of their talent, this is probably the next most important ingre-dient to contribute to success.

Phil Mickelson won in Miami on Sunday having led from day one. I would imagine he slept as well as if he were on vacation: leading tournaments is part of a superstar's make-up.

No psychologist can teach it to players who have not won and are not used to leading.

I listened and read with trepidation the pre-Scottish rugby match chatter last weekend and shuddered at the thought of a great team playing great rugby listening to the same probing questions about the Grand Slam.

I don't know what mechanisms the Irish rugby back-room team has for sheltering their players from the optimism and focusing on the future, but they seem to have done a good job of it.

Whether it is sheltering them, or just dealing with it face on, it has worked so far.

When I caddied for Retief Goosen in the US Open at Pinehurst in 2005, he had to sleep on a three-shot lead going into the final round. He had won at Shinnecock Hills the previous year. Pinehurst was a completely different scenario.

In Shinnecock, he had played great golf for the first three rounds. In Pinehurst, he had held it together for three rounds and his statistics revealed the fact he was not really playing that well.

To make a comparison between Retief in Shinnecock and Pinehurst and the Irish team's current flow of external expectation from an otherwise flagging nation, I hope I don't hear or read any Irish player speculating about next weekend. I look forward to hearing from them after the game.

There were virtually no interviews for Retief in 2004 until he actually won the event.

In 2005, he gave a TV interview on the morning of the final round. It may well have been the start of the demise in front of that TV camera on that Sunday morning in June 2005 in South Carolina. Retief had a catastrophic final round.

I have never seen Tiger Woods give a pre-round interview before his multiple major victories, only post- ones.

Padraig Harrington had an untimely – or timely – accident before his defence of his British Open Championship title in Birkdale last year. It deflected the conversation full of expectation of defending his title to whether he would get a chance to tee off in the first place.

There is no doubt that flying below the radar is helpful no matter how experienced you are.

A young Michael Campbell was rather insensitively asked by a Scottish interviewer as he led the British Open in 1995, "Well Michael, it's all yours to lose now?" while thrusting the microphone in his face expecting a civil answer.

There is a sensitivity rule which prevails among competitors and caddies in golf which means that the awkward, doubt-triggering questions will never be asked, and certainly not at an inopportune moment around the course.

So who gives a fiddlers if Brian O'Driscoll scored a hat-trick of tries at Lansdowne in 2002. It has zero relevance in the preamble to a game of monumental importance in 2009.

Or who cares if Ireland has not won a Grand Slam since 1948.

It will have no relevance to how they play a multi-layered, strategic game at the Millennium Stadium in Cardiff next weekend if they stick to their clearly laid-out professional approach which has got them into this position in the first place.

It must be a hair-raising and stimulating position for the Irish team to be in with a chance for the Grand Slam.

It will be a great success of their collective lives if they win. Before it, of course, it is just another game where the sound strategic principles they have adopted throughout this campaign must prevail.

I have the utmost of faith in them to do their best next Saturday and if they do they will have earned immortality in Irish rugby lore.

Enforced holiday set to continue

MARCH 24: I had just pulled into the car park of my golf club last Saturday for a game in the weekend singles competition. It is a rare luxury for someone who spends the majority of his life on the road.

On my second week on holidays at home I was actually settling into a routine of planning to play in the club competitions.

I felt normal, peeking into a world where the weekend came to many of my fellow members with a sigh of relief – it was playtime.

As I squeezed into a packed car park – it was never this full in boom time – my phone rang. It was my boss, Alexander Noren, calling from Stockholm, keeping me informed about the prognosis on his wrist injury which he had been carrying for much of our recent trip to the Far East and Australia, but which had deteriorated to such an extent during our final event in Bali, as to warrant his contemplation of withdrawal.

It had been hot, his wrist was sore and particularly painful at impact with the driver. Having hit three balls off the 16th tee in the second round we had a little chat walking up the fairway both wondering which ball we would find and what number we would clock up on the hole: nine was not unrealistic number.

He actually found his first ball in an unplayable lie and miraculously made a par. This is what good players do, they salvage their round from probable disaster.

Alex decided to continue playing, went on to finish the tournament and had a putt on the last hole on Sunday to possibly force a play-off, confirming the wide-held belief on tour to "beware of the injured golfer".

When a golfer has an injury it is a difficult decision for him to withdraw. With internal niggles, as anyone who has suffered with a bad back or a stiff neck will testify to, we are always hopeful of feeling better in the morning.

Hope can sometimes be the worst quality in man. Sometimes it is best to be realistic and take the break your body needs to recover.

This is essentially what we talked about walking up the 16th fairway in Bali. Our consensus was that at 26, Alex is young, he has a long year and hopefully a long career ahead of him, so why risk competing in what was a relatively obscure event and possibly compromise the rest of his year and more? Why, because he had a chance to win and, of course, that is why all these competitors play.

Of course we have had a couple of very recent high-profile cases of injuries with Tiger Woods and our own Padraig Harrington last year which highlighted both the physical prowess and decision-making ability of both gritty major champions. The sight of Tiger limping around southern California in the play-off for the US Open last June would have left an observer, who knew nothing about golf, wondering why he was putting himself through it. Answer: because he is a competitor. Of course the result was another title and almost eight months off with surgery and rehab on the damaged knee.

Padraig of course made the correct decision to play the British Open Championship last July despite carrying what appeared to be a serious wrist injury. Dealing with an injury questions not only your pain threshold but also your thought process about what damage you are doing yourself by playing through the pain. Golfers are one of the few sportspeople who can have a very long professional life-span; it is important not to be short-sighted.

Padraig's decision that "it will probably be all right in the morning", in hindsight of course, was the right one as he not only competed but went on to win his second Claret Jug. My ex-boss Retief Goosen once played a round in an event with a broken arm, such was his tolerance for pain.

So as I listened to my boss tell me of the MRIs and X-rays and poking and prodding of Scandinavia's finest physicians at his left wrist, I quickly realised that I may well become a permanent fixture on my club's timesheet. My relatively new boss had been told by the experts it would need at least another three to four weeks before he could play again.

They fortunately came to the conclusion that although it was a limiting injury, the ligament restriction that he was experiencing in his left wrist was not a career-breaking problem, as long as he rested.

Not hitting golf balls for professionals creates many types of withdrawal symptoms. For a young Swede to be banned from the range for so long could result in him going cold turkey; it is an extremely tough ask.

It must be very frustrating for Alex, who had such a strong start to the year, to have to sit out for so long. It is also a relief that he does not have a serious injury. So for him it's the couch and for his caddie it is time to slot into the weekend golf routine on the other side of the bag.

Why Augusta Masters is so special

APRIL 7: The great landmark in the annual golfing schedule is almost upon us; the Masters Tournament in Augusta, Georgia, will be decided on the not insignificant date of Easter Sunday.

Augusta, Georgia, to those who are not familiar with the southern parts of the United States is like most surrounding towns south of it; bedecked with churches. It is a deeply religious part of America and it wouldn't surprise me if the green jacketed gentlemen who run this iconic event would aspire to have their prestigious event as the high altar of golf.

Arguably I suppose it is and this comes largely from the fact there is a permanency at Augusta that has not been established at any other event. No other event of such prominence returns to the same venue year in year out. This sense of returning to an institution is what makes the Masters so special.

My first visit was in 1993 when I was bursting with suspense before my arrival. This expectation is heightened by the fact if you tell people where you are going their eyes widen and a sense of adventure vicariously spreads across their face: then the inquisition begins in search of what it is really like to be there.

When I arrived at the top of Magnolia Lane in the 1990s I had to present my passport to the security guard in order to gain access through a water-tight looking perimeter fence around the property. My name had been written beside my player of the time – Anders Forsbrand – which meant I was "good to go". I was to find the caddie shack at the bottom of the road running parallel to the famed lane.

I had caught a glimpse of the brilliant white-painted clubhouse through the magnolias before I diverted to the caddie shack. It was a Sunday morning, there was little to indicate the biggest event in golf starting the next week.

When I entered the forbidding caddie shack I instantly got the feeling I was somewhere special. But not the elitist special that the sight of the pristine clubhouse through the trees would suggest, this was what I imagined I would encounter if I took a wrong turn on the wrong side of the tracks.

I stepped down to the tatty caddie shack. The door squeaked open and the inmates of the shack turned to see who was entering. Another one of those tour caddies was the collective look that welcomed me.

Four local caddies dressed in the standard Augusta caddie overalls were playing cards in the corner, above them a sign alarmed me, it read; "No weapons allowed on the property, all guns and knives must be left outside".

I decided to head for the toilet and some privacy to digest the scene I had just walked into. There was no door on the toilet. That was 15 years ago and just as the caddies' lot has changed in general for the better over the decades the same applies to Augusta National.

There was always a serenity and an air of tranquillity about the place. Everyone moves at an even pace (the rules state clearly that running is not permitted on the grounds). From members to staff it was like they had been programmed to move at three miles an hour.

There was a southern politeness that seemed to infect even those players who would not be known for their warmth during an average week. "Gid mownen" was delivered at the same pedestrian speed that they walked at, deliberately.

The sense of permanence pervades both inside and beyond at Augusta. The same people present you with your credentials, just a little heavier and greyer than the previous year. Likewise in the renovated caddie shack which now has showers and lockers and doors on the toilet. Even the security guards are mostly the same as they were when I first came to Augusta, they even guard the same areas each year and you get to know them by name.

We wait for our players, having donned the dehumanising boiler-suits, on the tranquil balcony outside the locker-room. No clubhouse access in Augusta and there probably never will be. The gardeners tend the hanging plants on the deck at seemingly the precise same time as they did the previous day.

The emerald green paint that adorns the areas that are not painted pristine white never overlap. Much like the grass verges are as carefully cropped as the nape of a soldiers neck. Everything is very much in order at the National, from the consistent texture of the painted walls to the even height of the surrounding grass verges.

No wonder then that a colleague who visited Augusta once as a caddie heavily armed with an overdose of scepticism replied tersely on return to Europe when asked of his impressions of the sacred and secret golf club: "Chelsea flower show with a flag pole in it."

Despite the elite sense of order prevailing inside the compound, there is a similar sense of a different order beyond the fence: outside is truly America. Just as the green-jacketed gentlemen inside look like they have emerged from a wood and leather-bound chamber in the old cities of the east coast the patrons scurrying around the neon-lit Washington Road beyond look like they have emerged from a mall.

For the first time in almost a decade I will not be at the high altar of golf next Sunday. I will be observing from afar on my couch with the most amenable peculiarity of Augusta, the condensed television transmission, beaming out the unique green-jacketed sense of order.

Cabrera not quite what the Augusta doctors ordered

APRIL 14: There is always a desire in the final scene of a major for the heaving throng to rally behind their favourites and act as the 15th club, if you like. The choice pairing in the final round of this year's Masters was the American dream duo of Tiger Woods and Phil Mickelson. The patrons and TV producers just couldn't keep their eyes off them.

With the momentum the star pairing gathered on the front nine it was a wonder there was anyone left watching any other group; it was, for a considerable part of the day, the only show in town.

The real contenders are often elsewhere, but it is hard to let go of the dream. It is not like it is purely a patriotic sentiment, because two of the three final protagonists were good old American boys: Chad Campbell from Texas and Kenny Perry from Kentucky. But the natives seem to have an insatiable appetite for superstars, and not even other in-form Americans could detract from the Phil and Tiger shoot-out.

> "Watching Cabrera shoot up the leaderboard last Friday, he exuded the air of a player getting the very best out of his huge talent. He stared down his iron shots like they were going to knock out the flagstick."

There was a dearth of spectators with the final pair of Perry and Angel Cabrera. The gaps in the meagre rows of followers along the fairway ropes were so big on some holes that the distant azaleas looked more prominent than the people.

Having watched the coverage since Thursday, I began to get a sense of who was really in form. Of course, the leaderboard is an obvious indication of form. But watching the players' rhythm and reaction to the shots they hit tends to be more revealing about how the player feels.

I would categorise players into two groups at this level. The superstars, who tend to be able to turn on the form at majors like it is simply a decision to flick a switch and perform regardless of how they are playing, and the other group, the quality golfers who happen to find themselves on form during a major.

Tiger and Phil were just "making it happen" because their willpower to produce at majors doesn't relate to their form books. The quality group was the three who reached the play-off, Cabrera, Perry and Campbell. I always remember a former boss of mine admitting his weakness at performing consistently. But in the same breath he confidently suggested that, on any given week he may hit form, he believed he could beat anybody in the field.

So it is for most top golfers; if they hit form they are all good enough to beat whoever their main challengers are, whether it be Woods or Shingo Katayama.

Watching Cabrera shoot up the leaderboard last Friday, he exuded the air of a player getting the very best out of his huge talent. He stared down his iron shots like they were going to knock out the flagstick. If he missed a green, he seemed to see his chip shots clearly and execute them delicately, especially for such a big man. He appeared to move at a constant pace.

His sports psychologist would have been proud. Routines are the key to success, in their minds.

Of course, the lurching Argentine does not have a mind man: he admitted after his US Open victory in 2007 that cigarettes sort out his agitated golf mind. He seems to have substituted the tobacco with chewing gum.

So despite the force of the patrons rallying behind their "chosen ones", the reality of talented golfers in form was starting to manifest itself at the top of the leaderboard. With Cabrera competing in his 10th Masters, the course was unlikely to surprise him.

As is the trend at modern Masters, the top of the leaderboard was littered with the best names in the business heavily armed with talent and experience around Augusta. The bottom of the leaderboard was laden with veterans and novices, the former too old to perform, the latter too raw to understand.

Naturally, even the fluid form of Cabrera from Cordoba was compromised with the pressures that grip a player when the finishing line is in sight and a new dynamic is added to the game: the vision of victory and with it a heightened awareness. This causes errors and a lot of unease.

As Angel got closer to capturing his second major title he chewed his gum more vigorously and guzzled water more liberally.

By early evening last Sunday at Augusta even the big-bellied frat boys who seem to make up the bulk of this sacred event's patrons list couldn't deny their chosen ones were out of it. Who better to embrace as the alternative Masters heroes than the full-faced Perry, Cabrera or Campbell?

They love a winner in America, especially a home-grown one. So the concept of the lurching, hulk-framed South American, raised on generous portions of barbecued Argentine beef, probably didn't really fit into their plan. These relative unknowns, speaking their own tongue, can be welcomed, but maybe not celebrated as enthusiastically as the local superstars.

Not even the will of the expectant mob of patriotic patrons could outweigh the determination of a gifted golfer from Cordoba who found the form and finesse to take the 73rd US Masters title and work his way into superstar status, in South, if not North, America.

Baltray's garbage men should be on their guard

APRIL 21: There are very few sports where you as an amateur can gauge yourself directly against the best. We can all watch soccer and marvel at the skills of the world's best, but we could never pit ourselves against these players for real. Same goes for a tennis player or racing car driver. Golf, however, is the exception to the rule.

On a weekly basis throughout the hectic calendars of world golf there is an opportunity for amateurs of all shapes and talents to play with the world's best golfers the day before their tournament proper begins. A bizarre phenomenon which would never apply at the top of any other sport, but such is the culture in professional golf.

Okay so maybe I have over-simplified the opportunity to play with the stars in a real situation, but with this year's 3 Irish Open there is a realistic chance to play in the Wednesday pro-am through the national club qualifying competition. This competition is being run throughout the 392 clubs across the land until the end of the month.

Knowing professional golfers as I do, and having witnessed the bum-twitching experience us amateurs feel if a passing stray dog stops to look at you as you make a pass at the ball on an isolated golf course, the thought of presenting your idiosyncratic swing to the world's finest golfers and their baying fans beyond the ropes is one that fills most with fear and the creativity to make up endless mental excuses as to why you couldn't do it.

The majority of the amateurs in these events are guests of the sponsors both from a business perspective and from a tournament promotional view. On the US Tour the fourball teams that enter the weekly pro-am cough up as much as $20,000 a team for the pleasure of five hours with, hopefully, a professional that they have heard of. From a spectators perspective the Wednesday pro-am can be a hair-raising spectacle and I have often thought the best head-gear for the day is a hard hat and not the customary golf course baseball cap. The roping system at a professional event is set up with the pinpoint accuracy of a professional in mind.

The mis-directed tee shot of an 18 handicapper with limited talent, trembling knees and facing a strong south-easterly wind on the exposed Baltray links does not bode well for the expectant gallery peeking over the fairway ropes in anticipation of a glimpse of John Daly. They might get more than they bargained for.

In fact, as a caddie, you are in peril of getting hit unless you exercise extreme caution. Those of us who loop for good golfers every day become complacent about where we stand in relation to where our golfers are hitting their ball. The rules change on a Wednesday. Most of us bagmen and many of our employers have been hit at some stage of our careers, whether by bad luck or carelessness.

My own experience of pro-am terrorism dates back to the Tour Championships in Altanta five years ago when my former boss, Retief Goosen, was in his prime and the amateurs who played with him were not pulled from a hat; they were the sponsors' favourites.

As the round progressed, Retief and I edged perilously further down the fairway in front of our amateur partners. Suddenly I found myself with the 20kg bag on my back looking at this little white missile honing in on me at speed and the screech of one of our amateurs as I desperately tried to jump out of the way. By the time I got to the green my ankle had swollen to the size of a cricket ball.

The offending golfer was both embarrassed and extremely apologetic. By the time we got to the 10th hole, which ran adjacent to a road, a garbage truck was easing its way towards the tee with the windows down on a very hot day. At about 150 yards from the tee our errant amateur hit his tee shot and immediately shouted fore. The driver was obviously not a golfer. Our man had managed to hit the poor individual on his arm which was draped nonchalantly out the open window!

The Wednesday pro-am is supposed to be an enjoyable day out for the participating amateurs even if it is a necessary evil to those professionals who are obliged to play in the event. It is the price of success where the pros are chosen from last year's order of merit.

Unfortunately for many of the amateurs the day fills them with fear. I have seen the terror in many of our partners eyes over the years as they twitch with anticipation on the first tee. In Sweden many years ago, when golf was in its embryonic stages, one of our players managed to hit himself on the foot as he nervously contorted his body in a effort to make contact with the golf ball. It was hard not to laugh as he leapt around the tee clutching his left foot in agony.

If you are lucky enough to be invited or good enough to qualify to play in Co Louth next month then you are in for a treat. Most pros and their caddies will make every effort to make your day both enjoyable and memorable.

Remember people are not there to see you play, so try not to be self-conscious and look outward; most will not even notice your swing.

Local looper recalls a Royal old time in Dollymount

APRIL 28: In 1943, the old pavilion-styled wooden clubhouse that stood on the North Bull Island in Dollymount burned to the ground. It was the clubhouse of The Royal Dublin Golf Club, and with it went much of the club records and folklore that had been passed down from members and associates.

Earlier this year two of the club's locker-room attendants retired from their duties and, at the risk of their recollections and stories about the club going with them back over the wooden bridge and up to Clontarf, I met one of the recent retirees, Anthony Birney, to catch up on some of the memories he had in his association for over half a century with Royal Dublin.

In 1954, the young Birney, or Anto as we all knew him as he gave us his personal welcome in the locker-room on arrival, was one of the 20 caddies that looped for the members back in the post-war era. There were 20 caddies but only about 10 members took caddies. So the local loopers were always on the look-out for a car, and particularly a strange car, trundling gently over the famous Dolly-mount bridge.

One particular day Anto and "Clicky" Brown were waiting in the car-park as an unfamiliar vehicle entered the club. The car was driven by a chauffeur and his boss was, naturally, in the back seat. There was the shuffle of optimism in the caddie shack.

The boss was, in Anto's recollection, an American businessman and, as he had nobody else to play with, he got his chauffeur to peg it up with him. Anto was guiding the industrialist and "Clicky" had the unenviable task of steering the errant chauffeur around the links. The chauffeur was better at driving his boss's car than driving his golf ball.

Royal Dublin is a classic, old-fashioned links with nine holes more or less going in one direction and the homeward nine running the opposite way. At the bottom of the course lay the old St Anne's clubhouse, which of course was welcome relief to golfers who had a rough outward nine. It was also the end of many a bad round, as the St Anne's refreshments often proved more enticing than another nine holes of bad golf.

The American and his driver spent a while in the neighbouring course's clubhouse and as they re-emerged the boss realised that, in boredom, Clicky had hit a huge drive down the 10th hole. When he realised who hit it he immediately took the bag off Clicky's back and threw it over the chauffeur's shoulders. The caddie had been elevated to player status due to the driving limitations of the driver.

Anto also recalled the time when the same caddie, who was not that familiar with foreigners at the time, turned up looking for work at the inaugural international Jeyes Pro-Am. The caddie master had arranged for Clicky to work for a big, tall Englishman with an equally large golf bag. When asked by his fellow caddie who he was caddying for, he replied, pointing to the tall man beside the big bag, "Yer man over there, the long fella, Wolfe Tone". His employer turned out to be the English professional Guy Wolstenholme.

Caddying in the '60s at Royal Dublin was not a reliable source of income, so Anto got a job with Bertie Smyth, the club-maker. His workshop was located behind the pro-shop, past the first tee. There were about 14 people working in the club manufacturers then and Anto was employed as a gripper. He put on the grips and packed the clubs which were then retailed mainly in Clerys Department Store in Dublin. Bertie Smyth had maintained the tradition of club-making handed down by his father, Fred, who was employed as the club professional between 1920 and 1941.

In the late '50s, Anto saw the arrival of Christy O'Connor Snr, who brought three of his nephews with him to Dollymount. Seán, Frank and Christy Jnr all served their time in some capacity in the club. Anto struck up a relationship with Christy Jnr, who at the time did not have a car so Anto's Beetle was Junior's means of transport.

There is a dying breed of associates to older golf clubs called artisans. The original idea of the artisan was developed in times when there was less pressure on the course from the membership and the club let the artisans play at off-peak times. In return, they helped out on the course, or on big competition days. In the '60s they were invaluable in the summer months at directing pedestrians safely across the links to Dollymount Strand.

> "In the late '50s, Anto saw the arrival of Christy O'Connor Snr, who brought three of his nephews with him to Dollymount. Seán, Frank and Christy Jnr all served their time in some capacity in the club."

Back then the beach-goers would take the bus to the Clontarf Road and walk over the wooden bridge on to the North Bull Island and cross the right-of-way over the links at the back of the 16th and out the other side by the second green. The perimeter fence only went as far as the fifth hole and Anto recalls the embarrassing moments the artisans had in the grassy mounds alongside the fifth fairway which was a popular spot with courting couples.

The worst artisan golfer at the time was a six handicapper, so they obviously had plenty of time to hone their skills on the links on completion of duties. The Royal Dublin Artisans won two interclub championships, and one involved a fourball final of Mick Murphy, off scratch, and Syl Edwards, off two, who beat the legends Tom and Joe Craddock from Malahide.

Anto moved into the clubhouse in 1994 as locker-room attendant and served there until his retirement earlier this year alongside his colleague, Luke Maher. There was a presentation in the clubhouse to the two long-serving locker-room attendants in the club last month.

There are really no caddies left at the links and the artisans are a dying breed – the youngest one now in his 60s – and the locker-room attendants have gone.

On Tuesday, May 12th, there is a Christy O'Connor pro-am at the links to acknowledge Christy Snr's 50 years of association with Royal Dublin.

It might be a good time for a story-teller to collect some anecdotes of what it was like to be golfing on a wind-swept links in the summers of the 1960s. Who knows what tales are lurking behind the marram grasses of the old links at Dollymount.

Bush crawlers are a thing of the past

MAY 5: A week before the 3 Irish Open starts at Baltray's Co Louth links I find myself wondering if I have forgotten the art of the profession that I stumbled into as an inquisitive wanderer and have since been condemned to a lifetime sentence due to modest success and lack of any viable alternatives.

My current employer has been sidelined due to a wrist injury which he incurred in February earlier this year and so I have enjoyed an unprecedented early season sojourn from travel. Not only have I avoided the humdrum ritual of weekly caddying at a professional event, I have not spent so much time in planes, trains and automobiles either. I think for those not used to a constant life on the go it is the unsettling nature of spending no more than seven days in the one location that takes most getting used to.

The good old days of the last recession was an era when I had little thought of investment in shelter beyond a two-man tent and the idea of purchasing an onward ticket to the next event seemed like hasty forward planning. Some decades after my first adventure across the well trimmed fairways of Europe I find myself reminiscing about my early experiences with the Irish Open when it was one of the highlights of the annual sporting calendar.

I had a wanderlust from my youth, probably born from the fact that our family holidays had normally involved a car trip within the 32 counties. The one time my parents ventured for a family holiday as far as London I ended up on my own at the age of eight on the wrong side of the Central Line tube doors as the train took off with my parents and sister inside and me waving goodbye to them from the platform. It was my first sense of independent adventure and may be attributed to my accidental peripatetic lifestyle.

The Irish Open qualifier came to my club in Dollymount in the early 80s and I remember observing well-tanned golfers with elegant, rhythmical swings I had previously only associated with ballet as they cut their dashing swathe across my home course. I thought that it looked like "the life" and the next week they would be doing the same in France, the week after in the Netherlands and so on along an exotic trail through Europe playing golf, earning money and living, what appeared on the surface, the dream.

The Irish Open had set up camp back in the late 70s at the famed Portmarnock links. With its standing as a top-quality course, its proximity to the city and enough extra space to host a major international event it was the obvious choice for the then sponsors, Carrolls. It was a time when golf fans were starved of golf viewing and live events attracted huge crowds. The tented village was strategically positioned to catch you on the way in and trap you on the way out if you had a thirst on you. There was the buzz of something really special to savour about north Dublin when Europe's finest and some chosen American stars came to town to test their seaside golf skills and take on the unique links challenge.

The art of caddying back in those days was as much about getting around Europe on a shoestring as helping your player make decisions on the golf course. Being a savvy traveller was imperative to survival. I remember one of my colleagues recalling there was a new sewage system being installed on the road leading to Portmarnock on his inaugural visit. He instantly recognised the huge concrete tubes as a strategically situated resting place for the week. As long as the wind didn't blow straight down his lodgings for the week it would be a successful one.

It was indeed a very different era on tour three decades ago from everyone's perspective, but especially for the bagman. For many caddies their main objective was to present themselves on the first tee not looking like they had crawled out of a bush (which of course some of them had). The chances were the tent that had been put up to shelter the loopers in daylight while waiting for their players had probably housed many of them at night time when the bars had closed. Ablutions, if any, took place around a cold outside tap.

Back then knowing where the next tee was located was probably a sign of professionalism. Today you need to know which direction the tee faces and what elevation it is at. If a caddie provided yardage to his player 30 years ago it was an added bonus, now if you don't have a laser hanging from your belt, you would be considered unprofessional.

Today as caddies we have the choice of two yardage books at our disposal to guide us around each course we go to. We have lap-tops, satellite navigation, tour travel agents and a caddies association which helps all of us arrive at our destination in a more civilised manner than we might have done some three decades ago. Instead of worrying about an east wind whistling down your pre-installed sewage pipe lodgings there could be remonstrations if the hotel did not have hot and cold running satellite television.

It is very much a different era of living on the golf tour. Watching Europe's and Ireland's finest battling around Co Louth next week will offer a rare chance to see an exhibition of this unique form of links golf. It is also an opportunity to see how the quality of the life of bagmen has changed for the better.

Daly's attire well-suited to colourful Italian scene

MAY 12: You would have had to turn a lot of crispy pink pages of *La Gazetta della Sport* before you got to any mention of the Italian Open last week. The daily national tabloid reports mainly on soccer and whatever else might be of passing interest to the minority of sporting Italians who have time for any other form of sport.

The Giro D'Italia featured on the cover page beside more soccer news last Saturday and if you leafed from back to front, buried on page 47 of some 50-odd pages you would have come across a piece about Matteo Manassero, a young amateur golfer who probably plays soccer too. He is a 16-year-old from Verona who shot four-under in the second round to make the cut and already he was being compared to our own child prodigy, Rory McIlroy.

Italy's best golfer Francesco Molinari and his older brother, Edoardo, who grew up and still live in Torino, were carrying the nation's realistic hopes for a home win. Particularly Francesco.

The venue was Royal Park Golf and Country Club which is situated behind the exclusive walls of the regal park, once a place the royalty in Italy came to hunt. Torino was the residence of the royal family and the city does have an air of majestic glory.

The course winds its way through the mature trees of the park with the backdrop of the Alps framing many of the holes. With the foliage and late blooming flowers you could not find a more pleasant area in which to amble. Combined with near perfect temperatures, it was one of those weeks where most of us on tour agreed life is indeed good.

The club is an exclusive place where the patrons of the stylish clubhouse seemed to prefer the more mundane black and white broadsheet newspapers and not the pink tabloids. As visitors we got to experience part of the true Italian culture and its unique form of queuing.

We mingled with the membership in a haphazard fashion as everyone milled around the cashier from whom you had to purchase a ticket to present in turn to the waiters behind a bar. This led to another chaotic mill for a panino and a cup of coffee.

If you are a black bean lover then it was worth all the jostling. It would also make you seriously reconsider what we drink at home and refer to as coffee.

When you emerged from the melee you got a chance once again to appreciate some more cultural intricacies, like the style of couture expected from such a sophisticated gathering in the land of fashionistas.

The weekend was the real fashion show. The trend, a golf-course chic that would look misplaced in any other country: cerise, electric blue and canary yellow trousers. John Daly's recent change of threads by replacing the standard drab chinos and plain golf shirt for bright-coloured and gaudy-patterned pants didn't look quite so bizarre amongst the loud-coloured Italian crowd. Ironically, the Italian professionals were sporting a more demure attire adopting a more global golfing dress sense.

The Carabinieri (Italian police) are, from a formal-elegance perspective, still head-turners. For those of us not accustomed to the imposing stature that a well-cut policeman's uniform, coupled with a towering cap and an eye-catching emblem, bring to the fashion parade, their presence was distinguished. With their black suit, and white sash holding a little leather man-bag and their thick red stripe down their trousers they looked interesting if somewhat misplaced in this strange golf land of Royal Park.

It was our annual chance to catch up with the Italian golfers who played the tour in earlier days. Costantino Rocca, Massimo Scarpa, Alberto Binaghi and Silvio Grappasoni all made appearances last week. From playing the seniors tour, commentating and coaching they have kept their links to golf and the tour.

The more I travel in Europe the more fascinating the concept of a United States of Europe seems. Apart from observing the unique traits of a modest crowd of golf spectators in Torino, I got a chance to look at how the subculture of the European golf tour behaves.

Most of the players and caddies stayed near the airport in the suburb of Borgaro. With the increasing amount of time we all seem to spend at the course these days, looking for the edge in a very competitive environment, we didn't seem to have time for much else apart from an evening meal in the vicinity.

One restaurant in particular became unofficial HQ, an innocuous-looking pizzeria which served quality Italian food. The tour invaded the restaurant and set up their obvious enclaves. The English and Scottish tended to be in earliest and set up at their favourite tables, the Swedes not far behind. The Australians had their spot and, of course, the French drifted in en-masse relatively late. Naturally the Spanish were always the last to arrive, in true Iberian fashion.

Having spent a bit more time on the practice range last week I also noticed the same applies there. No matter how you try to break barriers they are firmly entrenched. The one event that seemed to unite the tour's unofficial eatery last week was Chelsea's defeat in the Champions league. Barcelona's late goal had the restaurant cheering in unison. Unsurprisingly it featured prominently in the pink tabloid the next day, smothering the modest lines given to their national golf tournament.

GUI deserve credit for nurturing top talent

MAY 19: Not many would have heard of, recognised or feared the name Lowry at the top of the leaderboard for the Irish Open. I have to admit, I thought if the 22-year-old from Clara finished inside the top-10 it would have been a great result.

Let's be honest, you would want to be a huge gambler to have put money on the young Irish international, and even then only if you were a reckless optimist.

I came across one such person who put on €20 at 1,000 to 1. Of course that is way more than the Irish Open champion of 2009 will take home for his victory on the battered Co Louth links which harboured a scene more fitting for a January day rather than May.

There have been many wonderful feats in modern Irish golfing history, but in my estimation, the victory by the jolly, portly and affable Shane Lowry last Sunday is the most important win for any Irish male amateur ever. If a rugby grand slam success can lift the spirits of the nation, then Lowry's title should send them through the roof.

You see, it is a testament to how these young golfers are nurtured in the amateur system in Ireland. The huge midland crowd did their best to shelter Shane from the stiff south-east wind on Sunday and perhaps make him feel more at home in a foreign play acted out on a familiar stage. The Offaly gang brought as much if not more oomph to the event than any named player on advertising hoarding could have done. We all love an underdog, especially one who might be more representative of the people who are following him; not particularly athletic looking, happy-go-lucky and quite simply an ordinary punter.

> "What the astute Manchip did with his young talent was make the game enjoyable to play by creating a relaxed environment around his team camps, which of course included Rory McIlroy until recently."

He didn't arrive in a helicopter laden with excess luggage and a pointy attitude. He didn't get cocky when he shot five under in the first round.

As the wind strengthened and the frighteningly low scores of the first two rounds started to soften in the gale that swept the course over the weekend, the previously benign links started to recoup some dignity, with the stragglers falling into blue figures by Saturday afternoon after an astonishing, four-under-par cut.

We had our star cut casualties in Padraig and Long John Daly, and quite frankly the leaderboard didn't look too terribly interesting.

That was until the lad from Esker Hills began to look like he was going to stay near the lead no matter how tough or late in the day it became last Sunday.

With a two-tee start, those of us who teed off on the back nine first, tend to keep a keen eye on the leaderboards. So in a few idle moments myself and my boss, Alex Noren, glanced at the leaderboard and agreed that Johan Edfors would likely be the one to come through.

Shane made us all dream. But those who know these young amateurs better were more realistic about their chances of winning a big one. Neil Manchip, the coach of the Irish national teams, has spent a lot of time watching Lowry improve under his attentive but hands-off guidance.

It is no surprise that a top modern amateur is accustomed to the demands of four-round tournaments, or at least lengthy bouts in strong international events.

Although last week would have tested the patience of the most seasoned pro, Shane did not seem put out; it meant more time to savour mingling in the nucleus of the professional scene.

Manchip, as the national team coach, first came across Shane in 2005 on the Irish boys squad. He remembered that the teenager had a natural, free-flowing swing. There was nothing much to work on there. What the astute Manchip did with his young talent was make the game enjoyable to play by creating a relaxed environment around his team camps, which of course included Rory McIlroy until recently.

Where he spent most time with his team was on the short game, putting, distance control and attitude.

Having heard Lowry's interviews last week it sounded like he was gifted with having a simple perspective on golf. This is what any coach or mind-man would want their pupils to believe. It is obviously Manchip's mantra: the game is not so difficult, just play.

I think it is more than a coincidence that we are enjoying a group of good young male amateurs in Ireland – there are six on the Walker Cup panel. Apart from embracing the challenge of working with talented players, Manchip has created a "hit it, find it, hit it again" approach in his headquarters in Carton House.

This is not to say it is simplistic or unsophisticated. He is getting his players to be more professional about being amateurs. There are always post-round debriefings for his players to assess their progress, but the emphasis is on enjoyment.

With another of Neil's star pupils, Niall Kearney from Royal Dublin, winning the Brabazon Trophy in Leeds at the same time his team-mate was beating the pros in Baltray, Irish men's amateur golf seems to be in good shape.

If the young hero from Offaly decides to keep playing for the love of the game and not the booty, perhaps my colleague Tom Humphries will rediscover a grá for the beautiful game of Irish amateur golf.

Festering logo issue may come to a head

MAY 26: It is difficult to imagine any hardships in the world when you enter the tranquil surrounds of the Wentworth Estate in the stockbroker belt of Surrey. Mature cedar and pine trees hundreds of years old, dense rhododendron bushes and the twittering of contented birds in their thick foliage all conceal the elegant dwellings of the wealthy inhabitants of one of the most beautiful places to live in Europe.

It would also be difficult to tell that to either the contestants or their caddies in the PGA Championship, the flagship event of the European Tour, were finding the going tough. The West course is cut through the lavish mansions of the estate and, once on the course, you could be oblivious to the outside world, it is like a cocoon of contentment.

The caddies' lot has improved dramatically recently. A couple of weeks ago in Ireland we were housed in an ample marquee and fed two hot meals a day. In Wentworth, BMW seemed to be going for one-upmanship with their all-day cheese platter, and they even added afternoon tea to their hospitality service.

It was only a couple of years ago we were queuing with the public for some frozen burgers and greasy sausages, which was totally inadequate sustenance for a day's looping around the demanding Burma Road.

Many of we bagmen, pleasantly shocked by the quality of the caddie hospitality, extended our gratitude to those responsible for our plush conditions in the European Tour and at BMW. Not that we have been immune to the general financial malaise worldwide over the past six months, but the world golf tours have been somewhat sheltered from the harsh realities of it. Of course, this cannot go on forever.

So when we did say our individual and collective words of thanks to the authorities, I got a humorous reply that we should enjoy it while it lasts, because we'll probably be back to the burger stand next year.

We have already had a hint of times to come with the belt-tightening of the manufacturers manifesting itself at the start of the year. There are some faces missing from last year's extensive posse of the manufacturers' support service, and despite many players still resembling swinging sandwich boards with the amount of branding which their patchwork clothing bears, I get the feeling in the next few years we will be able to see more of the fabric.

The European Tour car-park is a good economic indicator when it comes to unemployment figures. Casting my eyes over the players' car-park in Wentworth, through the gleaming windscreens of the Bentleys, Maseratis and Lamborghinis, I spotted about 10 porters shuffling in anticipation of a potential employer emerging from one of the flash motors. No repossessions yet in the players' car-park.

The club-makers have been operating in an extremely competitive market for years and they have tried many different angles to maintain their market share. From employing avionic experts to design more aerodynamic balls to marketing gurus who know how to make their latest offerings look indispensable to the gullible, no stone has been left unturned in the battle for sales. Some of the manufacturers have come up with a system that obliges the caddie of a contracted player to sport the company logo on his cap or visor.

Despite much muttering in the caddie-shack over the years about the legality of such a condition and just how the obligation affects the relationship between player and caddie, little has been done to challenge the system.

At a time when there are far more caddies around than available players, it would seem like a petty argument for a caddie to reject a player and employment because of the principle of respecting the caddie's choice to wear or not to wear a logo on his head.

But there is such a case looming where an extremely principled bagman, who has already left a player this year because of the obligation to wear a manufacturer's visor, is facing a similar problem with his current employer.

The same caddie has been consistent throughout his career and has indeed rejected some top bags because of the obligation to wear a sponsor's cap. He emphasises it is not a question of money, but purely a right to choose. He has since found himself a sponsor of his own in Amnesty International. It will be interesting to see what happens over the year if what seems like a suspect arrangement between players and manufacturers concerning their caddies will be challenged legally.

With the Magna Carta having been signed about 800 years ago just a few of miles from Wentworth in Runnymede, recognising the rights and privileges of the barons, church and freemen, maybe it is time for bagmen to exercise their freedom to choose, too.

As I cast my eye across the patchworked fairway of the third hole on the West course at Wentworth last week, I was alerted to the reality of recession even in such a leafy haven. There were a considerable number of "for sale" signs on mansions about the place. We are not, after all, impervious to the wicked world beyond, even in the plush Wentworth Estate.

Challenge events offer aspirants top golf without the hassle

JUNE 16: If you are not Shane Lowry and you don't barge on to the European Tour during a wet weekend in Co Louth by winning the Irish Open you might have to consider the long road to a Tour card, through the Challenge Tour.

Another of Ireland's exceptional young talents secured his playing rights through invitations to play on the Tour and amassing enough money in so doing to get into the top 115 on the Order of Merit.

This entails aligning yourself to a good management group who can access to enough invitations to events for their hopeful in order to secure their tour card. This is how Rory McIlroy did it.

The other obvious avenue to your playing rights is by finishing well in the Tour School at the end of each year. If you don't finish in the top 25 you may find yourself in the holding area between the main tour and the secondary Challenge Tour.

Last week Ireland hosted the Challenge of Ireland, presented by Moyvalley in Co Kildare. The heady days of vast prize funds at the European Open in The K Club, and the global spectacle of the Ryder Cup at the same venue, have long gone and the staging of professional golf events in this country would appear to be more modest occasions.

I eased into the spacious car park at Moyvalley and found a slot four rows back just half an hour before the leaders were due to tee off last Saturday. What a pleasant contrast to parking in a swamp and being bussed in from another county to the course. I wandered into the clubhouse without credentials and there was a sense of calm about the place which got me wondering had I got my dates mixed up.

I drifted into the locker room and was greeted by the soft sound of slumber from a caddie curled up in a discrete ball with his head cradled on a shower towel. Ah yes, I thought, I am definitely at a tour event. In the foyer outside the main bar area a couple of caddies were tapping away on their lap-tops and speaking on skype to family back home.

In the restaurant the friendly and unstressed waiter suggested I should have been here yesterday, it was bedlam and he had served 230 lunches. I was struggling to decide where to sit because there were so many vacant places. A family with young children sat lunching beside me, seemingly there for the food with the golf being incidental.

Outside I witnessed two angry men with blue over par numbers beside their names on what turned out to be their last hole. The advantage of a dearth of spectators is you can whack a rake or toss a flag stick to relieve tension without anyone to observe your little tantrum.

I got the feeling that perhaps the boys get away with a bit more attitude on the Challenge Tour until I had a chat with Jose Maria Zamorra, tournament director.

Zorro maintained the Challenge Tour is where the authorities get a real opportunity to educate and groom aspiring young golfers. They have a rule that no hats are allowed in the clubhouse. Try enforcing that on the main tour and you would probably be sued by a sponsor for denying exposure. There is a respect and a courtesy that some of the egos on the main tour have left behind.

Despite the Challenge Tour being the kindergarten for the big school of the European Tour it seems you are never too old to learn. I talked to Nicolas Colsaerts from Belgium who played the main tour for years and is now reduced to invites on the secondary tour.

Despite the high stakes, there is a casual nature about these events that took me by surprise. As Colsaerts chatted freely I realised he was about to tee off in 10 minutes time. Players on the main tour wouldn't even look at you so close to show time.

As I wandered over to the range to see what type of balls they were hitting (good Titleists) I ran into Robert Coles (eventual winner), another Tour veteran who has tread the crooked line between main and challenge tours. He was also in a chatty mood just moments before he was due on the first tee.

Peter Baker, Ryder Cup player and multiple tournament winner, was out on the course and he had obviously taken the "crowd" with him. There must have been two handfuls of heads around the fourth green watching as he grafted over a birdie putt.

With €150,000 in the pot, aspirants are not playing to get rich, rather playing for the chance to get rich. There was €24,000 on offer for the winner and 10th spot got you €3,300. With players expenses probably running higher on the Challenge Tour without the courtesy car, players' lounge and free food, the costs are pretty high, with a lot less of a financial lure. So it is more common to see even the leading players carrying or pulling their own bags. If they were to take caddies it would obviously be a serious financial commitment.

Markus Brier, the amiable Austrian tour player, combines the resources of his sponsors to host a Challenge event in which he plays, in his native land. It is his way of giving something back to the sport that has served him so well. Henrik Stenson has taken a step further in altruism in his native Sweden by getting involved with the Challenge Tour event staged there in a few weeks time. He had put a lot of his own money into one of the biggest prize funds on the Tour at €300,000. He also stages an exhibition with himself and Adam Scott before the event.

The Challenge Tour is a breeding ground for the future hopes of the European Tour. It seems to provide a few opportunities for hopeful caddies too, I spotted caddie "available with tour experience" advertisements on the notice board. Having all the appearance of a tour event with scoreboards and roped off fairways, the Challenge provides the drama of real golf without the hassle. It is a wonderful opportunity for young players to hone their skills as a precursor to the bigger and bolder European Tour.

Standby game is a huge mental challenge for today's players

JUNE 23: So the USGA have now earned the lofty exclusive status of the Green-Jacketed gentlemen from Augusta; they too can defy the elements. It would appear nothing could stop them from completing the 109th US Open. It was not the carefully chosen land by the original course designer AJ Tillinghast alone that let the deluge seep through the Bethpage Black public course on Long Island, New York.

From squeegees to towels, it was the resources the United States Golf Association threw at the monsoon like conditions, that made the course playable. If the tournament was anywhere else you would have seen the players lifting their balls, cleaning them and propping them up on a lush piece of grass.

As is Major tradition no such activity is entertained by the authorities. It is, however, very much on the minds of caddies, players and anyone else with planes to catch somewhere else on Sunday night. Why don't they like players placing the ball in a golf tournament? For the same reasons as they don't like to see players with their bags on a trolley. It is tradition; it is how the game should be played. The only time you touch a golf ball is on the tee, when you are taking a penalty, on the green or when you've finished the hole.

No major will be decided with players placing their ball. Another reason is that it adds half an hour on to the already interminably slow rounds.

So you have had all the excitement of the US Open build-up, and you are looking forward to a morning time in the first round, and you get to the course where the rain is bucketing down and the course looks like the scene from the US Open Regatta.

You know you are going to have a long day waiting. The way the authorities deal with delays is they keep you on site and on standby until the end of the world if that is what it takes to complete the event. Proximity of accommodation to the golf course can aid your cause when play is delayed. If you are close enough you can hop home and wait for a call from your caddie with updates. Players have the best parking so access is easier.

The caddies' lot usually makes it a little trickier to get back to the course on time if there is a sudden break in the bad weather and play resumes. Humans are territorial and with constant long delays such as they had in Bethpage last week, you will have noticed the lairs that caddies inhabit in order to make the lurking a little more comfortable.

In a game of routines and careful planning the standby game is a huge mental challenge for professional golfers. The word trickles back to the locker-room, players' lounge and caddie shack that there is another decision being made in another hour.

So you pour another cup of coffee and nibble on another doughnut and peruse another newspaper and glance at the TV screen with the weather channel keeping you guessing about what time you are going to tee off.

By the time you get out on the course you've got coffee breath, a good stubble on your chin after the 4.30am rise and the last thing you are ready for is the first round of the US Open; more likely a siesta and a shower.

If you are not both flexible by nature, and rigid with resolve, professional golf may not be the game for you. Despite the necessity for routine in the sport you need a huge element of flexibility, especially for occasions like last week's rain delays.

Golfers have a strong propensity to grumble. The often seemingly indiscriminate nature of the game can get us whingeing like babies. So I listened to some interviews from post-early-round competitors who endured the endless delays and finally got out on the course in the worst of the conditions.

According to one it was like a two-shot advantage last week to be on the right side of the draw. That's like a 10-shot advantage to us amateurs, to put it in perspective. Some also mentioned that when they hit three woods into the bunkers they got plugged lies. Naturally after such extensive rainfall the ball was picking up mud which adds a further variable in to the decision-making process. You can make an educated guess about which way the ball will go depending on where the mud is on the ball, this is an art not a science.

After a stunted three and a half days of play, the hands-on New York mob got to watch and commentate on golf till dark on Sunday. It sounded like an intimidating atmosphere with a vocal reaction to every shot on the beastly Black course. It looked like the unravelling had begun with the surprise outside leader after three rounds. As the siren sounded for the end of play at 8pm on Sunday Ricky Barnes had hooked his tee shot into some dense fescue grass by the second hole. Darkness had fallen at the perfect time for the leader as he looked happy to be returning to the sanctuary of the clubhouse.

Bethpage Black is best faced by a novice leader in the less frenetic atmosphere of a relatively tranquil Monday morning. The nervy player could almost fool himself into thinking it was a practice round or at least a more sociable round than the last loop in a US Open final round.

The scene was probably not as the USGA had envisaged yesterday afternoon in Bethpage. The density of the sodden rough made up for the unprecedented receptiveness of the US Open greens. No matter what mother nature threw at the guardians of the game in America they ended up with a worthy winner in Lucas Glover – just a little later than anticipated.

Serious but civilised women's game a tonic

JUNE 30: I have to admit I had limited knowledge of women's golf until last week. I grew up playing in a club that had restricted access for women and, professionally, was fortunate enough to stumble upon the more lucrative male tours of the world. The result was that the closest I came to women's golf was walking by the red tees on my home course.

I had narrowed my counselling to professional males where the routine was pretty simple: get a player, negotiate a financial deal and prepare yourself for the worst if the putts don't drop. Most men are not emotionally mature on the course and many have two forms of expression: silence and rage. They want to know what club to hit, not your reasoning behind the choice.

The women like to talk through from tee to pin every detail. I have never contributed to decision-making as much as I did last week caddying for Hazel Kavanagh.

My first experience of "the girls" was as a spectator at the Ladies Irish Open at Portmarnock Links last year. I have always known somebody at a men's event no matter where I was in the world. I found myself on my backdoor step in Portmarnock as a total stranger observing what seemed like a very pleasant environment. I said to myself that, along with all those other things I must do, I must caddie for a female golfer.

> "The women like to talk through from tee to pin every detail. I have never contributed to decision-making as much as I did last week caddying for Hazel Kavanagh."

At the end of a long spell on the bench from the European Tour due to an unfortunate spate of injuries to my current employer, I arranged to work for the tenacious, charming and popular veteran of the Ladies' European Tour, Hazel Kavanagh.

Early in my career I had been used to standing in a car park looking for work and, in latter years, through text and e-mail, somehow my lines of communication kept me on a bag. This year the tournament promoter and dynamic force behind women's professional golf in this country, Roddy Carr, persuaded me to join one of Ireland's representatives on the LET.

As soon as I knew Alex Noren's injury was going to keep him out until this week, Roddy had me teeing up the next day with Rebecca Coakley at the Links.

We played a practice round on the Links at Portmarnock off the tees Rebecca remembered they had played from last year. I got my first experience of women's golf: an arrow-straight, elegant and uncomplicated game. It was neat and compact, a bit like the modern mini-cooper car, eye-catching and nippy but without the thrust of a big-engined beast. There was no dramatic back-spin, the divots were soft and discreet and the whole trip was a very civilised affair.

What a relief that the Wimbledon-style grunting does not apply to female golfers in competition. The loudest sound heard on the course was the click of a very blingy, glittering star-shaped ball-marker being removed from the magnet attached to Rebecca's pink visor.

For the first time in my career an employer wanted to meet for coffee to discuss how the week would hopefully unfold. I rather insensitively responded to Hazel that we were joining up for the week to finish as high as we could in the Ladies Irish Open and not to arrange coffee mornings. I suspect Hazel was a bit apprehensive about having a caddie from the world of men's golf on the other side of her bag.

When we got out on the course for our practice round on Tuesday last, Hazel realised I was there to try to help her, not intimidate her.

The Links at Portmarnock was primed for last week and, with the recent dry spell, the fairways had become very hard and fast. From a strategic perspective, this made laying up short of bunkers off the tees a little trickier, as the women tend to get more run on their shots even on softer terrain.

A further challenge on the many raised greens on the Links was that, even with mid-irons coming into the greens, with a flatter trajectory stopping the ball was not an easy proposition.

The tour referees put a dot of paint on the greens to signify the following day's pin position. I was almost alarmed at how tightly placed the pins had been proposed for the first round. Some other caddies concurred that the dots were in outrageous positions given the relative lack of spin the girls get on the ball.

Having suggested to the tournament director the pins were a little severe, she agreed to alter the most difficult ones to make them more accessible.

My week at my first women's event was enlightening. It was such a pleasant environment. The women are competitive but they are so in a very agreeable way. I have never heard "please" and "thank you" so much on the course as I did last week. I could never get to a divot quickly enough to replace it, my boss always assumed this duty.

And it was most definitely the first time I have kissed a professional golfer, as they all do on completion of the round.

Unlike the weather for the men's Irish Open, Portmarnock was bathed in unusually warm summer sunshine. On Sunday the mist rolled in from the Irish Sea and enveloped the links, leaving us all on standby to complete the final round.

The delay could not dampen the feeling of bonhomie. Spectators assembled around the farmers' market situated between the hotel and the first tee. With players and caddies mixing among the gathering, it had the appearance of a Sunday afternoon picnic by the seaside.

At most, the touring women professionals will play about 20 events this year, which makes it less stressful than the tournament-packed men's tour but also much less financially rewarding. There is a strong sense that the girls love playing golf and they are professional about it, but it is all kept very much in perspective.

I hope I have a free week next year during the Ladies Irish Open so that I can enjoy serious golf in a very civilised and elegant fashion.

Bagman from Bingley is taking a walk on the wild side

JULY 7: We caddies don't particularly like walking as a past-time. Strolling is something we do when we get paid, not an activity we engage in for fun on our weeks off. One of my colleagues, Billy Foster, is taking this week's walking a few steps further; he is going to caddie from Loch Lomond to Turnberry with a golf bag on his back but no player at his side.

Not only is he going to walk the 90 miles southwest to the Open Championship he is going to give up a week's work with his current in-form employer, Lee Westwood, in order to complete his mission.

Of course in keeping with caddie sentiment the walk is not for fun. Foster has had his heart-strings tugged by a visit to St James' Hospital in Leeds. It is a cancer care hospital for children and when Foster visited last December he made his mind up he was going to complete his walk and raise some money for the unfortunate kids that he saw in the hospital.

Back in 2000 Foster had come up with his original idea of arriving in St Andrews for the Millennium Open Championship having walked from Loch Lomond. For a caddie with a sense of nostalgia of course the home of golf would have been the most appropriate destination for an historic walk. It didn't work out and the veteran caddie vowed that if the opportunity arose again he would definitely make it happen.

Foster had been sharing Sergio Garcia's bag with Glen Murray last year. So when they were planning their schedule for this year he had requested the week of Loch Lomond free in order to make the long march to the west coast. When Sergio decided that he didn't want Foster to caddie for him anymore, his first thought was that this was going to disrupt his walk, apart from the obvious concern of who he was going to work for next.

Golf has been a vehicle to raise money for charity since hickory shafts gave way to steel. There are countless charity pro-ams which players are constantly trying to squeeze in between tournaments, many of them, of course, include a sweetener for the players so their intentions are not completely altruistic.

Every event you go to on the US Tour has got a very visible indicator of how much the event has raised for charity in the past and how much it hopes to raise during the present event. It would be reasonable to say that they don't miss the advertising opportunity of their generosity.

Foster has taken this project on board himself with no ulterior motive other than giving something to young cancer sufferers who have obviously had a profound effect on him.

Even the lodgings that he has booked on the carefully planned trip have been paid for by the generous bagman.

We got chatting about the proposed long walk to Ayrshire last week in the caddie-shack and of course the calculations began about how quickly Foster should take to reach Turnberry. He has taken no chances on caddie-shack seat-of-the-pants predictions and has sought the advice of a fellow member of his home club Bingley in Yorkshire, who is an experienced walker. Between them they figured a three-mile-an-hour average would be attainable.

Stuart Hooley is a hill walker who has completed a 100-mile walk in 30 hours. Of course the bravado in the caddie-shack suggested that nobody is more experienced at traipsing than us loopers. Constant walking, though, is a totally different type of foot challenge.

Foster himself admits the furthest he realistically has walked in over 25 years of international porter service has been about 300 yards after which he dumps the bag down and engages in idle banter, reads out a few numbers to his player, pulls a club out of the bag and waddles off towards the ball again for another chat and a break. Hardly as arduous as you would have some of us bag carriers dramatically lead you to believe.

So with Hooley's experienced tutelage in serious striding, Foster has had a number of trial runs from his home in Bingley along the least busy bye-roads 18 miles away to Leeds with a ruck-sack on his back. Of course he had blisters, aching ankles and throbbing thighs, none of which he ever suffered in the normal course of caddying duty.

He has also been guided by Westwood's mother with her own expertise in chiropody. The anti-blister trick is to apply surgical spirits to the feet a week in advance of the departure date.

Already the feeling of good spirit Foster has experienced is going to go a long way to motivating him over the final tough miles each day. His plan is to set off on Thursday next from the driving range at the Scottish Open in Loch Lomond and cover 17 miles, including a boat trip to Largs for his first overnight stay.

He will be accompanied by his marching mentor Hooley and his wife and friends will join him on his last eight-mile leg into Turnberry next Monday for an afternoon entrance to the British Open Championship.

He will be carrying a TaylorMade bag which he hopes to fill up with note donations, preferably, due to the weight that coin donations would add to his already burdened shoulders. Although he will be grateful for all support. Already the donations are flowing in and Foster has been astounded by the generosity.

So if you feel like supporting the altruistic bagman on his long walk to Ayrshire this week you can do so by logging into www.justgiving.com/billyfoster. All donations go to the Candlelighters Children's Cancer Trust.

With Lee Westwood's second place finish with Foster by his side in France last week it would appear that good karma is on his side already for this magnanimous gesture from the Bagman from Bingley.

Fastidious Villegas can do my rankings the world of good

JULY 14: I jumped about 100 spots up the world rankings last week after the French Open. I calculated my rise by picking up Camilo Villegas' white Cobra bag last Tuesday morning. You see, we caddies can leapfrog the rankings vicariously through players of a higher status.

Villegas had contacted me earlier in the year, or should I say he had tried to call me but by the time I managed to get back to him he had already arranged another porter for a four-week stint in America. He had parted company with his previous full-time caddie earlier in the year and had decided to try out a few available bagmen before deciding on a more permanent arrangement.

I was sort of in looping limbo myself having worked for Alexander Noren since January this year. He was unfortunate enough to end up with two injuries which have stunted a spiraling career. Just as he finished second in the Indonesian Open last February his steady progress ground to a halt with a wrist injury.

As he eased back in May after two months in convalescence, he suffered a knee problem that put him back on the bench again. When this happened, he suggested that I should maybe look out for another bag for a while given the uncertainty of his physical situation.

Caddying is a very strange profession which does not entail simply doing your job, serving your time and slowly rising up the ladder. The consensus tends to be that it is only a matter of time before the next top bag becomes available. This is not necessarily so. I have met some caddies who have won majors with players in the not too distant past who are now club caddying for amateurs in country clubs in Florida.

Of course it is nice to think top and aspiring players are always on the lookout for an available and experienced bagman - who knows for sure how the system works. There is a feeling in the caddie-shack that the penchant of players for extended family members to pick up their bags and do the right familial thing has made bag changes a little less predictable.

Anyway for some unknown reason Villegas decided I would be worth a few weeks on his bag, presenting me with a fascinating two weeks with the dazzling Columbian in the Scottish and British Opens.

Having worked for just the one player in Retief Goosen for almost five years, it is a refreshing challenge to be given the opportunity to assist different players. Even though the process of advising players is a standard procedure you are after all dealing with humans and of course everyone is different. So from 6.15am last Tuesday I have been observing just what it is that distinguishes a top-15 world-ranked player.

"He reminded me his ball marker, an Australian 50 cent coin, had been in the bag since he turned professional. I guarded that with more care than I did the clubs."

I suppose a 6.15am meeting is a telling sign of the hours that these top players put into their weekly tournament preparation. I am not suggesting that lesser players are not prepared to roll out of bed as early in order to fit in as much as possible into a limited period, but there is a sense of the early bird catching the worm with Villegas.

I was instantly impressed by the order of the golf bag when I started trying to figure which pocket held what – it seemed like everything was very much where it should be in each designated pouch. The rain gear was folded in a meticulous manner, the towel draped evenly over the clubs and everything was just so. He reminded me his ball marker, an Australian 50 cent coin, had been in the bag since he turned professional. I guarded that with more care than I did the clubs.

His enthusiasm when I agreed to do these couple of weeks gave me the impression of a player with a purpose as he journeyed to Scotland to ultimately challenge for the British Open.

When we got on the Loch Lomond course I could see he absorbed every detail about each hole like a sponge. His observations off the tee were to hit the club that would land in the widest part of the fairway. Although there are generous fairways at Loch Lomond, he did hit a huge percentage of the fairways over the four days.

His next mission was to plot his path around the greens, giving a lot of attention to where he wanted to be for certain pins. While he played his practice round he didn't necessarily hit a lot of shots but soaked up the nuances of each hole. On a couple of up-turned saucer greens he pleasantly surprised me by suggesting that even with a wedge in his hand he didn't need to shoot at the pins – the middle of the green would do just fine. In this aggressive age of the young golfer with modern equipment, that statement was a revelation as to how the man from Medellin has got to where he is today in world golf.

Villegas carries his own yardage book and I noticed on the second day we played, he had stamped his own compass points beside the already detailed compass points printed in the sophisticated yardage book.

Villegas had lines representing not just north and south, he had north east and south east and so on. He was particular about the elevations between shots. He added numbers to his yardage to include how cold it was, how up- or downhill the shot was, how much wind was involved. So it wasn't as simple as 150 yards and 10 to the pin. It was plus two for the hill, three for the temperature and four for the wind.

All this was going on as I grappled for the first time in six years with caddying for a player who works in yards and not metres. He had a little chart with the distances that he hit each club. Naturally they were not estimates; they were pin-pointedly precise. There is an attention to detail that of course I have witnessed at times before but not with the consistency the fastidious Columbian has. It is what he needs to perform, and it has served him well in elevating him to 12th in the world rankings. It is important as a caddie to recognise just what makes a player tick.

Golf is a game of inches and frequently those inches win, so if Villegas has every blade of Turnberry grass charted to the precision that his detailed surveying of the course would suggest, it may be a case of another jump up the rankings for this porter.

Ailsa Craig may well doff hat to Watson's heroic efforts

JULY 21: You don't need a meteorologist on the Ayrshire coast to tell you what weather to expect. Simply cast your eyes down the Firth of Clyde and consult Ailsa Craig, the granite island sticking out of the sea that looks like a big muffin, about 10 miles offshore .

According to the local caddies at Turnberry when Ailsa has got a cloud clinging to her it will rain. If the cloud surrounds her it's not going to rain. As one old codger put it to me in his best west Scottish accent: "When she's wearing her hot it's gonna be wot, but when she's wearing her tie its gonna be dry."

Maybe the rule doesn't apply during a British Open Championship because we seemed to get away with very acceptable weather relative to how it can be in Scotland in July, regardless of what Ailsa Craig was wearing.

You just cannot get up early enough to beat the players' traffic at a major championship. Last Monday at 6.10am, with crows still nonchalantly picking at roadside fodder and rabbits looking at you wondering why you were not still sleeping, I met my player, Camilo Villegas, hoping to be first on the course. We were there too late. Michael Campbell and Tiger Woods had beaten us.

All of the early starters were not there on holiday; they play early to finish early, so we had a swift but informative practice round and a day's work done well before midday. If you go out later than 9am it could take up to five and a half hours to play a practice round.

This is what happened the next day, so Camilo abandoned his clubs after seven holes and walked the rest of the way. It was a chance to stroll through numerous groups of players and caddies from the US Tour that I would not have seen for some time. It is easy to forget people you used to see on a daily basis but haven't for almost a year, but it is equally as easy to strike up a casual conversation as we rambled through some slow-moving groups of players as they prepared laboriously for the 138th Open Championship

It is the one big trip of the year for the Americans where they have got to dig out passports and fly though the night to an event. We played with Steve Marino who, along with his bagman, was shell-shocked with the effect of the six-hour time change. Three movies later and a couple of sleeping tablets taken, and they were coming to terms with their first case of jet-lag.

It is refreshing to see the reaction of the US contingent to this bizarre form of golf on the unique links terrain. As the southerly wind freshened across the championship links the novice US seaside golfers were somewhat in disbelief at hitting their three-irons 280 yards downwind.

There is an overwhelming sense of nostalgia at such a prestigious event. Spectators will tell you how many consecutive Opens they have attended and how they always plan their holidays around it. We get to see rules officials from such countries as Ecuador who are drafted in by the R&A to follow each group. Past champions get to play in the event until they are 60 years old.

This is how an eventually play-off-vanquished 59-year-old five-time past champion Tom Watson gained exemption to this year's tournament.

You get the impression the event is for aficionados only. The fans are there to see their golfing heroes who they only get to watch on television the rest of the year. The stroll into the amphitheatre of the 18th green is hair-raising, making even the most seasoned pro feel he is taking part in something very special.

As traditional as the Open is there is no doubt the R&A are moving with the times. On our pins sheets this year we were given the distance in yards-and-a-half to the hole; on the 13th last Thursday the pin was set 24.5 yards from the front of the green and 5.5 yards to the left. With a north-westerly gusting at 25 miles an hour by the weekend, the half numbers seemed somewhat irrelevant even for the most detailed number analyst.

Players favour certain courses. You have often heard golfers saying that particular holes just fit their eye. Well the Ailsa Course at Turnberry undoubtedly fits Tom Watson's eye. He mentioned that he didn't need any visual footage of the famous battle he had with Jack Nicklaus in 1977, he could recall every shot he hit 32 years ago in winning his second Open title.

Although it seemed outrageous that Watson should dare to present himself on top of the leader board on Thursday morning last and stay there until the very end, the silence in the locker-room as players and caddies hushed for his nine-foot putt on the last hole on Sunday to try and capture his sixth Open betrayed how those at the very heart of the modern era truly believed an ageing legend was going to win at almost 60 years of age.

I am not sure the nutritionists and physical trainers would have been enamoured with a senior player with a new hip raising the Claret Jug amid the applause of contending players young enough to be his super-fit grandchildren.

Just as Ailsa Craig has done meteorologists out of a job on the Ayrshire coast, so nearly did Tom Watson put the modern big-hitting golfer back in his place with a sublime display of savvy links golf where distance yielded to dexterity from a man who was supposed to play only as an act of nostalgia and not as a serious contender.

Swedes love their golf, but can get a bit intense

JULY 28: The Scandanavian Masters is the biggest golfing event in the region. Held near the gateway to Sweden, in the southern port of Malmo at the end of July, it is part of many Swedes holiday plans. But no matter how big the event is in Scandinavia, it can only be a let-down compared to the magnitude of the British Open held the previous week.

It is the perennial problem for those staging a tour event, staging your tournament straight after a major. Jesper Parnevik, once the luminary of Swedish golf having excelled on both the European and US Tours, has become active in promoting the somewhat flagging national tournament. He was both competing and organising alongside his wife, Mia.

It is refreshing to see a former champion adopting the role of ambassador. With a limited budget and a post-major lack of interest, the best Jesper could do to attract his US Tour colleagues was to lure James Driscoll and Will McKenzie to the southern part of his homeland on a combined cultural/golf visit. The rest of the Open contestants from the US Tour either opted for a break or the Canadian Open.

There were 38 Swedes on the original starting list, and for the Swedes, being a patriotic people, it was enough to bring the blue and yellow flags out en masse to support what is the extraordinary success story of a young golfing nation.

Last Monday most of us trickled over the expansive bridge that spans the Ore Sound which separates Denmark from Sweden, having flown into the busier Copenhagen airport.

The news from my colleagues who had arrived a day earlier at the caddies' hotel in the docklands of the elegant city of Malmo was the range had been busy that day and the majority of its occupants were members of the host nation.

There is a sentiment on tour that the Swedes are permanent range residents, they are likely to open and close it. It is as if the relative newcomers to the game are making up for lost time. When I suggested to Goran Zachrasson, the broadcaster and voice of Swedish golf for almost 50 years, that his fellow countrymen were hogging the range, he was quick to point out that Padraig Harrington was not averse to a few extra hours of divot duty. True, of course, but Padraig is the exception, not the rule. On tour there is no argument: the Swedes rule the range.

Who could argue with their perfect practice preference? Last year's Order of Merit winner is Robert Karlsson, this year's winner of the Players' Championship, and the biggest prize fund on the US Tour, is Henrik Stenson, and among the 38 native competitors this year, a host of them were serious contenders.

Karlsson was in Malmo despite being sidelined since May due to an infection that has affected his sight and balance.

The amiable Swede has been advised to do absolutely nothing. He has been told not to get his heart rate too high, and therefore cannot practice or exercise. So he is trying to make the most of the enforced hiatus by playing no golf and spending an inordinate amount of time – for a professional golfer – with his family.

It is a fickle existence being a golf pro, good or bad. Having enjoyed the fruits of a lifetime of labour and enjoying his best year in 2008, instead of building on this success Robert has suffered a serious career set-back. He is philosophical about the enforced break, and sees it as a chance to enjoy being around his young family instead of as a career-breaker.

As a caddie in Sweden there is a real sense of being part of the golf tour as a whole as opposed to being a necessary inconvenience. It was the sage Zachrasson who pointed out that the scene in the clubhouse at Barseback was unique on tour: players, sponsors, caddies, members and players' guests all mingling freely in the clubhouse. There are no barriers, no notions of being separate but equal, just a sense of individuals playing a role in the big circus. Despite our lot being improved dramatically world-wide in recent years, there is an unmistakable feeling of equality in Scandinavia for we bagmen.

I came across another local legend in sport, Sven Tumba, who was instrumental in popularising golf in the 1960s and 1970s. He organised the first Scandinavian Masters in 1970 and managed to get Sam Snead over to play an exhibition. He had been an international ice-hockey player, soccer player and skier, on top of his golfing prowess. So he was extremely influential in bringing newcomers to the then foreign game of golf.

I asked him what he thought of the modern golfer, to which he replied, without hesitating, that these talented young men all take too long and think too much instead of relying on instinct. I had met an army of coaches and Swedish Golf Federation trainers throughout the week while I followed the flight of divots down the range. It was difficult to see how the instinctive golf that the multitalented Sven Tumba mentioned had much chance of survival.

Then again, with 38 natives in the field there is a strong case for the methodology of modern Swedish golf. A sprinkle of Tumba's flare might add a natural balance to the theoretical thrust of the Scandinavian game.

First-class means of transport on trip down memory lane

AUGUST 4: The gist of travelling ideally is to enjoy the trip. It's the journey that is important, not just the arrival. Experiencing the trip is something most of us loopers on tour rarely get to do any more, no matter what our original intentions were of travelling the world, carrying a golf bag and maybe sometimes being enlightened about new and interesting cultures along the way.

The intensity of the modern professional game has curtailed the nature of moving between golf courses each week. It is a challenge at times to figure out what part of a new country you are in; orientation is course-specific only; range, first tee and clubhouse with a yardage book in our back pocket instead of a tourist guide.

The chances of enjoying an overland trip are greater in Europe when we have back-to-back events in a similar region. Last week's move from Sweden to the Czech Republic was an excellent opportunity to get back to how we used to travel through Europe in the old days.

Caddies are efficient at finding the cheapest flights from one event to another. It made sense for most of us to do a two-week stint instead of going home for a night. It gave some of us a rare opportunity to spend Sunday night at a venue. There was an unofficial meeting place in a lively square in Malmo town centre where the whole tour seemed to drop in at some stage of the week. The victorious player, Ricardo Gonzalez, dropped in to buy some drinks for the rest of us who were celebrating both the end of the week and the popular Argentine's win. The problem was the cheap flight from Malmo to Prague left at 7.45am on Monday morning.

One of my enterprising colleagues had organised a bus to take us from the caddies' hotel to the airport at 5.30am on Monday last. The bets were on early for the number of no-shows. It was a surprisingly civilised affair, I am told, with some even rising promptly enough to enjoy the early breakfast the hotel had prepared in our honour. Obviously not everyone had been in the celebratory mood the previous night.

Although we had all booked our flights individually it seemed like it was an organised collective trip. Half a plane load of caddies landed in Prague airport on a fresh summer's morning of a day that was obviously going to heat up in time.

Everything had run smoothly; Check-in, flight and bag collection. We all drifted out of the terminal and started filtering out to our different modes of transport to Ostrava, some four hours away by road. Some rented cars, others hired small vans to take them directly to their destination. Those of us with a sense of nostalgia opted for the public bus into Prague's elegant central train station and ended up getting a group train ticket to Ostrava. Again, it was all very civilised and easy. Once on board our unofficial leader made a decision that we should splash out and upgrade our little party to a first-class carriage.

The Czech rail catering staff were not ready for the thirsty party they encountered last Monday. We ran out of beer by the time we pulled into Pardubice, an hour east of the capital. The card school started in the central part of the carriage, we had music and banter going all the way east as we soaked in the scenic countryside of a relatively obscure land from a golfing perspective.

There were about 25 of us in the first-class carriage on the 11.23am rattler to Ostrava in the eastern part of the Czech Republic. There was even a couple of players who joined us and partook in the banter that flows when everyone is relaxed and not in a hurry to arrive at their destination. For those of us who used to use trains as our primary from of travel some decades ago, the stories of stolen belongings and the enforced journeys home without tickets, wallets or passports ensued.

At Olomouc, one of my colleagues got a call from a player wondering if there was an available tour caddie willing to work for him in the tournament. All caddies on board were gainfully employed for the week, so the player settled for a local caddie.

> "We dragged our belongings across a wasteland around the Frydek-Mystek station and into the grey lump of concrete that was to be our lodgings for the week, the Centrum Hotel. It had a sort of groovy communist chic to its interior that will be back in fashion soon. "

The card school masterminded by the Sunningdale contingent on the trip was consumed by tales of the British Open Seniors which was held at Sunningdale the previous week. As they gathered their cards up after each round of "crash" they discussed their mates from their home club who caddied for the seniors – "Milky" went with Denis Watson, they couldn't agree on who "Slug" looped for. A text message came through from a Malmo airport no-show. He was snoozing on his travel bag in a park in the city, being softened by a light drizzle as he waited for a later flight.

We eased into Ostrava's main station just a few minutes behind schedule, Gary Tilston marginally better off with his "crash" earnings and everyone generally relaxed after a painless trip. We congregated in the central station bar and joined some locals for an afternoon beverage as we waited for our connection to our final destination of Frydek-Mystek. The austere grey concrete buildings became more apparent as we neared our terminus. Czech architecture is made up of a mix of aesthetically-pleasing Romanesque to Classicist period buildings of previous centuries, and the harsh, crude and functional concrete blocks of the communist era.

We dragged our belongings across a wasteland around the Frydek-Mystek station and into the grey lump of concrete that was to be our lodgings for the week, the Centrum Hotel. It had a sort of groovy communist chic to its interior that will be back in fashion soon. Meanwhile, we settled into our lodgings from a different era in preparation for a stay in a country that still promotes the view that the journey and not necessarily the arrival is most stimulating.

Hard man 'Frosty' bids farewell to tour with grace and humility

AUGUST 11: I have seen players ramble through their days on the European Tour and sidle off down some obscure trail into oblivion without making a formal exit, their only mark in history being an amount of euros beside their names buried in golfing annals.

In many sports there is a decisive moment when players choose to retire, it is a black and white decision. In golf it is not such an easy decision, as older players can still compete quite effectively at times, as we saw in Turnberry a few weeks ago with 59-year-old Tom Watson beaten in a play-off for the British Open Championship.

We were in the Czech Republic a couple of weeks ago, a part of the world oblivious to the capitalist game of golf until recently. You can still smell the paint drying on the game there, and it is not somewhere David Frost, the veteran South African, would have visited in his formative days in the early 1980s.

It was, however, where Frost was to hang up his European spikes ahead of his debut on the Champions Tour in America. I was perusing the noticeboard at the Prosper Golf Club before the tournament, and there among bus schedules, starting times and other directives from the tour was a letter from David Frost addressed to his "Friends".

At first I suspected it might be about the state of his wine business back on the Cape. Over the years he regularly passed around samples to members of the tour and made use of the access he had to a large group of impressionable wine-drinkers.

But as I read the letter I realised it was a heartfelt missive from a man who had initially seemed, on the surface at least, to be just another hard-nosed South African bringing his gruff attitude abroad with little regard for where he was. For those of us who had little contact with South Africans in the 1980s, their language and manner was more direct than we were used to and could be off-putting.

I had the privilege of caddying for David in the Volvo Masters once, when I witnessed the finest display of putting I had seen until I started working for his compatriot, Retief Goosen. Accents can put us on the back foot at times. My lasting memory of the Western Caper was of an uncompromising man.

He grew up in the Stellenbosch area and worked as a cigarette rep and a policeman. There had been no successful golfers from his area at the time.

David couldn't watch international golf until his family got their first television in 1975. He had no exposure to the international influence in the game. When he was a five handicapper he started to read about the swing. He bought a book by Ben Hogan: this was his first lesson. He knew nothing of swing planes, separation, downward pressure or any other technical terms most modern pros are reared on.

What the younger and more inquisitive David Frost knew was that he would take nothing for granted, and there were no guarantees like so many younger golfers have today.

Having taught himself, he bought his first set of Hogan irons in 1978 and decided golf would be his career: no more township patrols, no more cigarette sales, he was destined for the fairways of the world with his self-made swing and attitude.

I remember a colleague telling me about Frosty back when he was a serious contender (he won 10 times on the US Tour). His mantra when he hit a bad shot was "now watch me get out of this". There was no lingering in the analysis of how he hit a bad shot. It is the telling difference between self-taught players and hands-on, coached golfers who don't take responsibility for their swing. The self-taught golfer is obviously more self-sufficient in the exposed world of competition.

Giving my observation about Frost, I would say the game humbled him, as he continued to play in latter years, without the form he enjoyed in his golden years. He learned humility and respect for all of us involved in the travelling circus of world golf.

He was grateful to the European Tour for giving him the opportunity to play in Europe in 2007, which helped him earn his card for the next two years. It kept his match game sharp in his transition to the Champions Tour.

There was definitely a sense of nostalgia and respect in Frost's farewell letter. He talked about the sense of belonging and being part of a homogenous group. "When others win we are all happy for them, and when we play badly we can all empathise with that."

He regrets he didn't interact with the crowd more now that he understands their appreciation for the professional's talent. "They love the game as much as we do and only wish they could do with the ball what we can." He wishes he had given the crowd "just a nod or a smile to make them feel special".

From tour officials to other players and to caddies, David had a touching word for all of us. Of the caddies, he realised our love for the game and our "understanding of the tough times that players have to endure, it is not something you can describe but the looks say it all".

So many players seem to drift off into the ether without a goodbye to the tour. David Frost, once considered a tough man of the tour, bowed out graciously and with humility.

It adds weight to the argument that the game of golf is a great leveller and can teach people about what is important in life.

The remarkable layout at Kennemer is among the finest links

AUGUST 25: It was a week on the coast in Holland last week when the North European gentlemen understood why they bought those finely tailored linen jackets. The occasion to sport the summer's finest wardrobe was the great outdoor spectacle of the Dutch Open at Kennemer Golf Club.

It was fascinating to come across such a gem of a links course amongst the dunes of the Dutch coast. It's not like you immediately associate this part of the world as a golfing destination. Well that's exactly how the Flemish coast was developed at the end of the 19th century. Not specifically for golf but in order to attract the British aristocrats to northern Europe for holidays and having a good golf course was a good way to do that.

It looked like the Dutch aristocrats had taken over the hospitality area last weekend in the elegant but temporary entertainment area constructed around the practice range on the spare nine holes of the Kennemer Golf Club.

It is the first time that I have seen such a set up at a tournament whereby the driving range became something of an amphitheatre. The paying public and invited guests surrounded the back and side of the range and enjoyed champagne and fine wine as the entertainers warmed up in preparation for their serious rounds of golf.

If this became a regular arrangement on tour I would imagine that even the players with the most acute hearing, and therefore the most likely to be distracted, would become accustomed to a brouhaha as they hit their shots and ignore on course noise as a result.

Holland is a country that is not known for golf, yet it has a curiously long association with the game. When you consider new golfing nations like Sweden and Denmark, who have produced a plethora of world players in the past two decades, without links to the origins of the game it got me curious about how the game developed here centuries ago.

When I asked about the history of the club it was suggested that I talk to the club historian Robin Bargmann.

What I thought was going to be a brief chat about the humble beginnings of his club, turned out to be a European history lesson.

So the story began with me overlooking the Kennemer links scorched from the recent heat wave and littered with spectators during the afternoons play on Saturday. I gazed across the links land from the thatch-roofed understated clubhouse as I listened to Mr. Bargmann muse over past centuries.

Until the end of the 18th century old golf was played in the Lowlands. When the preference moved to a French cultural persuasion, the old game disappeared.

We got into Waterloo and Wellington and the British being put back in their place, according to my source. I was informed that 50 per cent of the worlds wealth was concentrated in the Lowlands in the 17th century.

We skipped through the decades quicker than you could say "sollen met den kolve" which translates to play ball, which is the form of golf they played in Holland in the pre-industrial revolution era. With the industrial revolution came rubber and thus the gutta perch golf ball was created. In that era more golf clubs were founded outside Britain than within the British Isles.

It was in the colonies that the Dutch once again came in contact with the games that were introduced by the British; tennis, football, rugby and of course golf. So when the British and the Dutch met in the colonies and had the common interest of the defeat of Napoleon, the returning military men brought the modern game of golf back with them to their homeland.

Five clubs were founded at the end of the 19th century; De Haagsche, Doorn-sche, Rosendaelsche, Hilversumsche and Kennemer and they formed the Dutch Golf Federation.

> "Another Englishman greatly influenced the development of golf in Holland. Henry Burrows was a golfing dilettante in the early 20th century, who was well versed in all matters golf..."

Then in the 1920s there was a Colt Cult that hit Holland. Harry Colt, probably the original golf architect, broke the mould of previous designers who had come either from the caddie or player ranks.

Colt was a Cambridge educated lawyer and former secretary of Rye and Sunningdale golf clubs, who successfully turned his hand to course design.

Another Englishman greatly influenced the development of golf in Holland. Henry Burrows was a golfing dilettante in the early 20th century, who was well versed in all matters golf; from technique, teaching, playing, club making and repairs, course design, to maintenance and green keeping.

At a young age he decided to take his talent to Holland. He won his first Dutch Open title at Kennemer. He went on to win two more Dutch Opens. Having won the title as the best professional of the Dutch Open five times he got to keep the Wisselbeker for Golf Professionals trophy. The trophy is a permanent exhibit in the Golf Museum in St Andrews in Scotland. In the tented village the Burrows trophy was on display alongside the Dutch Open trophy.

In true keeping with the sense of history of the game in Holland Robin Bargmann had a surprise guest travel to Kennemer last weekend in order to present the trophy to this years winner Simon Dyson.

Henry Burrows' daughter Dolly, now in her eighties, proudly handed over the trophy behind the 18th green on Sunday to an Englishman who travels the world to ply his trade. Much like her father did 100 years ago.

Ice cold from Alex for maiden victory

SEPTEMBER 8: Sometimes you can say something in passing to somebody and despite thinking it was a casual comment, the person who heard it takes great heed. Dealing with top performers is a fickle business, you need to choose your words wisely and time the delivery to perfection.

I had been chosen through the haphazard, but somewhat efficient system on tour, that pairs caddies and players together. Through this web I got paired up earlier this year with one of the hottest young names in European golf, Alexander Noren from Sweden. I remember having been paired with Alex a couple of years previously and being deeply impressed by his talent.

Of course natural talent is what you look for in a young player but being a successful professional entails so much more than quality ball striking. Hitting it long and straight off the tee and hitting a high percentage of greens makes the game easy, but the art of the game, assuming a certain amount of talent, is getting the ball in the hole.

Alex is a quality ball striker but his statistics showed that perhaps he was not converting enough of the huge amount of chances he was creating. No golfer is a machine and despite enjoying some weeks where you play pure golf for four straight rounds the chances are you will have at least one round in four where you have to grind and scramble to turn a 75 into a 70.

Having observed top players throughout the years this is what they all have in common; the ability to salvage a bad round and return a respectable score when they are playing badly.

This is as much a mind-set as a talent. The frequent reaction for a good ball striker to a bad striking day is to panic and question technique and seriously undermine self-belief. A top player gets on with scoring and not self-examination.

Alex had enjoyed quite a promising start to his year and our first few events together. He finished top 10 in Malaysia and backed it up with a second place finish in Indonesia a few weeks later. He had played good golf tee to green but had not really converted the huge amount of chances he had created; his putting averages were quite high.

A wrist injury and a couple of months off, saw him almost restarting his season from scratch in May not having been able to practice. Another knee injury after a brief comeback set the frustrated Noren back even further, and almost had him viewing the year as a bit of a write-off.

Like most young professionals, he has had a strict work ethic instilled in him from the outset. As much as hours on the driving range can be beneficial they can also be detrimental if you over do it. There is no point in hitting your best shots on the range, the game is about hitting them with a card in your back pocket and ultimately as a professional on the back nine on Sunday when the pressure of winning has narrowed the target to the size of a needle.

Through regular open conversations about where we are now, and how we should try to get to where we want to be as an aspiring caddie/player team, we agreed we should spend more time on the chipping and putting green. Also our practice rounds should be played as much as possible on our own, spending as long as possible chipping and putting to the four possible pins of the week on each green.

With a detailed knowledge of the greens and their associated challenges plus a couple of hours of daily chipping and putting practice during the course of the last month, it seemed like the specific work bore fruit last week in Switzerland.

Most people will give different answers when asked about the art of good putting. The more a player practices, not so much technique as habit and expectation of holing putts, the more putts should be holed. I think a lot of players over emphasise technique instead of repetition and expectation. You don't need a perfect stroke to consistently hole putts. Holing putts becomes a habit the more you work on it and believe that you can hole your fair share.

With a flawless eight-under-par round on Saturday Alex had to sleep (badly) on a lead and the expectation of filling his own and many others' aspirations for him to win for the first time on tour. It was the first time since I had worked for Alex where I felt he squeezed his round dry, he could not have scored any better.

I had mentioned in passing to my boss about a month ago that he would win before the end of the year. I had also commented that working intensely on his short game would ensure he did. He was obviously paying more attention than I had thought, because his post-win speeches alluded to both comments that I had made to him.

You never know what is going to happen in the final charge for the line in a golf tournament. With talented golfers, anything can happen. Despite stretching to a four-shot lead at one stage of the front nine, a pitch shot of over 70 yards that went in the hole for eagle on the ninth and another chip in on 11 by our main challenger Bradley Dredge meant that we were suddenly tied for the lead.

Great players make it happen when the pressure is on. A holed bunker shot on 15 for eagle probably stopped Dredge's attack in its tracks.

The fact that Alex hit his lob wedge when I had been encouraging him to use his sand-wedge confirms my belief that the player usually knows best, but it takes a good working relationship to be able to discuss these decisions.

He parred his way back to the clubhouse like an old pro who was used to winning. I think it is the maiden win that will pave the way for much more success for the most amiable person that I have ever caddied for who has finally taken the first step to realising his golfing dreams.

Taking time out to deal with a first Tour win

SEPTEMBER 15: When you win a professional golf event for the first time your world is likely to change quickly and dramatically. Just compare Shane Lowry before last May and his first victory on the European Tour, a rapid elevation to professional status a week later, and now in September he is a regular tour player.

The euphoria of the dramatic victory has subsided and the reality of being a tour pro has set in; a big golf bag, brash branding, caddie and coach in tow. Shane is very much part of the tour now, dealing with the mundane duties of bringing in a good score four times a week.

Playing on tour as a novice is a big learning curve. Playing as a recent winner is another experience that of course you cannot be prepared for. The best way to handle a win is to take the next week off, go home, celebrate and come back on tour when the dust has settled on the tour's memory of the occasion.

As you may be aware my player, Alex Noren, enjoyed his maiden victory on the European Tour in Switzerland the week before last and not only got "the monkey off his back" as a much tipped prospect who had yet to deliver but also got himself into the following week's event in Germany, which was played in Cologne last week; he had to win to gain exemption.

As a winners' tournament and with a limit on the number of contestants to about half that of a normal tour event it was an exclusive affair for which most players were flattered to be included.

With the energy that is expended in winning and the extra media and other duties expected of the winner it is often best to take the following week off from tournament golf as the distraction makes it difficult to give enough attention to the event at hand.

For Alex there didn't seem to be any thought of not playing last week, but I sense, in hindsight, he may consider the options when it arises in the future.

He was as tired as I have seen the exuberant young Swede. The show goes on in golf as it does in any other professional sport. Alex had committed to a sponsor's evening on the Sunday night of his victory which would have been less inconvenient if he had not won.

His manager had made a decision to travel from Sweden early on the Sunday of the European Masters to witness his client's first victory. It was a huge effort on his part and something that only someone as conscientious as he would have done. Conveniently, he was able to accompany Alex to the sponsor's evening and help the new winner deal with the instant demands of victory.

So I was left in the rarefied air of Crans-sur-Sierre as the sole representative of the victorious Noren team to celebrate. With the following week being over the other side of the Alps in Germany it was a rare week where many players and caddies stayed around on Sunday night and we had a chance to celebrate at the scene of the victory.

When you win you have the usual initial congratulations from your playing partners and particularly in our situation in Switzerland, from our main protagonist, Bradley Dredge, and his caddie. With a holed 70 yards pitch shot, a chip in and a holed bunker shot in the space of seven holes in the final round, the talent of these golfers never ceases to amaze me.

When you have such a final round battle as we did with Dredge there is a huge amount of mutual respect and a sense of being part of something special that envelopes the final grouping as the unpredictable nature of the game of golf unfolds under the pressure of competition late on a Sunday afternoon.

I was touched by the support and heartfelt good wishes from my colleagues. With Alex being such a polite, friendly and considerate golfer there is no doubt the accolades were genuine.

Graeme Storm, who played with us during the first two rounds, along with Tano Goya were both very generous in their good wishes.

Tour officials, TV production crews, other players, caddies and friends all took the time to say a special word of congratulations to me, which of course is embarrassing when I am with my player because naturally, it was he who won. As I have been aware so many times with my previous employer, Retief Goosen, he could have done it without me, but I could not have done it without him.

Alex had mentioned in his recent blog he felt he had a caddie who was more famous than him and it was about time he changed it. He has, of course, a dry sense of humour.

As is the Sportsyard management team's democratic way, Johan Elliot, the group's founder, got the Noren team together last week in Germany. Each part of the Noren cog got to air their views on the present and the future. As important as it is to be successful it is equally important to manage that success efficiently.

It is exciting as a more mature caddie to be part of a rejuvenating young golfing team which is very much part of a bigger, close knit group of touring professionals and caddies who can play hard but very much enjoy each others' success at the end of each round. It only takes a week in golf to change your life considerably for the better.

The start of the great adventure

SEPTEMBER 29: There is no standard plan of attack when it comes to deciding how to make the transition from top international amateur golfer to the unknown world of professional golf. Rory McIlroy was recognised from an early age as a rare talent and was carefully shepherded towards the European Tour. He received the maximum amount of invitations to play on the tour a couple of years ago and earned his playing rights for the following year with events to spare.

Shane Lowry was catapulted on to the European Tour with his spectacular victory in the Irish Open when he was still an amateur. His decision a week after his outrageous victory to turn professional was a no-brainer and his Irish amateur team-mate Niall Kearney agreed he would have done exactly the same.

I recently met the amiable young Dubliner after a short practice session at his home course and mine, Royal Dublin. I am not there that often but when I am, chances are I will see the tall, lean figure of the 21 year-old in the garden, the practice ground at Dollymount, and usually in the short game area.

It is the part of his game he thinks is his weakest. I had a game with him during the winter and was impressed by his short game. Having been a close observer of one of the finest exponents of the green-side detail of the game in Retief Goosen, I am not easily impressed. So I was fascinated at Royal Dublin's first Walker Cup representative's opinion of his chipping and pitching – he obviously has very high standards.

It has been a whirlwind month for Kearney; having represented Britain and Ireland in the Walker Cup in Philadelphia a few weeks back he endured his first foray into the professional golf life on a successful recent trip to Germany to the first stage of the European Tour qualifying event.

Top amateur golfers are not unfamiliar with tough competition and the inconvenience of travelling to compete. Perhaps a sortie to the European Tour School might have got an ordinary amateur's golf juices flowing; it was probably something of a let down for a guy who had just played in front of 10,000 spectators, at the biggest event in team amateur golf in a country that knows how to make potential stars feel important.

The contrast of that with what must have felt like a field in a remote region of eastern Germany with a few rabbits and birds the only form of life apart from fellow competitors was stark.

Kearney was wearing one of his Walker Cup polo shirts when I met him and didn't need much prompting about his experience at the Merion Club. The Walker Cup started for the team members the previous week in London with a meeting with Prince Andrew at Buckingham Palace. The team played golf in Sunningdale, where ex-Walker Cup player and now successful tour player Nick Dougherty came along to have a chat with the team.

The night before they headed off in comfort to the States they went to the BBC studios for a tour and attended *Friday Night With Jonathan Ross*. A night at the exclusive Dormy House at Pine Valley preceded the team's arrival at the Merion Club, where the red-carpet treatment continued.

In contrast, the first stage qualifier in Fliessen See, outside Berlin, involved a cramped seat with a budget airline and a 100km trip in a rental car to his underwhelming destination. It represented Kearney's first important lesson to life on tour: it is not always glamorous.

I get the feeling the mature Kearney is well aware of the reality of playing golf for a living. He explained he understood from a very young age that golf is a lonely sport where you spend the majority of your time on your own and therefore the life of a touring professional would not suit everyone.

He said he was content with his own company and did not crave companionship. He is happy to read and watch TV, selectively. I suggested he might be anxious to get back to watch the final showdown in the Fed-Ex Cup in Atlanta last Sunday night. By his response, I don't think he was too sure what event was on in the States last week. This is rare in young golfers, who are usually aware of the stars' every move.

Having got into the game by caddying for his dad at Corrstown when he was 12 and a 24 handicapper, he was down to scratch five years later. The extremely modest Kearney suggested to me he was not talented. His philosophy is: "You can be what you want to be if you put your mind to it. The practice range is out in front of you, go and use it."

His highest accolade to date, to be chosen for the Walker Cup team, came from five years of hard work on top of – despite what he may think – a considerable amount of talent.

As a member of the Irish Boys, Youths and Seniors teams he is no stranger to high achievement. A key quality in the seemingly sensible beyond his years Brabazon Trophy holder seems to be his self-awareness. He tried the US college scene in East Tennessee and lasted about six weeks before deciding it was not the best way forward for him.

When I asked him what his weaknesses were he replied he wanted to be more decisive and committed on the course.

Decision making doesn't seem to be a problem if you can recognise as a teenager that golf in the US college environment does not suit you.

The remarkably balanced and courteous Niall Kearney would like to be making a good living on tour in five years' time but when it comes to his golf he has no limits. He is aware that already he has made sacrifices by losing touch with his mates through travelling in order to improve his game. But as long as he continues to achieve he is happy.

With his talent, modesty, work ethic, and judgment we can look forward to watching a young craftsman carve a long, fruitful career as a professional golfer.

Ends

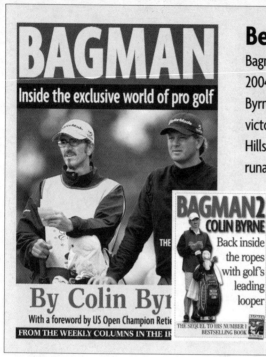

BAGMAN

Inside the exclusive world of pro golf

By Colin Byr[ne]

With a foreword by US Open Champion Retie[f]

FROM THE WEEKLY COLUMNS IN THE IR[...]

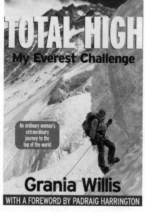

BAGMAN 2
COLIN BYRNE

Back inside
the ropes
with golf's
leading
looper

THE SEQUEL TO HIS NUMBER 1
BESTSELLING BOOK

Bestseller

Bagman was published in October 2004, the year in which caddie Colin Byrne guided Retief Goosen to a victory in the US Open at Shinnecock Hills. The book went on to become the runaway hit of Christmas 2004, becoming a national bestseller and garnering critical national and international acclaim for its author. The publication of Bagman 2 comes in the wake of demand for a second collection of Colin's work covering the years 2005-2009.

CATHERINA McKIERNAN

Running for my life With Ian O'Riordan

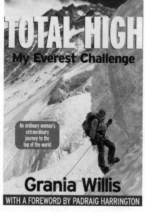

TOTAL HIGH
My Everest Challenge

An ordinary woman's
extraordinary
journey to the
top of the world

Grania Willis
WITH A FOREWORD BY PADRAIG HARRINGTON

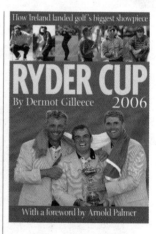

How Ireland landed golf's biggest showpiece

RYDER CUP
By Dermot Gilleece 2006

With a foreword by Arnold Palmer

Catherina McKiernan's life story detailing her rise from a humble, rural background to internationally acclaimed runner, as told to Ian O'Riordan.

A remarkable, inspiring and beautifully crafted account of Grania Willis's determination, ambition and bravery in reaching the top of the world's most iconic summit – Mount Everest.

Ireland's leading golf writer, Dermot Gilleece, gives a gripping, insider's account as to the money, power and politics that saw Ireland land the Ryder Cup. Superbly illustrated throughout.